# NIGHTCLUB CITY

# Nightclub City

## Politics and Amusement in Manhattan

BURTON W. PERETTI

**PENN**

University of Pennsylvania Press

Philadelphia

10  9  8  7  6  5  4  3  2  1

Published by
University of Pennsylvania Press
Philadelphia, Pennsylvania 19104-4112

Library of Congress Cataloging-in-Publication Data

Peretti, Burton W. (Burton William), 1961–
   Nightclub city : politics and amusement in Manhattan / Burton W. Peretti.
      p. cm.
   Includes bibliographical references and index.

   ISBN: 978-0-8122-2157-2

   1. Manhattan (New York, N.Y.)—Social life and customs—20th century.   2.
Nightclubs—New York (State)—New York—History—20th century.   3. City and town
life—New York (State)—New York—History—20th century.   4. Leisure—New York
(State)—New York—History—20th century.   5. Amusements—New York (State)—New
York—History—20th century.   6. Manhattan (New York, N.Y.)—Politics and
government—20th century.   7. Manhattan (New York, N.Y.)—Social conditions—20th
century.   8. New York (N.Y.)—Social life and customs—20th century.   9. New York
(N.Y.)—Politics and government—1898–1951.   10. New York (N.Y.)—Social
conditions—20th century.   I. Title.

F128.5.P47 2007

2006051092

*In memory of Lawrence Levine*
*New Yorker, historian, enjoyer*

# Contents

# Preface

In 1926, on 54th Street in midtown Manhattan, the entertainer Mary "Texas" Guinan's 300 Club glowed with color and resonated with activity. Stephen Graham, an Englishman, recalled his visit to the club with pleasure. "The walls are covered with pleated cloth and the roof tented with the same cloth softly toned in old rose, green, and sere yellow. There are hanging Chinese lanterns, and on the walls illuminated designs of parrots. There are twenty or thirty tables and a small space in the middle of them for intimate dancing. The lighting is wonderful." "A charming girl in blue satin trousers and wearing a crimson sash" sold cigarettes while "a smart girl in black with silver flowers on her hips" dispensed gift dolls. A guitar quartet strolled amid well-heeled patrons such as Harry Thaw (the wealthy playboy famed for his murder of the architect Stanford White twenty years earlier) and the mayor of New York City himself, James J. Walker, "flitting in elegantly to touch the hands of several of a large party and yield his charming smile to the ladies." Guinan, the mistress of ceremonies, appeared to introduce her "near-naked girls" and "a song about cherries." "Cherries!" the crowd shouted. One "girl . . . put a cherry into each man's mouth. One took the cherry and kissed the girl's fingertips. Another girl following ruffled up men's hair as she passed." A young man was recruited to dance with the chorines, the audience sang "And She Knows Her Onions!" and Guinan tossed finger-clappers and snowballs made of felt to the customers. The show concluded with a merry projectile fight. The hostess pelted a pair of newlyweds with rice and the clock struck five. "One of the waiters borrowed a horn from the jazz band and blew dreadful reveilles into the ears of the sleepers." By sunrise, even Guinan herself had become sedate.[1]

Shortly after Graham's visit, the 300 Club became a victim of official suppression. According to the *New York Times*, four hundred patrons were present that night, including two U.S. senators (whom the *Times* discreetly did not name) and twenty visitors from Georgia welcoming home the new champion of the British Open golf tournament, Bobby Jones (who was not at the club). Two New York City policewomen, "dressed and acting as if they were visiting flappers seeking a thrill," staked out the premises in advance. When vice officers and federal Pro-hibition agents announced the raid, some male customers tried to "fight it out" and were arrested. Also taken into custody were Guinan's father, Michael, the club manager, and seventeen-year-old Julia Dunn, a chorus member charged with "having taken part in an objectionable dance . . . in flesh-colored tights almost covered with imitation pearl beads." The site of the 300 Club was shuttered for six months. In city court, however, Julia Dunn was freed by the magistrate, who ruled that the narrow dis-tance between tables had forced her to dance amid the customers. Michael and Texas Guinan were acquitted after a trial, and none of their customers were punished as well. After the padlock came off of the front door, the old 300 Club venue housed similar liquor-dealing nightclubs, including the Club Argonaut owned by Larry Fay, the man who gave Texas Guinan her start in the nightclub business in 1922.[2]

The short life of the 300 Club is part of the fascinating and important history of Manhattan nightclubs between World Wars I and II.[3] This his-tory illuminates important dynamics in American culture in these dec-ades, such as gender relations, affluence, leisure, law enforcement, and urban commerce. *Nightclub City* explores these dynamics in one grand context: the interaction of nightclub leisure and civic life. The encoun-ter between clubs and government generated scandals, reform crusades, and regulations that helped to redefine the realities and the images of urban life in the United States. In addition, through this interaction nightclubs also transferred some of their style and cachet to the texture of city politics. By 1940 nightclubs were closer to the respectable heart of civic life, and the dream-manufacturing operation of the leisure industry had insinuated itself into politics. Since then, to the present day, the interwar mating of clubs and politics has continued to influence the culture of the city and the nation.

From their inception in the early 1920s, nightclubs in midtown Man-hattan's theater district were celebrated as representative institutions of that roaring decade. Boisterous rooms filled with illegal liquor, female dancers, well-heeled revelers, and multiethnic employees, surrounded by a nightlife environment of speakeasies, Broadway street life, taxicabs, dance halls, and all-night restaurants, exerted a pull on the national imagination. African American Harlem and bohemian Greenwich Vil-lage provided uptown and downtown counterpoints, respectively, to antics in the theater district. In the mid-1930s, after the repeal of Prohi-bition and the passing of the worst of the Great Depression, the night-club achieved a renewed prosperity and notoriety. Mostly because of the efforts of nationally syndicated gossip columnists and Hollywood musi-cals, the Manhattan nightclub remained an iconic presence in popular culture. Partly as a result of this, some clubs were able to survive the upheavals of the 1940s and stay in business for decades.

Previous histories of the nightclub have stressed two predominant themes. First, they have argued that the clubs' popularity illustrated the decay of Victorian institutions and values after the turn of the nineteenth century. They have also especially noted the role of nightclubs in the evolution of race relations. Southern African Americans migrated to Harlem in large numbers during World War I and established its cabaret culture. In the 1920s, though, white managers and gangsters forcibly took over black-owned clubs and controlled the careers of black entertainers. Their campaign facilitated the vogue for Harlem among affluent white patrons. At the same time, though, civil rights advocates and artistic modernists were inspired by the pioneering and intimate interracial contact that the new nightlife encouraged.[4]

My initial research into nightclubs strove simply to carry this story forward into the Depression decade of the 1930s. After a cultural institution reaches an apotheosis, it seemed logical to ask, does its influence wane and go into decline, especially if surrounding economic conditions worsen drastically? In such circumstances, in what direction would a nightclub rebellion against Victorian bourgeois domesticity and in favor of "modern" experimentation now go? Would depression America—which celebrated "the common man" and rural roots—encourage an antithesis of the classic nightclub, and perhaps a future synthesis of Victorian and modern values, of conformity and rebellion?[5]

As the project progressed I maintained an interest in these questions, but I also increasingly found myself stretching the boundaries of the topic and searching for the broader relevance of the Manhattan nightclub story. I became particularly fascinated with clubs' increasingly high profile as an object of social and political debate between 1924 and 1933. In these years, while literary figures such as Carl Van Vechten, Edmund Wilson, and Rudolph Fisher explored the implications of the nightclub experience for private sensibilities and social relations,[6] other observers tended to perceive clubs differently, through the lenses of public values, priorities, and policies. Critics blamed nightclubs variously for crime, the disruption of standard activity during the day and the night, the spread of illegal liquor, the corruption of young women, the spread of organized lawlessness, and the rise of public immorality. Clubs were said to represent both the growing pains and the signs of decadence that resulted from the city's often chaotic development in those years. In short, I came to be fascinated with the ways in which nightclubs became implicated in the civic life of the city.[7]

Contemporary observers' perception of the nightclub as a social institution expressed and popularized the notion that clubs helped to measure and indeed determine the condition of civic life in New York. At this point, a short definition of the notion is in order. By 1920 at least five major components constituted American urban "civic life." The citizenry, of course, was the central component of the regime, although the legal definition of citizenship (as well as the intensity of popular civic-mindedness) varied over time. Then there were city, county, state, and national governments, whose overlapping jurisdictions sought to adjudicate, legislate, and administer the city under the weight of precedent. Dynamic political parties and "machines" helped to channel countless private and public interests into official hands and to provide for the more orderly management of the mass electoral process. The mass-circulated press had long been central to what the historian Mary Ryan has called the rule of "politics by publicity." Finally, there were the urban reformers, issue-oriented individuals who sought to cure the city's ills through moral suasion, investigation, "expert" diagnoses, and insurgent politics.[8] All of these constituencies—citizens, government officials, party bosses, newspapers, and social reformers—acted upon the interwar nightclub, demonizing its moral influence and leading investigative and regulatory efforts.

Nightlife regulation in the 1920s represented a climactic effort by the Victorian reform tradition to shape the morality of New York City. In the eyes of reformers, the nightclub was the ultimate embodiment of urban depravity. Its doors were a portal through which sexual, ethnic, and criminal transgressions were funneled into a dense and lurid urban underground. Thanks to their efforts between the world wars, reformers and their allies in government turned nightclub regulation into a compilation of reform groups' truisms and tactics and government enforcement strategies. This reform spirit survived the upheavals of the Great Depression and was intensified by the triumphant entry of reformers into City Hall in 1934, in the administration of Mayor Fiorello H. La Guardia.

Change and influence, though, moved both ways. In the 1920s, the brazenly self-confident nightclub itself was representative of a more general rebellion in American culture against traditional concepts of civic life. This rebellion, exemplified by the mass flouting of Prohibition, would be poised to influence American civic life for decades to come.

To put it another way, while the public sphere sought to regulate and tame the nightclub, the clubs themselves helped to alter behavior and discourse in the public realm. Prime evidence of the latter trend could be found in the changing tone and substance of public leadership in New York City, which increasingly seemed to contradict that leadership's condemnation, investigation, and regulation of nightclubs. This tension was epitomized by the spectacle of a 1926 public hearing in which New

York mayor James J. Walker pressed the case for a closing time for night-clubs by offering his own eyewitness accounts of customer misbehavior in clubs in the early hours of the morning. It was also reflected in the eagerness of the anti-prostitution crusader George Worthington to pose for pictures with Texas Guinan, who some alleged to have procured young women for male nightclub customers. A decade later, in an echo of Jazz Age practices, lawyers in the office of the crime-fighting prosecu-tor Thomas E. Dewey treated sequestered anti-gangland witnesses—who were likely prostitutes—to nights on the town, complete with dinners and Broadway shows. Even as civic-minded New Yorkers were debating the contours of moral reform and regulation, then, they sampled the potentially forbidden fruit of nightlife in bites of varying sizes. They accommodated their behavior to the new "immorality" and revised their assumptions about public norms, propriety, and even their official decorum.

The cross-pollination of nightlife and politics continued unabated despite a change in political regimes halfway through the interwar era. It influenced both the tenure of "Jimmy" Walker and Tammany Hall from 1926 to 1933 and that of Mayor Fiorello La Guardia and his reform coalition beginning in 1934. Since the mid-1800s Tammany Hall, the governing Democratic organization in Manhattan, had invested in con-cert saloons and other pioneering entertainment venues. In 1925 it engineered the election of Walker, who as mayor became the city's most famed regular nightclub customer. Such involvement by politicians in nightclubs, as well as reformers' demonizations of the clubs as nests of civic corruption, helped to foment the scandals that eventually drove Tammany Hall and Walker from power. In the next decade La Guardia offered new condemnations of nightclubs and their allied institutions as part of his quixotic effort to remake the city's entire culture. La Guard-ia's effort culminated in his championing of wholesome public leisure at the New York World's Fair in 1939–40, but the fair ironically became the biggest promotional device for salacious leisure the city had yet seen. Less quixotic were the epic public works of La Guardia's parks commis-sioner, Robert Moses, whose accomplishments also included the demoli-tion of the Central Park Casino, the only nightclub owned by the city itself.

The passion with which New Yorkers addressed the new nightlife in part reflected interwar Americans' deep concerns about the general nature of their civic life. The 1920s yielded a steady series of laments from learned observers about the decline they perceived in citizens' commitment to public duty. Some thinkers, such as John Dewey, were guardedly optimistic about the future of participatory democracy. Oth-ers, most prominently Walter Lippmann, despaired about a general public disinterest in politics and advocated government in the future by "experts." Cynical modernists such as John Dos Passos, meanwhile, celebrated the demise of what they considered to be Americans' outmoded compliance with corrupt authority and awaited the rise of communism. All agreed, though, that modern culture, especially the city, popular culture, and the new leisure, had brewed what Lippmann called "the acids of modernity"—notions and practices in life, thought, and leisure that diminished earlier commitments to civic involvement.[9] This critique of modern urban culture helped nightclub controversies to intersect with loftier debates about civic life as a whole.

These debates have stayed with us until the present day. One scholarly component has explored the general significance of leisure in society. The pioneering scholar of human play, Johan Huizinga, was a contemporary of Dewey and Lippmann who shared their disdain for the mass-marketed entertainment and frivolity of the interwar era. Later historians have proved more amenable to the notion that modern, mass-oriented leisure, like the ancient games studied by Huizinga, has helped people to construct and to perceive their culture as a whole.[10] Similarly, labor historians in Great Britain and the United States have debated the nature of workers' leisure since the 1800s: did they engage in healthful and liberating play, or was their "free time" excessively constructed by the hegemonic forces of capitalism?[11] Today, more general comment is made about a perceived new crisis in Western civic life. Jürgen Habermas, Amitai Etzioni, Robert Putnam, and others variously blame bureaucracy, mass marketing, television, and the Internet for reducing populations—especially in the United States—to a state of disinterest, nonparticipation, and civic anomie.[12] Popular cultural critics such as Neal Gabler stress the dangers posed by the Hollywoodization of civic life, in which public events and personalities are packaged as mass-media entertainment, politicians are treated like celebrities, and unqualified entertainers are elected to public office.[13]

The interwar era is now distant from us and must never be viewed ahistorically, but I find it stimulating to note the similarities between that time and our own. Both eras feature a general disaffection with and cynicism about parties, leaders, and government; disgust with forms of official corruption; and a general abandonment of the hope that the public sphere can get anything done well. The First World War cast a long shadow over the civic mood in the 1920s, when journalists and the mass media found it more profitable to provide cynical, personality-driven political coverage instead of civic-minded analysis.[14] In our time, owing in part to the cultural impact of American wars past (Vietnam) and present (Iraq), ideals of an informed and active citizenry have been overshadowed in journalism and in public expression by pessimism, tabloid trivia, celebrity worship, and the "spin" of political consultants. It is important for historians to pay closer attention to the origins of Americans' embrace of leisure and entertainment to the detriment of more consistent civic engagement.

Viewed through this lens of civic life, various social and cultural elements of the nightclub story take on a new richness. Race and gender, for example, are obvious examples. The interactions of blacks and whites in Harlem and men and women in Manhattan nightclubs have been characterized by some as "pre-political" or "infrapolitical" behavior, beneath the attention of the public sphere.[15] Much of the interaction was discriminatory and oppressive, while some of it was "oppositional" in nature, but could any of it truly be called the stuff of civic life? Race and gender in nightclubs—which seemed to be obsessed with perfecting the provocative display of black people and of all women—seem to belong more properly to the history of sexuality and performance than to the story of civic life. However, nightclub issues helped to raise the profile of race, gender, and sexuality in civic debate and policy. The design and staffing of nightclubs codified dominant notions regarding racial, ethnic, and gender hierarchy and produced conflicts about them. When we examine the anti-prostitution group the Committee of Fourteen, Jimmy Walker, the Seabury investigations (which forced Walker out of office), and the brothel keeper Polly Adler, we find existing notions of race and gender imposed on nightclubs but also transformed by their powerful cultural appeal. Notions about nightclubs, in turn, infused government investigation and regulation with a special passion and some of the cultural characteristics of the clubs themselves.

The intersection of clubs and civic life also highlighted other important trends of the era, such as the evolution of social stratification and of capitalism, the genesis of urban planning and policy, and reforms pertaining to the administration of justice. Each of these trends had an important impact on New York's evolving civic identity. The financing and evolution of nightlife businesses offer a revealing case study of class conflict and competition in the economic realm. The content of nightclub entertainment, as well as the interaction of individuals in clubs, especially brought the status of women and homosexuals into greater relief. And the city, state, and nation's efforts to govern in the metropolitan age centered in part on combating the perceived threat of nightclubs to the civic good.

*Nightclub City* interweaves a history of the nightclub with chapters that reveal its close relationship to major civic trends: moral reform and policing, Prohibition, the fight against public corruption, the Great Depression, and the New Deal. What emerges is a story of a city, and a national culture as a whole, redefining its civic life through its leisure.

Chapter 1 chronicles the precursors of the Manhattan nightclub, discusses Larry Fay's seminal "bootlegger club" of 1922, the El Fey, and follows the industry to its peak of popularity in 1928. It also sketches the clubs' collective identity, in which entrepreneurs' careful commercial, financial, and technological calculations blended with the sexual, social, and spiritual rebelliousness found in the clubs' decor, entertainment, and social interactions.

The clubs' rise to notoriety in the late 1920s caused a spate of nearly simultaneous efforts at reform and regulation. To make sense of these efforts and their cumulative impact, I examine them separately. Chapter 2 explores the Committee of Fourteen's campaign to expose nightclubs as the new breeding ground for prostitution. The committee's investigations of New York's nightlife and its efforts to encourage regulation offer a case study of traditional reformers' special difficulties in the new cultural climate of the 1920s. The group's ambivalence toward uninhibited "new women" on the nightclub scene, particularly hostesses and other club employees, showed traditionalist reformers struggling to comprehend new trends in gender roles and sexuality. Chapter 3 describes the highly ambivalent attitude of Tammany Hall and Mayor James J. Walker—rulers of city government in the late 1920s—toward nightclubs. Tammany's and Walker's juxtaposition of traditional morality in the Irish Catholic style with long and deep involvement in Manhattan nightlife illuminate the government's tortured effort to control nightclubs with new licensing and closing-time laws. This effort, in turn, suggests the larger difficulties faced by the Tammany government in its attempt to reconcile its grassroots identity with its large-scale business interests in the 1920s. Chapter 4 reflects the fact that New York's civic life was not merely a local concern: federal Prohibition regulators targeted nightclubs as special incubators of the illegal liquor trade. A "war on the nightclubs" in 1928 encapsulated the paradoxes of both Prohibition regulation and of the Republican administration's own indecision about nightclubs, which blurred the boundary between public misbehavior and private intimacy. The failures of all three efforts—by the Committee of Fourteen, the city government, and Prohibition forces—indicate government's inability to define or subsume the new nightlife under its regulatory reach.

Chapter 5 returns us to the nightclubs themselves, describing their decline during the early years of the Great Depression (1929–33) and the genesis of their subsequent revival. The Depression created a general sense that civic life itself was in crisis, so it is necessary to explore

how the decline of nightclubs was entwined with New York's general pessimism in the middle of the slump. The chapter also suggests how the
Depression redefined many of the attributes of the Manhattan nightclub, making it more amenable to the new economic and regulatory
realities of the 1930s. The early 1930s also brought the destruction of
the Tammany-Walker regime in city government by means of the state
legislature's investigations under the direction of Samuel Seabury. Seabury, in turn, was instrumental in launching Fiorello La Guardia's successful bid to become a reformist mayor. The apparent revolution in
civic life revealed many scandals and changed many aspects of municipal
government. Nightclubs now were less often the main focus of reform,
but the roll of perceived social ills that had been associated with clubs
in the 1920s—deviant sexuality, misbehaving womanhood, prostitution,
liquor, nocturnality, price gouging, organized crime, and public
nudity—remained central targets of official concern. In Chapters 6 and
7, the stories of Seabury and La Guardia show how, even after the
Depression and the change in regime, the new nightlife continued to
influence what was problematized and investigated—in other words,
what was made into an important "issue"—by actors in the public
sphere.

The final two chapters return to the milieu of the nightclub. Chapter
8 explores the political and social crosscurrents on the nightlife scene
in the late 1930s, updating trends in Greenwich Village, Midtown, and
Harlem and gauging the impact of new cultural politics (including those
of the New Deal and the Popular Front) on the clubs. Chapter 9 concen-
trates on the career of Billy Rose, the most successful and influential
nightclub entrepreneur of the decade. Rose's evolving concept of the
nightclub featured surprising adoptions of non-urban influences—from
the circus, Wild West shows, and the outdoor aquatic spectacle, the latter climaxing in the spectacularly popular Aquacade at the 1939–40
World's Fair. While these innovations helped to boost his revenues to
record levels, they also threatened to deconstruct the urban identity of
the nightclub. By 1940, nightclub regulation reached a kind of equilib-
rium and the business had reached new plateaus of profitability, but
signs of an imminent "posturban" future for American culture and leisure were also becoming apparent. As war around the world resumed,
therefore, the defining era of the nightclub in American life came to an
end.

An examination of this story transforms the colorful legend of the
New York nightclub into a chapter in the important story of leisure and
its regulation. By 1940, two decades of government intervention had
helped to shape the contours and content of nightclubs, while the clubs
made regulators far more aware of (and complicit in) popular entertain-

ment's influence on the public sphere. Notions and practices relating to sex, gender, race, and leisure that the clubs had introduced became officially recognized as targets of regulation, but Broadway's culture of leisure and celebrity also managed to infiltrate the behavior and the public image of political figures. While show business became increasingly regulated, government increasingly became more like show business. These trends continue to persist. The municipal regulation of leisure continues unabated in New York City today. Manhattan's story contains national significance as well. Its example shaped leisure in other cities, and in regions of all kinds Americans shared New York's ambivalent stance between Victorian morality and modern frankness and tolerance. In these ways and in others, the interwar nightclub was an instructive cultural artifact of Americans' struggle to define the balances between work and leisure, freedom and authority, and civic identity and anomie.

# CHAPTER 1
# The 1920s New York Nightclub, a Modern Institution

According to Manhattan lore, the originator of the interwar nightclub was a tall, sad-faced Irish-American named Larry Fay (see Fig. 1). A native to the island, Fay was a taxicab driver with a long record of traffic and parking violations who dabbled in controlling his own fleet of cars. In 1920 Prohibition had begun and speakeasies had sprung up to sell illegal liquor. That year, legend has it, Fay took on a bootlegger as a fare. They drove 400 miles to Montreal, where the passenger picked up a crate of liquor. Earning a sizeable wad of bills for his effort, Fay decided to buy his own cache of Canadian whiskey. On his return to Manhattan he sold it to speakeasies and scored a large profit. Fay first poured his liquor earnings into an effort to build the most distinctive taxicab fleet in the city. He outfitted his cabs with blinking lights, tune-playing horns, polished metallic trim, and inlaid black swastikas. His personnel director, a recently paroled thief named Owney Madden, hired tough and aggressive drivers and ran the racket, using threats to scare other cabbies away from railway stations and prestigious hotels.[1]

In 1922 the bustle of nightlife around Fay's Times Square office apparently lured him into the cabaret business. The financial history of the Club El Fey is difficult to reconstruct. Fay's bootlegging revenue provided him with sufficient start-up capital to lease a long second-floor room shared by neighboring townhouses on West 45th Street and purchase simple furnishing and decorations. Fay asked Nils Thor Granlund to manage his club. A pale, ill-tempered immigrant from Swedish Lapland, Granlund seemed an unlikely Broadway impresario, but he had a decade of experience as a talent agent and restaurant owner and now helped to run the pioneering New York radio station WHN. Granlund would later produce shows at the El Fey, but on that day he declined Fay's offer and recommended a former business partner in his stead. Mary Louise Cecilia Guinan was a veteran lasso twirler and vaudeville and film actress, now working at the Beaux Arts speakeasy on 40th Street. Nicknamed "Texas" for her childhood in Waco, she was never-

Figure 1. Larry Fay was credited with creating the prototypical Manhattan nightclub, the Club El Fey, in 1922. Fay was also notorious for his taxicab fleet, milk racketeering, and violent death at the hands of an employee in 1933. Billy Rose Theatre Collection, The New York Public Library for the Performing Arts, Astor, Lenox, and Tilden Foundations.

theless a thoroughly urbanized Irish Catholic. While she led an unassuming private life, the twice-divorced hostess excelled at crafting a vivid public persona and piles of self-serving publicity. Fay hired Guinan, and she began to organize and host the entertainment at the Club El Fey.[2]

At first Fay perceived the El Fey mainly to be the sales outlet for his liquor cache. He bought protection from police raids by making the Tammany Hall district leader James "Jimmy" Hines a secret partner in the business. Fay was tiring of bootlegging, though, and soon focused his energies on the club's concept and design. Entertainment costs eventually required additional investors from the underworld economy, led by the notorious gambler and high-interest lender Arnold Rothstein. Fay yearned to provide a dazzling stage show modeled after the Folies Bergères and Florenz Ziegfeld's revues. The former taxi driver once again struck gold. By the end of 1922 Fay's various enterprises had earned him perhaps as much as half a million dollars and fueled what Nils T. Granlund called his "yen to hobnob with class." Thrill-seeking elite clients braved the tight security and forbiddingly high prices to make the El Fey the success of the season. Included among them were elected officials such as the state senator James J. Walker.[3]

Fay's explosive success epitomized Manhattan itself, which was in the throes of its newest business bonanza. New York City in 1920 was America's economic and statistical colossus. Six million people called it home; one-fifth of the nation's monetary wealth sat in its vaults; and that year $6 billion in goods—half of America's entire trade with the world— passed through its port. Urban centers were growing across the United States, but no city challenged New York's dominance in finance, trade, publishing, corporate headquarters, and human capital. The world's greatest cluster of towering buildings stood on Manhattan bedrock. During World War I the heavily protected city became the portal for most American soldiers and materiel. Five million immigrants had streamed through Ellis Island in New York Harbor, and many of them still called the city their home. Politicians ritualistically praised New York as the largest Irish city, the largest German city after Berlin, and the largest Italian city after Rome. In a few short years the African American population had reached a quarter million. Service industries of all kinds catered to every class and need and pioneered new methods of mass marketing and distribution.[4]

Nightlife was one of the most colorful and well-known service industries in this colossus. Generations of leisure establishments in New York City had variously provided drink, food, entertainment, and social mingling. Pre-Civil War stages and tavern floors featuring song and dance were succeeded by concert saloons, which began to standardize the inte-

gration of performance with dining. Meanwhile, vaudeville, genre theater, and circus-like spectacles made Broadway the national capital of
live entertainment and the home base of national touring companies.
Massed electric lighting, pioneered at amusement parks on Brooklyn's
Coney Island, transformed Broadway into "the great White Way." The
dens of gambling and prostitution that thrived in the shadows of Coney
Island and Broadway illustrated the early association of socially disreputable practices (or "vice") with nightlife. Songwriters based in Tin Pan
Alley, south of Times Square, provided rich and increasingly idiomatic
musical material for stage shows. Early film studios competed with live
entertainment, but the movies also reinvigorated some theaters and
infused show business with a new concept of glamour.[5]

By 1920, though, the term "nightlife" especially referred to specific
kinds of places for dining, drink, socializing, and intimate entertainment. These were first known as cabarets, a hybrid of the exclusive
Broadway restaurant (the "lobster palace") and the working-class concert saloon. By 1915 black ragtime musicians and Latin American dancers mixed informally in cabarets with white Anglo-Saxon socialites. That
same year, Florenz Ziegfeld, Jr., who earlier had imported the Parisian
chorus show to the Broadway stage, created his Midnight Frolic revue
and made female display an integral part of the cabaret formula. Some
cabaret owners bought up New York state charters that had been issued
to now-defunct voluntary associations, to evade the city's closing-time
laws. The concept of the "nightclub" thus was born.[6]

The arrival of Prohibition caused convulsions in the nightlife business. Restaurants and cabarets tried to adapt to the ban on the sale of
alcoholic beverages that began in January 1920, but dwindling patronage forced most of them to close. The leisure economy was drastically
reconstituted.[7] Illicit liquor traders sold their wares in thousands of so-
called speakeasies, which could be found in every kind of space in Manhattan. The liquor distribution network created a new source for capital
and a new class of entrepreneurs in nightlife. Arnold Rothstein, one of
the major investors in the Club El Fey, was a famed gambler who had
positioned himself adroitly to become the principal lender of funds to
underworld capitalists. Emulating Larry Fay, other bootleggers borrowed from Rothstein to make their own entrances into the nightclub
business. In later years the occasionally violent exploits of gangland club
owners and investors such as Owney Madden, Frankie Marlow, Jack
"Legs" Diamond, and Dutch Schultz provided colorful notoriety for
their clubs. Nils Granlund, though, characterized gangsters as "essentially . . . just a tough breed of businessmen," and in any event less colorful investors—some of whom were bootleggers, some of whom were
not—dominated the new nightlife business community.[8]

The lure of immediate windfall earnings attracted investors. The song lyricist Billy Rose's club "amortized itself on opening night," while the singer Harry Richman spent wildly on liquor and gifts at his new establishment to reap even greater profits. The Plantation, Moulin Rouge, Café de Paris, Palais Royale, and Piccadilly Rendezvous imitated Larry Fay's formula. In 1926 clubowner David Stone estimated that nightclubs represented an investment of $5 million and employed 11,000 entertainers and 19,000 musicians. Stone also guessed that 20,000 outsiders traveled to Manhattan every night to visit nightclubs. In a decade that saw the rise of retail chains, partners Samuel G. Salvin and James N. Thompson created the first chain of nightclub franchises, Salvin-Thompson, which extended to Greenwich Village, Long Island, and eventually all the way to Florida. Don Dickerman opened a chain of themed nightclubs that catered largely to college students. Nightlife thus demonstrated the potential of becoming a service industry for a mass audience. Socialites soon got into the act and spent lavishly on pretentious and expensive new nightclubs, mostly in hotels and roof gardens.[9]

Nightclub owners needed all of the investment capital they could muster. Regular expenses for club entertainment alone were extraordinary. In 1930—when many Americans earned less than $1,000 annually—Les Ambassadeurs on Broadway near 50th Street paid its star trio of Lou Clayton, Eddie Jackson, and Jimmy Durante $2,700 a week. The club's other performers, including twelve dancers, earned a weekly total of $890; the eight-piece orchestra and its conductor, $940; and waiters, cashier, and doorman, $370. The club space was rented for $250 a week, costumes cost $200, advertising cost $50, and other expenses totaled around $100, leading to a weekly expense total of $5,500. While the food service earned about $400 weekly, and the cloakroom and cigarette concession privileges made $250, Les Ambassadeurs still had to earn about $4,900 from weekly receipts in order to break even. Such clubs thus imposed high cover (or admission) charges—usually three to five dollars a person—and high prices for drinks, set-ups (glasses with ice), and simple food. Along with Prohibition raids, high regular costs forced many clubs to fail. One room might host as many as seven different nightclubs in two or three years, and from 1924 to 1929 the transient headliner Texas Guinan worked in at least eight venues.[10] Entertainers and clubowners were deeply dependent upon the army of Broadway publicists and tabloid gossip columnists who kept their names advertised in the newspapers.

In many ways nightclubs were a typical booming service industry of the 1920s. However, nightclubs become popular—and notorious—because of attributes they possessed that were more difficult to quantify. The historian Bryan Palmer has argued that Georgia O'Keeffe's painting

*New York Night* (1929) evoked Manhattan's "heavy air . . . shadowing the explicit acts, daring desires, and unconscious mediations of a multitude of night wanderers." For contemporary New Yorkers, the same aura was attached to nightclubs. Nightlife reporters and other journalists, tabloid gossip columnists, cultural critics, and other literary observers especially described nightclubs as sites in which new sexual attitudes, ethnic and racial interaction, and explorations of new leisure behavior were indulged. For a wide range of participants and observers, 1920s night-clubs became an encapsulation of Americans' strongly ambivalent feelings about modern life.[11]

By 1927 midtown nightclubs had almost completely supplanted its most illustrious antecedents, the after-theater restaurant and the cabaret, and were found everywhere in the theater district. A patron touring the area in December 1927 would find Texas Guinan and her company performing at its northern border, in the Century Theatre building on Central Park West. Chez Helen Morgan, on 54th Street east of Broadway, featured the star of the hit musical *Show Boat.* The bandleader Vincent Lopez fronted his own establishment, the Casa Lopez, at Broadway and 50th, on the site of Lew Leslie's old Plantation Club. (Lopez's first Casa, on West 54th, had burned down the previous spring.) A revue enlivened the Chez Florence at 117 West 48th—the site of two clubs previously operated by Texas Guinan and still run by her brother Tommy. The Montmartre featured the acrobats Mitty and Tillio; the Yacht Club on 45th Street offered Pancho, a ukelele-playing Argentinian; the Little Club on West 44th presented the accordionist Phil Baker and the comedienne Marian Harris; and the Parody Club presented the "complete idiocy" of Clayton, Jackson, and Durante.[12]

By this time, though, the theater district was only the central anchor of a three-part Manhattan nightclub circuit, which also featured Greenwich Village, thirty blocks to the south, and Harlem, eighty blocks to the north. Greenwich Village's wartime reputation as a site of bohemian radicalism had faded, as zealous self-promoters and tour buses had reduced the scene to a crowded parody of its former self. Barney Gallant's restaurant on West Third Street inspired a new nightclub scene in the Village, however, and was joined by the Four Trees and the Spanish-themed El Chico restaurants. Don Dickerman lured bohemian-seeking tourists and collegians to his elaborate Pirate's Den and County Fair clubs. As the sociologist Caroline Ware noted, "Village cabarets were relatively low-priced and were patronized more by college boys and girls out for a good time and less by 'sugar daddies' with chorus girls than were the midtown night clubs."[13]

Ware also observed, though, that the Village was being "eclipsed by the rising fame of Harlem." The mecca of African American migrants only attracted the fancy of white New Yorkers after 1925, when, according to a *Variety* reporter, Arthur "Happy" Rhone "virtually invented the Harlem night club." Rhone created a "millionaire's club" with floor shows that attracted the Barrymores, Charlie Chaplin, and other celebrities. Barron Wilkins's Exclusive Club was a pioneering Harlem cabaret of the early 1920s, which acquired white management after Wilkins's murder. The former world heavyweight champion Jack Johnson sold his club to Connie Immerman, who made Connie's Inn the next big nightclub sensation. Its fame was surmounted in turn by that of the Cotton Club, which like Connie's served only white customers. The Exclusive Club had generally excluded blacks as well. (Barron Wilkins's brother Leroy, the owner of Leroy's Club, was virtually the only black operator to ban white customers.) Small's Paradise, the 'Bamville, Tillie's Inn, the Nest Club, and Pod's and Jerry's were also thriving by 1929, when the trade journal *Variety* claimed that Harlem nightlife now "surpasses that of Broadway itself." Accompanied by less reputable "buffet flats" (brothels) and homosexual-oriented clubs, Harlem caught the fancy of affluent white New Yorkers tiring of the scenes in Midtown and the Village.[14]

Nightclub entertainment almost always began at about ten-thirty or eleven in the evening, after the conclusion of theater performances. Second sets by club performers began at one or two in the morning and were followed by miscellaneous entertainment concocted by waiters, hostesses, masters of ceremonies, and the customers themselves that might last until dawn. At Barney's in the Village the revue began at midnight. Lois Long, the nightlife columnist for a new magazine, the *New Yorker*, argued in 1926 that "life in New York only begins to get really amusing around two-thirty" when "professionals wander in after the night's work and do a little impromptu entertaining." The 44th Street Club, the Yacht Club, Texas Guinan's, and other midtown clubs "wake up and get jovial very late." In Harlem, Long found the Club 'Bamville deserted on Sunday night "until about four A.M.," when "hordes began arriving for the Monday morning breakfast-dance." In general "the colored habitués of the clubs" in Harlem arrived after their "daily toil cease[d] at three o'clock." Writing only days before a three o'clock legal closing time took effect, Long noted that establishments possessing state club charters "are fondly expecting to get away with" remaining open later.[15]

Many other clubgoers stayed very late into the night. Edmund Wilson reported on a visit to Texas Guinan's nightclub that lasted until four o'clock, while Stephen Graham persisted at a later Guinan venue until dawn. In 1926 Mayor James J. Walker publicly acknowledged his past patronage of cabarets after three o'clock. The diary of Carl Van Vechten, the music critic, photographer, and novelist, is a detailed record of one dedicated clubgoer. Van Vechten was a celebrated white "pioneer" in Harlem who made it his regular nightly destination in 1924 and 1925. (These visits provided material for his novel *Nigger Heaven*, published in 1926, which helped to stimulate the white stampede into Harlem nightlife.) In November 1924, Van Vechten recorded, he followed a dinner at Alfred Knopf's apartment (attended by George Gershwin) with a visit, in the company of the artist Miguel Covarrubias and others, "to Nigger land in Harlem"—Small's Paradise and the Capitol Palace. "Home at 4." In January he returned home from a party at Walter White's Harlem apartment at 12:45, but the next month he spent the entire night at a succession of Harlem cabarets, returning home at seven-thirty in the morning. In March he returned to Small's, and again the following month—"Home at 5."[16]

Late-night leisure was not new to Manhattan. Decades earlier taverns and other working-class establishments gained notoriety among the middle classes for their gaslit activities, and the wealthy had stretched the length of reputable evenings in lobster palaces and prewar cabarets. But the 1920s seemed to bring a wholesale reorientation of the average day for a large number of well-to-do New Yorkers, making them into entirely nocturnal creatures. Carl Van Vechten regretted waking, hung over, at ten in the morning, while Mayor Jimmy Walker gained fame for rising regularly at noon. Besides nightclubs, other leisure businesses accommodated the trend. Restaurant chains such as Childs's, Horn and Hardart/ Automat, Schrafft's, Stouffer's, and Longchamps sought the patronage of both the vast middle class and nightlife denizens, keeping their franchises open at all times. Midtown Childs and Automat locations often played host in the predawn hours to raucous gatherings by homosexual men and prostitutes.[17]

The nocturnal behavior centering on the nightclub districts posed a new challenge to the daytime norms of "respectable" New York culture. The presence of homosexuals and prostitutes was the most blatant indication that the night was a culturally alternate, liminal, or "inverted" time. Bryan Palmer has stated that the culture of the night in the West has consisted of "moments excluded from histories of the day, a counterpoint within the time, space, and place governed and regulated by the logic and commerce of economic rationality and the structures of political rule." Night, Palmer argues, provides the "resources of otherness," its "imaginative creations and challenges."[18] In 1920s New York, as we have seen, nightlife was a somewhat rationalized business, upon which investors and employees depended. The twenty thousand taxicab drivers who ferried people such as Carl Van Vechten to their watering holes, for example, helped to impose a kind of cash nexus on nightlife.

Furthermore, unlike the European nightlife that Palmer and historians of cabarets have described, American nightclubs were bereft of any political radicalism.[19] Nevertheless, Manhattan nightlife in the 1920s always featured a tension between the rational and the irrational, between the economic and the cultural enterprises that took place within its bounds.

It was already a time-honored myth by 1920 that Manhattan's nightlife contained danger, luring individuals from the day's bright world of order into a dark kingdom of crime. For a century moralists had warned New Yorkers that nighttime leisure was rife with confidence games, extortion, entrapments, and other risks for gullible or unwary patrons. Some nightclubs lit their façades brightly and cultivated an elite atmosphere to banish shadows from their corners of the night, but the old criminal image lingered and other clubs were eager to perpetuate it. Some journalists noted that hundreds of taxicab drivers steered unknowing customers to "clip joints"—nighttime establishments that robbed patrons—for a share of the ill-gotten proceeds. Complaints flooded into newspapers and city offices about customer victimization in nightlife venues, focusing on new forms of fraud. Employees at clip joints, it was claimed, drugged, clubbed, and robbed customers, or at the very least appended extra zeroes to the sums on their personal checks. Broadway, the newspaper editor Stanley Walker argued, was "the clip street of the world, the slaughter house of Moronia."[20]

Various confidence games infected nightclubs and the surrounding sidewalks. As John O'Connor wrote in a detailed exposé, "The beer and alky runner, the junk pusher, the cannon mob and the booster; the hoop dropper, the fire-proofer and the stock-steerer; also the tat-man and the hijacker" plied their trades in Midtown, all targeting "the half-smart egg who thinks he is three jumps ahead of Broadway himself." Since the rackets functioned openly in public, victims were led to confuse legitimate transactions with illicit ones. Phony acting academies and schemes that bilked investors in nonexistent theatrical productions also fostered corruption on Broadway. Illicit (rather than merely sensationalist) tabloid newspapers extorted money from celebrities to scotch embarrassing stories, while "puff rackets" promised illusory reams of beneficial newspaper copy in exchange for high prices. In clip joints, waiters, bartenders, and bellhops, as well as taxi drivers, steered victims toward racketeers. In some clubs, coin-matching, dice, cards, and watered-down liquor figured in small-time scams.[21]

References to "morons" and "half-smart eggs" reflected the privileged resident identity and knowledge with which many Manhattanites—including journalists such as Walker and O'Connor—smugly credited themselves. Nocturnality, in their view, was a part of modern urban culture, and those who had not adjusted to its ways were outsiders in the city—tourists, perhaps, or newcomers. New Yorkers' contempt for "rubes" and "jakes" from the hinterlands dated back at least a century.[22] The particularly strong disdain toward out-of-towners in the 1920s may have been a function of their increasing number. Automobiles, new conduits such as the Holland Tunnel and the George Washington Bridge, and trains now brought a million workers into Manhattan each weekday, as well as five million visitors annually. These hordes turned many nightclubs into tourist attractions. These were the customers greeted by Texas Guinan's famous line, "Hello, suckers!" The new chronicler of nightlife, the *New Yorker* (which proclaimed that it was "not for the little old lady from Dubuque"), lampooned the "typical First Nighters" on Broadway and dissected the know-it-all attitude of the "Out-of-Towner" who "has viewed all the plays, visited every night club, done Chinatown. . . . He knows the exact address of Texas Guinan's new rathskeller and where Mrs. Lennox Uppeldyke is spending the weekend."[23]

Some, however, accused New Yorkers themselves of the same gullibility. An advertisement for a new play ridiculed natives for "trying to guess tomorrow's styles or trying to determine what night club to visit to be seen among the smartest people." A *New Yorker* informant argued that confidence men picked "as their clients only real New Yorkers, who have such an inherent fear of ridicule that they have never been known to 'squawk.'" Lois Long noted that the magician at one nightclub "enthralls New Yorkers so sophisticated that they, apparently, have never been to a county fair in Dubuque and seen the shell game put over on the yokels." Boasting aside, almost every kind of club customer harbored some fear of losing face and lucre to con artists in a treacherous corner of nightlife.[24]

Even if they had not been contaminated with confidence games and clips, nightclubs nevertheless appeared to visitors to be a dark, closeted, and different environment. Club spaces usually aspired to cut patrons off from the outside world. Many of them had no windows at all. In 1925 Edmund Wilson described Texas Guinan's club on West 48th Street as a "compact room" simply decorated by a swath of brightly colored cloth covering the ceiling. A year later Guinan worked in a larger room that was decorated with a similar simplicity.[25]

The closeted and windowless nature of nightclubs differentiated them from the traditional restaurant and tavern. Saloons, private clubs, and cabarets had tended to be walled up, though, and in the same manner the speakeasy of the 1920s provided a ubiquitous and decisive new influence. The speakeasy was Prohibition's main contribution to the shaping of urban public space. These protean watering holes could be located in any enclosed area that might evade the gaze of law enforcement. The *New Yorker* writers Niven Busch and Wolcott Gibbs found speakeasies in abandoned structures, below tailor's shops, above nightclubs, in apartments and brownstones, above and below banks, and in the back rooms of restaurants, grocery stores, and butcher shops. Another writer, Edward Hope, counted seventeen speakeasies on one block of 49th Street, between Fifth and Sixth Avenues. Official estimates of the number of speakeasies in New York City as a whole ranged from twenty-two thousand to one hundred thousand.[26]

Speakeasies almost invariably shut out the rest of the world. One establishment decorated its walls "with a translation of the skyline of New York into terms of bottles" and its blacked-out windows with "the counterfeit presentment of policemen peering in." Most speakeasies were furnished with expendable items in the event of destructive Prohibition raids. Rituals of entry heightened the liminal nature of the speakeasy experience. Special cards (some made out of wood or steel) admitted trusted individuals. "Spy-holes, moving shutters, padlocks, chains, bars, [and] a password" might also be used. False wall panels, electric dumbwaiters, and drains underneath the bartender's work space allowed for the quick disposal of liquor in case of raids.[27]

While most of them were crude and anonymous, speakeasies (like nightclubs) catered to diverse socioeconomic clienteles. Some establishments resembled old-time saloons, such as one on Eighth Avenue that was patronized by retired coachmen. Former restauranteurs offered excellent dining, while other owners operated circus and gypsy-style speakeasies, complete with entertainment, or resorts in "swank six-storey mansion[s]" replete with Italianate plaster busts and ruby-red upholstery. Charles Shaw noted that "speakeasies are owned to-day by bootleggers, stockbrokers, publishers, detectives, and (among others) by peroxide blondes in their early twenties."[28]

The speakeasy was a liminal space that also transformed behavior, especially with respect to consumption of alcohol. Many city residents embraced drinking with a new fervor. As the historian Michael Lerner has shown, Prohibition served as a spark for cultural rebellion among many in the white middle class, who abandoned their families' temperate self-discipline in a spirit of rebellion and liberation.[29] The new drinking was often unrestrained as well. Even in New York City consumption of alcohol became a highly private affair. Deprived of its traditional social trappings, drinking became a surreptitious, even obsessive act that brought out latent alcoholism in middle-class patrons. In 1929 Frank Ward O'Malley lamented the decline of "the old Cocktail Trail," which had been replaced by covert speakeasies that "completely shot Manhattan's whole mentality to hell." A humorist at the *New Yorker* noted "the present endurance-test method of drinking," while another argued that "drinking in New York has ceased to be an art. . . . It has become adventurous and intoxicating. The esthetes who drink for taste, conviviality, or any other purpose except the natural one, may go abroad." The British novelist Ford Madox Ford found that in New York, "few people object to your getting far drunker than a lord at any [European] social gathering," while Lois Long noted Manhattanites' preference for "drinking without interruption in the smokiest place they could find."[30]

To some extent the closeting of public drinking reduced public leisure; observers noted that many people increasingly cooked their own meals at home, or relied on deliveries from restaurants. In contrast, though, nightclubs generally adapted the speakeasy's closeted environment and drinking to a somewhat more public setting, blending it with a raucous leisure that offered an illusion of quasi-private intimacy.

The nightclub experience, unlike that of most speakeasies, played down individual self-absorption and consumption and emphasized group hilarity. Edmund Wilson's description of Texas Guinan's club show in 1925 shows how distant the bootlegger club's atmosphere was from that of many speakeasies. The young writer generally found Guinan, "driv[ing] all along through an evening of entertainment without gaiety, of speed without recreation," to be a distasteful manipulator of both her female chorus dancers and her audience. The evening began with a harem show of barely draped female forms and gradually evolved into a maelstrom of orchestrated excitement. By four o'clock fistfights threatened to erupt among the customers. As the preface to this book noted, Stephen Graham witnessed a similar scene the next year at Guinan's 300 Club, but unlike Wilson he found much to praise, including the "smart girl in black with silver flowers on her hips" selling dolls, the four strolling guitarists, and Guinan's "near-naked girls" who sang "a song about cherries." Graham's evening ended not in fisticuffs but in exhaustion, as the clock tolled five times and the weary guests staggered out under a brightening predawn sky.[31]

Observers associated the consumption of such nightclub frivolity with the hedonistic and carefree leisure of New York's wealthy. The antics of well-heeled customers in nightclubs sold many newspapers and magazines. As in the cabarets of the 1910s, nightclubs at first seemed to be the plaything of affluent youth, whose leisure behavior was promoted by F. Scott Fitzgerald and others as a cultural vanguard of the 1920s. A signal early event was the publication in 1925 of Ellin Mackay's two-part *New Yorker* essay, "Why We Go to Cabarets," which caused a sensation. The daughter of one of the world's richest men, Mackay wrote that wealthy youth "go [to cabarets] because we prefer rubbing elbows . . . with all sorts and kinds of people . . . to dancing at an exclusive party."

Mackay's essay boosted sales of the struggling new magazine. In the following year her love of diversity was expressed anew in her marriage to the Jewish immigrant composer Irving Berlin, which became a society scandal. In the same spirit, the adolescent saxophonist Roger Wolfe Kahn, the scion of a wealthy Wall Street family, fronted his own band in nightclubs before he opened his own, Le Perroquet de Paris, on West 57th Street in 1926.[32]

Roger's father, Otto Kahn—a Jewish German native, a British peer, and the chairman of Kuhn, Loeb—led the movement of older wealthy New Yorkers into the nightclub scene. Kahn combined business and philanthropy with a love for a wild good time. The *New Yorker* called him "our favorite millionaire," and clubowners agreed. At the Hollywood Restaurant, the impresario Nils T. Granlund recalled, Kahn often arrived with "twenty or thirty heavy eating guests" in tow. One night a dancer "came down and covered [Kahn's] face with lip rouge," and the next evening he brought the troupe of the Metropolitan Opera for dinner.[33] Other very wealthy New Yorkers also were drawn into the nightclub orbit. The heiress and sculptor Gertrude Vanderbilt Whitney, for example, attended the opening of the Chez Fysher nightclub and briefly succeeded Texas Guinan as hostess at the second Club El Fey.[34]

"Class clubs" sprang up to exploit this new elite conspicuous consumption in nightlife. These included the Lido-Venice, the Beaux Arts Gold Room Supper Club, and later the Heigh-Ho Supper Club (which replaced the Lido-Venice at the same site). The decor was ornate and French-influenced, but the clubs also introduced elaborate mechanical devices that modernized the simple genre of room pioneered by Larry Fay. Roger Wolfe Kahn spent a quarter of a million dollars of his father's money installing goldfish tanks and mirrors in the floors and tabletops and a silver stage proscenium at Le Perroquet de Paris.[35] The novelty of air conditioning allowed the Club Mirador to remain open for the summer, when most other indoor clubs closed. The Chateau Madrid on West 54th Street featured a retractable roof, which Lois Long called "the most original night-club idea of the [1927] season." Revolving and sinking stages soon also came to the more lavish nightclubs. In their pursuit of social loftiness, the class clubs also encouraged physical elevation. While only business executives were welcomed in the Cloud Club on the seventy-seventh floor of the new Chrysler Building, the world's new tallest structure, all well-heeled customers could savor the open-air summer roof clubs at the Alamac, Astor, Biltmore, Cascades, McAlpin, Majestic, Pennsylvania, and Waldorf-Astoria hotels. The work of the Vienna-born artist Joseph Urban, seen in many roof gardens, became the signature style of the elite nightclub.[36]

While other nightclubs could not compete with such lavish spending on locales, decor, and technology, other attributes of the elite venues were widely copied. By 1927 diverse dress codes gave way to a general requirement for formality in men's and women's wear. The *New Yorker* added symbols to its nightclub listings that indicated whether one "must dress" formally, had "better dress," or did not need to dress formally at all to receive service at an establishment. Pretensions to etiquette also emerged. At the Ivory Tower in Greenwich Village, for example, a posted notice advised customers that "the hostess has not time for verbal combats. . . . Familiarity is not to be tolerated. Admittance to the 'Tower' implies a compliment. It is not for social errors, the over-robust." While this notice read like a parody, Lois Long did detect extreme "snootiness" on the part of the Ivory Tower's staff.[37]

Nightclubs' sizeable investments in skilled waiting staff indicated a general effort to mimic the environment of the idle rich. While some waiter-performers mixed dancing and singing with their chores, more pretentious clubs offered sober and sycophantic service. Much of this was a bid to flatter customers into spending more. A head waiter, Jimmy Durante argued, was "the most important person in any club. . . . He is the front man, the contact man, the salesman for the house."[38] Favoritism toward the biggest spenders—possibly along with sheer overwork— also caused the haughtiness and rudeness of waiting staff to become a rich part of nightclub folklore. Similarly, coat-and-hat check and cigarette concessions (rented to clubowners by specialists) were club fixtures, adding overdeveloped services and superfluous fees to the customers' bills.[39]

Excessive spending, by middle-class and wealthy customers alike, was so central to clubgoing in the 1920s that it became a main component of the nightlife experience. It mattered not if a patron entered a clip joint or a reputable venue: funds inevitably seemed to evaporate in the dark. The high cover charge or *couvert* best illustrated this fact. Don Dickerman's Pirate's Den pioneered the admission fee in 1923, charging each puzzled customer fifty cents. By 1926 Lois Long indignantly noted that opening night at the Club Richman cost "ten dollars a head. The Mirador, not to be outdone, is placing it at twenty. Roger Wolfe Kahn . . . is murmuring something about a one-hundred-dollar couvert. I ask you—." (Kahn's club actually charged only twenty-five dollars on opening night, but that was still half of Long's weekly *New Yorker* expense account.)[40] Due to this trend, Long soon sensed "a revolt against the high couvert charge on the part of almost everybody except the [wealthy] butter-and-eggers." The new Villa Venice on East 60th Street advertised itself as a club where costs were "not crowded with extras, couvert, tax, etc.," but within weeks it was charging a cover of fifty cents a night, doubled on weekends. As late as 1929 Paul Whiteman's Club and the Midnight Frolic each imposed a cover of $6.60, and the Casanova Club charged $5.00. Clubs holding state charters made a pretense of collecting "dues" from "members" as the price of admission.[41]

Prices at tables were excessive as well. "The native New Yorker," Gilbert Seldes wrote, "goes to a night club with three friends, brings his own liquor, buys two bottles of White Rock [mineral water], and departs at the end of thirty minutes, paying twenty-two dollars exclusive of tips." The Club Mirador eventually charged two dollars "for the scrambled eggs that used to be included in the five dollar [cover] charge." H. I. Phillips of the *New York Sun* accused the average nightclub of being "a poorly ventilated room over a garage, or under a banana store," in which "the moment you take a seat you are in debt from $3.00 to $5.00" and eventually "spend from $20 to $100 to have less fun than [you] could get at home for $3.75, including the cost of the oranges and ice."[42]

The widespread criticism of high prices indicated that for many customers, the magical thrill of nocturnal leisure could evaporate along with the bills in their wallets. High prices also reminded participants that despite their mountainous revenues and free spending on amenities, nightclubs were confronted with hard economic realities. The threat of Prohibition raids, in Lois Long's words, gave clubs serving liquor the impetus to "boost couvert charges higher so that the cost of new decorations can be met," while "dry" clubs raised their rates *because* they earned no liquor revenue. If a police raid did not cause a club to close, then overspending probably would. Roger Wolfe Kahn's Le Perroquet de Paris had unsustainable expenses and closed after a few months. The Lido-Venice and the Beaux Arts were both quick casualties of the competition, and the Trocadero later failed at the site of the former as well. The Villa Venice's reversal of policy in favor of cover charges came too late, and it also was forced to close. A rough calculation indicates that only a handful of the hundreds of nightclubs founded between 1925 and 1928—Barney Gallant's, the El Chico, the Silver Slipper, and the Club Richman, to name a few of them—survived long enough in the same site and under the same owner to face the later perils of the Great Depression.

For most of the late 1920s, though, it was almost an article of faith in nightlife that these realities could be kept at bay. The nocturnal setting kept luring customers and observers away from a rational appreciation of the circumstances in which they shed their savings, their sobriety, and their wakefulness. Stephen Graham wrote one of the most glowing paeans to Manhattan escapism, *New York Nights*, which was published in 1927. Broadway, he argued, "is not reality, it is transfiguration" of the mind and body. "Broadway is a great place of health. It is a free electric-ray treatment. It is a tonic light-bath. Here voices are clearer, eyes brighter, and the whole body more vivid than anywhere else in New York." "Poe's man in the crowd," he continued, "is walking there every night, back and forth, forward and back again, his eyes lit by some dream." Graham acknowledged that it all is "the artifice of night." Everyday life in Manhattan "is almost intolerable," so "a great deal of New York night life is purely escape from New York."

> The night club disenchants New York. You pass the portals of a guarded house, leave the throngs in the Avenue, and straightway you are transported to another clime. You are in a village street in Millen, Georgia, with wisps of cotton blowing about. There is dancing in the village square. . . . Old wooden lamp-posts stand round the square, with smoky kerosene lamps in the quaint lanterns above. Lamp-dazzled Emperor moths are on the wing, and float above in the dim light. Men and women sit about at tables, talking or listening or merely existing. . . . Inside all is unreality, sentiment, indulgence and relaxation. New York has been banished.[43]

Similarly, despite his distaste for Texas Guinan, Edmund Wilson admitted that the flower on her bosom, a "great closed glowing peony that melts from pink through deep rose to orange," was "hypnotic to drunken eyes," while her "shining white teeth" were a "formidable trap." Even the carnival-inspired theme clubs of Don Dickerman, directed at college audiences, lured customers with a complete package of surreal escapism. The Pirate's Den featured costumed attendants, a sinister lighting scheme, eye-patched sea-chanty singers, and wisecracking parrots; the Blue Horse club evoked the popular surrealism of George Herriman's Krazy Kat cartoons with fantastic murals; and the nearby Daffydill featured what the *New Yorker* called "entertainment, hey-hey dance music, [and] coo-coo decorations." Dickerman's County Fair club on East 9th, meanwhile, recreated rural America, complete with haystacks, fiddlers, white picket fences, and square dances.[44] Such escapist themes encapsulated the appeal of these strange, expensive, closeted new leisure venues to a mass urban audience.

While atmospheric imagery redolent of pirate dens, southern villages, and other exotic locales might have offered nightclub customers a kind of escape from everyday life, it also provided customers with extended references to ethnic and racial diversity in the real world. This was not new to Manhattan nightlife. In the 1840s a tavern called Aladdin's Cave opened its doors, and in ensuing decades P. T. Barnum's museum, circuses, carnivals, stage shows, vaudeville, and moving pictures had portrayed various peoples in elaborate and racially derogatory representations. Throughout this time, the portrayal of ethnicity in New York held a special import. More than any other locale in the United States, the city was constituted by a vast array of immigrants and their offspring.[45] New York's unparalleled immigrant population put the city at the vanguard of cosmopolitan diversity in America.

By the 1920s, though, in the view of traditionalists, this diversity had created a crisis. The United States was linked to the rest of the world like never before, through trade, communications, finance, war, immigration, and colonialism. Heavy immigration made European identities problematic to natives and newcomers. While a xenophobic Congress in 1924 had shut off most immigration with a restrictive quota system, New York City already was home to more than three million first- and second-generation Americans. In the 1926 Manhattan telephone book "Smith" fell to second place behind "Cohen" as the most common surname. Socially, as Ford Madox Ford observed, Manhattan was "a place for ever receiving accessions of populations that for ever pass on . . . the situation is one of a constant flux and reflux."[46]

To nightlife participants and critics alike, nightclubs were simmering with disturbing new interethnic encounters and relationships. As a result, ethnic motifs in the decor, personnel, and entertainment of nightclubs reflected the insecurities of native-born white Americans in an increasingly diverse society. These portrayals both fulfilled white customers' taste for exotic escapism and expressed their anxieties about the world outside nightclub walls.

Representations of European ethnicities, while stereotyped, were generally positive. Postwar French and Russian vogues, filled with strains of artistic modernism, deeply influenced nightlife of the early 1920s. Since the last century fashions in New York nightlife decor had been dominated by French styles. Originators of cabarets and revues such as Florenz Ziegfeld copied belle epoque motifs, and the more elite nightclubs of the mid-1920s followed suit. In 1927 the Moulin Rouge, Bal Tabarin, Beaux Arts, Montmartre, and Monte Carlo clubs opened within months of each other, mimicking the belle epoque mode.[47] Parisian nightlife itself had been caught up in a vogue for Russian culture and design, and this trend also affected Manhattan, beginning with the influential 1922 visit of the Paris-based Russian revue *Chauve Souris* ("The Bat"). A colorful series of Russian-themed "tea rooms," including the Russian Inn, Samarkand, Kazbek, Cave of Fallen Angels, Little Bear (known as "Moscow-on-the-Elevated"), Russian Art, Kretchma, and Russian Bear entertained audiences in Midtown and the Village.[48]

Many "Russian" entrepreneurs were Jewish immigrants who chose not to broadcast their religious affiliation. The marginal status of Eastern European Jews in Manhattan in the 1920s obscured their prominence in the new nightlife. Jewish entrepreneurs, ranging from veteran restaurant personnel such as David Stone (of the Club Maxine), Louis

Schwartz (the King's Terrace), and Joe Moss and Jake Amron (the Holly-wood Restaurant) to the entertainer Harry Richman (the Club Rich-man) and the underworld financier Arnold Rothstein (who invested in many clubs), were central to the financing and the organization of the nightclub business. While the press highly publicized some of these indi-viduals, it rarely described their religious and ethnic backgrounds and often subtly denigrated them as social outsiders. (This was why Irving Berlin's marriage to Ellin Mackay in 1926 caused her family and social circle to react in horror.) Some Jewish entrepreneurs remained content out of the glare of publicity. Arnold Rothstein did not trumpet his night-club investments or his underwriting of the biggest theatrical hit of the decade, *Abie's Irish Rose*—a comedy portraying a Jewish-Irish romance. Some never practiced the faith; Harry Richman, for example, claimed, "I don't know a thing about religion." Beyond the usual comedian's dia-lect routines, virtually no acknowledgments of Jewish culture were made in most nightclubs.[49]

The issue of Jewish patronage of nightlife received more overt gentile criticism. Some argued that Jews tended not to patronize nightlife; one bartender told Konrad Bercovici that legal access to sacramental wine during Prohibition obviated the need for speakeasies on the Lower East Side. More typically, though, the early *New Yorker*, which was dominated by Anglo-Saxons, expressed a satiric but real concern for the influx of Jewish customers in the "class" clubs. In 1926 Lois Long predicted that as a result of high cover charges, "the *Gus Eismans*, dragged thither by the *Lorelei Lees*, will be in the majority." The next year Long regretted that Paul Whiteman's and other new clubs "deliberate[ly] cater[ed] to the wholesale hat trade of Thirty-fourth Street or its wealthier equivalents"—the Jewish middle class—and that Chinese restaurants on Broadway were "jammed with jaunty clerks and woiking goils, all having an elegant time."[50] Illustrators also satirized the social fluidity of nightlife with a veneer of anti-Semitism. In 1929, Peter Arno depicted a middle-class Jewish man ordering his dinner at an exclusive roof garden, asking the formidable waiter: "Why dontcha make a suggestion—like they do at the Ritz?" Such caricatures typified the ethnic anxieties of white Protestants in Manhattan. Some of them criticized the new prominence of Jewish songwriters and entertainers, and some "exclusive" venues (such as Don Dickerman's Heigh-Ho Club) banned Jewish customers.[51]

Non-European, nonwhite cultures encouraged even stronger ambiva-lence, a potent blend of attraction and repulsion, in nightclub patrons. In the early 1920s fascination with the exotic had been stimulated by the highly publicized adventures of T. E. Lawrence and the discovery of Tutankhamen's tomb. Sophie Tucker's 1925 novelty song "King Tut" and such Nile-themed businesses as the Sakele Salon on Fifth Avenue (featuring incense, a "ceiling . . . depict[ing] a starlit Egyptian garden," and "statues, delicate carving and paintings with Egyptian themes") reflected the latter influence. Nightlife designers often resorted to wildly eclectic, often Orientalist styles. A "Moorish arch arrangement" greeted diners at the Grill at the McAlpin Hotel, while movie theaters in the Loew's chain featured "Indo-Persian decor" on 72nd Street, "an indescribable marriage of Classical, Islamic, Mayan, Indian, and Oriental motifs" on the façade at 175th Street, and an "Italian Baroque fantasia" in the gigantic Paradise Theater in the Bronx. Stephen Graham explicitly linked Middle Eastern exotica with the basic escapist allure of the nightclub, which replaced the stresses of modern life with "dreamland, or Nirvana, or a Mussulman's paradise where *houris* beguile." East Asian motifs were scarce, but the Ka Launa O Hawaii tea room on West 51st Street did gain a following.[52]

Perhaps surprisingly, ethnic traditions from the Western Hemisphere were largely missing from nightlife in the 1920s. The tango vogue of the 1910s persisted in nightclub dance acts such as that of Rosita and Ramon, but the Latino influence in Manhattan was now relatively quiescent. Puerto Rican migration and Cuban immigration were only beginning to grow, and their leisure institutions largely went unnoticed by outsiders. In 1930 the reporter Morris Markey described new sites in Spanish Harlem such as the Puerto Rican nightclub El Moderno Billar, the Teatro Campoamor cinema, and the Club Mella, but he concluded pessimistically that these venues represented "a way of life that must ever remain impenetrable to us." The year before, Dorothy Parker had made the opposite (but equally inaccurate) prediction about Native American influences: "The Negro age is passing; the Indian age is upon us. We shall be flooded with Indian music, Indian art, and so-called Indian books."[53] A Native American revival never touched Manhattan nightlife.

Conversely, representations of black life filled nightclub environs. African art and cuisine were hardly honored in New York's clubs and restaurants; African culture was accorded little majesty. Instead, whites' "jungle" caricatures of blacks in nightclubs dominated, giving a new face to their traditional identification of black people with private, covert, and illicit urges and behavior.[54] For all of its championing of Harlem nightclubs, for example, the *New Yorker* exhibited a large residue of anti-black stereotypes—more comical than vicious, but racist all the same. In 1926, for example, Ben Hecht derided white clubgoers' "Caliph Complex" in Harlem nightclubs, "giggling condescendingly . . . from the moment we step out of the taxi," but he also felt contempt for Harlemites, noting that "only five years ago a negro was somebody you gave your old pants to." Lois Long warned white readers to go to Harlem with "a friend who knows his way about" since "the liveliest places don't welcome unknown whites." Her views were shared by white pleasure-seekers in Harlem, such as the "dauntless crowds" at the Savoy Ballroom "who have heard that real razor fights sometimes go on there."[55]

Nightclubs in Harlem meant far more to the district's residents than they did to white visitors from downtown. As the historian David Levering Lewis has noted, black-controlled cabarets, clubs, speakeasies, and dance halls were community centers, the frequent sites of charity and fundraising events, family celebrations, and political organizing. The sociologist and civil rights activist Charles S. Johnson used venues such as Pod's and Jerry's as meeting places for strategic discussions. Performances by jazz musicians were a frequent component of gatherings in nightlife venues. The pioneering orchestras of Fletcher Henderson, Andy Preer, and Duke Ellington, the pianists James P. Johnson, Luckey Roberts, and Willie the Lion Smith, and countless small ensembles proclaimed black Harlem's cultural renaissance with the greatest spirit and originality. Beginning in 1927, when his orchestra began its residency at the Cotton Club, Ellington coupled his role as Harlem's most original musical ambassador with a commitment to civil rights organizations such as the NAACP. While white customers caricatured Harlem jazz as the expression of jungle and plantation clichés and the aptly named bandleader Paul Whiteman crowned himself the "king of jazz" in Midtown's Palais Royal, black musicians created music that balanced tradition and modernity, individual release and community identity. It was music that would help Harlemites to cope with grinding poverty and injustice and would inspire innovative creative endeavor for generations to come.[56]

White-operated Harlem nightclubs mostly rehashed and confirmed fantasies about the docility and incorrigibility of black people, whom some whites thought had barely changed since the time of slavery. Stephen Graham, for example, was easily taken in by the plantation setting of a Cotton Club revue: "A group of Negroes are singing a Dixie song, and the Negroes are like slaves and they are like children. They are fondly unified in a sentimental group, and they croon and beguile with notes of long-drawn sweetness and sadness."[57] Black performers, inseparable from the plantation myth, were perceived not as representatives of a significant new population in Manhattan but as the facilitators of white escapism.

The escapism of Stephen Graham and others grew out of their conscious blindness to the realities of the Harlem nightclub business. The wealthy white vogue for Harlem first encouraged and then was served by an orchestrated campaign by liquor bootleggers to gain control of the uptown entertainment industry. The campaign was a violent one. The black clubowner Barron Wilkins was murdered in front of his club by a Harlem rival, "Yellow Charleston," and the nightclub investor and "numbers king" Casper Holstein was muscled out of business by the white gang leader Vincent "Mad Dog" Coll. (The white gambler Connie Immerman, the owner of Connie's Inn, also became a victim of gangland kidnapping.) In 1926 Larry Fay's associate Owney Madden, assisted by "Big Frenchy" DeMange and Arnold Rothstein, took over a tavern on Lenox Avenue and 142nd Street and transformed it into the Cotton Club, the most lavish whites-only "jungle revue" in Harlem. Other "exclusive" Harlem sites after 1926, such as Connie's, also banned most or all black customers. By 1927 the African American writer Rudolph Fisher could note that "the best of Harlem's black cabarets have changed their names and turned white."[58]

For that reason it proved easy to import the Harlem "experience" into Midtown. A number of successful Harlem-themed clubs opened in the theater district in the late 1920s, saving many white customers uptown cab fares. Gangsters poured investment money into the Plantation Club on 50th Street and Broadway, the Club Alabam' on West 44th Street, and the Black Bottom on East 56th Street, which Lois Long denigrated in the *New Yorker* as "a dull dump" featuring "two or three very unattractive girl entertainers." (Perhaps, she allowed, "you would have to be in just the right slumming mood.") Long was slightly more enthusiastic about the popular Club Alabam', which featured a "Creole Follies" with male tap dancers and comic acts, such as a pantomime poker game. Meanwhile, on Broadway theatergoers were treated to a parade of all-black revues, including *Shuffle Along, Chocolate Dandies, Africana,* and *Rang Tang.*[59]

No aspect of the Manhattan nightclub environment generated as much comment, though—or revealed as much ambivalence and anxiety about modern urban life—as the presence of the so-called new woman. Young or old, black or white, rich or poor, women who flaunted traditional notions of femininity became completely associated with the notoriety of the new nightlife.

Tireless promotion—orchestrated by her skilled and devoted publicist, John Stein—made Texas Guinan the most ubiquitous representative of a subset of these new women, middle-aged nightclub hostesses. Revealingly, though, Guinan eclipsed the fame of other middle-aged hostesses (such as Belle Livingston) by both inflicting and receiving public ridicule. Guinan aggressively flaunted her bulging waist, overpainted face, shock of wavy red hair, and expansive and flamboyant gowns and jewelry. Drawing on hundreds of audience-pleasing and attention-getting tricks

Figure 2. Mary "Texas" Guinan entertaining in an unidentified nightclub. First employed at the Club El Fey, Guinan was the most highly publicized club performer in the late 1920s—largely due to her self-promotion and frequent arrests. Billy Rose Theatre Collection, The New York Public Library for the Performing Arts, Astor, Lenox, and Tilden Foundations.

she had learned on the vaudeville circuit, Guinan won over patrons—especially males—with superficially insulting words or gestures that actually flattered them with attention (see Fig. 2). Her trademark greeting, "Hello, sucker!" had been a standard vaudeville line, inspired by the various "sucker" sayings of the veteran humorist Wilson Mizner. "Let's give the little girl a big hand" was also a well-worn line, but Guinan's characterization of "butter-and-egg men" (big spenders in the audience) apparently originated with her at the El Fey.[60]

Guinan mastered the flow of time in the nightclub show, controlling the pace of action, directing her performers, and bluntly manipulating the reactions and the behavior of her customers. In doing so, as Edmund Wilson suggested in 1925, Guinan projected a rare form of public female power as well as a good-humored but very real new kind of coercion in a place of leisure. Her persona relied on existing stage conceptions of the overweight, middle-aged comedienne, a type first popularized in the 1910s by Marie Dressler, Sophie Tucker, and others. As the historian Susan Glenn has shown, these earlier female stage performers, as well as Sarah Bernhardt and Fanny Brice, had struggled to gain control over the depiction of women and female sexuality. Their alternately bold, vampish, and extroverted performances offered early models for a feminist theater. Texas Guinan, by contrast, diluted the subversive elements in these middle-aged female personae with a relentless and often frenzied mixture of officiousness and insult. As Stephen Graham detected, customers were won over by Guinan not by her intellect or brashness but by undertones of vulnerability and an aching for acceptance, which softened the impact of her barbs.[61]

In large part, though, the publicity that Guinan generated about herself and that journalists, photographers, and artists propagated presented her as a grotesque example of womanhood. (Reginald Marsh's portrait of Guinan in action, a typical example of his lurid renderings of Manhattan nightlife, perhaps best sums up this derogatory image.)[62] The main function of Texas Guinan's gaudy, ill-mannered, and paunchy persona seems to have been to offer a contrast to the images of youthful beauty presented by the members of her nightclub choruses. The young chorus dancer, not the middle-aged hostess, was the most highly publicized female persona in nightclubs, and she also became the focus for most of the gender discourse about the clubs.

Since at least the 1800s the male gaze in saloons, riveted on isolated females such as barmaids and prostitutes, had created a new objectification of women in urban society.[63] Florenz Ziegfeld's adaptation of the French chorine to American tastes in the decade after 1908 incorporated elements of the athletic, companionate "Gibson Girl" persona but also presented a rebuke to the nascent feminism of middle-aged singers, actresses, and comediennes. The Ziegfeld dancer was scantily clad, daringly physical, and thoroughly at home in the modern city, but she was also adolescent, cheerful, and Anglo-Saxon, notable (in Edmund Wilson's words) for her "peculiar frigidity and purity."[64] (Fanny Brice's Jewishness and anarchic comedy offered a contrast in the Follies, the exception that proved the rule of the chorus members' femininity.) The Ziegfeld formula put stage women back on a new kind of pedestal. Blending "idealism and voyeurism" (in Susan Glenn's words), Ziegfeld created a sexualized yet playfully unthreatening female image that was exclusively Anglo-Saxon. For a time he also employed a unit of the Tiller Girls, the chorus-line enterprise operating out of Britain which many observers criticized for its bland, mechanical precision. Larry Fay emulated Ziegfeld's formula in his nightclub, but Texas Guinan branded the El Fey dancers as her own "little girls," whom she took with her on outings, public appearances, and eventually to her own nightclubs. Some of the dancers were young indeed. Ruby Keeler was hired by Fay at the age of fourteen; two years later she met her future husband, Al Jolson, at the El Fey. (The original corps also included the acrobatic dancer Ruby Stevens, later known as Barbara Stanwyck.) Guinan's domineering treatment of very young dancers became a model for club impresarios of the 1920s, and enhanced the exploitative, anti-feminist nature of the chorus line in American culture.[65]

At the same time, though, nightclubs proved popular with female customers. The clubs offered them an arena in which they gained a rough social equality with their male companions. The nightlife reporting of Lois Long in the *New Yorker*, for example, contained no condemnations of the objectification of chorus dancers; she generally praised or panned establishments in a genderless voice. Long expressed no sense of sisterhood with the women—her critical authority was brandished with too much pride—and she almost never suggested that male and female customers might react differently to the clubgoing experience. Histories of the magazine, as well as memos exchanged between Long and her editor, Harold Ross, indicate that the nightlife reporter reveled in a sense of equality with her male colleagues.[66] Her attitude seemed to have been shared by nightclub performers, such as the Yacht Club Boys and Muriel Johnston of the Salon Royal, who "all sing songs, and insult each other, and deplore the ficklenesses of the sexes with the proper gay disdain. Just good, clean, casual romping." In the same vein, a *New Yorker* humorist suggested that the old-fashioned "leer" of men in saloons had vanished in the new environment of the speakeasy—"unless an effect is produced on the ladies the leer is nothing." A poem in the magazine, "Night Club," portrayed men and women engaged in a frantic dance that played down gender differences: "Fat men shifting; thin gals swaying; . . . That's what the mammas and the daddies keep a-saying; / Flogging dead nerve-ends—flogging and flaying, / Gulping down pleasure to the utmost crumb!"[67]

Journalists in the 1920s quickly hardened the image of the freedom- and equality-seeking female at leisure in the nightclubs into a stereotype. Ziegfeld's wartime American "girl" was now perceived as a sexual and economic challenge to men; still denigrated for her immaturity and lack of breeding, she nevertheless now seemed to employ negotiating styles that drove up her "purchase price" on the nightlife market. The *New Yorker* repeatedly presented versions of this caricature of the insouciant yet calculating "gold digger." Theodore Pratt quoted a line from a sermon by a young female Salvation Army officer on a Bowery street corner: "If I hadn't come to Jesus Christ when I was a little girl I would be out now having a good time like all the other girls." Frederick Lewis

Allen analyzed the department-store mannequin on Fifth Avenue who "has nothing in [her] expression at all. . . . she had gone beyond sophistication, beyond ennui," implying that the dummies reflected the behavior of real, contemporary "Fifth Avenue girls." "Where does this leave the capable-and-efficient-modern-girl theory, the brilliant-and-athletic-modern-girl theory?" Even Lois Long, reviewing nightclubs, recycled the gold-digger trope, while John Held, Jr. perfected pictorial representations of the "flapper." On college campuses, men instituted rating systems to evaluate potential dates for their sexual appeal, while women rated men's ability to treat them. In spite of the genuinely companionate new elements of the leisure environment of the 1920s, then, young women faced continued objectification and new male machinations.[68]

Sometimes women in nightclubs faced overt hostility from men. The proximity of the sexes occasionally released latent misogyny and provoked the violent abuse of women. With lawbreakers and racketeers in charge of many establishments, an element of violence existed. As we have seen, the threat of violence was part of nightlife's transgressive appeal, but it also led to damaging clashes. At the Club El Fey, Larry Fay's associate Tommy O'Neal used his fists to keep customers in line, and Fay himself was a "bruiser" who bullied his staff and once chased a patron around the club with a fire axe. Texas Guinan encouraged male customers to compete for dancers and promised them "a fight a night or your money back!" Extreme incidents included the 1928 death of Bessie Poole, a visitor from Massachusetts, who was killed when an employee at Tommy Guinan's Chez Florence struck her during a dispute.[69] The story of Harry Richman, the star of the revue in his own nightclub, is also instructive. Richman cultivated a reputation as the "Romeo of Broadway." However, in addition to luring female chorus performers to his dressing room and his Long Island home, he also abused them. "My anger at women was always beyond love, beyond everything else," he confessed in his autobiography. One woman struck him in the face with flowers he had sent her; during ensuing sexual relations Richman "kept at her until her nose was bleeding and her face was brilliant red. . . . My arm was so tired from beating her I was ready to give up." The woman may have been the dancer Ellen Franks, who sued Richman in 1929 for inflicting injury. When an explosion on Richman's pleasure boat killed the nightclub dancer Helen Walsh and injured Virginia Biddle, also a dancer, Biddle also sued Richman.[70]

Along with high prices, such violence, misogyny, and general unpleasantness in nightclubs helped by 1927 to create a backlash of sorts among participants, a critique of the value of clubgoing, and an indictment of modern pleasure-seeking that echoed the critiques of contemporary moralists. As mentioned earlier Edmund Wilson had characterized Texas Guinan's showmanship as "entertainment without gaiety" and "speed without recreation," while the *New Yorker* poet saw dancers in clubs "flogging dead nerve-ends—flogging and flaying." Lois Long tempered her general enthusiasm for nightlife by arguing that "the night clubs thrive on the average man's fear of going home" after the theater. "The moment four people reach the sidewalk after the theatre the cry goes up 'Don't break up the party,' and he who succumbs is lost for the night." When "the occasional individual . . . has the courage to desert," "broken and tired men and women watch him bitterly and enviously as he lurches toward the street." Within the clubs, Long argued, "the majority of chronic night-life-goers make up a pretty sad bunch. . . . They look ineffably bored with each other. . . . You can't tell me that there isn't something fatally wrong with [them], that they can squander dollars and hours in this way." The clubs thus were "the tawdry, pitiful, desperate, glittering refuge of lost souls." "This," she concluded, "is why Europe is hurling at us the accusation that we certainly take pleasure hard in this benighted country."[71]

Long's editor, Harold Ross, generalized in similar tones about the entire nightclub district. "Broadway has its moments of glamorous beauty when it shines forth, but for every one of these moments there are long dull hours of the day and night when it is as tawdry as Coney at its worst." At three in the morning, he claimed, "the dreary street sprawls slant-wise across the town in all the ugly meanness of disuse." In such observations we detect the limits of what Lewis Erenberg has called the "action environment" of the nightclub.[72] The frenzy, sexuality, and conspicuous spending on alcohol and cover charges liberated and diverted the individual but rarely guided her to a purposeful new sensibility or identity.

Perhaps in recognition of such shortcomings to modern leisure and other novelties, a nostalgia for the Manhattan of the previous century was revived in the mid-1920s. As the historian Max Page notes, it was in these years that affluent New Yorkers began to fight to preserve old buildings and to slow the pace of "creative destruction" in Manhattan. Nostalgic books on the "gay Nineties" appeared regularly. The *New Yorker* ran articles on gardening and roof farming next to its Broadway reviews, as well as Babette Deutsch's memoir of privileged city life in the 1890s, a "picture-book world" of soda fountains, strolling mandolinists, and barbershop balladeers: "Sentimental. Unjazzed. Jolly." A large 1927 cartoon in the magazine showed a couple riding in a Central Park carriage while surrounded by automobiles, trucks, buses, and horse races: "Let's just sit back now, Wilmot, and pretend we're living in grandmother's day." The magazine revealingly juxtaposed nightclubs and this yearning for the past. A cartoon by Helen Hokinson depicts an elderly woman asking a costumed employee outside Don Dickerman's Pirate's Den, "Please, sir, can you direct me to Ye Chintz Cat Tea Shoppe?" John Held, Jr. concocted an elaborate, deliberately archaic woodcut illustration for the magazine depicting Manhattan clubs as inns of the 1830s.[73]

Escapism from the modern city also took the form of literal flight toward leisure that seemed the antithesis of the closeted nightclub. For the affluent, vacations in the tropics became the rage. In 1928 a New Yorker could take a nine-day cruise to Havana for $175, while the Gulf Coast Limited train took passengers to Fort Myers, Florida in thirty-six hours. Such forays were widely viewed as alternatives to wintertime leisure in nightclubs and similar city venues. Enough of the *New Yorker*'s readers pursued distant vacations to lead the magazine to begin a new column in 1929 called "Out of Town"; the first installment explored mayoral election politics in Palm Beach. Hawaii's tourism board specifically solicited the clientele of the "class clubs" and roof gardens by announcing that "the smart Winter Throng is gathering at Waikiki."[74]

These countervailing tendencies should not be exaggerated, though. Nightlife boomed, and clubs kept multiplying. In 1927, the first year in which the city government specifically regulated nightclubs, 334 of these institutions were licensed; the number rose to 376 the following year.[75] Conflicting opinions about nightclubs—and about the cultural sensibility they represented—expressed the unavoidable ambivalence that people feel about experimenting with new behavior. What was important, though, was that the experiment was taking place at all, and that it was thriving as an economic and social institution. It was the vocation of social activists and reformers to recognize and evaluate such institutions, and it was the duty of government to regulate them for the public good. As the nightclub emerged as the signal site of modern life in urban America, filled with complex representations of the class, racial, ethnic, and gender distinctions found in contemporary New York City, reformers and administrators began to make it a target for investigation and regulation.

# CHAPTER 2
## "The Hostess Evil"

In 1928 Texas Guinan's instinct for publicity brought her to the office of the Committee of Fourteen. The committee was the city's celebrated anti-prostitution reform group. For more than two decades it had closed brothels and successfully lobbied for new anti-prostitution laws. In recent years the committee had accused nightclubs such as Guinan's of helping to revive the clandestine sale of female sexual favors. On this occasion, though, the reform group's staff welcomed Guinan as she arrived with some female nightclub dancers. The hostess attempted to photograph George Worthington, the committee's general secretary, together with an entertainer from the Silver Slipper club. Worthington later told the committee that he agreed to pose with Guinan because he believed that the group "gained more than it lost by the publicity."[1]

This vignette is highly suggestive of the curious encounter of New York social reformers with the nightlife of the 1920s, and of the general predicament of civic life as well. The city had a long tradition of reform, driven by Victorian Protestantism and the city's history of poverty, crime, and moral offenses or "vice." For decades these articulate and affluent reformers—guided by their class, ethnic, and racial biases—expressed the dominant vision of civic life in the city. This vision demonized working-class and immigrant homes and leisure, denied the existence of a healthy female sexuality, and associated nocturnal leisure with immorality and crime.[2] Prostitution inevitably became a flashpoint of reformers' investigations, since it stimulated their most potent fears about female sexuality, class interaction, and "vice" after dark—and, of course, because its patronage by well-off white men particularly threatened the elite concept of moral order.

By the 1920s, though, much had changed, in nightlife and elsewhere. In the eyes of traditionalists, public behavior by women, the working classes, and nonwhites had undergone a revolutionary liberalization. The national experiment in the prohibition of alcohol was being roundly rejected by New Yorkers. The city's population was now overwhelmingly immigrant and non-Protestant. Taxicabs, telephones, and other new inventions were restructuring travel and communications and changing people's experiences of day and night in the city. Texas Guinan's visit to the office of the Committee of Fourteen also showed that ideas about journalism had changed, too. George Worthington apparently believed that a jaunty, ironic photograph of himself posing with Guinan would be helpful to his cause, and that reformers might benefit from using the hostess's techniques of self-promotion. (Guinan, conversely, was relying on the current celebrity of the committee as a moral reformer to provide publicity for herself.)

Most important, though, Worthington's calculation that the committee "gained more than it lost" from such a photograph reflected the ambiguous status of Guinan and the other female performers. They may be suspected of engaging in prostitution, the solicitation of male customers, or the procurement of prostitutes for men, but they were also appealing and exciting presences who enlivened a traditional office's daily routine and mundane image. To what extent, and how, did their attractiveness also cause them to embody a new sexual immorality or illegality?

The ambiguities of Guinan's visit, and Worthington's response to it, indicated how, for reformers, prostitution was an elusive target in the modern age. Already in 1913 the young Walter Lippmann had taken a Chicago vice-reform group to task for proposing to eradicate prostitution in that city. "What the Commission advocates," Lippmann argued, "is the constant repression and the ultimate annihilation of a mode of life which refuses discovery and measurement." Prostitution, he claimed, "has woven itself into the texture of city life." He ridiculed the report's attempts to suppress "not alone prostitution . . . which lust seeks out, but lust itself," and challenged reformers instead "to think of the social evil as an answer to a human need." Lippmann targeted this report as the epitome of wrong-headed reform thinking and proposed a new "preface to politics" as a clear-thinking gateway to an effective modern civic life. To abolish prostitution, Lippmann argued, "means to abolish the slum and the dirty alley, to stop overwork, underpay, . . . [and] to breathe a new life into education, ventilate society with frankness, and fill life with play and art, with games, with passions which hold and suffuse the imagination."[3] His argument posited a role for eroticism and play—and probably for prostitution itself—in the incremental improvement of social and civic life in the city of the near future.

The New York Committee of Fourteen set goals and reached conclusions that represented an interesting middle way between the musty moralism of the Chicago reformers and the bracing tolerance of the young Walter Lippmann. For many, especially at the time of the group's greatest triumphs in the 1910s, it seemed to offer an enlightened, effective, and "modern" response to an old problem. Since 1905 the committee had succeeded in passing new laws and better police enforcement and in largely eradicating once ubiquitous brothels and pimps. Such reform activity itself can itself be viewed as an element of urban modernity—dynamic, empirical, brutally realistic, eager to get to the bottom of social problems. Behavior in the 1920s, though, caught the committee off its guard. It was forced to confront the impact of new morality, economics, gender roles, and leisure institutions. The committee reacted with alarmism, claiming that New York City faced a revival of prostitution—a more covert prostitution, in which cab drivers, waiters, and hostesses subtly steered customers toward "call girls," who stayed off the streets and used apartments for their assignations.

The committee's search for prostitution in nightclubs—and in dance halls, Broadway employment agencies, and other institutions related to nightlife—problematized them as alleged sites of vice. Along with government regulators (discussed in succeeding chapters), these reformers sought to investigate nightclubs, determine the essence of the threat to civic order that they posed, and formulate remedies to that threat. In the committee's daily work, therefore, we find New York reformers applying their old methods of investigation to new social and cultural conditions, wrestling with new interpretations of those conditions, and struggling to define the proper government remedy.

This chapter uses the group's voluminous papers to explore two important topics. The first one is the variety of male-female interaction in nightlife. The committee paid undercover investigators to pose as male solicitors of prostitution. Hundreds of reports of their interactions with suspected pimps and prostitutes have come down to us. Taking the biases and assumptions of the investigators into consideration, we find rich evidence of gender interaction in nightclubs and similar venues in their reports. Despite the detectives' frequent claims to the contrary, many of these interactions seem to have had nothing to do with prostitution. The reports do, however, reveal generally exploitative trends in the treatment of female employees in businesses involved in nightlife. Prostitution appears to have been a shadowy segment of a broader market in female favors. Women in nightlife may have been outspoken and free to move about the city, but they remained heavily dependent on employers (usually male) and on a male clientele that almost always set the price for their time and services. Committee records also allow us to step outside nightclub doors with investigators as they followed men and women into hotel lobbies, restaurants, taxicabs, massage parlors, and dance halls, as well as apartments and other largely private sites, where the terms for intimacy were negotiated.

The second revelation about the committee's work that I will explore concerns the difficulty faced by a traditional reform movement in its effort to define and guide civic virtue in the 1920s, an era of dramatic cultural change. The committee considered itself a modern reform group that employed the newest scientific techniques in a spirit of realism and frankness. It consulted and worked with social workers, business leaders, the police department, the courts, and city hall. The group's self-image, though, was undermined by the elusiveness of its target, the "new prostitution" of the 1920s. Despite its bold pronouncements, the committee's pursuit of prostitution was hampered by ambiguities in the city's leisure economy, class and ethnic hierarchy, and gender relationships. Its annual reports identified new prostitution in nightclubs and dance halls but could not explain its growth. The committee did seek to explain the causes of the new prostitution and it recommended new legislation, but after 1928 its position of influence within the city's power structure weakened. Within five years the Great Depression and quarrels with affiliated reform groups caused the committee's demise, which effectively ended progressive reformers' campaign against nightclubs.

Anti-prostitution efforts in New York had been sporadic and ineffective until the 1890s, when the energetic clergyman Charles Parkhurst explored the city's underworld and shocked high-minded elites with his reports. The clergyman claimed, for example, that he had met pimps and boy transvestites and had been solicited by no fewer than fifty women on a short street in Greenwich Village. Parkhurst accused Tammany Hall, Manhattan's Democratic party organization, of profiting from prostitution, and he persuaded the state legislature to launch investigations in 1894 and 1896. In 1900 two other clergymen, Henry Codman Potter and Robert Paddock, founded the Committee of Fifteen, which worked to expose prostitution and Tammany Hall's connection to it. Anti-Tammany groups rallied to its cause. In 1901, with the committee's support, an axe-wielding city judge named William Travers Jerome raided a series of brothels and hauled their proprietors into his court. Jerome's and the committee's target were the so-called Raines Law hotels, buildings with ten or more beds that were permitted under a statute to sell liquor on Sundays. Exploiting this loophole, saloons and brothels had stocked their rooms with enough beds to qualify for the lucrative Sunday trade.[4]

The group, soon renamed the New York City Committee of Fourteen for the Suppression of the Raines Law Hotels, began a highly successful campaign to rewrite the liquor laws, investigate patterns of prostitution, and recommend further legislation. The Prentice Act of 1906 eliminated about half of the Raines Law brothels. A city night court dedicated to the trying of prostitution cases was established the following year and was later folded into a reformed magistrates' court. New laws also for-

bade illegal saloons and prostitution in buildings with rented apartments. While the pursuit of "white slavery" rings in the 1910s produced
more headlines than results, that decade also saw the virtual elimination
of the brothel in New York. The committee's 1920 annual report hailed
that year as "the low water mark in prostitution," in which the number
of annual arrests had declined 75 percent since 1911. In 1922 the committee confidently dissolved a special fund it had created nine years earlier "for special proceedings against pimps."[5]

The committee seemed to have achieved results far beyond its goals.
Unlike Parkhurst and others, the organization had striven not to eradicate prostitution, but merely to ameliorate its effects. Its philosophy of
sexuality actually anticipated the tolerance of the 1920s. The committee
acknowledged that "sexual desires are an essential part of life" and
argued that "the belief that commercialized prostitution can be wholly
suppressed, is [now] commonly held to be Utopian." George Worthington noted in 1927 that the group was "proud of the reputation which it
has for [the] soundness of its program and of its scientific approach to
the problem of combating commercialized vice." The *New York Times*
agreed. "The committee does not suggest a panacea. . . . The choice
seems to be between complete enforcement of the law on the one hand,
and drastic modification on the other."[6] This pragmatic approach
attracted public health professionals, social workers, and politicians
from all ethnicities and religions to its ranks.

This pragmatism was reflected in the identity of the fourteen directors, who almost always included well-known figures from business,
social work, medicine, and the clergy. They included William McAdoo,
a former police commissioner; Mary Simkhovitch, the director of a set-
tlement house; Belle Moskowitz, an investigator of "white slavery" and
an advisor to Governor Alfred E. Smith; Katharine Bement Davis, the
first female head of city corrections and later the director of the Bureau
of Social Hygiene, which was funded by the Rockefeller family; Lee Beat-
tie, a minister and the head of the Church House mission; George Alger
and Edward McGuire, both attorneys; Agnes McKernan, the women's
prison secretary for the Salvation Army; and Percy Straus, the president
of Macy's department store. Guiding the enterprise daily was the general
secretary. Frederick Whitin served in that position for two decades until
his death in 1926, when he was succeeded by the attorney George E.
Worthington. Harry Kahan served as a full-time investigator for the committee for most of the decade. Other investigators included Raymond A.
Claymes, an African American graduate of Yale University.[7] The committee jealously guarded its autonomy, boasting that "all the work of private
organizations for the repression of prostitution is now centered in the
Committee of Fourteen." The group thus became the clearinghouse for

any voluntary association with some interest in prostitution. Its fame inspired imitators. Chicago had its own Committee of Fifteen, Buffalo and Montreal their Committees of Sixteen, Minneapolis a Committee of Thirteen, and Utica, New York, a Committee of Twenty.[8]

At the dawn of the 1920s the committee celebrated its apparent victory over prostitution in New York City, but it quickly came to realize that its success had been fleeting. The 1920 annual report's widely repeated proclamation that "there is less *open* vice in New York City than in any other of the world's large cities" pointed to a qualified triumph. Public brothels and promenading streetwalkers and pimps were gone, but the committee soon acknowledged that prostitution was making a covert comeback. Its 1920 annual report referred to "an increase in perversions"—probably oral sex and homosexuality—and the following year, for the first time in a decade, the committee noted a rise (of 7 percent) in yearly prostitution arrests. A newspaper story in 1921 suggested that taxicab drivers were becoming "aids to immorality," bringing passengers to assignations. Furthermore, the committee noted that "the man with means, who seeks the prostitute, can find her in restaurants and in hotels through bellmen and waiters. The present day prostitute takes her customer to a quiet flat, or is to be found there by him." The year 1922 brought another 7 percent increase in arrests.[9]

These new conditions led the committee to reassess its methods and goals. Some members suggested proposing more laws restricting the use of buildings in the city, but others were unsure of their chances for passage (since numerous statutes already existed). In 1921, attempting to change with the times, the committee hired its first female investigators. One of them "assumed the role of a prostitute and as such occupied, for very short periods of time, various bedrooms in the hotel with police officers" in efforts to entrap hotel owners. This tactic proved to be too provocative for committee members, though, and the group soon set stringent limits on its employment of women, effectively ending their use as decoys.[10] The committee also strove to criminalize the participation of the male customer or "john." State vagrancy laws had always targeted soliciting women, pimps, and those who made rooms available to prostitutes, but the laws had never penalized male patrons.[11] In 1923 the committee proposed a "customer amendment"; "Punish Sexes Alike, Says Vice Society," a newspaper reported. Its main ally in this fight was the important feminist group the National Women's Party. Strong and reactionary opposition met the idea. Judges called the amendment "unenforceable," while other critics reiterated timeworn defenses of johns' rights. They called the amendment "in advance of the times" and "an [improper?] attempt to make people moral by law" that neglected

male "sex necessity." In an astounding concession, one lawyer proclaimed that the proposed amendment should not be passed because
prostitution was "a necessary evil." The amendment, it was also argued,
would lead to the widespread blackmail of men.[12] Such opposition led
the committee to abandon the "john amendment" and redirect its energies toward liberalizing the admissibility of evidence in the Women's
Court.

Against this shifting background, the committee began to associate the
revival in prostitution with the new nightlife. In 1924 it first targeted
dance halls, speakeasies, and other relatively new kinds of venues. Its
report that year noted for the first time that "immoral women who were
formerly to be found in the rear rooms of the saloons and in the cabarets, now frequent the cheap restaurants and dance halls, though in
greatly decreased numbers." The committee ordered its investigators to
make a door-to-door canvas of midtown Manhattan in June and July
1924, during the prolonged Democratic national convention at Madison
Square Garden. The conclave deadlocked on the presidential nomination and lasted for two weeks, giving the committee an extended opportunity to search for prostitution amid the mass of frustrated visiting
politicians and journalists. A rumor spread among worried conventioneers that the committee's detectives were masquerading as delegates to
catch johns and prostitutes.[13]

The probe centered on hotels in the theater district, the locus of convention socializing. In the lobbies of the Hotel de France and the Astor,
McAlpin, Claridge, and Pennsylvania Hotels, the investigators found
"many professional prostitutes, cabaret girls or actresses," as well as
"rounders, sports, bootleggers, bookmakers, pimps, and thieves." Taxi
drivers picked up conventioneers and shepherded them to liaisons.
"Pimps and prostitutes hang out" at Jack's Restaurant on 47th Street
and at Lindy's on 48th. A block away, the Longacre Association Club
employed three "professionals" as hostesses. An investigator was solicited at the Clover Gardens at Lexington and 46th Street, and during the
convention the well-known prostitute "Jew Bessie" was arrested in Times
Square. In the thirties blocks to the south, though, fewer assignations
were reported, and investigators found few prostitutes and no delegates
in Harlem.[14]

The committee's worries about a revival of prostitution in New York
City were reinforced by ensuing findings. The 1925 report noted a three-
year decline in the number of arrests, but it also detected prostitutes
working "as instructresses in dance halls," and for the first time it
warned of foul play by hostesses in "the smaller night clubs, or 'speak
easys.'" The next year the group argued that prostitution was still

"almost entirely clandestine," but took little comfort in this: arrests had risen by 17 percent, and nonclandestine prostitution was emerging in Harlem and in speakeasies. The committee immediately solicited John D. Rockefeller, Jr. and others for additional funding. The year 1927 was the watershed. Prostitution arrests in 1926 had climbed 31 percent and the trade was now said to have a strong foothold in nightclubs and speakeasies. "We have again the old and vicious connection of prostitution and alcohol, in perhaps an even more inviting form than previously." Proprietors earlier "connected with the white slave traffic" now ran speakeasies, where hostesses "hooked" clients, and there was a "growing exploitation in colored areas such as Harlem."[15]

By 1927 the committee perceived nightclubs to be potential sites for the new prostitution, or at least vulnerable to immoral neighborhood conditions. Katinka on West 49th—George Kosloff's exotic speakeasy featuring Hindu and dagger dances, among other entertainment—was found to be free of soliciting, but it was a few doors down from the vice-ridden Chesterfield Hotel, the suspicious Green Room restaurant and the Club Monterey, and various furnished-room apartments (which often played host to assignations). The Silver Slipper on West 48th Street was not mentioned in the committee's reports, but it stood next to the tainted President Hotel (run by the gangster Waxey Gordon), was two doors down from the equally sordid Louis's speakeasy, and was within a stone's throw of suspicious tenement apartments.[16]

The committee also accused nightclubs themselves of housing the illicit trade. Confident that it could distinguish nightclubs from other kinds of venues, it gave only 6 of 157 so-called clubs "a clean bill of health" with respect to "any laws other than the Volstead Act." (The "clean" clubs might have included the Silver Slipper, Club Alabam', Casa Lopez, and such short-lived society clubs as the Chez Fysher and Perroquet de Paris.) The 45th Street Yacht Club, a popular night spot, was determined to be a site for soliciting. Dancers at the Chez Florence, or Guinan's, nightclub on 48th—run by Tommy Guinan—were also suspected. The investigators' suspicions also extended to such midtown "clubs" as the Wintergreen, Maxine, One Eleven, Scranton, and Monterey. It is uncertain whether most of these were nightclubs or merely speakeasies; at this time the definition of "nightclub" was still in flux. The reports were on firmest ground in arguing that the "lower grades" of speakeasies, "in which the illicit sale of liquor is only a blind," were hosts to prostitution.[17]

In 1928 the committee launched its most detailed studies of possible prostitution in the new nightlife. This probe resulted in street-by-street, often door-by-door descriptions of conditions in Manhattan, as well as the Bronx and Brooklyn.[18] Investigators made detailed reports for each street and block, providing readers with walking tours of these districts. Their findings about Midtown and Harlem had the most impact on the committee's perceptions of prostitution in Manhattan nightlife.

In Midtown the investigators worked their way up from the southern streets, finding first that some supper clubs, chop houses, and furnished-room apartments in the thirties blocks harbored suspected prostitutes. Speakeasies were found in vast quantities in the low west forties, and the investigators determined that the hotels and furnished-room apartments above them were sites of frequent assignations. On West 44th Street soliciting was detected in numerous basement and office speakeasies. West 45th Street featured a speakeasy above a news service office and a brothel above the Princeton Grill next door. The high forties and fifties, between Sixth and Seventh Avenues, featured the thickest area of suspicious sites. Basement speakeasies yielded varying evidence of prostitution, while at the Chesterfield and Flanders Hotels soliciting was unmistakable. The Club Monterey received a passing grade, though. The low west fifties featured more restaurants, often with ethnic cuisine. Places such as the Romeo Restaurant and the Red Moon Supper Club seemed most suspicious. Black prostitutes gravitated to West 53rd Street. One side of one block of 51st Street alone held six speakeasies, half of which gave evidence of prostitution. Further north, the Great Northern and Circle Hotels also permitted soliciting.[19]

The other detailed committee probe of 1928 took place in Harlem. The 1925 annual report had first alleged "special problems in colored areas." Since "the colored areas of Harlem seem to be inadequately policed," the "curiosity" of white tourists "is rapidly being capitalized [on] by exploiters of both races." In 1927 the Bureau of Social Hygiene pledged ten thousand dollars to the committee for a study of prostitution in Harlem, which was undertaken by the investigator Raymond Claymes the following year. Claymes's report concluded that prostitution was "four to five times as prevalent" in Harlem "as in other sections of the city."[20] His investigation of West 131st Street in Harlem provided the most detailed portrait of sexual activity on any street in the city. Important jazz venues such as the Bandbox, Connie's Inn, the Lafayette Theater, and the Rhythm Club resided here, but Claymes also found a two-block stretch of the street to be crammed with prostitution. At number 40 was "Peg Smith's" brothel. A few doors down was the Blue Ribbon Chile Parlor, where the hostess "Miss Williams" offered to "lie down" with Claymes for five dollars "once the food was ready." In the basement below the parlor were two women and five men, "two of whom were said to be 'noted faggots' (fairies)"; here too the rate was five dollars (plus two for the room). At the Foot Lights Club at number 115, liquor and gambling flourished in the back room and two hostesses kept male customers company. At the Entertainers and Performers Club down the street, two female employees took white and black customers to an apartment. Across 131st Street was the Kewpie Doll, a brothel where a pianist encouraged dance hostesses of different races to take male customers to the back rooms. Fourteen speakeasies on the two blocks seemed to contain no prostitution, although some "women looked questionable."[21]

Claymes claimed to have been approached by prostitutes, homosexual men, white female visitors, and cabbies in the general area between 129th and 134th Streets. A prostitute solicited the investigator at Small's nightclub for six dollars, while a streetwalker in her forties asked for half that amount. Claymes also visited a lesbian party on 137th Street. In general, his reports indicated that while prostitution certainly existed across downtown Harlem, it was merely part of a sexual continuum of experimentation and female exploitation. Harlem was a violent milieu as well. Two women fought in one speakeasy; a pimp beat up a prostitute; a theater manager threatened a cab driver. In the committee's view, Harlem bore all of the earmarks of a frontier boom town, with a feverish, racialized emphasis on sex especially shaping the character of its nightlife. In 1929 George Worthington traveled to Harlem to meet with black ministers about the problem, and sought action from the city police commissioner, Grover Whalen. (Whalen claimed to be "astounded" by the report and promised to hire black officers as a remedy—a vow he did not keep.)[22]

The Committee of Fourteen's findings seemed lurid to middle-class reformers, and inspired them to demand the cleaning-up of nightclubs. In 1928 the Reverend Christian Reisner called them "the most contemptible places in the city. . . . They are hotbeds of vice." Rabbi Nathan Krass of Temple Emanu'el was "utterly opposed to night clubs . . . where men and women indulge themselves and thus violate the law quite brazenly [in] a modern form of the ancient Bacchanalian orgies." Mrs. George J. Anderson, a donor to the committee, was "particularly anxious to find out if the night clubs fed houses of prostitution." George Worthington responded to Mrs. Anderson with conviction: "The main centers of prostitution in New York . . . are the undesirable night clubs and the speakeasies."[23]

Anecdotes from other sources suggest that activity resembling prostitution did take place within nightclubs. The madam Polly Adler recalled in her autobiography that in the mid-1920s she attended nightclub openings, where owners allowed her to publicize her call house. "When I'd walk in, surrounded by my loveliest girls, it was always a show-stopper. . . . The clubs were a display window for the girls. . . . Some of the club patrons would follow after us and end the evening at the house." Texas Guinan encouraged her hostesses to escort men, although these liaisons were ambiguous. The singer and prostitute "Tanya" claimed that Guinan, her one-time employer, "compelled us girls . . . sometimes to take a ride with her gentlemen friends in a car to the outskirts of New York." The Committee of Fourteen did determine that a few clubowners were active pimps. In 1926 the female owner of La Menagerie on West 52nd Street "could be approached and she will produce young girls for [the] purpose of prostitution." Organized crime appeared to have little involvement in prostitution in the 1920s, but occasionally a gangster would operate a call-girl ring out of a nightclub. One bootlegger hired prostitutes to solicit patrons for his club, the Melody Box, which operated briefly on West 54th Street, while another did the same at his Longacre Association Club on West 45th Street. More commonly, taxicab drivers, elevator operators, and waiters in nightclubs, as well as restaurants and hotels, offered to take male customers to prostitutes.[24]

Such evidence inspired the committee in 1928 to begin to refer to prostitution as "the hostess evil." Seven years earlier the committee had endorsed a "requirement that [cabaret] performers should not entertain between their numbers the guests of the restaurant." In 1927 it had warned that the new "night clubs and speak easies are now boldly advertising for girls as hostesses, entertainers, cigarette and check room girls." While most of these employees performed "perfectly legitimate" functions, they "work . . . under hazardous influence in many of the clubs" and were exposed to amoral influences. The hostess was "the modern American counterpart of the geisha girl," and her place of work was the "new cloak for prostitution."[25]

Committee investigators alleged that they had obtained empirical proof of this trend. The 1928 report, summarizing the door-to-door surveys, claimed that 1,134 out of 1,443 prostitution violations that year had occurred in nightclubs or speakeasies. As the *New York Times* summarized the report's findings, "the lower one goes the less important the liquor traffic becomes and the more important the traffic in 'immorality.'" Out of the 392 establishments that were visited, 360 featured some evidence of prostitution, and 185 distinct procurers in the clubs were identified. Four nightclubs had connections with the elite "call flats" that charged the highest rates for wealthy customers. "—— Society, Inc.," a club on West 48th Street, was "used as a clearing house" by a madam who employed her high-priced prostitutes in the club. "Mademoiselle Fifi," working at a club on West 51st Street, was offered $200 a week by a "notorious" call madam—undoubtedly Polly Adler, who then ran her business at a flat eight blocks to the north. Another madam, "Trixie," said that "she frequented night clubs and speak easies . . . and . . .

secured a constant supply of new girls." Prostitutes were welcome as hostesses in all but seven of the eighty-five Harlem speakeasies surveyed by the committee.[26]

The reports suggested that illegal activity became folded into the work of female nightclub employees for diverse reasons. The hostesses' work was difficult and exploitative. The women were usually poorly paid, and heavily dependent on customer gratuities. One hostess noted that tips were "the only thing that keeps me up, because my expenses are big." (Like most hostesses she had to purchase her own wardrobe, but she also financed an opium addiction.) Women working at clip joints, of course, were required to use their sexuality to steal from male customers. A woman who worked at the Gypsy Cave on Third Avenue confided to a female investigator that she was expected to "smile and lead [men] on as far as you can while the boss sees you, and then try to shake them on the outside." (Tearfully referring to her boss, she cautioned that "I'll get fired if he thinks I have been crying.") At the New Capitol Club hostesses altered patrons' personal checks to inflate their charges. Similarly, an investigator noted that at the Peek Inn on 48th Street "every girl which is introduced by [the hostess] from the chorus must be a prostitute or a thief, otherwise she cannot be employed here longer than a week."[27]

The committee's investigations also shed light on working conditions in nightclub chorus lines. Chorus dancers, the central embodiment of femininity in clubs, faced intense competition from younger women and the constant threat of unemployment. In 1928 the Chorus Equity Association estimated that nationally there were at least 25,000 young women struggling to gain 4,500 nightclub dancing jobs. Customer taste increasingly favored younger women. The "tall and stately," Ziegfeld-style showgirl, the New York American noted, was the reigning queen of the nightclub stage, but competition from the "chorine," "the more petite and sparkling type of girl," was growing. The latter "type . . . has the best chance of landing a 1928 chorus job." An executive with the Chorus Equity Association favored sixteen-year-old aspirants, since "the average stage life of a chorus girl is three years. 55% of our membership is new every year. The others just fade away" or marry. The union's oldest member was twenty-six. Out of almost 5,000 members only "about 140 chorus girls a year progress to small [theatrical] parts and principal roles." Uncertain career prospects drove some chorus dancers into prostitution. The chorus mistress at the Club Paddock, beneath the Earl Carroll Theatre, invited the investigator to visit her apartment. The dancers at the Shadowland speakeasy on West 53rd were also suspected of prostitution.[28]

The committee even believed that concessions workers in nightclubs might fall prey to prostitution. Coatcheckers were usually unskilled women who were hired mainly for their attractiveness. (At the Club Paddock Harry Kahan encountered a coatchecker who also helped to "bounce" customers at closing time, but she was a rarity.) A "syndicate for concessions" that operated in 160 nightclubs may have exposed them to criminal activity, but most coatcheckers apparently avoided prostitution. In 1929 a female committee investigator posing as a checker in the Romeo Restaurant found that the waitresses "made a lot of money on the side and didn't usually keep their positions . . . very long," but no one at the restaurant encouraged the investigator herself to become friendlier with the male customers. At the Bavarian Braukeller in Yorkville, the Princeton Grill, and the Parisian Restaurant, though, coatcheckers were found also to be engaged in prostitution.[29]

This information suggested to the Committee of Fourteen that widespread illicit sexual activity was taking place in nightlife. Elizabeth Butler of the city corrections department wrote George Worthington that in "nearly every history of minors which I take at the [Harlem Women's] Prison, the girl tells of having been employed as a waitress or dance hall hostess." In 1929 the committee gained the support of the police commissioner, Grover Whalen, who echoed its central argument in a public statement: "This question of a night club hostess is a very serious one. It is becoming close to something else long since driven out of this community." Whalen subsequently used the prostitution issue as an excuse for a wave of nightclub raids and closings.[30]

The committee's findings also seemed to indicate a general exploitation of female sexuality in the Manhattan economy. In 1926 the investigator Harry Kahan dined with two unemployed young women who typified "many girls traveling around Broadway trying to pose in motion pictures. . . . [They] are promised by lobby guys to be put in some motion picture concern, but they take advantage of them and gradually they become prostitutes." The committee argued that some unscrupulous theatrical employment agencies placed unsuspecting young women as hostesses to feed the demand for casual prostitutes in clubs and speakeasies. Investigators infiltrated eighty-six agencies in 1928 and found that twenty-four of them had sent clients to "place[s] of bad repute." Beyond the entertainment industries, prostitutes were found to be employed by real estate developers to entice clients to buy property in New Jersey. One of these women advised a committee investigator, "first buy property and then I'll invite you up." The woman was seen a week later in an apartment in Harlem, trying to attract investors among slumming whites from downtown.[31]

As the 1920s drew to a close, the committee's mound of data on sexuality in nightlife seemed to offer city officials guidance on how to proceed to reform behavior. Its annual reports sported impressive-looking statistics that demonstrated its "scientific" approach to the problem. The raw investigators' reports, though, show far more ambiguity. Cold and hard-looking statistics on "prostitution" often masked a spectrum of complex interpersonal encounters between male investigators and women in nightlife, which only occasionally seemed to prove the existence of commercialized sex. Much of what the committee called prostitution was actually noncommercial interaction between consenting men and women, as well as other varieties of economic exploitation of women in the nightlife industry which could not be classified as the sale of sexual favors.

Flaws in the committee's sampling of city behavior caused some of its problems. The investigators relied heavily on citizen complaints for leads, many of which led nowhere. In addition, their ability to explore nightlife venues was inhibited by their meager expense accounts. In a yearlong period from 1927 to 1928 Harry Kahan's monthly resources ranged from $36.20 to $576.70. Investigative expenses usually rivaled George Worthington's salary as the largest budget item of the committee, but they still did not enable Kahan and others to infiltrate the most expensive nightclubs and brothels. Some of the most celebrated venues remained beyond the committee's reach. In 1924 Harry Kahan lamented that "this place known as 'EL FEY' Club . . . would require a lot of money to obtain evidence." High-priced brothels enjoyed a comeback, but the committee rarely could afford to enter them or secure evidence for convictions. In 1925 investigators helped the police to raid four such brothels, but conflicting testimony by officers led to acquittals in court. Polly Adler became notorious for her exclusive call-girl ring. Arrested many times under assumed names, she always avoided conviction. When a prostitute mentioned Adler's name, the committee investigator actually replied, "I have never heard of that woman before." George Worthington scrawled on this report, "Locate Polly Adler *positively*—GW." But the committee never did.[32]

The flawed assistance of New York City police officers, who in plain clothes often accompanied committee investigators on their searches, also distorted their findings. Committee detectives and police officers shared similar backgrounds and outlooks, and they worked together smoothly through the early 1920s. Like the investigators, vice officers posed as customers and gathered data, but they also made arrests and shut down businesses. However, in the 1900s and 1910s police officers had regularly taken bribes from madams and pimps to allow them to operate. In the 1920s rumors persisted that these payments continued, and that some officers maintained close relationships with prostitutes. In 1924 the police commissioner, Charles Enright, attempted some reforms, abolishing the district vice squads, creating a single Special Services Division, and introducing the "green sheet," a form that officers were to fill out when making arrests for vagrancy.[33] The problems persisted, though. The committee found that use of the green sheets actually increased the frequency of distortion in officers' court testimonies. It also learned that a narcotics officer was married to a speakeasy hostess suspected of prostitution, and that a vice officer "brings with him on each visit police officers" to "Bedroom Dolly's," a basement speakeasy uptown, "for immoral purposes." A prostitute slipped a letter to Kahan warning about "a notorious cop . . . who works from the office of Commis Enright . . . shaking down all the girls on Broadway" with the help of a black female acquaintance. A police captain was reported to have arrived at a raided midtown speakeasy to supervise the collection of bribes. Such payments from affluent brothels supplemented the graft that officers received from many speakeasies.[34]

Publicly the Committee of Fourteen showed sympathy for vice officers and dismissed calls for police reform. Rumors that officers were entrapping innocent women in prostitution arrests actually led the committee to offer an endorsement of the practice: "Should not [an entrapped prostitute] be convicted and restrained for her own and the civic good?" Privately, though, the committee fretted about its forays with the police, which also might have violated Prohibition laws: "Such cases as might be made, would most likely contain a serious degree of entrapment, since the women found in these places require to be wined and danced before suggesting unlawful intimacies."[35] After 1925 the group relied less often on police partners and collaborated more with city court personnel (who would also prove to be fallible, however).

Even when they were free of police involvement, though, the committee's investigations proved problematic. The most serious difficulty was one of perception. In the 1920s it became more difficult to determine which women in nightlife actually were prostitutes. In the 1800s the streetwalker's inviting, painted smile (usually accompanied with an offer) had been a virtual trademark of her profession. While on vacation in Europe in 1928 Harry Kahan found such easily identifiable street prostitution in Warsaw, Berlin, and Paris. In New York City that same year, though, streetwalkers were scarce. Women (and men) of all backgrounds flaunted their sexual attractiveness in ways that resembled those of the traditional prostitute. A male investigator thus was not sure what to think in 1929 when, on the corner of Broadway and 136th Street, "a woman smiled at me" and said she had "been thinking about getting a sweetie, but they are hard to find." He was similarly confused when, at

Broadway and 168th Street, "this woman smiled and nodded as I passed," or when "a girl smiled at me" at the Pennsylvania Hotel. Another investigator was greeted by a smile on Broadway and 140th Street. He noted that the woman "was found to be respectable. She, however, took me to a speakeasy."[36]

The behavior of women in public nightlife perplexed the committee's investigators, who (like many others) were still adjusting to the increasing tendency of many young women to initiate intimate contact with men in public. The boundaries between liberated female sexuality and prostitution were becoming less clear. The 1922 annual report stated that the committee's mission included "bring[ing] under reformatory influences many women and girls who have not become hardened"—certainly a large population of women in nightlife. Or perhaps not; a large group may have already fallen into the clutches of immorality, as some critics of the committee averred. "It is being argued now, that the currently believed increase in the immorality among women is due to the repression of the prostitute; that men, unable to find professionals, induce other women to yield to their desires." ("The automobile and . . . the present freedom of discussion of sex problems" were also blamed by these critics, whom the committee did not name.) The committee obviously disagreed with this argument, but it also never really confronted the possibility that new social mores were creating the illusion of an increase in prostitution. George Worthington observed that many speakeasies "are filled with girls of varying degrees of respectability—not only prostitutes—and in varying stages of intoxication," but he rarely grappled with the larger behavioral trends that the scene apparently indicated.[37]

The reports detailed many ambiguous, sexually charged encounters with women in the city. A hostess at the Blue Bird dance hall asked an investigator to "step out with me," but he eventually concluded that she was not a prostitute. A woman on Times Square acted very suspiciously, but she explained to the investigator, "The reason I winked at you was that I didn't want anybody else to see me. You have to be somewhat careful around the City of New York." The woman wanted to find a room for the two of them, but she was not selling her time. In other instances these gestures were preludes to solicitation. On Sixth Avenue and 34th Street a woman smiled at the investigator and then solicited him for ten dollars. In other instances the detectives tried to glean conclusions from the most ambiguous female body language. Many women mentioned in the reports did not smile at investigators but rather simply sat, stood, or walked; nevertheless their status became the subject of speculation. Harry Kahan believed that two "unescorted women" in a basement speakeasy on West 72nd Street "appeared to be probable prostitutes," but he did not pursue the matter. At the Fireside Club on West 71st Street an investigator observed five hostesses sitting in male customers' laps but guessed that they were not prostitutes.[38]

The committee's information gathering was more far more situational and erratic in nature than it was scientific. Every encounter was a tiny human drama in which relationships and economic exchanges defied attempts at simple classification and quantification. The detectives were confidence men of a sort, liminally taking on the part of the eager john on the streets and in the clubs. (Conversely, the occasional clubgoer masqueraded as an investigator. In one restaurant washroom a Committee of Fourteen detective scornfully knocked false badges from the state police and the committee out of a man's hand.) Sometimes the women refused to cooperate, such as when an investigator pursued two wary suspects from a restaurant on 22nd Street—"I followed them trying to pick them up, but they got in a taxi cab." Suspected pimps or procurers slipped away as well. At an Italian grocery on Commerce Street, Harry Kahan pursued a lead by asking the clerk if a girl was there; the clerk sensed a trap, though, and at the appointed meeting time, the store was deserted and locked.[39]

When female suspects did seem to lure investigators into acts of prostitution, the men then ran the risk of temptation. This had been a perpetual problem for police vice squads; as the committee noted, the local units had been abolished in 1924 in part because "unreliable" new officers fell prey "to the temptations of the prostitution situation." As a result of this trend, the committee worried about public perceptions of its own investigators' work amid prostitutes, "to the effect that constant association with vice must and does warp the minds and the attitudes and the points of view of those constantly associated with it." Searches for prostitutes in massage parlors were a particular concern. In 1929 Bascom Johnson of the American Social Hygiene Association argued that the method the committee followed with regard to a Harlem massage parlor was "not safeguard[ing] the investigators from undue temptation, as per the terms of the cooperation agreement." In response to such concerns the committee first banned masquerades by female investigators and then codified behavior by males. In 1930 all investigators were "forbidden to 'pick up' persons of the opposite sex and are cautioned that the initiative must come from the other person. Unlawful sexual intercourse or other immoral acts are prohibited."[40]

There was cause for such concern. At the Dreamland dance hall in Harlem in 1931, a hostess exposed her breast to detective "B" and suggested that he kiss it. On his second visit in 1932 to a massage parlor on West 70th Street an investigator disrobed for a session. A masseuse removed the towel from his loins, put oil on her hands, and tried to "stimulate his private parts," while another offered him a "tongue bath."[41] Presumably this investigator pulled back from his "john" persona just in time, as his colleagues did on other occasions. In 1927, for example, a detective retreated from a liaison with a Harlem prostitute, protesting that he wanted a white woman instead. On another occasion in Harlem a detective beat a hasty exit from a prostitute by "convinc[ing] her I was afraid her old man might come in and pleaded that as an excuse for not staying with her and gave her [a] $1 tip." At other times investigators feigned sudden illness or lack of cash to dash out of assignations. In such ways, the investigators' forays into the ambiguous underworld of nightlife prostitution were often awkwardly cut short.[42]

The sheer quantity of detail in the Committee of Fourteen's investigators' reports remains compelling. If historians proceed with caution, the reports can be found to provide an interesting composite portrait of active, struggling, and often victimized women in nightlife, the vast majority of whom almost certainly were not professional prostitutes. However, the empirical flaws in the committee's body of evidence—even regarding the alleged prevalence of a "hostess evil" in nightclubs—cast serious doubt on its usefulness as a guide to prostitution in the 1920s. The committee's successes and confident image, won in earlier decades, discouraged it from adapting to changing times. In addition, limited financial resources and a narrow desire to find statutory evidence of prostitution filtered the investigators' perceptions of nightlife. In a larger sense, the flaws in the reports indicated the Committee of Fourteen's difficulty in maintaining traditional anti-prostitution reform activity in the new urban culture of the 1920s and 1930s.

By 1928 George Worthington and his fourteen employers had persuaded themselves that the investigators' reports proved the existence of rampant new prostitution in New York's nightclubs and dance halls. Portents of a revival of "the social evil" seemed to herald a long, active, and productive future for the committee. The group ambitiously strove to lead an effort to eliminate not only prostitution in the city but its environmental *causes* as well. This was not a new goal; in 1920 the committee had claimed that its "fight has . . . become one for industrial and civic efficiency and morals," for "repression through law enforcement and by education" in combat against the "underlying factors of prostitution."[43] Now, though, with public interest in nightclubs at a peak, the launching of such a grand "fight" seemed imminent.

The committee made a start in 1927 by successfully lobbying the state legislature for the Red Light Abatement and Injunction Law of 1927, which required the state licensing of hotels. Now, somewhat messianically, the committee proposed to smite and eradicate the underlying causes of vice. Self-interest inevitably was involved; as one committee member noted, "we cannot dodge the alternatives of a considerable expansion to meet present needs, or of going out of existence." The committee now stressed "a wider outlook than that of mere suppression." An inchoate landscape of sexual tolerance and vice challenged it; "those phases and factors which are now most prominent [in prostitution] are identified very closely with other factors and problems which are not easily disassociated from it. It is for that reason that our work unintentionally has of necessity broadened." The committee also believed that new rhetoric was needed. "The fear element" stressed in earlier campaigns no longer worked in the 1920s: "as the result of a dabbling in psychology and psychiatry by many people, either a conscious or unconscious opposition to the words 'repression' and 'suppression'" had appeared. Thus, a "message of faith, happiness, joy *and the prevention of suffering*" was now paramount.[44]

The concept of crime prevention was newly popular in the late 1920s. The life-history approach developed by sociologists at the University of Chicago became popular among criminologists, who lobbied now for effective measures in schools and communities to forestall future deviant behavior. In New York a state commission on crime—chaired by the state senator Caleb H. Baumes, the famed author of a harsh new penal code—included an influential subcommittee on the causes of crime, whose work particularly inspired the Committee of Fourteen. George Worthington claimed in 1930 that his organization "is now broadening its purposes to include the prevention of organized crime as well as commercialized vice." A prospectus envisioned the committee making "investigation[s] of crime rendezvous; resorts of gangsters and gunmen; vice resorts of all kinds, including vice and crime-breeding speakeasies." (It added, though, that "gambling, prohibition violations as such [and] indecent literature" would be left to other investigators.) Worthington, using the language of social hygienists, proposed a new police crime prevention bureau: "The modern police head must attack not only the social swamps and morasses whose existence is more or less patent, but he must seek out and combat sources of criminal infection and contagion wherever they exist in city life." New "crime prevention officers"—actually trained social workers—would "ferret out conditions deleterious particularly to our boys and girls." In June 1931 Mayor James J. Walker made Worthington's bureau a reality. The Crime Prevention Bureau created new police regulations and threatened dance halls and cabarets with closing if they failed to report the presence of "gangsters, racketeers or other undesirable characters" on the premises. Establishments were required to compile data on employees, female entertainers were forbidden from mingling with male customers, and closed eating booths were banned.[45]

Gender and labor politics complicated the committee's reform plans, though. A proposal by a state assemblyman sought to exempt restaurant workers from a 1927 ban on the employment of women in nighttime service industries. Many "waitresses in bonafide restaurants," Worthington was told, had found it "a real hardship . . . to be idle during the very hours when as a rule the work is lightest and the tips largest." A fledgling waitress's union, as well as a nurses' union with similar interests, supported the bill, as did the National Women's Party, which argued that the ban had been a plot to win jobs for men. The Committee of Fourteen opposed the bill, though, fearing "an influx of hostesses in establishments closely resembling restaurants, but actually operating as speakeasy clubs." The committee apparently agreed with the assessment of the union leader Rose Schneiderman, who accused the bill of "trying to close the speakeasies with the one hand [in other provisions] and making them more attractive with the other." It did not become law.[46]

The committee's effort to reform the city magistrates' courts was more sustained, but in the end it caused the group considerable grief. Members began to argue for court reform in 1925. The committee's report that year recommended the "reconstruction of our criminal courts on a basis of present-day advances in science, sociology, and business administration." In 1927 the Women's Court presided over more than four thousand arraignments, including a 41 percent increase in prostitution cases—an increase "so tremendous," the committee argued, "as to seriously affect the machinery of the . . . Court." The following year George Worthington joined the municipal Committee for the Centralization of the Magistrates' Courts, which was headed by the venerable reform judge William Travers Jerome. Worthington was also invited by a Women's Court judge "to sit beside him on the bench" as an observer. In 1930 the committee supported a bill in Albany that would have centralized oversight of the magistrates' courts, and it proposed the regular rotation of judges around the five boroughs. More generally the group advocated making the Bureau of Crime Prevention permanent and establishing a new court "for male sex delinquents."[47]

Few of these proposals became law. Compared to its earlier conquest of the brothel, the pimp, and the Raines Law hotel, the committee's reform record from 1920 until its demise in 1933 was slim. Its frustration derived in large part from the new elusiveness of its target, the semi-private nature of the new nightlife that blurred the line between licit and illicit consensual sex, and the growing unreliability of the police as a trustworthy agent of law enforcement. The Parkhurstian certainties of the progressive era—about the nature of the problem, the perpetrators, the locations, and disposition of "good" and "evil" actors across the city geography—were giving way to substantial confusion. Also, perhaps, the committee suffered from too much advice. Theologians, hygienists, social workers, psychologists, business people, politicians, police officers, and others brought differing and conflicting perceptions of prostitution, city women, and sexual behavior to the committee's work and competed against each other to influence its priorities and its initiatives. The group, as it called itself, was indeed "the medium of contact between the busy citizen and the recognized public authorities," except that the point of contact was now a very windy cultural crossroads.

Meanwhile, the committee made an underfunded attempt to investigate dance halls. Unlicensed, surreptitious dance "studios" had long been suspected by the committee to be fronts for prostitution. In 1929 the committee member William McAdoo argued that the descriptions of the dancing in some halls observed by undercover police were "so revolting and almost unbelievable that I would not care for any of the women stenographers connected with these courts to have read them." The fact that white female "taxi dancers" at particular halls often serviced interracial or even mostly nonwhite male clienteles—often East Asian or African American—especially disturbed the committee. In 1931 investigators infiltrated two halls owned by the gangster Morris Goodman, who was alleged to be violent toward his female employees and a facilitator of prostitution. Goodman's alleged relationship with a city magistrate temporarily allied the committee with the current state government investigation of the municipal bench, which was conducted by Samuel Seabury. This relationship soured, though, when a longtime committee associate, the assistant city district attorney John Weston, confessed to Seabury that he had taken bribes to help frame innocent women for prostitution. Even more than its earlier partnership with the city police, the committee's ties to the court severely tarnished the group's reputation among other reformers.[48]

  These other reformers included the committee's main benefactor, the American Social Hygiene Association (ASHA), whose disapproval of the committee's investigative strategies now boiled over. Relations between Worthington and the director of the ASHA, Bascom Johnson, had long been strained. The "frank" language of the committee's annual reports, what Johnson perceived as its bias against African Americans in Harlem, and its alleged lack of safeguards against the temptation of investigators by prostitutes and masseuses were sources of friction. In 1930, in a sign of John D. Rockefeller, Jr.'s displeasure with the group, the association discontinued its substantial funding of the committee's investigations. Further body blows were delivered to the committee by the Great Depression. Pointing to the depletion of their stock portfolios, the merchant Arthur Curtiss James, the committee's other major benefactor, and others withdrew their support. The committee launched a bid to raise $38,000 in contributions to double its budget, but during the economic slump, public opinion had turned against it. The *New York Mirror* protested, "If New Yorkers subscribe $38,000 let them give it for immediate relief of girls who are fighting hunger with their backs to rooming house walls." The Communist Party's Office Workers Union advised the committee that the business executives in the group "can give you first hand information as to the miserable earnings of office workers in our city. . . . These reverend gentlemen have a daily opportunity to expose the organizations in our city by name who are not paying a living wage to the girls of New York." In late 1932, Worthington and the fourteen directors agreed to disband the committee.[49]

George Worthington's comment in 1928, suggesting that the Committee of Fourteen "gained more than it lost by the publicity" of the visit by Texas Guinan and her dancers to his office, indicated that the committee was not adverse to the tabloid-style self-promotion of the times. In fact, the oxygen that kept this gaslight-era reform group alive in the 1920s was its annual sounding of the alarm about the rise of prostitution in the new nightlife. Its legislative achievements in the decade were meager compared to those of earlier decades, but its warnings of "the hostess evil" told many New Yorkers what they wanted to hear: that the moral relativism and tolerance of the modern age, and the nightlife they had bred, were allegedly fostering criminal immorality.

The committee paid little attention to Prohibition violations. Although George Worthington regularly corresponded with federal Prohibition enforcers, he also concurred with a *New York Times* editorial that accused the Volstead Act of contributing to the spread of generalized vice. The public's view of the group's stance was summarized by one speakeasy owner's statement to an undercover investigator: "The Committee of 14 don't give a damn about the whiskey—[they] are only after prostitutes."[50] Instead, the committee offered a "scientific" exploration of prostitution that mapped the evolving terrain of urban sexuality. Its frank reports helped to bring homosexuality, obscure corners of commercialized sex, interracial liaisons, and the occasionally violent exploitation of working-class women into the public discourse.[51]

But the city did not respond to these alarms and to this information the way the committee hoped it would. The group suffered from exceedingly poor timing. It remained allied with the police department in the early 1920s, just as scandals erupted in the vice department. Later, as it began to work closely with the magistrates' courts, a major state investigation exposed corruption on the city bench. The committee plotted the dramatic expansion of its mission and budget in 1929, on the eve of the Great Depression. George Worthington was a resourceful reformer, but the times still outwitted him, and in general they sounded the knell of reform organizations rooted in the moralistic muckraking of the gaslight era. Good-government organizations persisted past 1930—the New York Society for the Suppression of Vice, for example, labored until the 1950s—but for the most part moralistic reformers in the city became casualties of changing times. In the light of those changes, some thoughtful enforcers of the law themselves revised their judgments about gender interaction. Echoing Walter Lippmann's earlier critique, Jonah Goldstein, one of the least corruptible city magistrates to have worked with the committee, questioned the wisdom of targeting prostitution in the age of the nightclub. "Prostitution was an odd crime," Goldstein argued, "in that it took two to commit it, and only one was brought in [to court]. Furthermore, if the man gave her an automobile and showered her with expensive clothes and supported her in an apartment, it was not prostitution. But if he gave her two dollars in cash, that was prostitution."[52]

In the mid-1920s, even before the Committee of Fourteen's demise, government agencies and investigators took up the task of "scientifically" investigating and regulating alleged illegality in nightlife. The mayor, the police commissioner, and others in power occasionally associated their efforts with the committee's anti-prostitution crusade. In general, though, the city's attack on 1920s nightlife was guided by other major concerns. We turn now to these concerns, and to the municipal officials who acted upon them—officials who, ironically, belonged to the club-friendly Tammany Hall organization, including "the nightclub mayor" himself, James J. Walker.

# CHAPTER 3
## Tammany Nights

The earnest reformers at the Committee of Fourteen wrestled with the perplexing modern challenge posed by nightclubs. The clubs helped to promulgate gender interactions that often looked like prostitution, but which usually were not quite the genuine article. Paradoxically, though, the new interaction seemed more pervasive, more insidious, and thus potentially more threatening to the social order than the old streetwalking regime. The committee's efforts were complicated further by declining support from its benefactors and by allegations of corruption involving its official partners, the police and the courts. The corruption issue resurrected an old fear of New York reformers—the fear that the municipal government was not a model of civic rectitude and could not be trusted as a partner in the fight against social ills.

What was that government really like in the late 1920s? What was the condition of civic life in these years? And what was the position of nightclubs and other leisure institutions in this general civic context?

In the 1920s, as in the past, New Yorkers might look to their mayor as an embodiment of civic duty and official policy toward leisure. As it happened, the man they elected to the position in 1925 spent many of his waking hours in nightclubs and seemed to embrace its ethic of consumption, excess, and hilarity as a complement to his concept of civic involvement.

James J. Walker, the state senate majority leader, was sworn in as mayor on New Year's Day, 1926. Walker did not lack intelligence and skill. One colleague recalled that "I have never met a man with greater ability to absorb knowledge and express it to the public," while another claimed that "Walker as mayor got more things done in two hours than the rest of us could do in ten." He was considered one of the leading figures in Tammany Hall, Manhattan's storied Democratic Party organization. But since his youth, Jimmy Walker also had been immersed in the world of show business. In his twenties he strayed from his legal studies to Tin Pan Alley, where he was credited with the lyrics for successful songs such as "Will You Love Me in December as You Do in May?," "In the Valley Where My Sally Said Goodbye," "Kiss All the Girls for Me," and

"There's Music in the Rustle of a Skirt." He married the vaudeville performer Janet "Allie" Allen the same year he was elected to the state senate. Walker later told his biographer that "always my heart was in the theatre and in songs." He indulged in Broadway's flexible morality, conducting affairs with actresses. In Albany Walker became known for his acquaintances in New York City professional sports, which enjoyed close ties to show business. A law that Walker shepherded to passage earned him the nickname "the father of Sunday baseball."[1]

Walker's mayoral candidacy was pressed most lustily by his show business friends, especially by members of a new Broadway fraternal group called the Friars' Club. The club pursued a high public profile and introduced theater folk to political and financial elites. On 2 July 1925, the veteran showman George M. Cohan, the "first abbott" of the Friars, led five hundred musicians, marchers, and flag-wavers into Tammany Hall to plead for Walker's candidacy. Joining the marching Friars were members of the Grand Street Boys' Association, the Jewish Theatrical Alliance, the Music Publishers' Association, and the Motion Picture Producers' Chamber of Commerce, as well as the Sons of Erin.[2] These groups announced Broadway's increased presence in city politics.

Easily elected that November, Walker took office and quickly gained more notice as a public celebrity. He and his staff heartily promoted a showman image. At an "Inner Circle" banquet held two months into Walker's term, the mayor's secretary, Charles Kerrigan, toasted him as "the Duke of Jazzland," joking that while "under the old regime the symbol of power was the blackjack[,] we have made it the night club. We have made it a clean city; there is a bathtub on every stage." (This was a risqué reference to the producer Earl Carroll's recent scandalous party in his theater, during which male guests dipped glasses into a naked woman's champagne bath.) The mayor then joined in: "Let Charlie K. be Duke by day, / And I'll be Duke by night. / By every test, I'm at my best, / Beneath electric lights." In 1927, en route to his first European vacation, Walker traveled to Boston to attend the Ziegfeld Follies, where Eddie Cantor mimicked him. Upon his return from Europe the mayor celebrated on Broadway by making a surprise onstage appearance in the musical comedy *Manhattan Mary*. Summoned from the audience by the producer, George White, he replaced the actor playing "the mayor" and welcomed Mary (played by Ona Munson), improvising a wisecrack about appointing her a commissioner. Later that year Walker and his wife were filmed arriving at the premiere of the latest edition of the Ziegfeld Follies; Paramount included the footage in its big-budget fictional musical of 1928, *Glorifying the American Girl*. Walker was almost certainly the first American public official to appear in a Hollywood feature film.[3]

Walker's Broadway flamboyance was evident in his manner of dress (see Fig. 3). His tailor created unique clothes for his slight frame in which shirttails never became visible and "his clothes seemed to cling to him perfectly, no matter what his posture." Walker's single-button suit jackets (pinched at the waist), "toothpick"-pointed shoes, fedoras and derbys, narrow cravats, and garish colors received much notice. On a 1927 European vacation he toured Venice in "purple striped trousers and a green sweater" and arrived in Paris wearing a brown hat, "a tie of emerald and brown stripes, a blue shirt . . . , a blue-striped suit, low black shoes, a beige sport coat, and, completing the picture, a lavender hand-kerchief with dashes of purple and brown protruding from his only coat pocket." The public took notice. Each day boys in an ungraded public school classroom, in which Walker's portrait hung, named the best-dressed, cleanest boy "the mayor." A reporter was told that this boy's duties were the "same as Mayor Walker's. Sit around and look nice."[4]

The real mayor's widely publicized short workdays were built around nocturnal activity. Usually rising at midday, Walker dispatched official business quickly. At sunset he presided at political conferences and public hearings and then began long nights at the theater, restaurants, and nightclubs. Walker did not frolic in public to make himself available to the populace. He was a claustrophobe who feared crowds and elevators; in nightclubs he specialized in grand entrances and exits, but otherwise isolated himself in private booths and hidden tables. Like the gambler Arnold Rothstein, another Broadway habitué, Walker was a hypochondriac who inhabited his body uncomfortably.[5]

He was also strikingly passive. He went to baseball games, he confessed in a revealing interview, "because there I found the thing I liked best—a game, the drama, the spectacle, the emotions of human-beings." "When I go to the theatre I do not go to criticize. I go to be entertained. I give myself over to the player, and I do not want to see the inconsistency in the plot. I want to live in that make-believe world, the theatre. . . . Broadway is nothing but the world passing in review." Walker was a 1920s New York version of a modern archetype that first gained notice in Paris in the 1800s, the *flâneur*—the lover of public display and artifice who disdains personal intimacy. Walker's individuality was bound up in the generally passive consumption ethic of the era of Broadway shows and the cinema. The passivity of spectatorship militated against the nightclubs' encouragement of customer participation, but it also suggested that even in clubs, individuals might retreat into their own private subjectivities. Mayor Walker, for his part, reveled in keeping a safe physical distance from other people in order to gain the most pleasure from their social and artistic performances.[6]

Even in nightclubs, though, political issues continued to press in on the mayor, compelling him to blend his distancing act with frequent par-

Figure 3. New York City mayor Fiorello H. La Guardia, left, and former mayor James J. Walker lead the funeral procession for the Tammany Hall leader Nathan Burkan in 1936. During his Tammany mayoralty (1926–32) Walker's sartorial style and affinity for nightclubs helped to define the era. The rumpled and puritanical La Guardia, elected in 1933, symbolized anti-Tammany reform. La Guardia and Wagner Archive, La Guardia Community College. By permission of United Press International.

lays. And Walker did love to banter with like-minded people. In the back rooms of nightclubs he often met and did business with city officials and cemented his relationships with private citizens. Walker blended public and private business in a new and theatrical way. His biographer Gene Fowler later argued that Walker would be doomed by his "inability to see the difference between personal and public relationships," but the situation was somewhat more complex.[7] Walker's off-hours meetings in places of public leisure *were* semi-official business, which eradicated the boundaries between leisure and statecraft.

The mayor gave journalists on the city hall beat little to work with besides clever phrases and anecdotes. Stanley Walker, the *Herald-Tribune*'s city editor (and no relation), was struck by the fact that before 1931, "the administration of James J. Walker as mayor of New York furnished so little news. James had a way of charming his newspaper friends, of beguiling them with 'off the record' revelations, so that much news of actual administrative happenings never saw print." This suggests that Walker either wanted to hide a great deal or was carelessly obscuring the accomplishments of his office. Both were probably true; the mayor's "intimate" contact with journalists (and others) masked a deep aversion to outsiders, while his narcissism outshone any effort he made to promote his policies. But Stanley Walker's comment also reveals the complacency of the city press corps during the 1920s—a group of reporters who seemed to lack even a trace of the investigative urge. Throughout his first term they were only too happy to promote cheerfully what the *New York Times* termed "government by wisecrack."[8]

In the place of real news, newspaper readers often were given spectacle. The first two years of Walker's term, 1926 and 1927, coincided with what Grover A. Whalen later called "the high water-mark in many ways" of parades on lower Broadway. Whalen, a Greenwich Village Irish compatriot of Walker's and a veteran organizer of city hall functions, masterminded the development of the "ticker-tape blizzard," and in those years Charles Lindbergh, Admiral Byrd, the Crown Prince of Sweden, Ramsey MacDonald, Guglielmo Marconi, and others received the honor. While many in city government agreed with the police commissioner, George McLaughlin, that the parades were "a lot of nonsense," they brought some of nightlife's celebrity-in-performance onto a dramatic daytime concourse, Manhattan's "canyon of heroes." As Walker rode next to Queen Marie of Romania during her parade, workers on an unfinished skyscraper were alleged to have shouted, "Hey, Jimmy! Have you made her yet?" to which the queen was to have replied, "You Americans are so droll."[9] Tabloid columnists such as Walter Winchell broadcast such stories, even when they had not concocted them in the first place.

While the "the nightclub mayor" may have generated "little news," during his tenure nightclubs became a serious political issue. Complaints about the noise and disorder that occurred around some clubs in the predawn hours led traditional leaders of opinion such as ministers and reformers, as well as aldermen and the mayor himself, to call for the regulation and licensing of the establishments. The result, commonly called "the three o'clock curfew," was New York's first nightclub regulation of any kind, a comprehensive local statute that took effect on the first day of 1927.[10] The law was the signal effort by city government in the 1920s to impose its will on the new nightlife.

It may have seemed paradoxical that Jimmy Walker led the crusade to regulate clubs and impose the closing time. His effort, though, was in accordance with the wider moralistic campaign he led against traditionally objectionable forms of popular and mass culture in the city. This chapter considers how nightclub regulation reflected the vision of civic life projected by Walker and Tammany Hall. It was a vision that embraced both traditional and modern goals, typical of the so-called New Tammany approach to governing that blended old-fashioned cronyism and graft with a new commitment to innovative social legislation. The moralistic cultural crusade helped the political machine to bridge, or at least to mask, its own contradictions. The crusade's popularity, in turn—like that of the Committee of Fourteen—showed leaders and the public vacillating between moralistic regulation and the new social tolerance. The new law's ineffectiveness during the first year of its enforcement exposed some of the latent weaknesses in the Walker-Tammany concept of civic life, and it encouraged New Yorkers to begin to reevaluate their own civic commitments and the demands they made of government.

Jimmy Walker's ascent to the mayoralty in 1926 was the latest in a series of victories for Tammany Hall. The Democratic organization of Manhattan and the Bronx was plainly in charge of the city government. It had regained all of the top city offices in the election of 1917 and controlled almost all of them for the next sixteen years. Tammany's success in the 1920s was largely due to the strategy of Charles Francis Murphy, the organization's leader since 1902. Ending direct investment by district leaders in gambling and prostitution, which at the turn of the century had prompted state investigations and the election of an anti-Tammany mayor, Murphy cannily positioned the organization so that it would obtain maximum benefit from the imminent explosion in private and public construction in the city. Tammany Hall regained the mayor's chair in 1905, and as subway lines were dug, Manhattan grew skyward, docks were expanded, and the Bronx and Queens were developed, the leaders of the organization profited immensely.

"New Tammany Hall's" success was heavily weighted at the top. Murphy, who served as a harbor commissioner, set up a trucking company that leased docks from the city at bargain rates, and he made 5,000 percent profits. In a three-year period Murphy's company also won $15 million in city contracts; the Tammany-owned Metropolitan Street Railway Company manipulated ledgers and stocks to earn at least $30 million in graft; and Tammany milked the New York, New Haven, and Hartford Railroad of $100 million from inflated construction costs for tracks in the Bronx.[11] Unlike the doings of bosses Tweed and Croker in the 1800s these transactions were public and legal, vetted by Tammany's attorneys and "brokerage services" through "blind" contracts. In the words of the socialist reformers Norman Thomas and Paul Blanshard, "For every type of exploitation [Tammany Hall] has developed a technique for coming within the limits of the law. . . . The new Tammany is the old Tammany with the wisdom of age and experience added. . . . To-day it has a legal device for every possible type of looting and a moral explanation for every bribe."[12]

Reformers such as Thomas and Blanshard frequently sounded that refrain, and like-minded observers (and later historians) also portrayed the 1920s as an era of total Tammany dominance that inevitably stimulated a subsequent movement for reform. Conversely, after the mayoral victory of the reformer Fiorello H. La Guardia in 1933 sympathetic observers claimed that the Tammany "tiger" had been tamed for good. Historians recently have revised this dualistic interpretation of New York City's politics. They first note that Tammany Hall itself was a force for reform. It was Tammany Hall, not reformers, that generally presided over the growth of municipal social service agencies run by professional managers. Kenneth Finegold argues that "the most important links between administrative reformers and city government were established under the Tammany-elected administrations of George B. McClellan, Jr. [1905–9], and William Jay Gaynor [1909–12], in response to [William Randolph] Hearst's mobilization of an antimachine constituency." The Bureau of Municipal Research, the first public-interest policy think-tank in the nation, began work in 1907 with Tammany's backing. The reform mayor John Purroy Mitchel, in office from 1913 to 1917, actually spent less money annually on social reform measures than John F. Hylan, the machine mayor who succeeded him.[13]

Tammany Hall under Charles Murphy benefited from a disunited opposition and the resultant growth of opportunities for expanding its power. The machine faced a wide array of opponents, including independent Democrats such as Franklin D. Roosevelt and Samuel Seabury;

the Republican-dominated state legislature, the *Herald-Tribune*, and Wall Street; a strong local Socialist Party; and good-government groups such as the Citizens Union. However, during Mitchel's term Tammany's foes began to squabble among themselves and failed to mount another successful "fusion" campaign. Murphy, meanwhile, rolled back progressive "good government" reforms. In 1911 his lieutenants in the state legislature, Alfred E. Smith and Robert Wagner, put through the so-called Murphy Charter, which diluted civil service classifications, adding thousands of unclassified jobs to the city payroll. The historian Stephen Erie has called the 1920s "the Irish machine's heyday." By 1925 fully one-sixth of all Tammany voters had a city job.[14] Now governor, Al Smith pushed through a reorganization law that made him the most powerful executive in the state's history, and on the national stage he sought the presidency.

Tammany Hall certainly dominated city politics, but its critics (and its first historians) tended to exaggerate its machine-like power and cohesion. Brooklyn's Democratic organization maintained a stubborn independence, and within Tammany itself district leaders usually pursued their own interests to the detriment of the organization's solidarity and general strategy. The enormous profits from graft flowed mostly to these semi-independent public entrepreneurs. Meanwhile, Tammany patronage rarely offered its voters avenues to upward mobility. Most city jobs paid poorly and offered few opportunities for career advancement. In addition, the bosses' persistent bias in favor of Irish American employees alienated members of other ethnic groups and made Tammany Hall vulnerable to significant future opposition.[15]

Charles Murphy's unexpected death in 1924 at first did not seem to threaten the machine's dominance. In retrospect, though, it is clear that his passing deprived Tammany of crucial imaginative leadership and marked the beginning of the end of a halcyon era. In 1925 district leaders rejected their own mayor for the first time, forcing John Hylan into a party primary and engineering the victory of Jimmy Walker. The state senator's success was followed quickly by the first, seemingly minor blow to Tammany Hall's fortunes. Reform groups issued warnings of a revival of gambling in the city. Walker's deft response to these warnings, as well as his colorful exploits as "the nightclub mayor," at first helped to obscure the problems confronting his organization.

The gambling issue helped to remind New Yorkers that Tammany Hall itself was a club. It was one of New York's oldest fraternities, founded in the 1780s by Aaron Burr and his allies. For decades, to divert attention from its political schemes, or perhaps in jest, members had insisted that the Society of Tammany or Columbian Order was merely a social club, numbering in the hundreds. In the 1920s it still performed traditional ceremonies and bestowed hoary titles such as "wiskinkie" and "sachem." The wizened Grand Sachem John R. Voorhis, who had joined Tammany during James Buchanan's presidency, still served as president of the city board of elections in 1929, when he celebrated his one-hundredth birthday. In other ways, though, the "club" visibly changed with the times. Tammany Hall itself was updated when a new headquarters was constructed on 14th Street and the 1850s "Wigwam" three blocks to the north was razed. Tammany stalwarts also patronized a space that resembled a modern cabaret in some ways: the Tiger Club, atop a building at Fourth Avenue and 23rd Street. The Tiger Club was owned and operated by William F. Kenney, a Tammany member and a businessman. The theatrical producer Eddie Dowling recalled that the club's main area was "a tremendous room [with] highly waxed and polished floors and tiger skins all over it," the place where "many of the Mayors of the City of New York were chosen" and where Walter P. Chrysler was first pledged the capital for his automobile company.[16]

Tammany's leaders maintained district clubhouses that also served as sites for political and business deal making. For decades many of these clubs were also active incubators of nocturnal leisure. Tammany Hall had, in fact, long been an ally of the entertainment business. Before the turn of the century Charles Murphy's saloons offered floor shows, while "Big Tim" Sullivan managed several theaters and concert saloons. Sullivan and other Tammany leaders introduced the first moving-picture nickelodeons to Manhattan and also formed business and personal relationships with Broadway theater producers and other leisure personnel. Irish theaters in Lower Manhattan enchanted such young future Tammany stalwarts as Jimmy Walker, Mary Sullivan, and Alfred E. Smith (who acted theatrically as a youth, between stints at the Fulton Fish Market and as a machine ward heeler). Good-government reformers, many of whom were Protestant ministers, associated Tammany Hall publicly with "immoral" new amusements. In 1907 they persuaded Mayor George McClellan (who broke with Tammany after his election) to close moving-picture theaters in the city to stymie Sullivan and other district leaders. Popular protest soon forced him to rescind the ban. Jimmy Walker's affinity for Broadway and show business thus conformed with a general tendency in the culture of Tammany Hall.[17]

After Walker became mayor, though, events forced him to deal with the scandal that linked Tammany clubhouses with gambling. In his 1925 campaign Walker was rarely compelled to discuss the issue of gambling, all forms of which were illegal in New York State. Very soon after his election, though, reports circulated that gamblers were "com[ing] into the city in seeming belief that New York is to be a 'wide-open' town." Walker promised to "stop anything like organized gambling before it fairly started." His claim that "Tammany assistance will be of great help," while disbelieved by reformers, was supported by his appointment of the youthful and able George V. McLaughlin, a reform-minded state official from Tammany's ranks, as police commissioner. McLaughlin reinstated the so-called Confidential Squad, an elite police unit that had investigated gamblers' payments to officers in the 1910s until it was disbanded due to pressure from Tammany Hall.[18]

The head of the Confidential Squad, police captain Lewis J. Valentine, later testified that the Tammany clubhouses "were semi-political clubs, but they were really gambling clubs." In these clubs lucrative gambling rings lured "Wall Street barons, society blue-bloods, city officials and Tammany leaders" into poker games, made book on horse races, and paid police officers to ignore the lawbreaking. Valentine considered "Nick the Greek," "Nigger Nate" Raymond, and Arnold Rothstein to be the gambling ringleaders. Court-sanctioned wiretaps also indicated that the Tammany clubhouses hosted card and dice games and liquor sales. The club's front windows were "covered with a heavy copper mesh wire," and their portals were secured by steel icebox doors encased in four-inch-thick wood frames. When Confidential Squad officers failed to infiltrate the clubhouses in disguises, they used sledgehammers to bring down the doors.[19]

Raids of the Tammany clubhouses became major news stories. Informers leaked warnings of the raid on the Yorkville clubhouse of the New York county sheriff Tom Farley, where 26 men greeted the squad mockingly, "playing with children's skipping ropes and rubber balls." More successful raids took place at Billy Warren's clubhouse on 14th Street and city clerk Michael Cruise's establishment on East 32nd Street. Then, in August, the squad broke down the door of the late congressman Tim Sullivan's clubhouse in the Bowery, which was now operated by his widow's stepson, the city courts clerk. Two gamblers (one of whom was employed by the state senate) had recently been killed at the club during a dispute. Henry Perry, the courts clerk, was not present during the raid, which resulted in the arrest of 101 suspects.

Into 1927 Mayor Walker continued to back McLaughlin and the raids, and Charles Murphy's successor as the general leader of Tammany Hall, George W. Olvany, lent his public support. The Tammany district attorney refused to bring indictments, though, and magistrates were obligated to free everyone who had been arrested in the raids. Lewis Valentine's lieutenant, Ezekiel Keller, later testified that "professional gambling could [not] continuously exist in the City of New York unless it were protected . . . [by] certain politicians in whose bailiwick or district the games might be operated." In their 1930 testimony Keller and Valentine would reveal that Arnold Rothstein coordinated the activities at

Billy Warren's clubhouse, while George McManus tended to Michael Cruise's operation, Baldy Frolich and Gus Mayo managed Tom Farley's gaming, and Johnny Baker ran Harry C. Perry's place as well as "sham" Democratic clubs called the Philo and the Pericles.[20] For more than three years, though, Tammany used various forms of intimidation and pressure to keep these details from becoming public. The first major political coverup of the nightclub era had begun.

On 12 March 1927 the Confidential Squad raided three non-Tammany clubhouses in Brooklyn. The most notable resulted in the arrests of 158 people at the People's Regular Democratic club, including its patron, the alderman Peter J. McGuinness. The next day McGuinness and 150 others were absolved of all charges by a city magistrate. This development finally compelled Mayor Walker to express a vague public endorsement of the raids, but Democratic-leaning newspapers launched a coordinated attack on the Confidential Squad. Even the *New York Times* reported erroneously that the officer who arrested McGuinness had shouted "to hell with Mayor Walker" when the alderman protested that he had Walker's support. In the Democratic newspapers Lewis Valentine was likened to the notorious police lieutenant Charles Becker, who had used a similar position a decade earlier to enrich himself with bribes from gamblers. For Valentine the raiding "game . . . was rapidly becoming a bitter and deadly conflict." Lieutenant Keller was arrested and charged with violating a suspected gambler's rights. The crusading police commissioner, George McLaughlin, was talked into resigning his post to take a position in business. The new commissioner was the mayor's former law partner, Joseph Warren, who retained Valentine and the squad and vowed to continue the gambling raids. But Tammany Hall had begun to close ranks to protect its interests and its image.[21]

Jimmy Walker's ambivalent crusade against clubhouse gambling was fairly representative of the general tenor of his first two years as mayor. In 1926 and 1927 Walker attempted a political and cultural balancing act, blending progressive-sounding rhetoric, business-friendly policies, and Irish American sensibilities in a manner fairly typical of the "new Tammany Hall" of the Charles Murphy era. Among city residents Walker was perhaps most popular for the deceptively difficult achievement of maintaining the five-cent subway and bus fare, in the face of a major transit workers' strike and lawsuits by the private companies that provided municipal transport. Walker had a good understanding of the city's desperate need for improvements in transportation infrastructure and working-class housing. He effectively browbeat obstinate landowners who refused to sell their parcels to the city for public housing construction, accusing them of "holding out for exorbitant prices." The

Walker administration can be credited with the upgrading of services at Bellevue and other city hospitals and a highly publicized modernization and professionalization of the police force. Soaring real estate tax revenues kept the city treasury reasonably solvent.[22] The economic boom of the mid-1920s helped to make Walker look like an effective head of government.

The mayor's occasional gestures of effective leadership conformed with Tammany Hall's general effort to steal the thunder of reformers and deflect the attacks of political opponents. While Walker himself had little contact with the Committee of Fourteen and its new crusade against prostitution of the 1920s, his police commissioners and magistrates were vocal advocates and frequent correspondents with the committee's staff. (Grover Whalen, the official city greeter who later served as police commissioner, even became one of the fourteen directors after he departed the latter post.)[23] The committee's anti-prostitution campaign had its roots in 1800s Protestant reform, but its alignment with the police department and indifference to moral condemnation and Prohibition violations made it culturally palatable to Tammany Hall Catholics.

Much of the same moralistic spirit characterized Walker's campaigns for public decency in New York City, a series of efforts that culminated in his effort to regulate nightclubs. The mayor launched efforts to regulate "immoral" stage performances and printed matter at about the same time as the clubhouse gambling raids. Protestant-dominated groups such as the Society for the Suppression of Vice had been attempting for decades to legislate against "obscene" literature and artifacts. The New York branch of the society, headed by the Reverend John R. Straton, remained active in the mid-1920s, hauling burlesque theater managers and "lewd" authors such as Ben Hecht into court under state laws written by the society's founder, the late Anthony Comstock. Early radio stations were attacked for "indecent" on-air jokes and for broadcasting on Sundays. The Roman Catholic Church joined the effort. The city's archbishop, Patrick Cardinal Hayes, condemned modern "playwrights who wrote only of the darker side of life and . . . unbridled realism in the drama or in fiction." The cardinal also praised Mayor Walker's commitment to maintaining "a clean, wholesome stage in New York."[24]

While it may seem an obvious target for moral reform in the 1920s, the stage became a site of contention almost by accident. In 1923 New York's highest court ruled that under the state constitution a theater's operating license could be revoked only by a judge, not by the agency that had granted the license. No new law remedied this decision, so the city licensing department launched an experiment and created a citizens' commission that would judge the suitability of all new presentations. (The district attorney's office soon oversaw the commission.) In early 1927 the "play jury" permitted three controversial productions to open: *The Virgin Man*, the story of three women who seduce a naïve Yale student; Mae West's *Sex*, concerning prostitution; and *The Captive*, a French import with a lesbian theme. Public anger caused the police to raid all three plays on 9 February and arrest theater owners, producers, cast, and crew for disturbing the peace. Mayor Walker, who had been present at the premiere of *The Captive*, called in Broadway producers and asked them to police their own material. Within weeks the state legislature obliged moralists by passing the Wales Law, which banned indecent stage plays and required the closing of the theaters that produced them. Mae West served ten days in jail for writing and producing *Sex*; she later faced Wales Law prosecution for her homosexual-themed play *The Drag* (1927) and for *The Pleasure Man* (1928), a backstage melodrama about a womanizing singer (based on Harry Richman). Walker himself ordered the raid on the latter production, but West's rather raucous trial (which featured a flamboyant visit from her "supporter" Texas Guinan) resulted in a hung jury.[25]

Walker and the district attorney Joab Banton were criticized from both sides for their moralistic crusade. From the left, one newspaper editor protested that "in this modern, liberal era . . . —when sex is a part of the curriculum of colleges and high schools—prudes and so-called reformers are largely in the minority. The public patronizes shows to be entertained, edified, and enlightened." Republicans conversely claimed that Tammany censorship crusades were mostly bluster that masked the organization's longtime alliance with Broadway. The new federal attorney in Manhattan, Charles H. Tuttle, criticized Walker for "slap[ping]" the play producers "on their wrists, and hav[ing] his picture taken" with them. Tuttle also accused the mayor of doing nothing after he pledged to revoke the licenses of newsstand operators who sold "magazines specializing in pictures of the undraped female form and other salacious illustrations." Moralists also frowned when Walker declined to ban the motion pictures of Charles Chaplin during the comedian's sensational divorce, commenting that "I am not a Judge of the Court of Domestic Relations." Such attitudes helped to split Walker ideologically from Protestant and Republican reformers with whom he might have found common cause on moral issues, but it did not cause his crusade to abate in 1927.[26]

Walker's general campaign for civic morality helps us to understand the tangled motivations and actions surrounding his campaign to regulate nightclubs, which resulted in the three o'clock closing or "curfew" law of 1926. As with their effort to promote decency in theaters, Walker and

Tammany Hall regulated nightclubs both to cultivate an image of traditional, censorious rectitude and to encourage longtime friends and business partners to reform their ways. This balancing act showed New
York's leadership attempting to keep its options open in a time of
change in public tastes and morals. Mayor Walker's own preference for
the new nightlife, though, both added an element of farce to the crusade and underlined the deep ambivalence of the government concerning the regulation of nightlife. The regulation, as a result, largely would
fail. More generally, Tammany's ambivalence about nightlife reflected
the increasing unsteadiness of its control of city government.

For a dozen years before 1926, cabaret closing laws in New York had
come and gone. The idea of using a statute to cut the night short had
long animated the hopes of social reformers. In 1913 Mayor William
Gaynor, probably the most progressive Tammany mayor, pushed
through a one AM curfew in response to fears about the "white-slave
traffic" and gambling in all-night restaurants and saloons. Gaynor also
wanted to counter the purchase by establishments of old, state-issued
club charters, which permitted operations at any hour. Gaynor's law also
reflected politicians' concern about the explosion in the number of
dance halls. Like restaurants, dance halls were required to register with
the city's department of licenses. (Licensing, in fact, was the true heart
of closing-time laws; observance of a closing time was simply a condition
an establishment had to meet in order to keep its license.) Clubs with
state charters then obtained state court injunctions that halted enforcement of the closing law. Gaynor's successor John Purroy Mitchel
relented, pushing the closing time back to two AM and granting some
"all-night licenses." He also allowed three o'clock closings on New
Year's Eve. (Mitchel, a foe of Tammany Hall who was supported by Protestant moral reformers, thus was a surprisingly liberal proponent of
nightlife.)[27]

Under the next mayor, John F. Hylan, Prohibition reshaped the landscape of nightclub enforcement. The Volstead Act and New York's own
"little Volstead," the Mullan-Gage Act, superseded most earlier laws governing establishments where liquor was served. Since speakeasies existed
in order to violate the law, their operators naturally ignored city licensing. In 1923, then, Governor Al Smith and the state legislature decided
to repeal the Mullan-Gage Act. In addition to reshaping Prohibition
enforcement in New York (as the following chapter shows), the repeal
encouraged cities to revive campaigns for cabaret regulation through
licensing.

In the 1920s New York City seemed to be infatuated with licensing. For
reformers especially, licensing seemed to promise control over countless
untidy components of city life. In 1925 the licensing commissioner

claimed his office's "purpose" was "the inclusion, as far as possible, of all city licenses in one department." His agency that year issued permits for bathhouses, billiard parlors, bootblack chairs, "dirt carts," employment agencies, hand organs, junk shops, boats and carts, massage parlors, motion picture and legitimate theaters, pawnbrokers, taxicabs, small vending stands, and many other facilities. In 1924 and 1925 the department lost its most populated classifications, as taxicab, horse-drawn vehicle, and pushcart licenses were transferred variously to the police department and the Department of Public Markets. Still, during the next year the department's staff of eighty-five issued over fifty-five thousand licenses.[28]

More than half of the licenses were for billiard rooms, horse or motor carts, and dancing. Fewer than a thousand dance hall permits were issued yearly, but ten times that number were granted to sponsors of one-time dance events. The issuing of dance licenses yearly provided the department with its main experience in policing nightlife. A licensed dance or ball could be investigated if the dancing and the "conduct of patrons" was not "proper," if arrests or "disorder" occurred, or if other irregularities were discovered. Most dance hall permits were actually granted to restaurants, where dancing accompanied dining; revocations of these licenses were almost always due to violations of Prohibition laws. The department claimed that owing to its quixotic effort to regulate all city dancing, "it has succeeded . . . in keeping some of the more undesirable organizations from getting dance permits." In 1925 the licensing commissioner first noted that increasing numbers of restaurants and dance halls had organized as private clubs to avoid licensing and to facilitate liquor sales. This phenomenon indicated an abuse of the club concept that far exceeded the scope of the nightclub business.[29]

However, in 1926 the nightclubs themselves inspired a new era in municipal licensing. Under the existing law, Commissioner of Licenses William F. Quigley later recalled, "the dance hall license was not applicable to the night club, an institution that has grown up with Prohibition enforcement, and its hold on the cabaret was somewhat slender." The cabaret, he explained, was difficult to classify as a dance hall since it was really a restaurant in which "entertainments of the variety-show order were [the] real attractions." Nor could it be licensed as a theater. Chartered nightclubs "were also beyond the provisions of existing laws and were in a position to defy regulation. The only thing they had to fear was a Prohibition padlock, but even this need not abolish them as they could re-incorporate and move to a new place." In short, Quigley argued, "the night amusement life of the city was under a loose system of legal regulation outside of what might be enforced by exercise of general police powers."[30]

How could the new nightlife be brought under effective government oversight? Citizen complaints about late operating hours, drunkenness, disorderly conduct, gambling, and prostitution did not indicate clearly what kinds of nightlife venues were most to blame. To impose some control, the city initially attempted to investigate violations by nightclubs of various existing ordinances. In February 1926 the police commissioner, George McLaughlin, announced that building codes, especially bans on overcrowding, would now be vigorously enforced in nightclubs. As Harold Ross of the *New Yorker* noted, this campaign introduced an unexpected note of strictness in the new administration of Jimmy Walker, who "was familiar of many a night club before he fell heir to the mantle of Hylan." Since building-code enforcement attacked nightclubs "on the score of comfort, rather than morality," though, Ross predicted that no significant policing of nightlife would result.[31] As we have seen, though, Walker's stances on cultural issues tended toward censorious moralizing. The recent sensational arrest of the thieving Whittemore gang at its headquarters, the Club Chantee, encouraged officials to propose stricter enforcement. By April Walker was publicly calling for a three o'clock closing time. Confusion then ensued in June, when McLaughlin issued an "order" to police officers to close nightclubs at two o'clock. Complaints forced McLaughlin to rescind his order, which he claimed was merely an attempt to gather information for the Board of Estimate (the city's upper chamber, consisting of the highest elected officials). Walker, urged by all parties to act, then made a formal proposal to the board for a 3 AM closing.[32]

Walker proposed a local law that would regulate "public dance halls and cabarets." Both terms were defined very broadly. A public dance hall was "any room, place or space in the city . . . in which dancing is carried on and to which the public may gain admission, either with or without the payment of a fee." A cabaret was defined as "any room, place or space in the city in which any musical entertainment, singing, dancing or other similar amusement is permitted in connection with the restaurant business or the business of directly or indirectly selling the public food or drink." In addition to these sweeping definitions, "membership corporations," "clubs," and "associations and societies" were "deemed to be conducting a cabaret within the meaning of this local law." The proposed law, therefore, required licensing for virtually every space or occasion that featured music or dancing. The only exemptions were for hotels with more than fifty bedrooms, religious, charitable, or educational locales, or "premises owned by a membership corporation, club, society, or association." (Virtually all nightclubs were in leased locations.) Section five of the law contained the "curfew," requiring the closing of all venues between three and eight o'clock in the morning, except at the commissioner's discretion.[33]

This law was proposed by Walker a few days before he launched the most farsighted initiative of his mayoralty. On 21 June he established the City Committee on Plan and Survey and charged it with making a comprehensive evaluation of the city's needs. Walker's proposal illustrated Tammany Hall's continuing involvement in progressive-style reform, in this case with the growing movement among business and academic leaders for regional planning. The mayor ordered eight subcommittees to examine such topics as transportation, housing, and zoning. The latter issue had the most direct impact on the nightclub issue. In 1916 New York City had passed the nation's first municipal zoning law, which profoundly affected the subsequent shaping of the city. The graduated "wedding cake" setback of floors on new skyscrapers, for example, was mandated by the law to ensure sunlight on Manhattan's streets. Most significantly, the law created use districts, in which only specified kinds of residences or businesses (that is, those created after 1916) could be located. For example, "4B districts," which were "restricted retail districts," specifically excluded billiard parlors, freak shows, and "cabaret[s] other than a hotel," while "4A" districts had no restrictions on retail businesses. Residential or "3" districts allowed only noncommercial clubs.[34]

In 1926, as the cabaret licensing law was debated, zoning conflicts also raged. Influential figures, particularly the drafters of the 1916 law, now argued that the city's explosive growth warranted revisions. The Board of Estimate had already issued hundreds of amendments to the zoning law. Walker's city planning committee on zoning found that due to "shifts in the land market," the 1916 law was "too permissive" and "obsolete." Realtors, for their part, complained that it was too strict because it disallowed high-density housing for workers near factories. This dispute became indirectly involved with the nightclub issue late that year, when the Board of Estimate approved the reclassification of West 52nd and 55th Streets between Fifth and Sixth Avenue as business districts. Advocates of the changes argued that "virtually every house in the block already sheltered some sort of a commercial or industrial enterprise, although no display signs were hung out." Some of these businesses, they admitted, were operating "clandestinely . . . in the old brownstone front private dwellings from which residents had moved away when radical changes began in the neighborhood." John D. Rockefeller, father and son, lived on this block of 55th Street and resisted this change. No nightclubs apparently operated on these blocks, but the Club Florida was on 55th Street across Sixth Avenue while the Club Cameo was on 52nd Street another block down, and a dozen other clubs were located on the diagonally opposite block. Two years later, in 1928, investigators for the Committee of Fourteen found the Fifty-Nine West 52nd speakeasy (featuring Hawaiian musicians) and the Club Basque (recently raided by Prohibition agents) nested in the former roosts of Manhattan's elite.[35]

Thus the Board of Estimate, presided over by Walker, changed rules to accommodate the growth of the nightlife economy at the same time that the mayor was pushing for intrusive new regulation of that same realm. To the public, though, the mayor's well-known affinity for night-clubs burdened the bill with its greatest irony. At a board hearing in late June, Walker used his knowledge of nightclubs to moralistic advantage, jousting effectively with two clubowners arguing against the curfew. One of these opponents, David Stone, the owner of the Maxine Supper Club, asked, "Where are these people going to go after 3 o'clock if you close us up?" "Where I've learned to go—home," Walker retorted. He refused to consider a closing time on Elks or Masonic lodges because he believed that while the nightclub "is a detriment to the town," the fra-ternal organization "is an ornament." Expressing what became a com-mon argument during the debate, the mayor blamed "white-collar thieves" and "out-of-town visitors" for corrupting nightclubs and mak-ing New York "a cesspool." When Stone proposed the increased polic-ing of such people, though, Walker demurred and restated his support for a closing time.[36]

The main effect of the hearings, the *New York Times* reported, was to air the mayor's "familiarity with business of night clubs." Interrogating a lawyer who represented the Silver Slipper, Alabam', and other clubs, Walker pointed out that he knew "the closing time of all of them. . . . The Silver Slipper is open after 3. . . . So is the Three Hundred Club. The Richmond Club used to be. You see I haven't forgotten all I've learned. . . . The Lido is not open after 3 nor is the Montmartre, or the Mirador." "I know the class of people who stay out after 2:30, and I know where they stay and where they go after they leave the night clubs," he added, apparently referring to speakeasies. Others at the hearing also commented on Walker's clubgoing. The owners' attorney told the mayor that nightclubs "entertain people from all over the world" and that "you have been doing practically nothing else [besides such enter-taining] for months." Joseph McKee, the president of the Board of Aldermen, teasingly added that the mayor "never asks for the check." "I have been doing plenty of other things," Walker retorted.[37]

In October the Board of Estimate approved the bill with minor amendments. This led to more hearings before the local laws committee of the Board of Aldermen, which held the power of final approval. David Stone appeared again to express his disappointment with "our friend,

Jimmy Walker," and claimed that thousands of cab drivers, nightclub entertainers, and musicians would be harmed by regulation. Alderman Murray Stand of the Lower East Side opposed the bill on the grounds that it favored large hotels at the expense of smaller establishments; "if it be fixed for one class let it be fixed for all." Stand also criticized the government's general strategy, asking, "When did we get the right to set ourselves up as censors of the morals of the people of this city?" No supporters of the bill appeared at the hearing, but this did not stop the local laws committee from unanimously recommending the bill's passage to the aldermen. The committee's accompanying statement was the city government's first explicit verdict on the social impact of nightclubs, and it was highly unfavorable. "Simply dance halls . . . where food is served at exorbitant prices to the tune of jazz and tabloid entertainments," nightclubs encouraged "altogether too much running 'wild.'" "The 'wild' stranger and the foolish native should have the check-rein applied a little bit." Out-of-towners "tumble . . . out of these resorts at six or seven o'clock in the morning to the scandal and annoyance of decent residents . . . and return to their native heaths to slander New York." Neglecting the contradictory legacy of cabaret curfews, licensing precedents, and zoning decisions, the aldermen on the committee chose to make a fashionably moralistic indictment.[38]

Flaws in the bill's logic were noted when the entire Board of Aldermen met to consider its passage. Republican Ruth Pratt from the Upper East Side, the lone female on the board and a local laws committee member, said that she had signed the committee report "under protest" because she felt the bill was "a mere gesture and not even a step in the right direction." "Dance halls and night clubs which are a menace to the social life of our city should be wiped out entirely and not merely told when to close their doors." Pratt thus argued that the city, by abstaining from Prohibition enforcement and proposing curfews, was shadowboxing with a major cause of public disorder. Murray Stand repeated his class-discrimination criticism, but he and Pratt were drowned out by moralistic blarney such as that of Peter McGuinness. This Brooklyn alderman recalled that "Mike Murphy on the corner of Greenpoint and Manhattan avenues put out the lights at 1 o'clock and the guy on the opposite side of the street did the same. Them was the good old days. I vote aye." Michael Cruise, the clerk of the board (who, like McGuinness, would be arrested in Tammany clubhouse raids in coming months), recorded a 58–2 vote for the bill. The aldermen had attempted broader regulation that would have outlawed large illuminated signs, cover charges, and coatchecking fees in dance halls—the latter prohibition was sponsored by McGuinness—but these companion measures failed to pass. Mayor Walker signed the bill into law, which was to take effect on 1 January 1927.[39]

In his history of the city's regulation of jazz musicians, the attorney Paul Chevigny notes that the new licensing law was an anachronism. "By the time the City got around to regulating the 'cabarets,' in 1926," Chevigny argues, "they were gone, destroyed by Prohibition. When the City finally passed a licensing ordinance, it was regulating speakeasies. . . . just 'joints' with music and dancing. In the cabaret law, the City was seeking to apply its regulation to a genre that was already out of date." Furthermore, Ruth Pratt had noted in 1926 that the city sought to regulate illegal facilities that had no right to be open at all. Conversely, by defining virtually any site in the city where dancing regularly took place—such as a restaurant or nightclub—as a "dance hall" and any gathering featuring dancing as a licensable "dance," the city was vastly expanding its potential regulatory reach. Most important, though, as Chevigny implies, the new law was a blunt instrument that did not discriminate sufficiently in its choice of targets. In short, it did not strike cleanly at nightclubs. A massive enforcement policy would be required to ensure that even a few of the late-closing, peace-disturbing new venues would be shuttered.[40]

The enforcement of the curfew in 1927 produced disarray in the nightclub industry but also an ultimate admission of failure by the city. After record-setting business in the early hours of New Year's Day, when the city exempted clubs from closing, the curfew received vigorous enforcement. Licensing inspectors visited "30 or 40" of "the larger Broadway cabarets" in response to citizen complaints about "scantiness of dress of the female performers, or indecency of dialogue," but the task of ensuring that clubs closed at 3 AM "obviously . . . became a police job." The police generally logged every complaint against a single club, although the licensing department bundled them into one complaint. In addition, police often issued summonses to clubs for "exceeding the closing hour by only a few minutes"; Commissioner William Quigley, hearing their cases, usually let them off the first time with a warning.[41]

The Club Dover received the first citation on 4 January. Four days later Texas Guinan's 300 Club and two others received summonses for violating the curfew; Helen Morgan's, the Crystal Club, and the Capital Club were cited the next day. David Stone's Club Maxine entered the first guilty plea for violating the curfew, but this case was later thrown out by the magistrate. Eleven clubs were charged by January 10, but the courts were already tossing cases back to the commissioner of licenses. At this early point interagency conflicts began to weaken curfew enforcement. The police commissioner announced the cessation of court summonses, and the Supper Club Owners' Association began to bring pressure on the city to revise the law. In February Commissioner Quigley began hearing clubowners' appeals: four from Harlem one week, thirty others two weeks hence. He revoked the licenses of seventeen clubs, and the next month the courts had fined seven clubs for operating without a license. Thirty-three clubs had their licenses revoked by April, but by then it was known that most nightclubs simply avoided licensing to elude city enforcement. One owner publicly stated that his establishment was a speakeasy, not a cabaret, and thus did not require licensing. As Quigley acknowledged, his office could only regulate licensed businesses. In the summer the Committee of Fourteen made its proclamation that night-clubs were the new breeding grounds for prostitution; the arrests contin-ued, but the licensing commission was now demanding extra staff to do its duties. Jimmy Walker, returning from a long European vacation, made a strong appeal for the extra inspectors, noting a lack of coopera-tion from both the magistrates and the police. Meanwhile, though, reports of clubowners' bribes to inspectors put the entire enforcement regime into question.[42]

Problems arose on all fronts. The vagueness of the 1926 law, in tan-dem with the tangle of existing regulations, produced unusual judicial interpretations. Vague and obsolete definitions played havoc with enforcement; one judge argued that the introduction of a nickelodeon in a restaurant would make it a cabaret. The supremacy of the state courts over municipal law also caused problems. In October 1927 the Guinan family's Texas Restaurant Corporation successfully applied to the state supreme court for a stay of Century Club's closing order. Doz-ens of clubs now operated without licenses altogether to avoid curfew scrutiny. Also, as caches of liquor were uncovered by curfew enforcers at such sites as the second El Fey Club, the wisdom of New York City's turn away from Prohibition enforcement was seriously questioned. Officials countered with the argument—which had never been made during the earlier debates—that the curfew law's real advantage lay in giving the city the power to uncover illegal liquor. Walker ultimately admitted that "the enforcement of the 3 o'clock closing law has completely broken down" and asked for a tougher law, but none was politically possible. The city's will to regulate nightclubs seemed to be sapped. Advertise-ments for Texas Guinan's latest club mocked law enforcement: "Remember, there's *no* 3 AM curfew at the Salon Royale."[43]

As 1927 drew to a close, therefore, the city government, which was controlled by Tammany Hall, had been implicated in clubhouse gam-bling, had launched a general campaign to guard public morality from sexually indecent leisure, and had imposed regulation on nightclubs that, upon implementation, quickly failed. In the end Jimmy Walker, who was linked intimately in the public mind with the new nightlife, could not present himself convincingly as a moral reformer. In later years he would not try so hard to be a crusading mayor. The Democratic organization's muddled efforts to play to conservative cultural fears helped to revive the spirits of its traditional enemies, good-government reformers. The years 1927 and 1928, meanwhile, would be the period of nightclubs' greatest popularity and cultural influence. City officials' ironic disconnection from new leisure trends—at least during their work hours—suggested a weakening of Tammany Hall's traditionally close (and profitable) tracking of those trends.

Still, the combination of the Committee of Fourteen's anti-club campaign and the city's regulatory efforts increased the general public momentum of investigation and regulation of the world of nightlife. In 1928 it would be the federal government's turn to try to "make war" on Manhattan's nightclubs. In the process, the impact of Prohibition on the city's culture would reoccupy the center of civic discussion, and the debate about the value or detriment of the nightclub to the city's culture would be expanded to the national political arena.

# CHAPTER 4
## "War on the Nightclubs"

In the 1920s national policy had unprecedented peacetime impact on life in New York City. Manhattan's financial institutions dominated the considerations of the Federal Reserve Board, the decade-old institution that determined national monetary policy. The administration of the immigration portal at Ellis Island continued to shape the city's population. Most significantly, Prohibition had a greater influence on daily (and nightly) life in New York than any federal domestic initiative since the Civil War.

The Eighteenth Amendment produced dramatic action and reaction in the city. The Volstead Act (the amendment's enforcement statute) made the saloon obsolete, but it also stimulated the rise of a vast underground industry of distilleries and speakeasies. Prohibition's effect on Manhattan nightlife is difficult to understate: careers, businesses, and time-honored institutions and practices were disrupted continually for thirteen years.

The hectic professional existences of Larry Fay and Texas Guinan illustrate this fact. In 1925 Guinan left Fay's club, the El Fey, and opened her own venue on West 48th Street. Within months Prohibition agents raided and closed both the El Fey and Guinan's club. Such raids turned liquor-serving clubowners into nomads who jumped from one closed room to another, crossing each other's paths and even retracing their peregrinations. In the fall of 1925 Guinan reunited with Fay for a new venture in the old El Fey room, called the Del Fey. That too was raided, leading Guinan to headline at the 300 Club on 54th Street. Fleeing a 1927 raid there, she then opened a second Texas Guinan's club at the original 48th Street site; when it was padlocked, she started a club in the basement of the Century Theatre on Central Park West. She also appeared at her brother Tommy's club, the Chez Florence. From there, in the late 1920s and early 1930s, it was on to the Salon Royale, the basement of the Hotel Harding, the Club Argonaut (at the same site as the 300 Club), and finally a "roadhouse" in Valley Stream, Long Island.[1] Larry Fay meanwhile moved somewhat absentmindedly from the Del Fey to the Rendezvous, Winter Garden, Casa Blanca, and Club Intime outfits while he focused his energies on an effort to monopolize the city's milk-delivery business.

Such stories show how Prohibition enforcers, along with the Committee of Fourteen and municipal officials, became fixated on regulating New York City's nightclubs. The city and the state stoked this fixation by seceding from the effort to prosecute liquor violations. In 1923 Albany broke ranks with Washington by repealing the state prohibition law, the Mullan-Gage Act. Viewed by prohibitionists as the contemporary equivalent of the Confederate firing on Fort Sumter, the repeal of Mullan-Gage left the prosecution of all Prohibition cases to the federal courts. As they attempted to shepherd these cases, "dry" Justice Department officials in Washington found them to be a legal minefield, procedurally and substantively; even the department's own U.S. attorney's office in Manhattan proved difficult to control. Despite these setbacks, nightclubs provided too much publicity and notoriety to the Prohibition effort for officials to ignore them. Like the members of the Committee of Fourteen, federal attorneys and agents viewed these venues as the cultural center of a law-breaking psychology and behavior.

The year 1928 saw the climax of this most symbolic element of the "symbolic crusade" of national Prohibition. The city's own licensing campaign of the previous year, centered on the three o'clock closing law, had largely failed. Now the Volstead Act was applied to a "war on the nightclubs" that padlocked dozens of celebrated sites and made federal defendants out of Texas Guinan, Helen Morgan, and many others. The election-year political context encouraged observers to attribute the raids in Alfred E. Smith's city to the Republican administration's hostility to Tammany Hall. The Washington official in charge of the raids, the assistant attorney general Mabel Walker Willebrandt, engaged in blatant politicking, and journalistic observers figured Willebrandt—a rare female administrator in that era—into the already heated gender discourse about nightlife.

After the federal "war" came to an ambiguous ending, the city's police commissioner, Grover A. Whalen, retook the reins of the anti-nightclub crusade with great fanfare. Even then, though, Mayor Jimmy Walker was helping to open the Central Park Casino, the only nightclub that operated in a city-owned building. The federal government's ill-fated attempts in 1930 to squelch the presence of liquor at the Casino and other clubs illustrated the final phase of Prohibition enforcement, which in turn gave way to a new federal emphasis on tax-evasion prosecutions of criminal rackets that invested in nightlife.

From the beginning Manhattan was national prohibitionists' prime testing ground for enforcement. The state's Mullan-Gage Act, in fact, was a tougher version of the Volstead Act that had been drafted by "dry" forces to make an example of New York City. Even the application of both acts, though, could not disguise the fact that Prohibition enforcement was ill-conceived. Government lawyers feared constitutional challenges to a strong policing mechanism, and members of Congress refused to allocate most of the funds that enforcers demanded. The hastily constructed and underfunded federal apparatus was split between the Justice and Treasury departments, and it relied heavily on the integrity of supervisors and agents in the field. In New York City the celebrated exploits of agents Izzy Einstein and Moe Smith, masters of disguise who raided three thousand speakeasies and confiscated five million gallons of liquor, contrasted strongly with the indictment of dozens of other agents for "extortion, bribery, solicitation of money, illegal disposition of liquor or other property, intoxication, assault, the making of false reports, and theft." The rampant untrustworthiness of agents caused the federal government to depend upon the city police department for most Prohibition enforcement even after the repeal of Mullan-Gage (although the NYPD itself was not a model of integrity).[2]

Federal action against cabarets and nightclubs originated with the so-called padlock provisions of the Volstead Act. Taken together, sections 21, 22, and 23 of the law provided for the issuance of court injunctions that could shut down and bar entry to "common nuisances," or the premises on which liquor sales took place, for up to one year. In 1921 these provisions were first used by federal raiders to shutter a restaurant in Brooklyn and venues in some cities in western states. Soon the strategy would be applied to Manhattan.

Cabarets, the forerunners of nightclubs, were first targeted as a category in 1922. In February the Paradise Restaurant on 58th Street and Eighth Avenue became the first Manhattan property of any kind to be raided for the purpose of imposing a padlock. The Paradise occupied the former site of Reisenweber's restaurant, a center of nightlife in the 1910s. The potential longtime shuttering of some of the most lucrative commercial properties in the world received comment. A *New York Times* editorial claimed that "when a piece of valuable real estate is made unproductive for a year, other owners of such property are likely to take notice, and to be wiser, if not better, men." In October, after the Paradise padlocking appeared to have survived legal challenges, the Light House Cabaret on West 48th Street was inspected by the police. Days later the Knickerbocker Grill on Broadway, the Shuffle Inn in the heart of black Harlem, and the White Poodle Club in Greenwich Village were closed. During the raid of another restaurant in the Village the owner's wife clubbed a federal agent with a rolling pin and knocked him unconscious, but the padlocking effort still succeeded.[3]

This initial campaign, though, ultimately ended in failure. On 18 October a daytime crowd gathered outside the Paradise to watch the U.S. marshal apply the establishment's second padlock. "When the big official seals were placed on the doors [of the Paradise], the spectators thought that they had witnessed the end of a landmark which had been in existence nearly sixty-five years." Employees emerged and dumped their personal effects on the sidewalk to the accompaniment of "many good-natured jests from the throng." Within hours, though, a second federal judge stayed the padlock injunction and the Paradise was reopened. "At 8:30 o'clock [the marshal] was amazed to find the place in full operation as on the previous night. A number of diners were in the place." The process was repeated for the other raided clubs.[4]

The repeal of the Mullan-Gage Act in June 1923 made New York the first state in the union to divest itself of Prohibition prosecutions. In his repeal message Governor Alfred E. Smith took pains to insist that the repeal "in no way abrogates a Federal statute" and that peace officers still had a responsibility to enforce the Volstead Act. However, Smith argued, courts had ruled that the state law had exceeded the authority of the Eighteenth Amendment, and thus it was the legislature's duty to repeal it. Political observers interpreted the repeal entirely as a "wet" challenge to Prohibition and the first volley in Smith's campaign for the 1924 Democratic presidential nomination. To legal scholars, though, Smith's action highlighted the perils of concurrent federal-state enforcement. Such enforcement—devised to keep the federal apparatus small—had been the major constitutional experiment embodied in the Volstead Act. The repeal of Mullan-Gage was a major setback for that experiment. Five other states from different regions of the country followed New York's lead. In each state the federal courts subsequently were overwhelmed by Prohibition cases. Mabel Walker Willebrandt, the assistant attorney general in charge of Prohibition enforcement, later likened the state repeals to "secession" and castigated the "Tammany ruthlessness" that torpedoed effective enforcement of the Volstead Act in New York. (In 1933, Richard Hamm notes, the amendment that repealed Prohibition would address these circumstances by returning virtually all liquor enforcement powers to the states.)[5]

In the immediate wake of the Mullan-Gage repeal, though, federal enforcers in Manhattan remained optimistic and soldiered on in their efforts. In 1924 the popularity of the first nightclubs encouraged federal authorities to attempt Prohibition raids of these venues. These raids were highly publicized. The Gypsy Land restaurant was shuttered, and the owners of the Silver Slipper cabaret pleaded guilty to Volstead violations (although their club was not padlocked that year). In one evening, the Prohibition agents Reager and Mittes, "posing as actors," made three arrests at a restaurant on 49th Street, "then blackened up as negroes and went to Connie['s] Inn" in Harlem, where they took the owners and waiters into custody. Days later the owners of the Piccadilly Rendezvous, Silver Slipper, and Ringside cabarets appeared together in the court of the federal judge Learned Hand.[6]

Subsequent raids shut down the New York properties in the Thompson-Salvin chain of cabarets, most of which were located in New York City. After the padlockings the owners, Samuel G. Salvin and James N. Thompson, disappeared, but the managers of their establishments appeared in the court of Learned Hand's brother, Augustus Hand. The Palais Royal (famed as the home of the Paul Whiteman Orchestra), the Moulin Rouge, and the Plantation restaurants declared bankruptcies that totaled over $100,000. In a separate action, Larry Fay, the originator of the "bootlegger's nightclub," became the final major victim of the 1924 raids when his El Fey Club was shuttered by a temporary injunction. "This is the end of the Gay White Way as we know it," an observer of one padlocking remarked, while a federal agent boasted that Broadway at night would soon be "as dark as Tenth Avenue."

Government officials were heartened by court successes and the apparent victory of their loose interpretation of the Volstead Act. An assistant U.S. attorney reported to Washington that he was "grinding out padlock cases" and that "our record has been pretty good," securing 101 shuttering decrees in 117 court hearings. "Splendid," Assistant Attorney General Willebrandt scribbled in the margins of his memo. Later that year, in another reflection of optimism, a lawyer on Willebrandt's staff informed her that prosecutors need not pursue the actual owners of the property in which Prohibition violations had occurred: "In these padlock cases the landlord, as distinguished from the lessee, is not a necessary party . . . the property affected is the leasehold."[7]

To capitalize on these advantages, though, Prohibition enforcers needed adequate personnel and funding. As with the anti-prostitution efforts of the Committee of Fourteen, widely shared good intentions surrounding Prohibition fell afoul of often antagonistic cultural and economic trends of the 1920s. In New York City as in other large cities, the generally low quality of Prohibition agents had become a scandal. The problems were attributed to personal corruption, the reach of Tammany Hall, and controversial methods of gathering evidence. Local federal marshals were responsible for serving subpoenas and other summonses to operators of liquor establishments. Lyman Ward, a special assistant to the U.S. attorney in Manhattan, accused these deputies of fealty to Tammany Hall. They "were all organization men," Ward reported; when the chief marshal "called one of them to task or threatened to remove them, he would be immediately beset by the deputy's District leader." A 1925 federal law began to impose civil service requirements on Prohibition agents, but it would be implemented slowly.[8]

In addition, the more creative efforts of agents to gather incriminating evidence inspired court challenges and public reproaches. The Treasury branch of Prohibition enforcement, headed in Washington by Lincoln Andrews and in Manhattan by A. Bruce Bielaski, pioneered the extensive use of telephone wiretaps and eavesdropping devices hidden in lamps. At first they generally neglected to obtain the required court orders for these tactics. Bielaski also recruited hard-boiled agents who applied the "third degree" to suspects during questioning. Most colorfully, the Treasury agents set up their own speakeasy-cum-nightclub to trap Prohibition violators. The Bridge Whist Club at 14 East 44th Street, opening in 1925, violated the Volstead Act in the name of its enforcement in too many pathbreaking ways for Washington or the public to accept. Those arrested at the club ultimately were set free.[9]

The dubious reputation of Prohibition agents was further debased by controversies concerning the serving of official documents. The procedures for serving notices of violations to speakeasies and cabarets contained grave flaws that doomed many cases in court. Overworked U.S. marshals had to contend with the huge caseload. At least fifty court orders had to be served daily to allow the cases to be dispensed with smoothly, but only five to ten documents were served on an average day. More seriously, judges had determined that a key Justice Department assumption was incorrect: the owner of the actual property, not the lessee who operated the venue, must also be served. In 1924 a government lawyer concluded that half of the three hundred padlock cases in the Southern District of New York[10] were invalid because the property owners had not been notified of the charges. While building owners remained completely unaware of the litigation involving their property, club operators escaped, and in their stead bartenders, head waiters, and other employees were charged in court. The chief U.S. marshal claimed that "the people who operate illicit saloons or speak-easies are irresponsible fly-by-nights who anticipate action being taken against them, and who, at the first intimation of trouble, disappear." Cases were delayed as long as three or four years because those who owned and operated establishments at the time of the violations could no longer be found or even identified. An early Prohibition case against the venerable Reisenweber's restaurant, from 1922, had unraveled largely because the establishment was operating under a tangle of subleases held by such entities as United Cigar Stores, the St. Regis Restaurant Company, and the White Rose Baking and Restaurant Company. Individuals were not required to be fingerprinted in padlock actions, and thus it was easy for them to disappear from the public record by changing their names and entering new business arrangements.[11]

Severe budgetary limits also hindered padlocking efforts. Every expense in the field, even minor ones, had to be approved by Mabel Willebrandt's office in Washington. In 1923 William Hayward, the U.S. attorney, hired a property title company to identify the current owners of two thousand suspected speakeasies, at the rate at twenty-five cents per property. An official in Washington quickly ordered the company to cease and desist and directed Hayward to hold a competition for the account and hire the lowest bidder. On another occasion the government, citing a law from the 1890s, refused to reimburse the U.S. attorney sixty dollars for the services of ten private detectives who helped to padlock fourteen cabarets. The Justice department also refused the chief marshal's request to continue the wartime practice of employing a used automobile and a driver for his official duties.[12]

The padlocks themselves—the symbols of federal power in nightlife—were also deemed by Washington to be special equipment, to be purchased only from the lowest bidder in an open competition. A department official declared further that "the purchase of these locks, etc., will be authorized, or they will be furnished, only in such number as are actually needed for immediate use in connection with execution of the decrees of the courts." Lacking a handy supply, marshals often bought padlocks at hardware stores on their way to speakeasy closings. Eventually, during the highly publicized nightclub padlockings of 1928, the local office was permitted to buy padlocks in bulk for $18.90 a dozen. In the meantime, though, officials in Manhattan and Washington had to process reimbursement applications as minuscule as $2.40 for screw eyes (which were also needed for padlockings).

Despite these obstacles, throughout the mid-1920s New York Prohibition enforcers maintained a crusading spirit, infused with moralistic and partisan zeal, and continued their pursuit of high-profile nightclubs. In 1925 the new U.S. attorney in Manhattan, Emory R. Buckner, declared that "one of my first duties was to bring injunction proceedings against 14 of the most prominent and exclusive cabarets in my district."[13]

Like the other federal prosecutors in Manhattan in the 1920s, Buckner was a Republican attorney who was a member of a prestigious city law firm. He also was a longtime participant in Protestant-oriented reform groups, working with John D. Rockefeller, Jr., the City Club, and the Citizens Union to eradicate police corruption and prostitution. Buckner was personally ambivalent about Prohibition. Before assuming his post he held a party at his University Heights home, where the guests helped him pour the contents of his well-stocked liquor cellar down sink drains. At the office he made his subordinates join him in a teetotaling pledge. In late 1925, though, he caused a sensation by telling Morris Markey of the *New Yorker* that a citizen who purchased alcoholic drinks "is not a criminal. . . . Such a man, presumably, is dissatisfied with a particular condition imposed upon him by society, and is making his protest against it by taking the matter into his own hands." Buckner added that he was "not very much interested" in Prohibition "except as a legal problem" and as "an amusing and intricate problem in creative administration."[14]

Nevertheless, the new federal prosecutor mounted a new campaign against nightclubs. Buckner mistrusted Prohibition agents, so he supplied four staff lawyers with $1,500 of his own money so they might gain entry to cabarets and collect incriminating evidence. He also enlisted the New York Civic League, under the direction of the Methodist minister Harry B. Fisher, to become an unofficial and uncompensated investigator of Prohibition violations in nightlife. During the six-month period ending on 1 March 1926, Fisher later claimed, the league had "provided the evidence for the padlocking of twenty-one 'elite night clubs' in New York City, fifty-five elite clubs elsewhere, [and] forty-one 'smaller clubs, restaurants, wineries, and saloons.'"[15]

In his first year in office Buckner faced many obstacles, which he recounted in frustration before a congressional committee in April 1926. He claimed that the biggest problem was the diversion of tens of millions of gallons of alcohol yearly from local denaturing plants to distillers, but his testimony placed equal emphasis on the antiquated federal court standards that hindered the prosecution of speakeasy cases. "The kind of Federal courts which we have," Buckner argued, "namely, those requiring jury trials for the smallest offense, . . . are not the kind of courts by which police laws can be enforced in such a congested district as New York City." Buckner hailed the assistance provided by the New York City Police Department and Commissioner George McLaughlin: responding to an average of fifteen thousand liquor complaints a month, "the special police officers were making more [Volstead] arrests than prohibition officers, far more in fact." However, he noted that the city and the federal government worked at cross purposes, since the NYPD largely used Prohibition as a pretext for ferreting out professional "crooks or gangsters" and cleaning up "particular little nest[s] of pus" that hosted diverse criminal activity.[16]

Even worse, the legions of speakeasy and nightclub denizens arrested by the police were choking what Buckner called the "toy machinery" of the U.S. courts. "I found the fifth floor of the Federal Building a seething mob of bartenders, peddlers, waiters, bond runners, fixers." The small-time employees of nightlife establishments mingled in the halls with often unscrupulous court hangers-on who "fixed" bail, counsel, and even the outcome of the cases themselves. These fixers bribed jurors, often in the stalls of the building's restrooms. "A very large percentage of the cases [were] thr[own] out for lack of evidence." Raids by federal Prohibition agents met particularly ignominious fates in court. These agents were given minimum quotas for arrests but not for convictions. They regularly neglected to have testimony recorded in writing, and on the stand—innocently or not—their memories of details of the raids often became cloudy. In many cases the judge manifested a "prejudice against a particular prohibition agent" owing to the latter's "demeanor, manner, contradictions, overzeal and bad personal impression." (Buckner soon began to import agents from other cities.) The backlog of cases was so great that it often took five months for a case to proceed from the booking office to the court clerk two floors below. A rare case against an actual "big man" in liquor distribution took four and a half years to proceed to trial, where it promptly failed.[17]

Ironically, few of these cases were criminal in nature. Only about thirty of them, Buckner testified, actually were prosecuted under federal criminal statutes. These prosecutions proceeded under much swifter circumstances and resulted in longer jail sentences. One major bootlegger was convicted for income tax evasion. The rest of the padlocking cases under the Volstead Act, though, were civil actions. In civil cases the federal government was the plaintiff, not the prosecutor, and it did not issue indictments, but complaints. Arrestees in civil padlock cases were never fingerprinted. In such a case there was no jury and the federal judge "sat in equity," a legal practice that was otherwise obsolete in the United States (except in Delaware's state courts). Judges imposed decrees, not sentences. In addition to a padlock the judge might also impose a consent decree (allowing the government to inspect and close an establishment at any time), a bond decree (which added the requirement that the operator post a bond, usually $500 to $1,000), and a personal injunction (forbidding specific actions by an individual) on liquor-selling establishments and their employees. Since the equity proceedings faced a two-year backlog, Buckner asked the senators for "a special padlock court sitting one week a month" to help him clear the dockets. In two months Buckner received his special court and dozens of new Prohibition agents.[18]

As a result, from 1926 to 1927—at the same time the city government debated and implemented the new cabaret law and closing time—Buckner's federal office pursued a wide gamut of targets and succeeded in padlocking hundreds of establishments. In May 1926 alone the U.S. attorney disposed of ninety-nine cases. Sixty-one of these establishments received padlocks lasting from two months to a year. While some were well-known nightspots, such as the Chauve Souris and Three Fifty Club, most were speakeasies outside of Manhattan, in other boroughs and in towns as far north as Poughkeepsie. Forty-one additional cases, including that of the popular Cave of Fallen Angels in Midtown, were postponed to later court calendars. Later that year Texas Guinan, her father and manager Michael, and employees and patrons of the 300 Club were prosecuted. In 1927 a padlock section of the U.S. attorney's office in Manhattan was created to handle the heavy caseload. During the summer of that year 236 padlocks were applied.[19]

As we have seen, though, 1927 and 1928 were also the peak years for nightclubs in the decade, especially in Midtown and in Harlem. Just as the Committee of Fourteen and the municipal curfew had ineffectively defined and disposed of the social problems perceived in the nightclubs, Prohibition enforcement also never came close to shutting down the liquor trade in nightlife. That situation bred an eagerness in Prohibition administrators to score highly publicized and politically helpful victories.

In early 1927 Emory Buckner happily resigned as federal prosecutor, and he was replaced by Charles H. Tuttle. Tuttle shared with Buckner a background in Republican politics, prestigious Manhattan legal circles, and Protestant reform. His grandfather had been a prominent Episcopal minister in Greenwich Village. At the outset Tuttle continued the heavy padlocking campaign of his predecessor, but his political ambitions led him to play down moralistic crusading. As Morris Markey reported, Tuttle "does not conceive himself to be a moral agent but a prosecutor. He will discontinue Mr. Buckner's raids. He will continue to padlock on justified complaints, but he will not be aggressive about it." As federal action eased, the city government's busy but increasingly fruitless closing-time enforcement dominated the headlines. In late 1927 Texas Guinan symbolically took on both the municipal curfew campaign and the federal padlocking effort. In the former instance, in court her attorneys successfully established the primacy of state law governing private clubs over the city curfew statute. Against the latter Guinan took aim by appearing in a revue at the Shubert Theatre entitled "Padlocks of 1927." As E. B. White noted in his review of the show in the *New Yorker*, "Texas induces a hilarity which culminates in a battle at the end of the first act, in a scene which is a replica of the Guinan Club. . . . The Guinan mob surges across the footlights, and whoopee is made." At her new autumn venue, the Century Club, Guinan sported a necklace of small padlocks in a mockery of the federal effort, which now obviously was waning.[20]

Around this time federal Prohibition regulators began to modify their tactics. As nightclubs became a prime symbol of modernity and a beneficiary of mass publicity, Volstead enforcers in Manhattan became enamored of pursuing a handful of high-profile clubs in order to promote their general crusade. Practical considerations had already predisposed prosecutors to reduce the number of raids. In January 1927 a government attorney argued in favor of "more active and aggressive prosecution of a lesser number of important cases only rather than the present routine manner of handling the great volume of such cases."[21] Such a strategy suited both the politically calculating Tuttle and the new federal Prohibition administrator in New York City, Major Maurice Campbell.

The city administrator was responsible for coordinating Treasury, Justice, and local Prohibition enforcement efforts. It was a job filled with difficulties. Maurice Campbell's predecessor resigned in protest against the meddling of municipal officials and the lack of support he received from Washington. In addition to his military service and brief employment as a Prohibition administrator in the Midwest, Campbell brought long New York residence and experience in journalism and show business to the position. Campbell's first jobs had been in theatrical press agentry. He later became a Broadway producer and the husband of the actress Henrietta Crosman. In the early 1920s Campbell was the director of such breezy silent films as *She Couldn't Help It*, *The Speed Girl*, *The Exciters*, and *Girls Men Forget*, but his fervent teetotaling inspired him to move to Prohibition enforcement.[22]

Campbell's personal blend of theatricality and moralism—so common among Manhattan officials in the 1920s—encouraged a heightened interest in Prohibition enforcement in nightclubs, and led to new controversy. In late December Campbell threatened raids of nightclubs on New Year's Eve and made good on his promise by targeting nine of them with a novel charge, income tax evasion. His office especially played up the raid on Chez Helen Morgan on West 54th Street. Morgan and seven other investors in the club were indicted on tax charges. The Morgan affair also generated headlines, though, because Campbell's agents had stripped the club of furniture and fixtures that were valued at $50,000. U.S. Attorney Charles Tuttle, ever cautious, invoked Prohibition statutes to rebuke Campbell publicly for the loss of property in the raid. Campbell responded by arguing that Internal Revenue Service law gave him "[the] right to seize everything in the place." Within three weeks a federal judge rejected this interpretation and ordered the return of the fixtures, including potted plants, buckets, a cash register, 188 chairs, 93 tables, draperies, two glass doors, a chandelier, "twelve spears," and eleven carpets, to Chez Helen Morgan. Tuttle ensured that charges against Morgan and the other principal owners were dropped, and minor fines were imposed on the employees. A final farcical conflict developed over Campbell's refusal to allow members of the press to take photographs of the club's belongings as they were taken on and off of trucks during their return to the venue. The tax-evasion tactic failed, but it was the seed of a later strategy against nightclubs and the underworld that ultimately supplanted the entire focus on illicit alcohol.[23]

Campbell's activity in early 1928 mainly was directed toward building a climactic campaign against liquor in Manhattan's nightclubs. What newspapers labeled the "war on the nightclubs" of the summer of 1928 deployed all of the strategies and rhetoric that had been used against cabarets and clubs for half a decade, a time during which the government helped to identify nightclubs as sites of modern misbehavior. As before, the federal effort showed that prejudice against New York City and its nightlife elsewhere somewhat irrationally drove and shaped policy. Election-year politics, in addition, brought anti-Manhattan attitudes to new heights. The year 1928 proved to be a watershed, in which Prohibition enforcers in the city made their biggest effort to reshape New Yorkers' opinions about public drinking. The ensuing failure of the "war" on the nightclubs encouraged most officials to scale back their enforcement goals. Others in the government in Washington, though, saw the failed "war" as merely another skirmish—so the Prohibition campaign in the city soldiered on, with increasing futility.

In the first few days of 1928 Maurice Campbell launched another multipronged assault on nightclubs, raiding and closing the Golden Gate, Jungle, European, Moscow, and Rainbow clubs, as well as Dinty Moore's restaurant. The court proceedings against these clubs produced mixed results, but Campbell planned an even larger dragnet raid. He began to import incorruptible agents such as Lon Tyson of Dallas and John Mitchell of Denver to supplement his force of New York customs (not Prohibition) agents. For six months they gathered preliminary evidence by infiltrating dozens of clubs, especially in Midtown, in the process spending over $60,000 in taxpayer money for fifty-dollar bottles of champagne and other overpriced nightclub beverages.[24]

On the night of Thursday, 28 June, a force of 160 mostly young male agents dressed in evening wear crammed into Campbell's office on Park Avenue. Fearing leaks, officials disconnected the telephones and kept the agents unaware of their mission until their departure. At midnight each team of eight agents was dispatched to one of twenty nightclubs in Midtown. The agents gathered evidence of alcoholic commerce and waited until the conclusion of the performances at around two o'clock. Members of the team then blocked exits as an agent stepped on the dance floor to announce the club's closure and the arrest of suspects. "In each case," the *New York Times* reported, "wild scenes ensued." A "mop-up squad" of agents from Washington combed the empty venues for further evidence and applied temporary padlocks. The twenty Broadway-area clubs were closed in what was correctly called the largest and most spectacular Prohibition raid ever held in New York City. The well-known establishments shuttered that night included the Jungle, European, and Silver Slipper clubs, Chez Helen Morgan, and Texas Guinan's Salon Royale. One hundred four persons landed in jail that night and were soon indicted, followed by another 130 suspects located later. The latter group included Texas Guinan, who somehow was warned and left her club moments before the raid inside a cluster of protectors, and Helen Morgan, who "chang[ed] costumes with her cloakroom girl and quietly slip[ped] out during the search."[25]

Federal enforcers boasted that the June raids were only the first assaults on wet nightclubs and that this campaign was merely the spearhead of the government's climactic effort to dry up metropolitan New York. National political currents seemed to many to have influenced this new attack on nightclubs. A few weeks earlier the Republican Party had added a stronger dry plank to its platform, and the raid itself came on the very evening of New York governor Alfred E. Smith's nomination for president at the Democratic convention in Houston—a fact that would later loom large in public discussion of the raid. Maurice Campbell denied any political motive, claiming oddly that the end of June—during the slow summer season—was the best "psychological moment" for launching the raids. Despite this protest, the padlocking of the twenty clubs stimulated what proved to be a pivotal public debate about the intersection of alcohol with nightlife, in which moral, political, legal, and even gender discourses collided for a season.[26]

The national notoriety of Washington, D.C.'s "war on the nightclubs" of New York City was enhanced by reports that Assistant Attorney General Mabel Walker Willebrandt, in Washington, had personally planned the massive raid. In New York only local Prohibition enforcers and prosecutors tended to become political celebrities, but now Willebrandt occupied the spotlight. Willebrandt's new celebrity resulted from Americans' ambivalent fascination with pioneering professional women and was amplified by her own calculated effort to use the raid to boost her career and the presidential campaign of Herbert Hoover.[27]

The assistant attorney general, like Hoover, was a westerner whose life had been a classic American success story. A largely self-taught teacher from the Kansas prairie, Willebrandt relocated to Arizona with her ailing husband, the former principal of her school. After they divorced, Willebrandt earned a law degree at the University of Southern California. Beginning as an unpaid Los Angeles county public defender in an all-male office, she rose quickly to the top job. In 1921, at the age of thirty-one, Willebrandt became assistant attorney general in the Harding administration, following her immediate predecessor Annette Adams as the second woman ever to hold such a high federal position.

Willebrandt became known for creating the first federal women's prison and arguing cases before the Supreme Court, including at least one concerning liquor prosecutions in New York City. Prohibition, however, consumed most of her time and energy. Under the ill-defined aegis of Prohibition administrator, she shared enforcement responsibilities with officials at the Treasury department (whom she believed "neglected their duties"). From 1926 to 1928 she almost obsessively pursued George Remus of Cincinnati, who evaded bootlegging prosecution but eventually would be tried for the murder of his wife.

Willebrandt's private papers from her Washington years reveal the person behind the bureaucrat, an intelligent and passionate woman who struggled to balance private and work life and remained genuinely ambivalent about 1920s attitudes and behavior. A progressive Republican, she despised laissez-faire conservatives such as Andrew Mellon, the secretary of the Treasury, and certain Supreme Court justices. Willebrandt simultaneously contemplated marriage to a Jewish law-school classmate and agreed with a Manhattanite that "the young Jew in N. Y. is the biggest crime problem in this country today" because "he has broken away from intimate contact with the faith of his fathers," refuses to convert to Christianity, and thus "has no code except to get what he desires." Willebrandt played mah-jongg with Congressman Volstead's wife and shared a Thanksgiving dinner with Justice Louis D. Brandeis. In 1923 she spent a vacation in New York City, where she watched with "pleasurable excitement" a boxing match featuring Louis Firpo, danced at the Biltmore Hotel, and visited Greenwich Village and the Bowery, where the sight of prostitution "made me blue." That same year she adopted a daughter.

Long before Willebrandt's war on the nightclubs in 1928, journalists applied standard gender rhetoric to her and to her career. In 1923 the *New York Herald* sized her up in a headline: "Attorney General, yes; but yet a woman." Four years later a magazine described Willebrandt as someone who "would have been content to play woman's biggest rôle . . . if she had been happily married," and quoted a prominent bootlegger as saying, "Imagine being sent to prison by a pretty woman you'd like to take to a dance!" Days after the June 1928 raid, the *New York Herald-Tribune* called her both "a woman with a woman's love of home and love of children" and "a modern Portia." (The Shakespearean cliché relating to women in courts of law, later famously applied to Willebrandt by Alfred E. Smith, had also earlier been used by the *Union Signal*, the magazine of the Women's Christian Temperance Union.) Even the obsessively "modern" *New Yorker* lapsed into trite sexism, arguing that "though she dislikes to think so, Mrs. Willebrandt is essentially feminine. At her office she wears tailored suits, at home filmy things." Such patronizing portrayals masked the fact that the assistant attorney general waged the nightclub "war" in a gamble for professional and political advancement. By 1928 she had outlasted most of her bureaucratic rivals, her friend Herbert Hoover was running for president, and she was yearning for a lifetime appointment on the federal bench. Manhattan became her focus of action.[28]

Political calculation also turned Willebrandt into a more dogmatic opponent of the new leisure and a more fervent champion of Prohibition. In the wake of the June raids she exploited the publicity it brought her and used it as a bully pulpit for her cause. Behind the scenes she sought to develop effective new techniques and sources of evidence. Willebrandt urged the federal attorney Charles Tuttle to obtain temporary restraining orders against speakeasies and not to hesitate to destroy liquor caches that were discovered. She ordered the city's chief federal marshal not to disturb fixtures in the nightclubs, though, to avoid a repeat of the Chez Helen Morgan fiasco. Reviving Maurice Campbell's most successful tactics from that case, Willebrandt also aggressively sought the recent income tax records of dozens of nightclub proprietors. Andrew Mellon personally forwarded the 1926 tax returns of several of them, and she later received the 1927 records of Texas Guinan and many others. Curiously, the assistant attorney general also urged subpoenas for George S. Worthington, the general secretary of the Committee of Fourteen, and the committee's investigators in order to force the anti-prostitution group to reveal information about liquor sales in nightclubs. (Only a typist in the committee's office was located, though, and Willebrandt's advisor concluded that "to serve a subpoena on her . . . is doubtful tactics.")[29]

Familiar procedural, legal, and political snarls—and some unusual new ones—slowed Willebrandt's crusade. New Yorkers criticized the ethics and the high cost to taxpayers of federal agents' covert infiltration of nightclubs, as well as the fact that some agents brought their wives with them to enjoy liquor at the tables. The most embarrassing conflict developed within the Justice Department itself. The U.S. attorney Charles Tuttle had no involvement in the June raids. As he explained later, his office had never taken part in such efforts. For reasons that remain unclear—probably related to his political ambitions—Tuttle publicly attacked Willebrandt's post-raid strategy. In August he openly opposed Willebrandt's subpoenas of 125 patrons of the padlocked clubs. Cutting short a vacation, Tuttle announced that he had no knowledge of the planned indictments and departed for Washington to compel Justice to revise its strategy. (The list of patrons was reported to include socially prominent New Yorkers as well as numerous NYPD officers, "a former employee of the Naturalization Bureau[,] and several prohibition agents.")[30]

An enraged Willebrandt refused to see Tuttle and sent a cable to the vacationing attorney general, John G. Sargent, to explain her strategy. The goal of the raids, she argued, had been to humiliate the elites who patronized and invested in alcohol-selling nightclubs, and she boasted that the "mass of documentary evidence legally seized and usable . . . implicates others besides waiters entertainers etc." Tuttle, in her view, "indicted only waiters entertainers etc." She accused him of sabotaging a grand jury hearing at which high-level police officials were to be implicated in nightclub liquor graft. Furthermore, Willebrandt claimed that she had "gone to exaggerated lengths to protect Mr. Tuttle's authority but his cheap newspaper grand stand play yesterday was indefensible and the issue now becomes whether this prosecution is to proceed in an orderly manner by the usual method employed in other districts and the one that ought to be usual in New York or whether it is to be interrupted according to Tuttle's misguided New York psychology on liquor cases."[31]

On 24 August the grand jury questioning of nightclub patrons was abruptly halted. This was interpreted by local newspapers as a "victory" for Tuttle. The next day a "truce" between Willebrandt and Tuttle was reported, but on 26 August the former vented her anger at the latter in a scathing telegram. "Your unfortunate publicity . . . has done untold damage to the government[']s opportunity to enlarge these cases. . . ." The patrons were being questioned for information, not indictments, so "there was therefor[e] no need for you to become their protector from anything except your own pitiless publicity beginning with leaks from official sources." She noted that Tuttle's prosecution of the Helen Morgan case earlier that year "accomplished absolutely nothing" and accused him of "build[ing] up your reports by large numbers of cases against small insignificant violators." Willebrandt now thought it would be "extremely difficult . . . to get [at] real parties financially interested or sources of supply," "to make [the] law effective against the powerful as well as the weak."[32]

When the Democratic presidential candidate Alfred E. Smith accused Willebrandt of political grandstanding, she asked her assistant to "please phone him or get Campbell to see him and positively guarantee no reference to me personally." At that very moment, though, Willebrandt took her political quarrel to a national audience and began to campaign widely for Herbert Hoover. "Manhattan is ruled by Tammany," she declared in a speech in Springfield, Ohio, "an organization that for underworld connections and political efficiency is matched no place else in America." Smith was its creature: "Tammany had reared him; gave him his power. Tammany's desires were his convictions." The Methodist clerics in her audience were praised in a way that inferred a critique of Smith's Catholicism: "Your church has always been interested in conditions that make for the welfare of mankind." A storm of criticism resulted. Willebrandt told supporters about "all the threatening letters that have come [to me] from New York City," which had "wounded [me] by so much attack on untruthful grounds." But the assistant attorney general continued her electioneering, and the criticism became more intense. Few encapsulated it more pithily than the *Washington Daily News* cartoonist H. M. Talburt, who depicted Willebrandt bent over a man's knee and receiving a lusty spanking. "Give the Little Lady a Big Hand," the prominent caption read.[33]

The cartoon's conflation of Mabel Willebrandt with Texas Guinan also reminded readers that for the moment, the nightclub hostess's fate was to be determined by the dictates of the assistant attorney general's office. The formally charged defendants from the June raids included many well-known personages: Guinan, Helen Morgan, the radio announcer Nils T. Granlund, and even the alderman Murray W. Stand, the outspoken foe of the three o'clock municipal curfew. In her court appearance Morgan was tearful and announced her retirement from nightclub performing. Texas Guinan, by contrast, appeared in court wearing "a black ensemble, a broad smile and an air of bored tolerance" and called the charge against her "a lot of bologna." Guinan's lawyers peppered the court with motions to vacate, while the entertainer gave belligerent interviews to journalists, promising to hire Clarence Darrow as her counsel. In mid-September, in a major setback for Willebrandt and Maurice Campbell, Guinan and other defendants managed to persuade a federal judge to vacate the pre-trial padlockings. Guinan still lost the Salon Royale, though, and was even publicly rebuffed by Darrow. She was acquitted on the charge of maintaining a nuisance, but days later her new venue, the Club Intime, was raided (see Fig. 4). Her brother Tommy Guinan, the manager of the Chez Florence, had even less luck in court, actually becoming convicted on nuisance charges.[34]

Mabel Walker Willebrandt and the other federal enforcers could point to numerous convictions and closings as the fruit of the celebrated raids of 28 June 1928. In one court in November, for example, ninety-two padlocks were applied to city locales. The jurisprudence of nightclub closings remained ambiguous at best, though. Federal judge Thomas Thacher's vacating of a number of temporary padlocks in September was a clear slap at Willebrandt. Thacher described her lawyers' performance in his court as "shocking." In a measured written reaction to the verdict Willebrandt showed an appreciation of the "difficult" legal issues involved, which were rooted in the complex history of fed-

Figure 4. Texas Guinan celebrates her acquittal on federal nuisance charges with her attorneys in September 1928. Billy Rose Theatre Collection, The New York Public Library for the Performing Arts, Astor, Lenox, and Tilden Foundations.

eral preliminary injunctions. Also, though, she rehearsed the reasons why temporary injunctions were needed. Without them, she wrote, "it is exceedingly difficult to discover the real parties owning an interest in the premises wherein the nuisance is maintained." Bartenders appeared to be "in charge" while the owners remained in the shadows; new "owners" appeared in court and complained that they had not been served; even the bartenders changed, and the business kept operating. "The temporary injunction is worthless save as against those who have been served." The Justice Department lost its appeal of Thacher's ruling, however. In March the fugitive club operator David Stone, who had fled the city after the Club Maxine was raided in June, resurfaced in federal court to plead guilty to a minor offense and pay a fine of seventy-five dollars—all in the presence of a compliant assistant U.S. attorney. Willebrandt and Tuttle had made peace by then, but the latter's weak defense of his lawyers' laxity must not have pleased the assistant attorney general. Nor, presumably, did the fact that another of Tuttle's attorneys was discovered by Prohibition agents in an inebriated state at the Furnace Club.[35]

Correspondents urged Willebrandt to keep fighting. A former Connecticut prosecutor urged her to play dirty, to "drive every nail through and clinch it on the underside." Referring to Texas Guinan's acquittal in the Salon Royale case, the Salvation Army's Agnes McKernan hoped that "the fact that she was liberated does not mean that drink can again be sold in the night club." "Doubtless if the lady worked for Shubert, she enjoys the kind protection of Tammany Hall," another wrote. "Do not surrender," a Manhattan resident counseled. "People like a fighter. Sometimes when things get dark the light breaks through." But Willebrandt's campaign to clean up Manhattan clearly had not succeeded. The *New Yorker* noted "the failure of La Willebrandt to put Mistress Guinan and Mistress Morgan in jail" and lauded jurors for "actually consider[ing] the case from the standpoint of justice." Willebrandt's moralistic, even sectarian campaigning the previous fall had also made her a political pariah. The Hoover White House deemed her too controversial for a judgeship. After resigning from office in May 1929, Willebrandt appropriately ended her celebrity moment by selling to a newspaper syndicate a series of articles (later reprinted in book form) that criticized Prohibition enforcement. She then made headlines by returning to California on a sixty-hour transcontinental air flight. In her suitcase was a vial of water from the Hudson River that had been presented to her by Mayor Jimmy Walker.[36]

The federal Prohibition effort stalled seriously in 1929. During the legal struggles of the previous fall, Maurice Campbell (who raided but did not prosecute) continued to beat the drum for eradicating liquor through nightclub raids. He insisted that the city had the power to zone nightclubs out of all commercial neighborhoods. Another big dragnet raid took place on 16 November 1928, duplicating the feat of 28 June by closing twenty nightclubs. At the same time, though, new civil service requirements forced many of Campbell's agents to resign, and his office underwent a wrenching reorganization. Campbell struggled gamely in his post for another year and a half, but after his resignation in 1930 he stormily demanded the repeal of Prohibition, which he claimed was "honeycombed with political insincerity, trickery and corruption radiating from Washington to every State, city and town in the United States."[37]

In the meantime, President Herbert Hoover had undertaken a sincere effort to explore the social impact of Prohibition, crime, and the social changes of the 1920s. The President's Research Committee on Social Trends thoughtfully explored the explosion of consumer goods, easy credit, and leisure in recent years. Hoover's National Commission on

Law Observance and Enforcement, known as the Wickersham Commission, acknowledged the class bias in Prohibition enforcement, which shut down saloons while it permitted private liquor consumption by the wealthy. "In some cities," the commission's final report noted, "night clubs have notoriously sold to a steady and considerable patronage." The commission added that "it is much easier to padlock a speakeasy than to close up a large hotel where important and influential financial interests are involved." It also acknowledged the constitutional quandary involved in attempting to align state and federal Prohibition enforcement—an effort that had failed spectacularly in New York State. The commission in the end made an expedient endorsement of Prohibition and only recommended modifications in its enforcement, but four dissenting statements by members of the commission were also published, including Newton Baker's call for outright repeal.[38]

The diminishing federal campaign against liquor in nightclubs in 1929 was accompanied by a municipal effort against disorderly establishments that was even more paradoxical than the closing-time raids of previous years.

Election night in 1928, 6 November, brought not only the defeat of Al Smith and the forces for Prohibition's repeal and victory for Herbert Hoover and the Volstead Act. It also brought the death of the underworld financier Arnold Rothstein, three days after being shot in a Manhattan hotel. The Rothstein murder may have been the most important political event in New York City in the 1920s, since it inspired investigations and reform movements that eventually toppled Tammany Hall from power and paved the way for Fiorello H. La Guardia's reform administration. In the short term, though, the case inspired a new wave of municipal crackdowns on curfew and liquor violations in nightlife venues, an effort that dovetailed with the diminishing federal Prohibition effort in 1929.[39]

The police department's suspiciously slow progress at solving the Rothstein case led Mayor Jimmy Walker to replace the police commissioner, Joseph Warren, with Grover Whalen. Whalen was an unusual choice. His work as an executive at Wanamaker's department store and as official city greeter was less important than his membership in Tammany Hall's Irish inner circle. The press portrayed Whalen as an independent force who would shake up the department and clamp down on a perceived crime wave. In reality the new commissioner was not eager to offend anyone at Tammany Hall, which he continued to serve. By his own admission one of his first actions was to retain a patrolman who was about to be terminated for repeated public drunkenness; "he was an old friend and I needed him around." Whalen told Walker that he "would tolerate no interference in cracking down on professional gambling, including any that might be going on in Tammany clubhouses," but he then dismantled the clubhouse-busting Confidential Squad and sent its head, Lewis J. Valentine, to a distant precinct in Queens. The commissioner ordered detectives to disregard laws that forbade the searching of dead bodies at crime scenes before medical examiners had arrived and embarked on a crusade against Communist Party demonstrations that often flagrantly violated the demonstrators' right to organize. Whalen continued the NYPD's adoption of scientific methods of investigation, campaigned against traffic congestion, introduced a widely praised new patrolman's uniform, and worked closely with the Committee of Fourteen (later even becoming a member). But his often stormy eighteen-month tenure did not prove to be a political advantage for Walker or a deterrent against the rise of organized crime (and not incidentally, he never found Arnold Rothstein's killer). As Whalen himself even later acknowledged, by 1930 he was a political liability, and he was asked to resign his position.

Whalen noted proudly later that his campaign to rein in Communist demonstrations "was laid out on military lines." Such actions indicated both a partial revival of the fortress mentality in city government that had prevailed during the Great War and that civic life in New York in the 1920s was undergoing an important change. Whalen's militaristic aspirations were also evident in the new series of raids on speakeasies that were launched in the closing days of 1928. On 29 December the police raided thirty drinking establishments and arrested eighty-one persons suspected of crimes. Whalen's "standing order" to "drive out of the city every criminal," inspired by the Rothstein affair, blended with the federal government's Prohibition campaign. Federal agents, in fact, joined the NYPD's new "strong-arm squads" that night, using axes to smash through speakeasy doors and false walls. A week later the *New York Times* revived the superlatives it last used after the 28 June raids: "Probably never since the passing of the Eighteenth Amendment was the lid clamped down on New York City as tightly as it was last night." Nightclubs now required identification from patrons to prevent the entry of law enforcers.[40]

Reportedly now formally cooperating with Charles Tuttle and Maurice Campbell, Whalen boasted of an unprecedented clampdown on liquor-serving nightspots. On 5 January 1929 he announced that his squads had closed 695 speakeasies in the city and pledged to determine the whereabouts of every major suspected offender still at large. This federal-municipal effort coincided with prosecutors' shift in tactics to charging Prohibition offenders with maintaining a nuisance, which resulted in high-profile convictions such as that of Tommy Guinan.

Helen Morgan (who did not retire after all) was tried on nuisance charges after a raid on her "summer home." By the summer of 1929, in addition, sensational murders at nightclubs such as "Legs" Diamond's Hotsy Totsy Club had intensified the focus on gangland ownership. The Committee of Fourteen, meanwhile, was enjoying its last high point of influence, fanning the flames of the "hostess evil" issue and proposing new crime prevention initiatives.[41]

This activity did cause the busy nightclub scene in Midtown to contract. Raids were too frequent and investments were too risky to permit the continuing expansion of the lavish Broadway club scene at the pace seen in 1927 or 1928. The municipal licensing department reported that in 1929 "cabarets are deserting Broadway to some extent," mostly for Harlem and the Upper East Side. Still, given the fact that out of 376 nightclubs licensed in 1928 the department revoked only one license and suspended only five for Prohibition violations and twenty-four for exceeding the closing time, it appears that the overworked licensing officials had very little power over the establishments they were supposed to regulate.[42] (Within two years, in fact, the police department would assume jurisdiction over nightclub licensing.) Meanwhile, turmoil in nightclub financing—owing to increasing unpredictability, the death of Arnold Rothstein, and raids by law enforcement—were causing a dramatic evolution in the industry, the outcome of which few could discern.

In 1929, while Grover Whalen made bold promises about eliminating crime, the strangest chapter in the history of Manhattan nightlife of the 1920s was being written by his superior, Mayor Jimmy Walker. Ostensibly leading an administration dedicated to the elimination of liquor-dealing nightclubs, Walker was covertly involved with the creation of such a venue: the Central Park Casino.

The Casino was Walker's lavish, even monumental official effort to turn a corner of the park into a semi-public haven for his own work and play. The "Ladies' Refreshment Salon" on the lower east side of Central Park had been designed by Calvert Vaux and erected in 1864. Carl Zittell, the publisher of *Zit's* theatrical weekly, had leased the structure since 1901, mismanaging it into a state of decay. In 1928 the Broadway entrepreneur Sidney Solomon approached Walker with the idea of renovating the building. Solomon told the mayor that if he, Solomon, were allowed to operate the new club, a group of Tammany Hall supporters and other investors would pay for a lavish renovation. He apparently did not tell Walker that there also were gangland investors who would handle the new club's liquor accounts. An agreement was reached between Solomon and the city in February 1929 that allowed the former to rent the structure for $8,500 a year.[43]

Solomon encouraged Walker to consider the project a gift from the renovation donors to both the city and himself. The mayor was a willing recipient. Since 1926 he had been pursuing an extramarital affair with the actress Betty Compton. A compliant city press had kept the relationship a general secret, but Walker still sought a more controlled nightlife environment in which he and his mistress might enjoy themselves. Solomon's group of donors provided $400,000 for the renovation and hired the noted decorator Joseph Urban to design the interior. The Casino, with its delicate floral wall patterns in the pavilion, wood inlay set against a modernistic silver background in the main dining room, and blackglass ballroom ceiling both looked backward to the Vienna of Urban's youth and forward to the *moderne* style of nightclubs in the 1930s. Walker and Compton demanded a relocation of the dining room's main entry in order to monitor arriving guests more easily, forcing a $20,000 alteration of the nearly complete renovation. Walker did not attend the Casino's opening in October 1929, but he and Compton soon became fixtures there, reveling in their own unique semi-private showcase. Walker, wearing a tuxedo with trendsetting shiny lapels, gave hatcheckers and bandleaders Emil Coleman and Eddy Duchin hundred-dollar tips, spending as freely as other customers. At the Casino champagne was cooled in a limousine whose engine was kept running in case of a raid, while nightly receipts frequently matched Sidney Solomon's annual rent.[44]

Over the course of two nights in June 1930 thirty-one federal Prohibition agents made visits to the Central Park Casino. Mayor Walker was not present, but the guests in attendance enjoyed liquor in abundance. The agents' terse notes described the evenings. A Mr. Mann was spotted pouring cognac into a glass under his table. Agents saw flasks on table tops. Without being asked, the waiters served "set-ups," glasses with ice ready for liquor, and uncorked bottles of wine for the agents. From 7:30 to 9:45 that evening the agents placed "bottles containing fluid resembling whiskey . . . upon tables" but received no admonishment from the restaurant staff. At 9:30 on the second evening, 24 June, the agents flung away their napkins and made a mass arrest. An agent found a bottle at the feet of the defendant Irving Schwenger: "Seized it—tasted it—rye whiskey. Claimed he was doctor. Arrested him." Eight other customers were also caught, along with the manager Sidney Solomon, the head waiter Rene Black, and eight other employees. This carefully planned raid mimicked an effort two months earlier at the Hollywood Restaurant, the large and popular new nightclub on Broadway. At around 9:45 on 25 April twenty-two agents had climbed the spiral staircase of the Hollywood. They collected evidence of alcoholic consumption and then shortly before midnight they made a flurry of arrests.[45]

These sensational raids were late tests of the public's and the government's resolve to enforce Prohibition in Manhattan's nightclubs. Maurice Campbell initiated the raids to revive the federal effort and to expand prosecutions to include waiters who served set-ups to flask-toting customers. The day after the initial spectacular foray at the Hollywood, though, the police commissioner Grover Whalen "emphatically" refused to cooperate with Campbell, insisting that the NYPD only raided nightclubs to search for gangsters. Customers who were present at the Central Park Casino raid, such as the Princess Obolensky (née Alice Astor), officials from the Cuban and Brazilian governments, and the subway builder Samuel Rosoff, expressed "outrage" and "astonishment" at the event. Weeks later Campbell and Whalen independently resigned their positions. In statements they essentially blamed each other for tensions between national and city officials over Prohibition enforcement.[46]

Politics mixed with jurisprudence to slow court action on these 1930 nightclub cases. Citing recent federal opinions, defense attorneys insisted that customers could not be prosecuted for purchasing and possessing intoxicating beverages for their own private use. In federal attorneys' offices, political considerations as well as potential legal obstacles were debated at length. In November 1931 Jackson Morris argued in a memo that the two nightclubs must be prosecuted for the sake of the Justice Department's image. "In no place in the country is the power of padlock proceeding more needed than in New York. Someone from almost every community in the country visits New York City and if its night life shows the scenes as described by the Prohibition Agents in the trial briefs, . . . no surprise can be shown if criticism of this Bureau is heard throughout the country and claims made repeatedly by the wets that Prohibition is a failure." Morris argued that recent court decisions allowed for the prosecution of guests who brought their own liquor into the venue. Nathan Morrisson disagreed, worrying about losing the two cases in the U.S. court of appeals. "The government has gained an advantage in the western circuits. Why should we risk it for the sake of the Second Circuit, especially when there is, as everybody knows, enough work to be done in New York City without engaging in doubtful cases?"[47]

The cases of the Central Park Casino and the Hollywood Restaurant—as well as a similar one involving the Argonaut, Texas Guinan's latest venue in Manhattan—went to U.S. Attorney George Z. Medalie. Medalie had replaced Charles Tuttle, who ran for governor that year (only to lose badly to the incumbent, Franklin D. Roosevelt). Like other successful defense lawyers from both political parties, Medalie was active in diverse legal, political, and intellectual circles, but the diversity of his interests and activities was unusual. A scholar of ancient law and a future

Republican candidate for the U.S. Senate, Medalie had also represented the clubowner and killer "Legs" Diamond and other nightlife and boot-legging figures. In his new post, though, Medalie was instructed by Washington to prepare prosecutions of the Central Park Casino and the Hollywood Restaurant, but he was also told to seek consent decrees and bonds that would eliminate liquor from the establishments without closing them. The Justice Department sought to gain a victory through finesse. A year later, though, Medalie was still haggling with the Central Park Casino's lawyers, who were "unwilling to accept a finding that a nuisance had existed upon the premises." Strangely, these lawyers included the former U.S. attorney Emory Buckner and one of his former assistants, John M. Harlan (a future Supreme Court justice). They succeeded in delaying a trial until December 1932 and then persuaded the judge to throw out the case. The magistrate declared that the Casino had "no earmarks of a speakeasy," did not encourage drinking by customers, and had even warned them that doing so would violate the law. Padlocking the Casino, the judge concluded, would be "pressing to the limit the Volstead act." The Hollywood and Argonaut cases unraveled in similar fashion.[48]

Into 1933, with Prohibition clearly in its last months, lawyers for the Justice Department were still debating the value of padlock decrees, the importance of serving subpoenas to owners of structures, and the symbolic significance of nightclub prosecutions. In June 1933 Washington instructed Medalie to obtain consent decrees in all remaining speakeasy padlock cases. By December of that year, though, more than six hundred padlock actions remained pending—but Prohibition had been repealed by the ratification of the Twenty-first Amendment. Medalie's assistant, Thomas E. Dewey, cabled Washington about "preparing stipulations of discontinuance for the entire list of cases." Nathan Morrisson, who had advised Mabel Walker Willebrandt years earlier and remained a consultant to her successors, responded with a line that brought the entire Prohibition adventure in Manhattan to a close: "Since there can be no further violations of the National Prohibition Act, there is nothing to prevent."[49]

The complex interaction of national legislation and politics with Manhattan nightlife during the era of Prohibition allowed government officials, journalists, and the public at large to develop new and conflicting ideas about the legality and social value of alcohol and nightclubs. As with the anti-prostitution efforts of the Committee of Fourteen in nightclubs and regulation by the municipal government, ironies and contradictions abounded in the largely federal Prohibition effort, obstacles that compelled enforcers to twist their words and actions tortuously as they sought to create tangible declines in the flow of liquor down Broadway.

These difficulties turned officials such as Emory Buckner, Mabel Walker Willebrandt, and George Medalie into cynics about Prohibition, and Maurice Campbell into a public opponent. It also gave anti-Prohibition municipal leaders such as Jimmy Walker and Grover Whalen plenty of opportunity to pose hypocritically as crime fighters. Meanwhile, persisting gender inequalities in the culture of the 1920s (including nightlife) compounded the public humiliation of Willebrandt in the wake of her political miscalculations. By contrast, Texas Guinan and others used the contradictions and hypocrisies of Prohibition to pose as victims of the state.

Animating the Prohibition story, underneath the morass of complex and cynical maneuvering involved in its enforcement, were the issues that had made nightlife of the 1920s a vital cultural concern in the first place: To how much freedom of leisure were all Americans entitled? And, did modern urban life provide new freedoms and rights for non-whites and women? Before a major scandal in city government placed these issues at the forefront of public debate, though, the Great Depression would profoundly transform daily existence—and nightlife—in Manhattan.

# CHAPTER 5
## Bargain-Counter Broadway

The bootleggers' and "class" clubs were the classic nightlife institutions of New York in the 1920s. Similarly, the concerns and responses that these clubs stimulated in New York's civic life also were deeply representative of their times. Public action on the nightclubs always hinged on their modernity, on their challenges to established notions of the night, gender roles, ethnicity, race, and economic legitimacy. The difficulties of efforts at reform and regulation showed the limited ability of reformers and governments to understand and control the new modern behavior. In addition, circumstances such as Mayor Jimmy Walker's clubgoing showed that civic regulators were often complicit in the behavior they were trying to regulate.

In the four years following 1929, though, the Great Depression caused a profound transformation in nightlife and in the civic context in which it grew. To some contemporaries, in fact, the Depression seemed to deprive the fertile culture of modernity of its nourishment. Wealth, innovation, excess, and abandon all fell victim to a crippling malaise. "As if reluctant to die outmoded in its bed," F. Scott Fitzgerald wrote, the 1920s "leaped to a spectacular death in October 1929."[1] Various cultural indicators provide compelling evidence of urban life and leisure undergoing a transformation. A cinematic example from 1932, a quasi-mythic distillation of cultural trends of its time, is one such indicator.

*King Kong* was rooted in its makers' globe-trotting adventures of the 1920s, but it was a product of the early years of the Depression. The film was conceived and written in 1930 and 1931, shot in 1932, and became the year's highest-grossing motion picture in 1933. Released in New York City in March and nationwide the next month, the film's innovative special effects depicting Kong, his dinosaur adversaries, and his final adventure in Manhattan made it a sensation. From the perspective of our topic, the film can be viewed as an oblique commentary on the primitivistic energy that underlay the modernity and nightlife of the 1920s.

In the movie, the film producer Carl Denham's crew, with the ingenue actress Ann Darrow in tow, drops anchor at a South Seas island where a dark-skinned people inhabit what resembles a large-scale Cotton Club jungle revue. (The shadowy lighting suggests that we only view the island at night.) Skull Mountain, the walled-up domain of Kong, functions as a sort of nightclub within the larger venue of the island itself, in which the murderous animal impulses that oppress the natives' society are contained. The nightclub performer Harry Richman boasted of having sex with multiple women nightly in his dressing room; on the island the primitives offer females to Kong to satisfy his raging id. In the style of Florenz Ziegfeld, though, Kong behaves somewhat more gently toward the all-American blonde, Ann Darrow (whose easy manner with an ape might explain the allusion to John Scopes's attorney in her name). Only just violating the code of behavior for male customers at a Texas Guinan nightclub, Kong removes Ann's nightgown and sniffs it. When Denham's crew rescues Ann, Kong breaks through the gate and destroys the native village. Primal animal energy, it may be said, has overwhelmed the jungle revue.

Next in King Kong's path is the "class" club, the playground of Anglo-Saxon civilization, represented by New York City in its entirety. The film features a variation on the human love triangle that was already a cliché in the infant genre of backstage musicals. Carl Denham is attracted to Ann Darrow, but the cynical producer is most eager to trap and to exploit Kong. Denham manages the romance between Darrow and the young ship's mate John Driscoll, announcing their engagement onstage at Kong's unveiling. At the end of the story Denham is still the publicist, supplying tabloid reporters with the "angle" for their articles: " 'Twas beauty killed the beast."

Viewers in 1933, however, hardly shared Denham's cool attitude at the end of the film. Kong's rampage through New York City—a disaster scenario entirely new to movies—gave the film an irresistible shock appeal. The prelude to this final act quickly sketches Manhattan as the site of empty and joyless exploitation in nightlife. Audience members gathering in the theater for Kong's unveiling express a jaded view of the spectacle. A middle-class husband, squirming uncomfortably in his tuxedo, chides his wife about high prices: "You would make us come to this. These tickets cost me twenty bucks!" A seated couple then alludes to aggressive masculinity in nightlife. "What is it, anyway?" one asks; "Some kind of gorilla," the other answers, while a burly man forces his way past their knees, prompting the woman to protest, "Ain't we already got enough of those in New York!" An usher then defines Kong as a modern celebrity, assuring a patron that this is not a performance but "more in the nature of a personal appearance."

The burst of photographers' flashbulbs in Kong's face underline the usher's words, but they also goad the beast into destroying the entire scenario. He breaks his shackles, destroys Denham's outsized nightclub stage, and rampages up Fifth Avenue. In the film, matte paintings of the Manhattan skyline (most evident in the establishing shot of the doomed elevated subway) provide shorthand allusions to the modernity of the 1920s.[2] Like a john pursuing a call girl, Kong "picks up" a woman in an apartment whom he mistakes for Ann Darrow. Once a denizen of the darkest, dampest cellar club, the beast finds Ann and carries her to the pinnacle of the man-made world, the new Empire State Building. To reverse the triumph of bestiality over civilization New York City reverts to a military regime, launches an air squadron, and in a foreshadowing of future warfare brings the ape down with a purely aerial assault. For 1930s moviegoers, Kong's wounding and spectacular quarter-mile death tumble undoubtedly only partially erased their unease at having witnessed the mock destruction of Manhattan.

*King Kong*, of course, should not be mistaken for a cultural history. The story was concocted by the English pulp novelist Edgar Wallace (who died while working on the film) and the American adventurers and filmmakers Merian C. Cooper and Ernest B. Schoedsack, none of whom had spent much time in New York.[3] Its portrayals of Manhattan and modern behavior owed more to Hollywood clichés about nightlife than to its actual contours. Films had been developing iconic representations of the city for at least a decade. In the late silent era many studios were located in the metropolitan region. Often they resorted to location shooting. *Night Life in New York* (1925), for example, was filmed in part at the Hotel Commodore "after midnight," according to studio publicity. The movie concerns an Iowa boy who is corrupted by an actress at the Club El Fey and swindled by a taxicab driver, but who is redeemed in the end by a chaste telephone operator (played by Dorothy Gish). Early "talkies" were virtually defined by representations of New York's nightlife. The very first picture with a soundtrack, *The Jazz Singer,* featured Al Jolson in the bosom of Broadway, and *The Lights of New York* was Hollywood's first all-talking film. Paramount's *Glorifying the American Girl,* an expensive tribute to the Follies made with Florenz Ziegfeld's assistance, featured footage of Mayor Jimmy Walker and others in a theater lobby. Rouben Mamoulian's drama *Applause* made imaginative use of New York locales and featured a strong lead performance by the nightclub star Helen Morgan. *The Broadway Melody*, the second Academy Award winner for best picture, originated the MGM movie musical and paved the way for the choreographer Busby Berkeley's elaborate film fantasies.[4]

Clichéd as it might be, *King Kong*'s anarchic fury nevertheless gives a taste of the upheaval that had shaken New York City and its nightlife from 1929 to 1933. Aside from Ann Darrow's initial financial woes the film makes little reference to the Great Depression, but Kong's story subtly traces the psychic devastation that attended the economic slump in the city. The Depression eliminated much of the purported wealth of the 1920s and bred a crisis of the spirit that had a powerful impact on the leisure, heedlessness, and sexual license that had animated nightlife. Nightclubs had channeled wealth and desire into carefully designed settings, but the Depression tore those settings apart, scattered wealth, and (according to some observers) threatened to unleash animal passions that the clubs had contained. The decline of nightlife seemed to bring modern decadence into the open and strip it of its glamour; to observers, what was left was mere prurience, exhibitionism, exploitation, and the real-life counterpart to King Kong: a dense, unsophisticated mob that choked the sidewalks of Broadway.

Tales of decadence, however, do not describe the complete evolution of nightlife during the Depression. This chapter argues that while most of the 1920s scene was swept away, enterprising promoters quickly developed alternative visions of the nightclub. The Hollywood Restaurant, guided by Nils T. Granlund, pioneered the no-cover, high-volume club that became the model for successful establishments in the 1930s. Granlund's famed chorus line brought female near-nudity to a mass audience, which encouraged criticisms of Depression-era prurience almost as quickly as it set the cash registers ringing. To many, the burlesque and female-impersonator crazes of the early 1930s were further evidence of a new sexual decadence. These three nightlife developments, though, showed how promoters cannily adapted to economic scarcity by playing to the desires of a less privileged mass audience into the theater district. The Depression terminated many nightclub trends and careers of the 1920s, but the vitality and innovation of the business as a whole persisted and laid the groundwork for a major revival in nightlife in later years. In reality, then, King Kong—or the urge for transgressive adventure that he symbolized—survived the Depression, adapting for the moment (with the help of promoters) to the chastened and thriftier environment of the mid-1930s.

In many ways the decline of nightlife in midtown Manhattan was evident months, and even years, before the Wall Street crash of October 1929. The year 1927, as we have observed, saw the high tide for both the bootleggers' and the "class" nightclubs. It was also a cultural turning point, in which high prices and general customer exploitation caused revolts and exoduses from the established clubs. By the following year observers first noted a process of decline, the onset of a certain seediness on the same Broadway blocks that boasted high-priced speakeasies. Owing to changes in taste and midtown microeconomics, enterprising promoters and curious customers disavowed the traditional pretense to refinement in nightlife and began to champion aggressive, confrontational, and consciously "unrefined" entertainment and behavior.

Despite prosperity—or more likely because of it—a new crush of small-time leisure peddlers, confidence men, gamblers, and prostitutes filled the Times Square area. The *Variety* reporter Abel Green recalled finding in Midtown in 1928 "Hubert's freak show on 42d Street. . . . Traffic worse than ever, and no solution. . . . The Garment Exchange with its models . . . arguing business men settling deals on the curb while holding up pedestrian traffic. . . . Street fakers offering their wares and watching for cops . . . handbook men, three-card monte boys, touts, tipsters and steerers for speaks." Broadway, Green claimed, "was more like the Bowery in 1928 than the Bowery in its heyday." "Class" nightclubs were giving way to disreputable speakeasies, "the main industry of the Square after dark. Few offer any entertainment of any sort save the usual prop conversation of the take-'em gals," the hostesses. The drama critic Brooks Atkinson noted that the Times Square block had been "one of the finest in the city and a splendid part of the theater district," but now it had fallen into gradual decline.[5]

Chinese restaurants occupied many old nightclub and restaurant venues. Their low-priced cuisine and entertainment (usually American, not Chinese) flourished beginning in 1928. Chinatown itself, on the Lower East Side, had not been a popular nightlife destination for white New Yorkers. The writer Niven Busch found it to be a heavily policed ghetto in which Chinese merchants controlled their interests in secret and bland storefronts dared outsiders to take note of them. Largely because of this, Chinese restauranteurs sought opportunities in Midtown. The Chinese eateries democratized nightlife considerably, offering much less expensive food and musical entertainment. The *New York Times* argued that Broadway "went Chinese" as "countless chop suey houses . . . attracted the one-time patrons of the night clubs," forcing the clubs to lower charges and offer cheaper food and drink; many of them, in turn, went out of business. The "Yellow Peril," as *Variety* called it, had descended on Broadway.[6]

While the October 1929 crash itself did not soon initiate a general Depression, it almost immediately encouraged big leisure spenders to economize. The result was a drastic decline in the remaining high-priced nightclub business. By January 1930 only half of the eight "class" clubs remaining were showing a profit. These were the Embassy (literally a club, subsisting on $250,000 in annual dues and bond sales), the Club Lido (with its five-dollar cover), the city-owned Central Park Casino, and the Montmartre. Club Richman, Villa Vallée, the Casanova, and Les Ambassadeurs were all struggling. The Chez Florence (resurrected without Texas and Tommy Guinan) was a rare success because, being in a hotel, it was exempt from the 3 AM curfew and thrived until dawn with all-black entertainment. During the succeeding spring over a dozen clubs in the Times Square area closed and then reopened in a spurt of hopefulness; by April the California and Parody clubs had opened (and closed) three times. The Chez Florence, California, and Parody clubs all required cover charges, and a reporter claimed that "others [with such charges] were also suffering heavy losses and will probably close any week." Even clubs attempting the no-cover strategy, such as the Everglades, Mayfair Roof, and Booby Hatch, were failing. The usual summer hiatus for indoor clubs now caused a near total drought, and by August Broadway professionals predicted that "no cabaret business" would remain in two weeks. Performers were fleeing for the burlesque circuit and "reframing their professional techniques to suit other lines of work."[7]

During the fall, some new "class" clubs appeared, but they also fell prey to the cycle of struggle established in the previous season. One of them was the Club Richman, rebounding from a closing and a fire, but now without its eponymous star. By the following spring it was closed, as were the El Patio and Texas Guinan's Club Argonaut. In 1932 Don Dickerman, the impresario of such theme spots as the Pirate's Den and the County Fair, declared bankruptcy. Even the low-priced Chinese restaurants were vanishing—"Yellow Peril Blowing Up; Chink Cafes Run Right Into Red," *Variety* declared. The 1920s-style nightclub seemed extinct to observers such as the newspaper editor Stanley Walker: "Night life definitely turned toward the home, the hotel grills and roofs, in inexpensive places in Greenwich Village, a few Harlem resorts, and the beer gardens and roadhouses in the suburbs." Harlem, though, was no longer in vogue; the Cotton Club and Small's Paradise persisted until 1932, but Connie's, Barron's, and other large clubs had all succumbed earlier to the Depression. This decline also reflected the pernicious ghettoization of Harlem that the "renaissance" of the 1920s had obscured but which the Depression had both exposed and accelerated. The black district became more vice- and gangster-ridden than ever, and working residents felt the worst impact of joblessness and poverty in the entire city.[8]

The economic devastation of New York City during the early 1930s has been well documented. By the winter of 1930–31 dozens of the city's lending institutions had failed. The spectacular (and much litigated) failure of the Bank of the United States wiped out the life savings of 400,000 city customers, most of them Jewish immigrants. Over a third of the city's 29,000 manufacturing concerns were closed. Apartment evictions multiplied; as Thomas Kessner has noted, "luxury apartments stood empty and foreclosed homes were without inhabitants." As surviving businesses hunkered down to weather the storm, workers' wages were slashed as much as 70 percent. At least 500,000 residents became unemployed. Tens of thousands of migrants from the hinterlands, seeking work, only worsened the problem. Under the gaze of the national press Manhattan became a giant exhibit of the Depression's urban ills. Employers and desperate black women turned Harlem's street corners into "slave markets," where day labor and even prostitution were contracted. The Great Lawn in Central Park became a shantytown of 10,000 drifters living in overturned crates and pasteboard boxes. Soup and bread lines became fixtures in Manhattan; there were eighty-two of them in the city at the Depression's height. By early 1932 1.6 million city residents were considered eligible for public assistance.[9]

In this general context nightlife looked like a ravaged victim of the times. It became popular to associate moral squalor with the economic depression surrounding nightclubs. Back in the mid-1920s, during Broadway's economic heyday, gossip columnists had already popularized the notion that Midtown's nightlife was a site of moral depravity. Walter Winchell made a good living writing condemnations of Broadway as "a hard and destructive community," "a pretty phoney avenue," dominated by "an army of racketeers and other shady manipulators." Others mimicked Winchell's attitude. The *Brooklyn Eagle*'s gossip columnist Art Arthur—who apparently made alliteration his métier—called Broadway the place "where a knife in the back is worth two in the hand . . . where they apply salve and the stiletto with the same suave salute."[10]

The economic devastation of Midtown and its physical manifestations now seemed to compound the depravity. Observers now wistfully recalled the cosmetic allure of mid-1920s nightclub interiors and perceived an even less appealing moral and spiritual atmosphere in Depression-era clubs. In a book published in 1931 that ostensibly was a guide to Manhattan's nightlife, Charles G. Shaw averred (in a string of sentence fragments) that "fundamentally, night clubs aren't gay places. But haunts for the dull and dejected. Those who would forget themselves, their cares, and a mad, mad world. In the main, night clubs are noisy, close and uncomfortable. . . . You are squeezed into a table with elbows digging you on both sides and served by a waiter . . . perhaps." A year later Stanley Walker echoed this threnody when he characterized Broadway as "a peculiarly excited condition of fourth-rate emotions," a street that "has degenerated into something resembling the main drag of a frontier town." The home of "cut-rate" nightlife, the Times Square area now held "seventeen dance-halls, with prices ranging from one cent to five cents a dance, 'with 200 most beautiful hostesses as your dancing partners.'" With its sideshows, quack lecturers, peep shows, touts, and

shoddy cafeterias, "Broadway has become a basement bargain counter."
By 1933 the Club Montmartre, one of the longest-lived "elite" establishments, had "[re]opened to take care of the strange people who go to
dance for five cents a dance." Besides joblessness Walker cited other
causes for Broadway's decline, including "the awful decline in real
estate values"—another result of the Depression—and "the growth of
radio and the motion picture." King Kong and Busby Berkeley thus
helped to finish off the urban leisure and nightlife that, directly or not,
had inspired their wildly popular celluloid fantasies.[11]

Stanley Walker's most intriguing claim was that Broadway was being
swallowed by a crush of people, an increasing density of human occupa-
tion. Charles Shaw had noted the nightclubs' "lack of ventilation, their
crush, and exorbitant prices," but Walker found the entire district
groaning under the weight of a thick crowd. He blamed in part the garment factories, which "have steadily inched their way northward" to
42nd Street; in the evening "their workers pour out of the tall buildings
and place a blight on the streets like so many ravening grasshoppers."
They were joined by thousands of gamblers and other thrill seekers,
"drawn by the irresistible urge to be among nice people," who helped
to flood Times Square. His aggregate description echoed the gritty, brilliant panoramic sketches of the cartoonist Reginald Marsh: "cauliflower
ears, beggars, sleazy crones, skinny girls who would be out of place in
even the cheapest dance hall, twisted old men, sleek youths with pale
faces, the blind and the maimed."[12] The Texan-born Walker's class and
ethnic prejudices are evident here, but his core perception—that Broadway nightlife had traded a certain past spaciousness and quality for a
new, densely packed, low-grade quantity—was a revealing insight.

Owing in part to this density, "prurient" leisure activities that had
taken place behind closed doors in the 1920s now spilled out into the
street itself. Much like the perceptible new streetwalking by desperate
jobless women, the new Broadway mass culture now choked the sidewalks, shocking observers who earlier had assented to bacchanalia in
basement clubs, furnished-room apartments, and speakeasies. One charitable observer, the writer Konrad Bercovici, felt that these activities indicated New York entrepreneurs' instinctive challenge to the gargantuan
modernism that had shaped the city since 1920. "Suddenly New York,
having grown with tremendous rapidity, remembered that it had lost
some of its old charm," leading hucksters figuratively to turn Manhattan
back into "a small town, making the most heroic attempts to imitate
Oshkosh and Greeneville and Memphis, Tennessee." Bercovici confessed his liking for the recent "size complex that has animated, and
still does animate, so many millions of people," but he also professed to
understand why skyscraper massiveness might have driven others to

street level. "There is no question but that a body breaks of its own weight."[13]

It is doubtful that a freak-show vendors' "small-village movement"—if there was such a thing—outpaced the Great Depression as the driving force behind Broadway's decline, or that it foreshadowed what would later be called "the new urbanism," the thoughtful championing of city life on a human scale. Bercovici's sidewalk reporting, though, does depict a kind of village carnival atmosphere. "Penny arcades, peep-shows, shooting-galleries, flea circuses, and burlesque theaters," "shoot-ing galleries, fake doctors, . . . freak-shows and hot-dog stands," and "Hindu yogis" "have moved their tents from Coney Island to Broad-way." The seaside carnival had decamped on the Great White Way "within the shadow of the Empire State Building, the greatest architec-tural feat of all time." Charlatan yogis pretended to mend people and wristwatches in storefront tent theaters, and automatic moving-picture booths allowed the customer to "see herself as she would look on the silver screen." For many, Hubert's Museum epitomized the presence of Coney Island in Midtown. Famed for its flea circus, in which the insects kicked balls and walked on wires, Hubert's also featured lectures on human conception, transvestitism (delivered by a practitioner), and boxing, the latter given by Jack Johnson, the destitute former world heavyweight boxing champion. A pig and a monkey in a baby carriage, Siamese twins, Asian dances, slot-machine films, and freak exhibits—including "Doraldina," "half man and half woman"—also graced the museum.[14]

The decline of Midtown's real estate, street traffic, and casual enter-tainment was accompanied by intensified violence. As the panic deep-ened in the early months of 1930, leisure in Manhattan seemed to make the transition from a nominally regulated economy into a blatantly pred-atory one. As elites and other legitimate investors pulled out of night-clubs, the general dearth of capital caused gangland financiers to initiate violent conflict over retail liquor and entertainment venues, door to door and neighborhood by neighborhood. Frankie Uale, Van-nie Higgins, and Joe Masseria were among the gang leaders who lost their lives in this struggle in the late 1920s. Daring young criminals now poached on more established gangsters' territories. Dutch Schultz invaded Waxey Gordon's West Side territory, and the following year he and Vincent "Mad Dog" Coll struggled over control of Harlem's num-bers racket. In 1931 Jack "Legs" Diamond and Frankie Marlow, both clubowners, and Francis Crowley, an investor in clubs and dance halls, were murdered, and early the next year Schultz's men killed Coll. Night-life became a battle zone. Walter Winchell was able to alter his persona from gossip columnist into something resembling a war correspondent after he received a mysterious advance tip-off about the Coll murder. Texas Guinan was drafted into the conflict, probably involuntarily, when Dutch Schultz blamed her for tipping off Winchell. Both nightlife figures paid a price for their notoriety, though; for months Winchell lay low in Florida, while Guinan worked in France to avoid Schultz's reprisals. Meanwhile Schultz found fertile territory in Harlem, cornering gambling and bootlegging there while reformers and police officers alike largely ignored him.[15]

Larry Fay, the originator of the bootlegger's nightclub and the prototype of the gangster clubowner, met a violent end in this era as well. In 1927 he reached the pinnacle of his entrepreneurial success, building a symbiotic financial relationship between his taxi company, the El Fey nightclub, and his racketeering operations. He applied the techniques that brought him early success to broader swaths of the city's economy. Fay tried (and failed) to list his taxi company on the New York Stock Exchange, as one paper put it, "to be on an equal plane, socially, with his former night club patrons." He then created a milk syndicate, demanding one cent in protection money for every quart of "loose milk" he sold over the counter to eateries and cafés and gaining a forty-cent profit from every ten-gallon can sold wholesale. The syndicate cultivated an ethnic following by labeling one racket the Jewish Grocers' Association.[16]

Succeeding years became increasingly difficult for Fay. Texas Guinan, his major talent discovery, struck out on her own, and the entertainment at Fay's clubs never recaptured its early exuberance. Indicted for racketeering in 1929, Fay saw his milk syndicate coming crashing down; his later acquittal was cold comfort. Two years later he was again indicted, this time for income tax evasion pertaining to his defunct Club Rendezvous. Fay managed another acquittal, but in the meantime the Depression ruined his taxicab business. He was forced to sell two hundred vehicles for five dollars apiece. Fay was resilient, though, marrying a chorus dancer and spending $100,000 to renovate a mansion speakeasy, on 56th Street near Fifth Avenue, that had previously held Tommy Guinan's and Owney Madden's Club Napoleon. The Casa Blanca opened in the fall of 1932. Its white and gold panels sought to recapture the heyday of the mid-1920s, but business was slow and at year's end Fay cut employee wages by 30 percent. Edward Maloney, a hulking former Prohibition agent turned doorman, allegedly feared that the wage cut jeopardized his repayment of a $67 gambling debt (in which Fay apparently played a role). Given his dismissal by Fay on New Year's Day, the drunken Maloney emptied a pistol into his boss, who died within minutes.[17]

The newspapers were quick to interpret Fay's death as a knell for the nightlife of the 1920s. The columnist James Whittaker argued that the murder "is suggestive, to anyone who remembers the Club Napoleon standards, of the pinch and poverty of the new times," in which "business is paralyzed, the waiters are in a daze and personnel and patrons are glumly nursing . . . hangovers." The Napoleon itself, in the same venue, had closed earlier during the Depression because it also had been "unable to settle supply bills and wage claims." A London journalist echoed Whittaker, pointing out that since Fay had been "killed by the man he could not pay" he was "another casualty of the American depression." It was widely reported that Fay had "died broke" with only three dimes in his pocket.[18]

The decline of celebrated individuals of nightlife of the 1920s also followed different and less violent paths. In the weeks following Larry Fay's funeral Texas Guinan was able to generate more publicity for herself by spreading the myth that she had risked her life to attend the funeral, braving an assault threatened by Dutch Schultz's henchmen. Guinan's own public persona came under press scrutiny during the hard times. The press depicted the sporadically employed hostess not only as a victim of the Depression but also as a perpetrator of it—or at least of the economic exploitation that had helped to cause the slump. Just as Henry Ford's earlier paeans to mass production were turned against him after 1929, Guinan's trademark greeting "Hello, suckers!" now made her complicit in an alleged plot to swindle nightclub customers. The columnist Sidney Skolsky noted that while Guinan (as well as others) had boasted that they had originated such brash nightclub expressions, "nobody's claiming those phrases now [and] nobody's using them now." A cartoonist for the *Philadelphia Record* made the link explicit in a sketch that alluded to European nations' war debt to the United States. A bemused Uncle Sam is poring over documents on his desk—"Poland Default," "French Default," "Belgium Default"—as Texas Guinan strolls into his office and bellows, "Hello, Sucker!"[19]

In March 1933 Guinan strained to redefine her image in the light of the economic troubles. Juxtaposing nightlife and the Depression—specifically, the current crises involving bank failures and the gold standard—Guinan told a reporter, "Why not let some of the 'gold diggers' dig it out and put it back in circulation [?] I've got some little girls working for me who could put the damper on some of this hoarding in no time. What the country needs is more and better gold diggers." Provocatively connecting the tired economy and the sexual exhaustion of the early 1930s, Guinan contrasted this scene with the vitality of the preceding decade: "The bankers went busted because they said 'Hello, Sucker,' and then took the customers for all they had. . . . We'll always give a guy carfare so's he can get home to the wife and kiddies. When you treat them too rough they don't come back. . . . The trouble with the 'tired business man' [today] is that he's too tired." Guinan offered to "take over" failed banks and resuscitate them with her hospitality. "You can't get a guy to spend his dough by greeting him with a sour pan."[20]

Advice, though, was all that Guinan could reliably sell in 1933. Her livelihood largely depended on a syndicated newspaper column, "Texas Guinan Says," which she had begun in 1930. She also toured the country, trying to piece together a living that New York City alone could no longer provide. In November of 1933, reaching the West Coast in the middle of an exhausting tour, Guinan contracted amoebic dysentery and died in Vancouver at the age of forty-nine. Guinan's funeral in New York attracted thousands. As with Larry Fay's demise, the press interpreted Guinan's death as the extinguishing of a spent candle, a symbol of the demise of the nightlife of the 1920s.[21]

Many other entertainers, of course, did not succumb prematurely to the crossfire, overexertion, or sheer hopelessness of the predatory economy of the Depression. Fay Marbe, a Manhattan-born singer, dancer, and actress, had returned to New York in 1928 after long and successful engagements in Berlin and London. Her ample scrapbooks from the following half-decade show a somewhat old-fashioned torch singer's tenacious and reasonably successful attempt to build a career in the splintered cabaret industry. A subscriber-funded residency in late 1932 at the Central Park Casino was short-lived, though, and it marked the end of Marbe's flickering nightclub career.[22]

Harry Richman, a major nightclub star and the "Romeo of Broadway," fared better (see Fig. 5). In 1928, tussles with Prohibition enforcers encouraged him to sell his interest in the Club Richman. Despite these distractions and the Depression, Richman's talents and some common sense—his own or his manager's—allowed him to remain successful. In 1930 he starred in the popular Hollywood musical *Puttin' on the Ritz*. Although he is coy about it in his memoirs, Richman seems to have adjusted deftly to hard times, reducing his nightly intake of a half-gallon of bourbon, five packs of cigarettes, and female sparring partners to keep in good professional trim. In 1932 Richman successfully defended himself in court against the dancer Virginia Biddle, paying out only fifty dollars in damages in the wake of the speedboat explosion that had injured her, and opened a new Club Richman in its original venue beside Carnegie Hall. The club accommodated hard times by requiring a cover charge of only $1.50 a person, but it still failed. Richman returned to Broadway revues. A writer in the *New York Evening Post* in 1934 noted his "stage gift of seeming to eliminate the footlights while he destroys all barriers between himself and his audience." Richman also made headlines by challenging the speed record

Figure 5. The singer Harry Richman, a former vaudevillian who became known as the "Romeo of Broadway" on theater and club stages. Beginning in 1927 he appeared in his own Club Richman, adjacent to Carnegie Hall. Billy Rose Theatre Collection, The New York Public Library for the Performing Arts, Astor, Lenox, and Tilden Foundations.

for a two-man transatlantic flight (his plane crashed in Newfoundland) and helping to form a new theatrical union in opposition to Actors' Equity. While he claimed much later that "I haven't got a nickel left from the thirteen million dollars I made," he nevertheless demonstrated a staying power that overcame many obstacles that struck New York's nightlife in the early 1930s.[23]

Harry Richman's decision to institute a low cover charge in 1932 was foreordained. Well before that year, all nightlife entrepreneurs had learned that the drastic reduction—or best of all, the outright abolition—of the cover charge provided the only hope of success in the club business. The passing of Larry Fay and Texas Guinan coincided with the extinction of their breed of nightclub. Although conspicuous consumption at high prices was the time-honored foundation of New York's nightlife, dating back to well before the Great War, customers' attitudes had undergone a sea change that far outpaced their discontent at being unable to pay the old rates. Largely but not entirely owing to the Depression, notions of exclusivity, waste, abandon, and irrationality were giving way to more practical ideas about the function of a night on the town.

No innovator in the business recognized this more perceptively than Nils Thor Granlund, the often arrested producer of revues at Larry Fay's clubs and the Silver Slipper Club. At the Silver Slipper, the most successful club to be operated openly by organized crime figures, Granlund began to develop ideas for a new approach to club entertainment. Recruiting little known but capable vaudeville acts, he essentially turned the Silver Slipper into a variety stage. Performers such as Jimmy Durante, George Raft, the tenor Morton Downey, and the young Imogene Coca and Ginger Rogers appeared there. "Broadway night life reached its peak in the Silver Slipper," Granlund boasted. Talent scouts soon attended shows to investigate Granlund's finds and to recommend new personnel to him. Granlund duplicated his formula for a time at Tommy Guinan's short-lived Playground club. Marrying and moving into an antique farmhouse in New Jersey, Granlund felt the lure of the suburban life. He always resisted becoming a clubowner himself, fearing both the underworld and the law. Nevertheless, in late 1929 Granlund's success encouraged him to form a partnership with Joe Moss and Jake Amron. In the second floor of the old Rector's restaurant on 48th Street and Broadway, the three men realized an innovative new club concept, the Hollywood Restaurant.[24]

The movie theme indicated by the name was fully developed inside the club. "We decorated it with giant photographs of motion-picture stars and Hollywood sights and scenes." Only a year after the general advent of talking pictures, the studios' glamorized version of New York's nightclubs had redounded back onto the clubs themselves. Hollywood clichés of nightclub design—the tuxedos, tinsel, streamlined staircases, and airy dance spaces between tables—were incorporated into a real Manhattan venue, lending them a bit of the new movie "magic." Moreover, at the Hollywood Restaurant the industry itself and southern California became points of reference and reverie for Manhattan's nightlife.

Business at the Hollywood Restaurant was slow at first, but word of mouth soon led to a brisk expansion, and by 1930 the success of the nightclub was assured. Even the highly publicized federal Prohibition raid that April (discussed in the preceding chapter) did not stagger it; no padlocking or conviction resulted. Virtually all other clubs were failing at this time. Even other no-cover charge venues faded, including the Mayfair Roof, which also was owned by Granlund, Moss, and Amron. The Hollywood Restaurant was a solitary success because it responded effectively to the exigencies of the Depression's economy. Just as Texas Guinan's reputation had been tarnished, Granlund argued, clubs and speakeasies of the 1920s had declined "for the simple reason that they were choking the geese that laid their golden eggs. The suckers were getting wise, and the wise ones were developing an awareness of the racket the cabaret business really was." Exploitative cover charges and prices had come about because of high liquor costs and decorating bills (fueled by competition for elite clienteles); thus nightclubs had been "small, tremendously expensive places."[25]

Granlund's restaurant-nightclub was not such a boutique, but rather a warehouse outlet for socializing, dining, and entertainment. The enormous room seated a thousand patrons. The club's key innovation was to do away with liquor sales and cover charges. The Prohibition Bureau's raid targeted customers' personal bottles and the waiters' tolerance for them but uncovered no liquor supply in the restaurant. The Hollywood's no-liquor policy was genuine and daring. Granlund and his partners gambled that the Prohibition-era culture of obsessive drinking had run its course and that a relatively dry restaurant clientele could blend with traditionally wet nightclub customers. No liquor, in addition, meant that organized crime would pay much less attention to the club's operation.[26]

Granlund's replacement of the cover charge with a restaurant-bill minimum received much comment. For a minimum of $1.50 in the early evening and for $2.00 after theater closings, a customer received dinner and an elaborate show. Three dollars put a diner at a table in front of the stage. Sime Silverman, the founder of *Variety*, visited the Hollywood, and in his review he marveled at the occasion as "the first time here or anywhere that a big floor show was virtually given away." Volume business made the low minimum charge profitable. Little extras bolstered the bottom line: a glass-and-ice set-up for brown-bag drinkers, costing the restaurant three cents, sold for one dollar. All told the club grossed an average of $30,000 a week—"phenomenal trade for a place of its kind."[27]

Four times nightly Granlund presented a lavish-looking stage show that presented low-priced novelties. He enlisted vaudeville performers such as the roller skaters Johnny and Mary Mason, the novelty dancers Mark and Marquette, the contortionist Mary Lee, and the juvenile singer Sidney Hawkins, along with the Jean Garber Orchestra and its featured singer, Harriet Nelson. A four-man troupe performed "Apache" and "jiu-jitsu" routines, and on occasion Texas Guinan sat on the edge of the stage and dispensed wisecracks. The plain-looking Granlund himself served as a quick-tongued master of ceremonies. The main attraction, though, was the chorus line. It was filled with the kinds of young female "talent" that Granlund was known for discovering—tall, "very young and good-looking" women.

The success of the Hollywood Restaurant's chorus line indicated a significant change in the preferences of nightlife's customers. The indulgence in the 1920s in anarchic play and in interaction with female performers in their twenties was giving way to passive gazing at nearly naked performers who had just passed the age of consent. As *Variety* put it in 1929, "most of the talented café performers [now] work in cities outside of New York. They can't get jobs here since the craze for young kids has become paramount. A girl who is good looking but who can't shake a foot has a far better chance than any real performer." As the action-based environment of the nightclub of the mid-1920s was supplanted by the floor show for immobile diners, the Ziegfeld- or Guinan-style "showgirl" gave way to the "chorus girl," whose career lasted only as long as her teen years. At the Hollywood Granlund tried to chaperone and isolate his young charges, "never allow[ing them] to mingle with the trade." (The impresario, however, enjoyed a double standard. The fortyish Granlund married Rose Wenzel, a seventeen-year-old member of the Hollywood troupe.)[28]

From the perspective of recent stage entertainment history, the extreme youth of the 1930 chorus line indicated a further disempowering of the female nightclub performer. The wisecracking drinking companion of Texas Guinan's era (although still present for a time stageside at the Hollywood, in the person of Guinan herself) was supplanted by a new archetype, a talentless, vulnerable "symbol of youth," a figure of wish-fulfillment for male customers whose sexual and social confidence needed reinforcement after the Wall Street crash. The new symbolic disempowerment of young women reflected their economic vulnerability in the Depression. Investigators for the Committee of Fourteen found that once a chorus girl retired at the age of twenty, she often was forced into work as a dance hall hostess, where she might fall prey to prostitution or to police framing on false charges.[29]

The devaluation of female talent and of dancer-customer interaction was also a symptom of a new trend toward mass marketing in the night-life business. Just as the streets of Broadway held a dense and diverse new crowd, Granlund's young choristers in the Hollywood Restaurant paraded before a much more economically varied audience. Movies of the 1920s had made Ziegfeld's "American girl" icon more familiar and less glamorous, turning her into "the girl next door." The "girl's" neighbors began to dominate the New York nightclub audience. Many commentators noted that Granlund's Hollywood Restaurant chorines introduced Ziegfeld-style near-nudity to a large middle-class clientele. The dancers "were mostly dressed in harnesses," Sime Silverman noted in his review in 1930. "Nothing could be more undressed than the Holly-wood show." The Hollywood Restaurant, ironically, promoted female nudity at the exact moment when its namesake, the film industry, launched its campaign to censor such display. Hollywood, California's more daring pictures from the era before the Production Code— including *King Kong*—introduced sexual themes and nudity to the American mass audience, but after 1933 these attractions migrated from the screen to the Hollywood Restaurant in New York City and similar nightclubs.[30]

Revealingly, though, the Hollywood Restaurant also boasted of its eth-ical integrity by publicizing its adherence to the Volstead Act, its orderly service and operation, and its openness to a wide cross-section of the public. This strategy enhanced its appeal to a broad audience. Otto Kahn and other elite luminaries often visited the restaurant, but the low prices ensured that middle-class patrons would fill most of the thousand seats for each show. As *Variety* noted, "No nite club [*sic*] has drawn the mixed crowd the Hollywood has." At this establishment clubgoers on a budget could celebrate the extinction of "gyp joints [where one got] not less than a check for $60 for one-tenth of the entertainment." An important transformation in consumer values was taking place. The movie palaces helped to initiate the transformation back in the 1920s, admitting anyone who could pay ten cents into ornate auditoriums that presented an oversized new celluloid dreamscape. Now, during hard times, the nightclub—a fantasy world of excess and abundance that had been the paragon of conspicuous consumption—became a place for lei-sure within a middle-class budget.[31] Granlund's big movie-themed room became the model for later high-volume nightclubs such as Billy Rose's Casa Mañana and Diamond Horseshoe, the French Casino, and the

International Casino (run by Granlund's partner Joe Moss), which created the new nightclub archetype in the popular culture of the 1930s.

This new archetype was part of a more general, indeterminate, and significant trend toward sexual frankness in American culture during the early years of the Depression. Social histories of this era tend to emphasize the decline in sex as a priority, citing falling birth and marriage rates and the advent of the Motion Picture Production Code. These trends gained dominance largely after 1933, though, in league with the nation's general new dedication to a comprehensive government response to the Depression, as part of what Warren Susman has called "the culture of commitment" of the 1930s.[32] In preceding years, though, the culture's general needs and desires were still being hotly contested in the wake of the startling discoveries of the 1920s and the social devastation of the Depression. While the prosperity and giddiness of the 1920s had vanished, the provocative alternative identities and behaviors the decade had introduced still remained. The explorations now cost less, as well. Nils T. Granlund's inexpensive chorus shows, the "charity case" (five-dollar prostitution plied by young streetwalkers from mill towns and farms), and Broadway's carnival-sideshow attractions gave evidence of the bargain-basement sexual smorgasbord of the early 1930s.

Alongside the carnival attractions and the high-volume, no-cover nightclub on Broadway of these years, two other popular nightlife trends—stock burlesque and pansy shows—especially confirmed the cultural significance of the mass consumption of sexuality and female nudity. In his 1933 survey of Broadway's apparent degradation, Stanley Walker identified a trio of blights as "the hallmarks of the New Broadway": "cheap dances, lewd burlesque, [and] filthy pictures."[33] Of these three, burlesque stimulated the greatest attention and attracted the most diverse audience. The so-called stock burlesque genre owed most of its formal properties to the burlesque tradition, but it also reinterpreted the chorus shows and revues of the 1920s for the Depression-era audience. While burlesque theaters did not serve liquor or permit their customers to interact with stage performers, they shared the nightclubs' mantle of sexual frankness, female display, and sarcastic cynicism. They sold a raw product that some clubgoing New Yorkers disparaged but that many others flocked to, and burlesque became the entertainment rage of 1931 and 1932.

Burlesque was a form of variety theater with roots in nineteenth-century European dance halls, in which exhibitions of the female form served as the fundamental attraction. In the 1860s Lydia Thompson's troupe of hefty British dancers introduced burlesque in the United

States, where dance numbers blended with skits that satirized more respectable theatrical entertainment of the time. Predating vaudeville and independent of its more family-friendly mission, burlesque built its own stable of performers, theaters, and a nationwide circuit centered in the big cities. As the historian Robert C. Allen has shown, burlesque appealed especially to wealthy and well-educated audiences that sought a subversive theater that avoided the crude ethnic stereotypes and self-censorship of vaudeville; it was perhaps the closest thing America had to European-style political cabaret.[34]

By the turn of the century, however, burlesque had become a male-dominated cultural arena in which producers and spectators increasingly lampooned new feminist concepts of American womanhood. They created a female image that objectified the body and disparaged the mind. When the Mutual burlesque "wheel" or touring circuit was founded in 1922, the old performance tradition made a comeback, but another innovation, commonly called stock burlesque, eventually surpassed it. Filling theaters during summer months when the wheel acts were on vacation, the stock companies of the Minsky brothers and others presented crude voyeurism, shows that consisted almost entirely of striptease and double-entendre skits. As the historian Rachel Shteir has argued, "beginning in the 1930s, striptease evoked emotional and physical comic excesses that could not be contained in civilized life" and "provided a relief from and a counterpoint to burlesque's raunchy, violent clowning." In 1931 stock burlesque moved into a few darkened Broadway theaters and became the district's big new success.[35]

Stock burlesque thrived while other theatrical forms waned and nearly perished during the early years of the Depression. As Konrad Bercovici noted, during the theater slump of 1930 two "burly houses" "were crowded to the brim" for five performances daily. Stock burlesque was in vogue among elites who had deserted the nightclubs of Midtown and Harlem. For men "in full dress and silk hats," arm in arm with "ladies wearing modern clothes (and as little of them as possible)," "the burlesque shows became the after-theater rage. . . . It was burlesque for society and not for sailors and poor immigrants." Despite its cachet, the new burlesque had few class pretensions. Customers were lured with the crassest forms of sidewalk ballyhoo. Barkers encouraged male passersby to "come see the girls" and harassed both sexes to a degree that female workers at the nearby McGraw-Hill building began to complain. The Central Theater, one police official observed, employed a woman to "advertis[e] the show vocally—and they had a big mechanical man beating on a bass drum." The visual lures were even more blatant. In the words of one critic, signs "plastered from the sidewalk to the roof" featured "vulgar paintings, large size and small, photographs of women in a more or less condition of nudity, with glaring electric light signs containing such inscriptions as 'Bigby Hind from Peoria' . . . in letters a foot or more high."[36]

In 1932 the Walker administration launched its last high-profile censorship campaign by summoning the burlesque theater owners before the city's licensing commission. In question were four theaters—the Republic, the Central, the Eltinge, and the Apollo, owned variously by Max Rudnick, Jack Rovenger, and Herbert Minsky—as well as Hubert's Museum (which also fell under the municipal designation of a "common show"). In the hearings lawyers for the anti-burlesque 42nd Street Property Owners' and Merchants' Association, including the former district attorney Joab Banton, publicized salacious details that filled many newspaper columns. Prurient books and magazines, they determined, were peddled between shows in the aisles. Each show offered about six striptease numbers, in which strippers actually undressed down to flesh-colored underwear. (Breasts were bared only in Ziegfeld-style tableaux.) Interspersed with stripteases were skits filled with double-entendres. Titles such as "Aileen Dover from Aiken" conveyed their flavor. A King Tut skit was built around the line "every girl has a tomb . . . mine is pink and white." Wordplay on current slang was the height of its sophistication, as in a skit about a young man who tells his father that he "went too far" while ice skating with his girl; "I'm afraid I put my foot in it." The father replies, "At least you weren't wearing your skates then." Brooks Atkinson, the charitable *Times* theater critic, attended three burlesque shows at the Republic Theater and found that while the stripteases were "plain pandering" the skits "had a kind of animal obscenity about [them]."[37]

The licensing commission especially sought to determine whether burlesque had crossed boundaries of propriety that nightclub shows, with their nearly naked chorus lines, had already stretched far. Brooks Atkinson testified that he could not compare burlesque with the Hollywood Restaurant's flesh-baring show since he had never seen the latter, and he declined to say whether the Republic Theater's advertisements "are any better or worse than others in New York." He did argue, though, that there was a considerable difference in artistic quality between the Republic's burlesque and the various Ziegfeld Follies. Similarly, Henry Moskowitz, the social reformer and director of the League of New York Theaters, testified that the Earl Carroll and George White revues (featuring substantial near-nudity, but in higher-priced theater settings) were not tarnished by "the same direct pandering to the lower instincts that you find in burlesque." He insisted that there was a difference in kind, not in degree, between the revues and stock burlesque. By contrast, the *New York Telegraph* critic Charles Feldheim countered that the Republic's shows were "just as moral as the $5.50 shows." The theater owners' attorney tried to deflect the immorality charge by reminding the commission that Moskowitz and other respectable men had attended burlesque shows and by suggesting that persons other than the theater barkers might have harassed passersby. Meanwhile, the attorney argued, "legitimate" plays such as "the eminently respectable Noel Coward's *Private Lives*" featured nudity as well.[38]

In the end the Republic and Eltinge theaters lost their licenses. However, as Robert Allen has noted, the city's decision was not so much a victory for decency than for established Broadway merchants who had hoped to slow the "cheapening" of their business environment; "the real issues . . . were economic and political, not moral."[39] While the 1932 hearings indicated a revival of reformers' efforts to police public entertainment—and in later years, the La Guardia administration would intensify the attack on burlesque—it also showed how the Depression, changing leisure behavior, and ubiquitous publicity had made all urban nightlife more sexually explicit. Like the line between new female public behavior and prostitution, the boundary between acceptable and unacceptable public entertainment had become more difficult to define. The crush of barkers, sideshows, cheap theater shows, and sidewalk hustlers on Broadway had made frankly prurient material much more common. The closeted sexuality of the cabaret and the nightclub was now in the open, on billboards lining New York's most visited street.

Like burlesque, the so-called pansy craze of 1931–32 also exposed more sophisticates, journalists, and middle-class customers to a nightlife genre filled with relatively raw sexuality. The most celebrated transvestite show took place at Dutch Schultz's Club Abbey, featuring Manhattan's premier "drag" performer, Gene Malin. Malin's two-hundred-pound physique and deft ripostes to homophobic hecklers helped to ease newcomers into the phenomenon of female-impersonator clubs (as did his surprising, albeit brief, marriage to a woman in 1931). After Harry Richman left the club that bore his name, the manager, Lou Schwartz, hired a transvestite act as the main attraction, as did other venues. Male masters of ceremonies with "a lavender tinge in their make-up," in *Variety*'s words, became ubiquitous. The opening in December 1930 of the Pansy Club, adjacent to the Hollywood Restaurant, was a high point of this vogue. New York was not the only drag-happy city. By late 1930 at least thirty-five new transvestite clubs had opened on Chicago's North Side, part of a decidedly unusual new underworld racket. "The world's toughest town," *Variety* claimed, "is going pansy. And liking it."[40]

The gay-transvestite nightclub vogue in New York in the early 1930s was the culmination of the nightlife audience's growing, decade-long fascination with gay male culture. As George Chauncey has shown in his study of gay New York, transvestite balls at the Hamilton Lodge in Harlem and the Liberal Club in Greenwich Village had long attracted heterosexual onlookers. In 1928 the gay presence in Harlem's nightlife had especially gained notice. Raymond Claymes, an investigator for the Committee of Fourteen, noted widespread gay and lesbian social activity and solicitations for sex. The commercialization of Greenwich Village in the 1920s exploited its perceived status as a center of gay life. By 1930 Times Square had become a leading site for male "cruising." Stylish hustlers trod Fifth Avenue in Midtown, while 42nd Street was the prime site for solicitation by working-class men. Later in the decade a Village-style gay community developed along what participants called "the Faggy Fifties."[41]

While society in the 1920s generally denigrated homosexuals and increasingly pathologized their sexual preference, the buildup in that decade to the pansy vogue of 1931–32 revealed the centrality of the gay experience in the new nightlife. To begin with, heterosexual observers of nightlife continually tended to link sexual transgressions with racial and ethnic mixing. As Kevin Mumford has shown, outside observers' identification of Harlem after 1928 with homosexual activity resulted not only from the presence of this activity, but also from their conceptual likening of gays and blacks as similar outsiders in American society. In the 1930s, for example, bookstores often shelved gay-themed novels in Negro literature sections. Even some white gay men cultivated this association, consciously adopting certain black dance steps as their own special styles. The mixture of blacks and whites and gays and straights in clubs uptown, midtown, and downtown signaled a new fluidity in sexuality and culture. Sociologists and other perceptive investigators of nightlife, Mumford notes, found that by the 1920s "cross-dressing itself no longer served as the privileged signifier of homosexuality."[42]

In this era, as many scholars have observed, both mainstream medical "experts" and gay men and lesbians themselves were redefining homosexuality along similar lines, changing it from a *gender* identity built around clothing and gestures into a *sexual* identity built around the choice of sexual relations and partners. Such changes made "the homosexual" less obviously flamboyant and garishly dressed. However, in the 1920s the definitional transition was still taking place, and as Chauncey puts it, "multiple systems of classifications" thrived. The sexual orientation of companions of the same sex in a nightclub, therefore, was often ambiguous. Concerned observers such as investigators for the Committee of Fourteen yearned for clear indicators but usually found none. In its 1928 annual report the Committee could identify only "14 homosexuals of both sexes" in only 13 of the 392 nightclubs it investigated.

Undoubtedly these sites actually teemed with many more gay employees and customers.[43]

However, the gay presence in nightlife in the 1920s may also have clashed with the rebellious male-female interaction for which nightlife was most celebrated. Chauncey even calls the new female freedom in clubs and speakeasies "a heterosexual counterrevolution" against the traditional homosocial (and sometimes homosexual) male dominance of saloon and street life before the Great War. The new attitude now encouraged men to have fun in public with women, while all-male leisure was classified either as a relic of the gaslight era or as an indication of abnormal homosexuality. Gay men in nightlife, therefore, were becoming more assertive and visible at the same time that the straight majority was increasingly stigmatizing them. The tensions were inevitable and strong, as is attested by the presence of hecklers at Gene Malin's act at the Club Abbey. Appropriation by straights may have been the most insidious threat. Even newly subtle gay men's fashion indicators—the red necktie, the lapel flower, or the marcelled hair—were picked up and publicized by the mainstream tabloids and other mass media. (Jimmy Walker's fondness for similar sartorial touches indicated either appropriation or possible hidden facets of his private life.) Mae West's notorious gay-themed plays *The Drag* and *Pleasure Man*, ostensibly sympathetic and tolerant, offered shallow and largely hostile portrayals of transvestites.[44] Like African Americans in Harlem, gay men surely doubted that the attention paid to them by affluent outsiders was in their best interest.

Against this background, then, the vogue of the pansy appears to have been homophobic, dependent upon rigid and hostile stereotypes of gay effeminacy. While the transvestite show, like the minstrel show or jungle revue before it, certainly permitted straight viewers to explore alternative identities, like those earlier genres it also showed them managing their latent insecurities about "the other" through ridicule and stereotype. To straights, female impersonators (like the performers at Hubert's Museum) were freaks who reassured a Depression-ridden audience that old standards of manliness—and the newer models of femininity—had not been shaken.

Like burlesque, pansy shows became the target of official repression. Chauncey demonstrates, in fact, that a new wave of anti-homosexual policing had been gathering in New York at least since 1923 (when a law banning gay solicitation was passed). In 1933 legislation was enacted that explicitly banned public assemblies by homosexuals, and a campaign of municipal and police repression was launched. Gay men in New York in the 1930s creatively developed "multiple sexual systems, each with its own cultural dynamics, semiotic codes, and territories" to evade detection and arrest. Depression-era nightlife, therefore, cut both ways culturally, offering glimpses of a liberated sexuality but also imposing cruel stereotypes and inviting official censorship. As it did in many other ways, the Depression increased violence and division in American culture and thus tended to make 1920s-style sexual adventurism very problematic.[45]

No real-life King Kongs wrought actual physical violence on Depression-era Manhattan and its nightlife, but culturally violent developments—economic predation, as well as the objectification of unclothed young women and the simultaneous vogue and repression of burlesque shows and homosexuals—reshaped Midtown's nightlife from 1929 to 1933. For nightclubs, economic conditions and the content of their entertainment had been significantly altered along lines that conformed to general reorientations in America during the Depression.

While most of nightlife in the 1920s had been swept away, Nils Granlund's successful high-volume, no-cover charge formula pointed the way to a post-Depression (and post-Prohibition) recovery for nightclubs. Like the New Deal, though, the future cultural terrain of nightlife would seek to salve the fears and stoke the hopes of average, heterosexual, and largely white "middle Americans," who sought honest, no-frills relief—in the form of makeshift government employment or an evening's entertainment—as an escape from fear and from drab, jobless daily existences. The business of nightlife somewhat contradictorily sought to stimulate in customers both the sexual adventurism of the 1920s and reassurances of familiarity and safety that were newly important in the 1930s.

Only as New York and the nation emerged from the worst of the economic crisis after 1933 did nightlife's new contours become apparent to observers and participants. In the meantime, the Depression also had caused a revolution in the city's political life. The toppling of Tammany Hall and Jimmy Walker by Samuel Seabury's investigations and Fiorello H. La Guardia's reform campaign created a new kind of civic life for New York City, an environment in which overt sexuality and nightlife evolved but also faced new forms of censure and regulation.

# CHAPTER 6
## "Where Fleshpots and Politics Together Meet"

The dancers that Nils Granlund paraded before customers at the Hollywood Restaurant were scarcely the only women to make headlines in New York City in the early 1930s. Among all kinds of women were Jean H. Norris, the first female judge in the city's history, who lost her position when her ethics were challenged; Vivian Gordon, a convicted prostitute who was murdered in the Bronx amid a scandal involving Tammany Hall; and Polly Adler, the notorious young head of a high-priced prostitution ring who was tied to powerful city leaders. Controversies surrounding these women helped to define the new links between nightclubs and civic life as the city worked its way up from the nadir of the Great Depression. All of these controversies were episodes in a general political scandal that toppled Tammany Hall and paved the way for a new reform-oriented municipal government. As Jimmy Walker fell from grace and Fiorello H. La Guardia saw his fortunes rise, women and men associated with nightlife gained new notoriety and celebrity.

From 1930 to 1932 the retired judge Samuel Seabury headed three separate state investigations of New York City's government. The first focused on alleged official misconduct by the city's magistrates or judges; the second investigated the city's district attorney; and the final inquiry explored graft and bribery among leading Tammany Hall officeholders, including Mayor Walker. Well before Walker resigned in disgrace in September 1932, Seabury's controversial and highly publicized efforts had discredited Tammany Hall and created a popular movement for extensive reform. It was a major turning point in the civic life of the city.

But what did the Seabury investigations have to do with the history of nightlife? This episode in New York City's history was chronicled by the press as sensationally as the latest Broadway scandals and in later decades it would be dramatized in a movie starring Bob Hope (*Beau James*) and a Broadway musical (*Fiorello!*). These treatments are somewhat misleading about the tone and the focus of the Seabury investigations. The connections between Seabury and nightlife were indirect at best, and in many cases they may be called tenuous or tangential. The vast majority of the work done by his team pertained to more prosaic financial and legal matters.

Nevertheless, the inquiries did explore, evaluate, and portray nightlife in a few revealing and significant ways. Like the Committee of Fourteen, Seabury's attorneys had to research and interpret modern mores and behavior to grasp the particulars of the street-level court and police cases with which they were working. The investigators thus probed the official treatment (and mistreatment) of working-class women and the nature of social interactions in nightlife (especially within the subset of Tammany Hall's clubhouses). In addition, Seabury probed the ties between nightlife and civic life in the era of Jimmy Walker. Seabury himself did not hesitate to exploit his own celebrity for political ends. Even his general lack of focus on nightlife (as well as on Prohibition and prostitution violations) may be considered significant. Like-minded reformers who supported Seabury had campaigned for decades for moral uplift in New York, but the judge expressed a strikingly libertarian opinion and modern tolerance for private experimentation, considering it much less of a threat to civic life than official malfeasance.

The Seabury inquiries directly inspired two new trends in city governance, which incidentally altered the official attitude toward clubs and related nightlife. First, while the early years of the Depression had witnessed the extreme objectification of women in entertainment, Seabury made the municipal government's often criminal abuse of innocent women—especially their framing on prostitution charges—into a major issue. The inquiry inspired more future protection for average city women than the Committee of Fourteen had been able to achieve in decades of work. Restrictions on police brutality had the further ironic effect of initiating a brief period of extreme freedom for prostitutes and other previously marginalized participants in nightlife. Manhattan in 1933 was said to have become a "wide-open town," and Seabury's witness Polly Adler became a minor celebrity. This development suggested, at least for a time, that the advent of "good government" would introduce a new libertarian standard to civic life.

Second, and more important, Seabury's investigations (and the difficulties of the Great Depression) turned enough voters away from Tammany Hall to ensure the victory of a reform "fusion" administration in November 1933. Seabury himself chose Fiorello La Guardia to be the leader of the fusion ticket. Far stronger than any other anti-Tammany mayoralty, La Guardia's administration attempted to reorient the entire moral thrust of government. This, in turn, altered the city's fundamental approach to leisure and "vice." In a kind of secular Reformation in New

York City, largely Protestant usurpers displaced a Catholic-dominated governing class. In the spirit of Luther or Calvin, though, La Guardia's team deserted Seabury's libertarianism and initiated a series of moralistic crusades that exceeded the ferocity of Walker's a decade earlier. The mayor's domineering personal style and strict moral code eventually produced a new kind of repression of nightlife. First, though, came the revolution.

In late 1928 the murder of Arnold Rothstein seemed to promise the exposure of the workings of underworld finance. A *New York Times* editor hoped that "New York will again be given a long view of that life which lurks in the shadows cast by the lights of Broadway. Since the Rosenthal murder [a celebrated case from 1912] the shadows have held their secrets. Now, with a mortally wounded man staggering into the light of a hotel entrance, the glare of publicity is thrown upon their precincts again."[1] The probe of Rothstein's finances uncovered little pertaining directly to nightclubs. The gambler's encrypted accounting books did reveal that he had invested millions in the narcotics trade, city buildings, suburban real estate, and union racketeering, but they indicated little about nightlife. The evidence most notably led federal prosecutors to redouble their efforts to use income tax records to trap underworld figures. The city's slipshod search for the killer and failed prosecution of one suspect cost the district attorney and the police commissioner their jobs. Grover Whalen's aggressive and punitive but grandstanding and amateurish eighteen-month tenure as commissioner followed. In 1929 the Rothstein affair inspired a spirited campaign for mayor by the Republican congressman Fiorello La Guardia. La Guardia's allegation that Rothstein had fostered corruption in city hall was met with considerable public apathy, though, and he lost to Jimmy Walker by half a million votes.

Within months, though, the Rothstein story began to create political headlines when his relationship with a magistrate was revealed. The city's fifty magistrates were the workhorses of the municipal court system. Sitting without juries, they handled lesser civil, criminal, and misdemeanor cases and presided over the night court and the special children's, family, traffic, and women's courts. One of the entries in Rothstein's account books indicated that the gambler had loaned twenty thousand dollars to the magistrate Albert H. Vitale. Demands during the 1929 campaign for a state investigation by La Guardia and the socialist mayoral candidate, Norman Thomas, gained fresh currency after the election, when a testimonial dinner for Vitale was interrupted by a spectacular hold-up that apparently had been planned by one of the suspected gangsters in attendance. The collapse of the stock market also revealed that many magistrates suffered losses to suspiciously weighty portfolios. In early 1930 journalists discovered that the money stolen during Vitale's testimonial had ended up in the judge's bank account. Growing public interest in the city's judges initiated what became a three-year-long general civic review of official morality. Acquiescing to demands by the Republican-run state senate in August (just before he faced reelection), Governor Franklin D. Roosevelt agreed to a limited investigation. After Samuel Seabury was appointed "referee," though, the inquiry was expanded to cover all magistrates (although it still did not have the power to indict any of them).[2]

Samuel Seabury came to this moment with rich experience in the city's politics, legal culture, and class structure. Politically he was unusual: an old-money, anti-Tammany, reformist New York City Democrat. He fit into none of the traditional Democratic factions, shunning Tammany Hall, its silk-hat allies, and their self-styled "populist" critic, the publisher William Randolph Hearst. Descended from two pioneering Episcopal bishops whose name he shared, the young Seabury simultaneously counseled well-heeled legal clients and supported Henry George's single-tax movement. After that movement faded he became a loyal but independent Democrat, winning a series of elective judgeships and reaching the state's highest appeals court at the age of forty. In 1916 Seabury cast his sights even higher, leaving the bench to run for governor. Losing a close and hard-fought race, Seabury quit politics, concentrated on his private practice, the city bar association, and the library in his home in the Hamptons, and took long European vacations.[3]

Seabury owed his initial appointment to public fascination with a provocative scandal that led the judiciary to be associated with the notoriety of Manhattan's nightlife. The case in question involved not a city magistrate but a state supreme court justice (in New York, a regional appeals court judge) named Joseph F. Crater. As Morris Markey noted in the *New Yorker*, for journalists "the Case of the Dubious Magistrates" had been "moving into half a dozen alleys that were encouraging, then doubtful, then palpably wrong" until Crater's disappearance riveted their attention. On 2 August Crater left his family's vacation in Maine for New York. He frantically removed documents from his office and asked his clerk to cash the latest in a series of mysterious and substantial checks. On 6 August Crater purchased a show ticket and dined at Haas's Restaurant on West 45th Street with the theatrical attorney William Klein, the nightclub dancer Sally Lou Ritzi, and her parents. After dinner he hailed a taxicab and was never seen again. The ensuing sensational headlines alleged countless sightings and ransom letters but few facts. It was discovered that Crater had a mistress, Connie Marcus, who was also missing. Markey speculated that the judge possessed at least "four rather sharply divided personalities." A jurist, professor, Tammany Hall stalwart, and family man, Crater also was "a fellow of the night clubs, good old Joe to a handful of pretty showgirls . . . in a mild emulation of Jimmy Walker." In the end, Markey argued, the judge had "foul[ed] himself astonishingly . . . running at last into a corner where fleshpots and politics together meet on common ground for his destruction."[4]

Such insinuations about Crater (who was never found)[5] helped give the city's judges' scandal enough public urgency to keep the state investigation in the limelight. Seabury revealed that some magistrates shared Crater's involvement in nightlife. Magistrate August Dreyer had been a Broadway theatrical attorney who had sought a judgeship after two actors' unions resolved their disputes and deprived Dreyer of his biggest case. Magistrate Amadeo Bertini had presided over the 1930 obscenity trial of Mae West's play *Pleasure Man*. Seabury accused Bertini of paying Tammany Hall one hundred thousand dollars for his position, a charge that led Roosevelt to push for his impeachment. (Bertini died before his case was considered.) Other middle-aged jurists, like Crater, had indulged in sexual as well as financial speculation. Magistrate Lewis Brodsky kept a hidden bank account in the name of his secretary, Kitty Carr, for whose mother he invested in mortgages. Sitting temporarily at the Women's Court, Jesse Silbermann dealt with two young female shoplifting defendants "arbitrarily," as Seabury put it; "with apparent bias [he] refused to hold [them] for trial." The magistrate, Seabury observed delicately, "was prompted by considerations outside the record." And in 1931 the Committee of Fourteen alleged to Seabury that Morris Goodman, a dance hall owner and known pimp, was a close associate and possible relation of Magistrate Henry Goodman, who had resigned earlier that month.[6]

Seabury shrewdly played up these headline-grabbing cultural elements. Although his efforts rarely broadcast a moralistic condemnation of modern leisure, they labeled the officials' indulgences in the "fleshpots" a serious threat to civic virtue. This was most evident in the case in which Seabury most directly connected modernity and gender with judicial behavior. Jean H. Norris had been appointed in 1919 as the first (and in 1930 still the only) female magistrate in the city's history. After the women of New York gained the vote, Tammany Hall appointed female co-leaders for each district; Norris, who ran the 10th District with the future Tammany boss George Olvany, was one of the few female leaders to gain a substantial city office. Like other magistrates Norris indulged in inside business deals, although her investment in a bail bond company that did business in her courtroom was particularly egregious.[7]

In addition, Seabury revealed that Norris, the most active judge on the

Women's Court, had regularly dealt out excessively harsh sentences for female defendants. In the more than five thousand cases that came before her bench—overwhelmingly related to prostitution and disproportionately involving African American defendants—Norris decreed guilty verdicts 40 percent more often than the other judges in Women's Court, and sentenced a much greater proportion of women to the workhouse. In the years when the Committee of Fourteen was encouraging the Women's Court to increase prostitution convictions, Norris clearly acted on their advice.[8]

The committee had found some evidence that vice officers had framed innocent women for prostitution. Now Seabury showed that many of these women were convicted in Jean Norris's court. A female accountant was arrested for prostitution after an officer entered her apartment and struck her. The woman was jailed, subjected to intrusive physical tests, and convicted by Norris, who dismissed the testimony of a defense witness—a black female custodian—in favor of the officer's version of events. (Another court later reversed the conviction.) In another case Norris refused to allow the testimony of five defense witnesses and later altered the court transcript to hide the fact. She erroneously ruled that a twenty-year-old woman was "a wayward minor" for living with her fiancé and violated procedure by sentencing the woman only two hours after her arrest. Norris convicted an alleged brothel keeper on the basis of a supposed police report that was phoned into her chambers by "some one at the office of the Committee of Fourteen"—an allegation that hurt the committee's image as much as Norris's.[9]

One of Norris's more obscure defendants was a fifteen-year-old resident of Harlem named Billie Holiday. In 1930 the young speakeasy singer was arrested for soliciting. Much later, in her autobiography *Lady Sings the Blues*, Holiday would blame her arrest on her accuser—a man named Blue whose advances she had resisted—and "some dirty grafting cop" (probably James Quinlivan or William O'Connor, vice officers in Harlem who soon became notorious). Her case was heard by Jean Norris, "a tough hard-faced old dame with hair bobbed almost like a man's . . . tougher than any judge I ever saw in pants before or since. If the girls had lawyers, they'd move heaven and earth to get their cases put off to some other judge." Lying about her age and defended by her mother, Holiday was given a relatively light sentence, four weeks' examination at a Brooklyn hospital. Nevertheless, as her memoirs show, the experience haunted Holiday for the rest of her life.[10]

Seabury attacked Norris's most symbolic transgression with particular zeal. A paragon of female advancement in the 1920s, Norris was willingly caught in the advertising net trolled by the Fleischmann's Yeast Company. Fleischmann's—the financial savior of the *New Yorker* in its first

months—was the major exponent of the print celebrity testimonial, publishing glowing endorsements by distinguished European physicians of
the health benefits of yeast. (The American Medical Association forbade
its members from appearing.) Judge Norris was paid one thousand dollars—twice the usual fee—for appearing in a magazine advertisement
for Fleischmann in which she claimed that yeast had cured "insomnia
caused by indigestion [which] threatened the impairment of the abun-
dant energy with which I have been blessed." In public testimony before
Seabury, Norris insisted that the endorsement "was not for my own
exploitation. I don't need any exploitation." But she also admitted that
"as I think of it now, I believe it was unethical." In his investigation
report Seabury singled out Norris's endorsement for scorn, arguing that
her posing in the ad "in judicial robes . . . discloses a willingness to
cheapen and vulgarize the judicial office and in my opinion, demonstrates a shocking lack of appreciation of the proprieties attaching to
judicial office."[11]

Jean Norris's case brought out Protestant prejudices against the Irish
Catholic brand of public morality that Tammany judges allegedly held,
a morality that blended leniency within the tribe with harsh condemnations of others' transgressions. For example, when Norris's counsel, Martin J. Conboy, argued that "Judge Seabury would have had Judge Norris
tell that girl [Miss Bodmer] to go back to her life of sin," Seabury
attacked Conboy's "most virtuous attitude," inferring that Tammany
Hall would break the law to enforce a rigid sexual morality. Protestants
like Walter Chambers, a journalist who wrote a biography of Seabury,
portrayed Norris as an Irish American woman with unwarranted pretensions and ambitions. He mocked her "frequent use of an obviously
acquired Oxonian accent," the fact that "twice in her excitement she
slipped back into her native language [sic]," and her "grand hauteur of
manner . . . dressed in a green sport ensemble . . ." Like Billie Holiday,
Chambers mocked Norris's alleged mannishness; removed from her
post by the appellate court, she "looked as if she was about to faint, but
recovered herself. Even then she could not obtain relief in womanly
tears." (Reformers also portrayed Tammany politicians as physically grotesque. Norman Thomas and Paul Blanshard described state senator
Louis Cuvillier as "an aged gargoyle," while Walter Chambers noted
state senator John McNaboe's "vain, pathetic attempts to display a
deplorably missing greatness.")[12]

Such sniping showed how the pervasive gendering of city life in the
1920s (which had been influenced strongly by the new nightlife) shaped
the language used by journalists and anti-Tammany Hall reformers.
Samuel Seabury, for his part, used Norris's misbehavior on the bench to
broadcast a thesis about working-class women in New York that differed

from the analysis of the Committee of Fourteen. In his evolving view, injustice in the streets and the courts—not nightclubs and prostitution—posed the greatest threat to the safety of the city's women. If Walter Chambers is to be believed, Seabury became the unlikely champion of some young women in the city. After one morning hearing Seabury left the courthouse and was greeted by a "crowd of several hundred young girls, out at lunchtime from nearby office buildings, [who] burst forth in a salvo of cheering. He stopped short in annoyed amazement. Quickly he assumed the impassive dignity of the judge and entered his car. The girls pushed and jammed about it as though he were a Lindbergh."[13] Despite his professed abhorrence of Norris's appearance in a yeast ad, Seabury probably perceived the advantages of his own celebrity.

The retired judge blended crafty investigative methods with a studied advocacy of what he considered the purest civic rectitude. Seabury's surface loftiness hid a Tammany-style adeptness at exploiting personal relationships. Individuals with grudges against various magistrates—particularly journalists—supplied many leads. Even Joseph Corrigan, Tammany's chief city magistrate, "quietly slipped a great deal of evidence" to Seabury that embarrassed his own judges. Other Tammany loyalists, though, argued that Seabury's zeal resulted in extreme violations of personal privacy. His staff pored over the financial records of dozens of jurists and took hundreds of depositions before calling witnesses in public. When speaking in these hearings, Seabury shrewdly played up his sober dedication to justice and truth and manipulated witnesses such as Jean Norris in ways that made them exude evasiveness, untrustworthiness, or, at the very least, Irishness on the stand. Seabury honed in on what later would be called "double talk"—witnesses' self-serving twisting of words and use of half-truths—and presented himself as the tribune of open, clean public discourse. A staff member quoted Seabury as saying, "It is only by humanizing this Inquiry that we can translate our findings into a language the great mass of the people can understand. The public will not be aroused [by] graphs, charts and reports. We must divorce it as far as possible from legalistic machinery."[14]

Seabury's approach had its liabilities as well, mostly rooted in the unyielding self-righteousness he projected. His moralistic approach often led him to dwell upon the shortcomings of personalities he deemed inferior to his own. The New York State official Frances Perkins, who was not a Tammany regular, considered Seabury's "the most arrogant face I ever saw . . . very disdainful," while the attorney Jonah Goldstein (then in Tammany Hall, later a Republican) found "Saint Seabury" to be an aloof know-it-all: "I know of no philanthropic social service agency that Seabury ever did any service for or gave any real money to."[15] Despite his loyalty to the Democratic Party, Seabury's impartiality certainly was diminished by a lifetime of hostility toward Tammany Hall.

The results of the first Seabury inquiry were mixed. Jean Norris was not indicted for her business dealings and sentencing irregularities, but the state courts' appellate division did vote to remove her from the bench. Other judges were indicted and tried in state court, with uneven results. One feigned insanity during his trial but was convicted. Others avoided conviction or won acquittal on appeal. Magistrate Lewis Brodsky, who among his many misdeeds had acquitted gamblers who frequented the clubhouse of his Tammany mentor, was acquitted of ethical violations by a panel of appellate judges. Brodsky's fate led Seabury to sputter in his final report, "is it consistent with the standards to which a judge must conform for him to be actively and constantly involved in heavy speculation in the stock market upon the hazard of a flimsy margin. . . . [or if] he becomes continually and deeply involved in extra-judicial activities for personal gain, necessitating the constant borrowing of money from numerous sources and the frequent kiting of checks . . . ?"[16] What Seabury did accomplish, though, was to stir public interest in possible further corruption in the municipal government, which he would be asked to investigate as well. No small part of the public's interest derived from Seabury's linking of magistrates' financial corruption with glimpses of their personal indiscretions in their leisure hours, especially in nightlife, and of the official mistreatment of working-class women. The retired judge would continue to mine these threads of cultural excavation in the months ahead.

As 1930 gave way to 1931, Seabury touched the rawest public nerves with his revelations about the treatment of women beyond the magistrates' courts, in wider fields of law enforcement. In the 1920s the investigation and regulation of nightlife made the fate of the "new woman" in the city a perceived major problem, a barometer of the moral health of the metropolis. Seabury's public hearings revealed that judges' sexual indiscretions were only a small indicator of the general exploitation of women by city government. Now, for a few months, Seabury and the city focused on defining this exploitation and considering the civic remedies that were needed. Along with other emerging scandals and the suffering caused by the Depression, the treatment of women encouraged New Yorkers to consider important changes in their civic life and government.[17]

Seabury's most disturbing revelations concerned a group of vice squad officers, lawyers, and bail bondsmen in the Women's Court who systematically framed hundreds of innocent women on prostitution charges. The inquiry uncovered the ring accidentally by exposing a participant who had been encouraged, albeit unknowingly, by the Committee of Fourteen. In 1928 John C. Weston, an assistant district attorney who was dismayed with the slow pace of prostitution convictions in the Women's Court, began to write weekly reports to the committee and to supply leads to its investigators. When Seabury called Weston as a minor witness, he discovered that Weston's savings account showed a balance of over $93,000. Weston eventually confessed that more than $20,000 of it derived from "gratuities" paid to him by defense lawyers in the Women's Court.[18]

The Women's Court was an early brainchild of the Committee of Fourteen, created in 1910 as a component of the Night Court to deal especially with the prostitution caseload. The court was based in Brooklyn, but its Manhattan branch was located on West 10th Street across the street from the old Jefferson Market building, "a dingy castellated pile of red brick" that housed offices for small-time lawyers and bail bondsmen. In 1926 some of the officers of the court began systematically to frame women on prostitution charges. Since the city's legal assistance program did not function effectively, defendants were usually at the mercy of the lawyers and bondsmen of Jefferson Market. Already in 1927 the Committee of Fourteen had received reports of "fixers, runners, professional and shyster lawyers" preying on defendants and had noted that "there is nothing more despicable on God's earth than the men of this type who hang out in the courts."[19]

The complicity of police officers in the framing ring was exposed by Seabury in 1930. As one of his lawyers described it, vice squad officers created the cases themselves. In a typical situation, the officers began by locating a woman with means and a reputation to protect. They then enlisted a male "stool pigeon" to lure the victim to a hotel room. After he entered the room with the woman, the man planted marked currency at a predetermined spot. Policemen then burst in and questioned the man. Officers "discovered" the currency, pretended to eject the man by force (he was not subject to arrest), and took the woman to the police station for booking. Bail was set at five hundred dollars. A bondsman pretending to be in the station by chance then offered to take her case. He obtained the keys to her home, retrieved her bankbook, and attached himself to her account. He posted bail for the stunned woman, who was then released. A few days later, before the trial, the bondsman introduced the woman to a lawyer. The attorney instructed her to plead not guilty. At the trial, if the woman's account held enough money to pay everyone's fees, the lawyer whispered to a complicit prosecutor, "This one is O.K." An officer testified that no incriminating evidence existed after all; the prosecutor moved for dismissal, and the swindled woman was set free. If the defendant could not pay the fees, the officer testified to her guilt and she would be sentenced—usually for sixty days—to the Welfare Island jail.[20]

Racketeers made enormous sums by splitting the fees from these framing cases. Over the years some vice officers made as much as $88,000. The prosecutor John Weston admitted to taking about six hundred bribes involving nine hundred framed defendants. A quarter of the framing cases were heard in the courtroom of Magistrate Jesse Silbermann. Ironically, it was Silbermann who had devised the "green sheet" that officers were to fill out during prostitution arrests to ensure accuracy. Defense lawyers involved in the ring in Silbermann's court included Abraham Karp, who derived much of his clientele from "a cabaret in Harlem." Karp on occasion had represented Polly Adler, the elusive madam sought by the Committee of Fourteen, who managed to avoid being framed. Evidence of a similar framing ring (connected with other graft) in the Brooklyn Women's Court also emerged.[21]

The exposure of the framing ring in early 1931 produced a sensation. Seabury's associate William Northrop stammered, "Incredible—unbelievable!—but it happened day after day, week after week, and year after year, in the Women's Court of Manhattan." The socialists Norman Thomas and Paul Blanshard proclaimed it "the most hideous thing in the whole history of New York." They laid the blame on the city's culture and institutions. While "in small towns" defendants had friends who would put up their own property as collateral to ensure that the former would not leave town, bail bonds had thrived "partly because New York is so large and impersonal." Completely unregulated by government, even typically reputable bail bondsmen were "extortionists pure and simple." Thomas and Blanshard's contemporary analysis might be challenged or supplemented—official criminality certainly had complex origins—but it illustrates the radical analysis and search for remedies that the scandal inspired.[22]

The stool pigeons themselves became valuable witnesses for Seabury, as well as minor celebrities in the press. Chile Mapocha Acuna was the first and most notable of these informers. As a waiter at Reuben's restaurant, Acuna began feeding policemen information on alleged Spanish-speaking lawbreakers, for which he was paid fifty dollars per lead. (This was an established practice on police beats.) In 1929 Acuna began working with officers in the Harlem framing ring, and he became a skilled "unknown man," the stool pigeon whose statements at the time of a woman's arrest guaranteed a conviction. Officers encouraged him to be an active seducer, pressing women for sex and virtually dragging them to hotel rooms. His every move and his every word in the room were carefully rehearsed. In each instance Acuna quickly removed an article of the woman's clothing and identified a physical characteristic that officers might later mention in their incriminating testimony. Acuna elided his identity as a crime-fighting informant with his role as a seducer of women, using his waiter's skills at manipulative servility and conforming to the stereotype of the sexually predatory Hispanic male. However, Acuna sometimes told officers on the spot that particular women were not prostitutes, which indicated that he may never have been aware that the operation was dedicated to the framing of *innocent* women. Testifying in one case in 1929, Acuna abandoned his planned testimony and accused the police of framing the defendant. He was indicted for perjury and convicted; after his release from prison a year later he was eager to testify for Samuel Seabury.

Seabury was unstinting in his praise for Acuna, calling him "a witness without parallel in the history of American jurisprudence." Showing "unquestioned . . . courage" at one hearing, Acuna correctly pointed out and named all but one of twenty-eight allegedly corrupt officers present in the hearing room. Lawyers for the officers, with apparent official assistance, launched a campaign to discredit Acuna, producing individuals who called him a pimp and a brothel keeper. Dozens of witnesses who were needed to corroborate many of Acuna's charges—especially the victimized women themselves—avoided subpoenas and fled the city. Other well-known stool pigeons, such as Harry Levey, also vanished. Forty witnesses in the magistrates' hearings also had left town by early February.[23]

The press made Acuna the subject of ridicule, defining him according to derogatory Hispanic stereotypes. Tabloid papers caricatured him as a predatory Latin lover and conniving service worker: "Chile Acuna, the human spitoona." They mocked the incongruity of such a man meriting an expensive round-the-clock armed guard and a secret hideaway. Later, when Acuna himself sold his story to two tabloids, rival newspapers scorned the deal in false indignation. Other Hispanic informants who surfaced—men called Angelo Chicko, Pinto, and Calleginto—were also portrayed according to stereotype. Even Seabury's biographer, Walter Chambers, wrote that a "Latin desire for vengeance" moved Acuna to testify.[24]

Fortunately for Acuna, stool pigeons who were not Latin American, such as Harry Levey, Meyer Slutzky, Eddy Mack, and "Harry the Greek," soon eclipsed him in notoriety. After Levey was captured in New Orleans in January 1931, he displaced Chile Acuna as Seabury's most useful witness. Levey charged that the Harlem vice officer James Quinlivan paid him $750 to leave New York, and that Quinlivan and William O'Connor had collected thousands of dollars in protection money from owners of speakeasies.[25]

Seabury's handling of Acuna especially demonstrated his skill at what he called "humanizing this inquiry" by giving victims a carefully prepared public platform. "There is more eloquence in the testimony of an illiterate witness telling of oppression suffered through abuse of legal process," he argued, "than in the greatest sermon or editorial or address ever written." Vulnerable figures, speakeasy owners as well as young women, had paid dearly for their "protection" by police officers, lawyers, and bail bondsmen. The judge ignored Prohibition and prostitution laws and welcomed all victims of official corruption who were willing to talk. In one month alone he signed over twelve hundred subpoenas.[26] The stories of these victims, championed by the more liberal New York dailies, brought new voices to the civic discourse.

The inquiry especially revealed an urban geography of female suffering and exploitation. Female boarding-house operators were highly vulnerable to framing. One such landlady, a French immigrant named Mina Landry, was convicted of keeping a brothel in the court of Jean Norris and sent to the state reformatory for one hundred days. Boarders in her lodge told Seabury that her male clerk was actually the individual guilty of procuring prostitutes, and that he had worked with a police officer to frame Landry of the charge.[27] Another woman was indicted for brothel keeping; although she was acquitted, her bank account was virtually emptied by her bail bondsman. A third woman who was similarly swindled by a "fixer" failed to regain her funds after spending seven weeks in a city correctional hospital and six months on probation.[28] Male acquaintances often recommended victims to the framers, who let the men in on the proceeds. In one case the elevator operator in a woman's building lied under oath to help convict an innocent woman of prostitution. The framers' frequent ineptitude did not stop the injustices from occurring. In one arrest situation Chile Acuna, playing the john, realized that he had forgotten to plant currency on the premises. The police officers forced the woman to plead guilty anyway, and on the strength of that "confession" she was sentenced in court to ten months in a Catholic halfway institution. (The woman later was pardoned by the governor, but by then a private detective had paid her to leave the state.)[29]

The violent abuse of framed women by police shocked New Yorkers the most. No other issue gave Seabury's argument for reform more emotional urgency. A police officer named Brady had broken the arm of a woman arrested for alleged vagrancy. Brady was indicted for this offense. The most lurid case was that of Genevieve Potocki, whose story highlighted the link between framing for prostitution and speakeasy protection money. Seabury and his supporters portrayed Potocki as a respectable woman, a single mother who worked as a waitress to support her two daughters, but she also sold liquor out of her home. One evening two plainclothes vice officers burst in and assaulted Potocki and a female friend, demanding five hundred dollars in protection money. The officers' beatings left the two women with bleeding cuts and contusions, but in the holding cell they received no medical attention. The charges against them were dismissed, but the officers were not disciplined. After they were questioned by Seabury, they notoriously danced a jig outside the courthouse. Newspapers labeled them "the Smirking Cops."[30]

The parade of mistreated women revealed the framers' exploitation of nightlife venues. Dance studios, especially those in private apartments, were vulnerable. Nina Artska, whom Seabury's lawyers called "eminently respectable," ran a legitimate ballroom dance studio on West 84th Street. A new male student turned out to be a stool pigeon. During his lesson two detectives burst in and arrested Artska and her sister. At the police station they were forced to pay a corrupt attorney one hundred dollars to gain an acquittal; John Weston received the twenty-five dollar prosecutor's fee.[31] Less "respectable" female performers than Artska were less publicized by Seabury, but they were even more vulnerable to mistreatment. One case involved the framing of two female nightclub employees, Rose Davis and Marion Godfrey. In a twist, two patrolmen were the stool pigeons, luring Davis and Godfrey from the club to a hotel room, where a third officer arrested them. Harry Levey's testimony showed that the framing of nightclub hostesses in particular—especially in Harlem—grew out of police officers' practice of extorting protection money from clubowners. The "hostess speakeasy," highly publicized by the Committee of Fourteen as a likely site of prostitution, was also a venue where framing victims were identified and pursued. Masseuses—also often investigated by the committee—were framing targets as well, including Sigrid Johnson, the first framed woman to testify in public for Seabury. Johnson lost eight hundred dollars in fees paid to lawyers and bondsmen, who simply advised her to feign illness in court to gain an adjournment.[32]

As 1930 ended and 1931 began, more revelations regarding the official mistreatment of young women followed in the wake of the prostitution framing scandal. In January the city took notice of the particular mistreatment of minor females in the Women's Court. A pattern of sentencing irregularities had emerged. Women under the age of eighteen were not convicted of crimes but were committed to a state reformatory in Bedford Hills, in Westchester County, for "medical" and "educational" reform. Seabury revealed that since 1926 dozens of young city women had been sent to Bedford by the Women's Court because magistrates had illegally scrawled on their dockets "guilty by reason of confession." As Seabury noted, "competent evidence" was also required for a conviction. H. Stanley Renaud, Jesse Silbermann, and Jean Norris had sentenced most of the defendants. Fifty-five of the seventy-seven women in question insisted that they had never confessed. Fifty of the seventy-seven women still languished in Bedford; some of them had been there for more than three years. These fifty women (who lived there with thirty-eight of their infant children) constituted one-seventh of the facility's total population. Many of the other convicted women were still on parole. Most of them were of Italian, Jewish, or Irish ethnicity, and African Americans made up one-sixth of the total. Seabury soon found more women in Bedford who had been improperly convicted.[33]

Securing the release of the seventy-one minors in question—a task for state officials, not for Seabury—proved to be politically difficult. Mayor Walker expressed his "obvious concern," met with city officials and the Committee of Fourteen's George Worthington, and sent the chief magistrate, Joseph Corrigan, to Bedford to investigate. In his report, though, the widely respected Corrigan apparently bowed to pressure from Tammany Hall. None of the women had been framed, he insisted. The confessions involved mere "technical errors," and "not one of the girls had any complaint to make as to the manner of their commitment." Seabury scolded Corrigan and Walker, and two days later the state ordered the transfer of forty-eight women from Bedford to institutions in the city. Journalists observed the transfer closely and indulged in some amateur sociology. The New York Daily News called the women "rather shabby little heroines, these girls of sixteen or seventeen, who know only the seamy side of life in a great city. One or two of them carry themselves with a defiant swagger, the belts of their 'mannish' coats pulled tightly about their waists, their collars turned nonchalantly up, their berets at a dashing angle." The Times noted that on the bus some of them sang "Hurray, Hurray, We're Going to Get Out." The Daily News, however, found them "stolid . . . their placid faces show that they have accepted without question everything that an unfeeling fate has dropped upon them in the way of a life."[34]

Thirty-seven of the forty-eight women were bused to detention, while the other eleven, who were mothers with a total of eighteen infants, were assigned to religious institutions. The city then made a deal with the state and sent all but one of them back to Bedford (see Fig. 6). The remaining woman, Anna Peltz, became the lead case in the appellate court. In April the court ordered a new trial for Peltz, which resulted in her acquittal and the eventual freedom of the other women.[35]

While Seabury and other reformers castigated the city and the courts for their behavior, others betrayed a moralistic and cynical attitude

Figure 6. Women with infant children being transferred from New York City to a state reformatory in January 1931. They were among dozens who had been unjustly convicted as minors in the city's Women's Court. The scandal, one of many exposed by Samuel Seabury, shed light on the treatment of working-class women in the nightclub era. *New York Daily News* Photo Archive.

toward the inmates' predicament. A *New York Times* reader, I. Montefiore Levy, characterized the framing and unjust sentencing of young women as an unavoidable pitfall of urban life. Levy quoted Emile Zola's *Nana* on the similar abuse of prostitutes in Paris in the 1800s: "[Police] laid hold of everybody, and greeted you with a slap if you shouted, for they were sure of being defended in their acts and rewarded, even when they had taken a virtuous girl among the rest." "In light of this quotation," Levy concluded, "is it fair to charge the abhorrent practices to a political party? Are not these the evils of individuals? . . . Here is a problem and a condition that are older than any man or party. They have defied solution since government existed."[36] Such complacency, in league with the tabloids' exploitation of the women and their circumstances, reflected the brand of sexism that had shaped the image of the hostess and chorus dancer in the new nightlife. It was an attitude that created serious obstacles for reformers such as Samuel Seabury, who sought to make the accountability of officials (not the alleged moral threat of sexually mature young women) the top public priority.

Seabury's campaign soon gave rise to another scandal mixing female exploitation, violence, prostitution, and official malfeasance. In February 1931 the judge questioned a woman named Vivian Gordon. In 1928 Gordon had been arrested for prostitution, for which she served a sentence at Bedford. She insisted that a police officer had framed her. Because Gordon had a considerable police record dating back to 1923, Seabury did not publicize her story. On 26 February Gordon was found, strangled to death, in a park in the Bronx. The police followed various leads and eventually located her diaries, which recorded her "fear" of certain men. The men were questioned but not charged. Sensational press coverage, labeling Gordon a prostitute, apparently led her sixteen-year-old daughter to commit suicide. Seabury considered Gordon's murder an attempt to intimidate him. The officer who had arrested her in 1928 denied involvement, but his large bank account came under scrutiny, Seabury exposed his role in the framing ring, and he was suspended. The police eventually arrested a career thief who was found to possess Gordon's fur coat, but he was acquitted of the murder, which was never solved.[37]

A sensational revelation of the Gordon case was the listing of the madam Polly Adler in the victim's address book. In the late 1920s Adler had defined the limits of the Committee of Fourteen's investigative powers; no detective's budget was large enough to obtain entry into her elite "call house." For Seabury also the madam was something of a lodestar, the ultimate notorious witness who might possess information on corruption at the highest levels. Adler had been arrested and brought to the Women's Court eleven times—only twice under her real name—and had never been convicted. She appeared to be immune from the framing racket, and John Weston alleged that the madam had considerable influence with the magistrates.[38] The Gordon murder and Adler's apparent connection to the victim led Seabury to theorize that Adler's testimony might tie up many loose ends and implicate her protectors, who were highly placed in Tammany Hall and the underworld, in a network of illegal activity. Adler eluded him, however, hiding in Florida for four months. Seabury revealingly enlisted the talents of a tabloid newspaper, the *New York Mirror*, which he later claimed was "instrumental in locating" Adler. Her sometime lover, a vice squad patrolman, encouraged her to return and take her chances with Seabury.[39]

In what proved to be the Seabury investigations' final detour through nightlife, Adler proved to be little help. Two of the judge's aides served Adler a subpoena at her West 69th Street residence. The madam offered them coffee, and her friend the vice officer helped them leave on the fire escape, to avoid the press. As Adler later recalled, though, she was aware that Seabury and the tabloid press remained in league, and she likened the penetrating gaze of Irving Ben Cooper, Seabury's tough inquisitor, to the exploding flashbulbs of photographers outside her building.[40] Adler perjured herself repeatedly, denying any involvement in prostitution or with city officials. She later argued in her memoirs that unlike the working-class women who were framed, her obvious guilt made her vulnerable to long-term blackmail. For years after, she claimed, her Tammany Hall lawyer extorted money from her as a sort of amortized payment for his services. By keeping silent before Seabury, though, Adler also maintained her reputation for total discretion— which was essential to her business—and preserved the basic assets of her floating elite brothel until a future time when the press and the law lost interest in her. The tactic succeeded with Seabury. Adler's listing in Vivian Gordon's address book became a dead end. She denied knowing Gordon, telling a reporter that she was "just another attractive woman out to feather her own nest."[41]

John Weston's allegations against Adler did not lead to further charges against any magistrates. Weston testified that he had split fees with Adler's defense attorneys in cases that appeared in the courtrooms of two judges. In one of these cases, Weston testified, he "laid down" for an acquittal. As he later testified at the disbarment trial of defense attorneys of the Women's Court, Weston had been "afraid of [Adler's] influence" in city government, and feared "more than" firing if he brought up her past arrest record. But Weston could not shed any more light on Adler's alleged influence. Seabury probed Adler's bank and brokerage accounts, which showed that she had made sizeable investments, as well as regular withdrawals that suggested payoffs to police officers and city officials. In questioning Adler, Irving Ben Cooper encouraged her to implicate "these framing cops" who demanded protection money from her, but she refused. She denied that she and her friend, the vice officer, were aware of each other's occupations. Seabury and Cooper eventually decided that Adler was of little use as a public witness, and she was quietly dismissed. The vice officer was stripped of his police badge and tried for graft, but he was acquitted; his was the only trial resulting from Adler's testimony. In late 1931 Seabury received a final rebuke in the Adler case when the judge's own bailiwick, the city bar association, found the attorney who represented Adler in the Women's Court—and eleven others—innocent of malpractice.[42]

In the spring of 1931 this flurry of scandals produced notable changes in the streets of New York. Intense negative publicity caused the police to restrict their usual vice policing. It was reported that there had been a "sharp decline in vice arrests" owing to the reassignment of vice squad members and the procedural elimination of the "unknown man's" testimony as admissible evidence. Adler herself rejoiced that "the Seabury investigation turned New York into a wide-open town. . . . The lawbreakers had a holiday, and proceeded to make the most of it." No longer could "a policeman's unsupported word be enough to damn a prostitute. . . . There was no more kowtowing to double-crossing Vice Squad men, no more hundred-dollar handshakes, no more phony raids to up the month's quota. . . . Thanks to Judge Seabury, . . . I was able to operate for three years without breaking a lease." The maverick police captain Lewis J. Valentine, while a supporter of Seabury's, agreed: "Things were so bad that policemen couldn't touch vice. They were afraid they'd be charged with framing. They wouldn't take assignments to vice duty. The town became overrun with vicious women. They flocked from other cities here."[43] Seabury had no interest in encouraging sexual license, but this development showed an unavoidable consequence of his effort to dismantle traditional moral policing—a dismantling that a future reform administration would work to reverse.

Seabury proposed structural reforms in his final report on the courts, such as the appointment of city magistrates by state judges rather than by the mayor, the combining of the Women's Court with the other special courts, the strict regulation of bondsmen and defense attorneys, mandatory "competent counsel" for defendants, and other measures.[44] The report also offered a mountain of data on the workings of law enforcement and justice in the city. Again, though, Seabury's hopes for widespread prosecutions and convictions were disappointed. Forty vice policemen, twenty-three lawyers, and thirty-eight bail bondsmen were implicated in the framing ring or in associated corruption and were tried in court. Some officers were punished. The two men who beat Genevieve Potocki were sent to Sing Sing prison; James Quinlivan was convicted of income tax evasion; and Sidney Tait was convicted of perjury related to the framing of a woman from Harlem. However, other trials and reviews failed to produce results. The first trial of an officer involved in framing activities ended in acquittal, and Quinlivan's partner was exonerated as well. To Seabury's disgust many accused officers evaded sanction by attributing their swelled bank accounts to family generosity. Most of the lawyers in the framing ring avoided disbarment.[45]

In addition, Seabury had become convinced that Tammany Hall was actively hindering his investigation. The defense attorney for one of the framing officers, who did not even bother to offer a closing argument at the trial, happened also to be Mayor Walker's personal counsel. Walker himself had proven to be obstructive. In 1930 the mayor had joined the Tammany leader John F. Curry in criticizing Seabury's demand that magistrates and others waive their immunity from prosecution. The next year Walker insisted that the magistrates' inquiry was unconstitutional, and he refused to pay the salaries of Seabury's lawyers. The city soon relented, but when a Tammany state assemblyman was among the first fourteen lawyers to be accused by John Weston of bribery, the Tammany district attorney quickly indicted Seabury's own chief counsel, Isidore Kresel, on embezzlement charges (related to the failure of the Bank of the United States, where Kresel had been a director). Kresel was forced to resign. With regard to protection money paid by speakeasies to officers, Seabury suspected that "the police were merely serving as collectors for others higher up." Accused officers meanwhile must have been encouraged by Mayor Walker's assertion that only "a few" policemen in the city "had faltered."[46]

This seemingly coordinated municipal effort to obstruct the investigation and prosecution of misdeeds of Tammany members led good-government reformers to beat the drum for another investigation by Seabury. Now, it seemed to them, was the moment to call for a revolutionary change in New York's civic life. The City Affairs Committee especially sounded the call, holding public meetings and publishing scathing and detailed pamphlets attacking the Walker administration. The liberal reform coalition's best-known members included the Socialists Norman Thomas and Paul Blanshard, John Dewey, the newspaper columnist Heywood Broun (also a Socialist), Rabbi Stephen Wise, and the veteran civil rights activist the Reverend John Haynes Holmes. The City Affairs Committee's high-minded crusade tended to emphasize personal morality more than the rather libertarian Seabury, as it conflated Tammany Hall with the small-time venality it perceived in Broadway's nightlife. Holmes, the personification of liberal eloquence, castigated Tammany Hall at a public meeting as an "unspeakable crowd of political gangsters, who have slain and robbed and burglarized in this city for decades upon decades," and he urged that they "be banished forever from the company of honorable men." Scorning the "politicians, the social vulgarians, the speakeasy gangsters and Tammany Hall racketeers" who ran the city, Holmes wished Walker to pursue jobs "to which he is properly adapted, the jobs that are to be found in the night clubs and the speakeasies of this city." (Following Holmes at the lectern, Broun dissented in part, noting that "I have been to just as many night clubs as Jimmy Walker; just as many speakeasies, and . . . I intend to keep up with that particular phase of his life.")[47]

With encouragement from the City Affairs Committee and other reform groups, anti-Tammany Hall legislators and officials in Albany broadened Seabury's mandate and put him in charge of two more investigations. The governor appointed him "commissioner" in charge of an investigation of the city's district attorney, Thomas C. T. Crain, while the legislature named him "counsel" to a committee, led by the state sena-

tor Samuel Hofstadter, that would investigate the entire city government.

Seabury concluded that Crain, who was alleged to have stalled a probe
of racketeering in the seafood business, should stay on the job. His investigation of city hall lasted longer, though, and it shook the political foundations of New York. On its face this effort, like the previous ones,
seemed to suffer from serious limitations. Seabury again had no power
to indict, and state and federal prosecutors proved hesitant to act. The
Depression remained a more pressing public concern; as Norman
Thomas put it, "Why indeed bother about civic reform when the question is: When do I eat?" In the end the governor removed only one person from office, and only one other was indicted—and acquitted. An
effort by the Internal Revenue Service to uncover tax irregularities
among officials also led nowhere.[48]

Nevertheless, utilizing his proven methods, Seabury uncovered dozens of illicit financial relationships between Tammany leaders and businesses. In public testimony the bosses gave homely explanations of their
enormous bank accounts—alluding to family generosity and "magic tin
boxes"—which gained wide ridicule and helped make the investigation
a potent political force. Seabury also revealed widespread corruption on
city commissions, where "expert" witnesses and fixers split sizeable fees
with Tammany appointees to gain permits and licenses for their friends.
Tammany members of the building, education, zoning, and transportation commissions were accused of having taken bribes. Party leaders in
the five boroughs were found to hold large sums in their bank accounts,
and further evidence of police officers' graft was also uncovered.[49]

This investigation also made public for the first time the full story of
gambling in Tammany clubhouses in the mid-1920s. In testimony before
Seabury the police captain Lewis Valentine, the former head of the Confidential Squad, and his erstwhile assistant, Ezekiel Keller, described
Tammany's heavy involvement in illegal gambling. The Tammany official Thomas Farley corroborated Valentine's story, testifying that it was
the custom for "executive members of the Democratic Party, where
there are arrests in the official club house of executive members of those
club houses, to bail out anyone who is arrested in there with other members of the club." Seabury was also able to show that the clubhouse
arrangements were a model for more widespread collusion between
legitimate developers and creditors, underworld gamblers, and bribable
city permit and zoning boards under the Tammany regime, deal making
that characterized the city's political economy in the 1920s.[50] These
incriminating linkages prompted Seabury to explore relationships that
led directly into the mayor's office.

New York newspapers were not known for their investigative reporting. As Norman Thomas noted, city hall reporters were "routinists rather than crusaders," who tended merely to reprint Mayor Jimmy Walker's witticisms. Even well-informed news readers, Paul Blanshard lamented, mimicked the "superior semi-satiric intelligent outlook of the editorial paragraphs of the *New Yorker*"; they "listen to a preacher or a reformer denounce Mayor Walker once in a while, and then . . . turn over to the sporting page." In early 1932, though, the *World Telegram* began reporting on the mysterious sources of the mayor's apparently limitless expense money.[51] Seabury then moved in, exposing a link between the awarding of city transportation franchises and money paid to Walker by one bidder. Businessmen, it was found, set up lavish lines of credit for the mayor, helped him to make lucrative investments, and even filled a bank account with more than seven hundred thousand dollars to cover his living and travel expenses. Seabury laid the groundwork at hearings of the Hofstadter Committee, where partisan arguments grew heated as Tammany members blamed Communists for many of the attacks on the mayor. Then, on 25 and 26 May, Seabury confronted the mayor himself in a climactic hearing, in which two master political showmen did their best to unnerve each other.[52]

Seabury's overwhelming evidence, as well as the city's near bankruptcy in the wake of the Depression, began to erode Walker's last line of defense, his political popularity. In the summer of 1932, though, the mayor's fate was held in suspense by the surreal maneuverings of Democratic presidential politics. Franklin D. Roosevelt was fighting off a number of rivals, including his bitter former ally Alfred E. Smith. (Jimmy Walker attended the convention in Chicago as a Smith delegate.) Samuel Seabury, meanwhile, succumbed to ambition and allowed admirers to promote him quietly as a dark-horse candidate. Walter Chambers wrote a hagiographic campaign biography. Roosevelt testily commented in a letter that "this fellow Seabury is merely trying to perpetrate another political play to embarrass me. His conduct has been a deep disappointment to people who honestly seek better government in New York City by stressing the fundamentals and eliminating political innuendoes."[53] Seabury posed no serious threat to Roosevelt, however.

With the nomination in hand Roosevelt—who as governor had the power to remove mayors—finally invited Walker and Seabury to Albany to hear their versions of the story. Roosevelt was prepared to remove Walker from office, but on 1 September, before the governor could act, the mayor announced his resignation. Walker and his mistress Betty Compton then departed on a cruise for Europe, where he waited in vain for a call from Tammany Hall to run for vindication in the special mayoral election to be held that November.[54]

The celebrated showdown between Seabury and Walker, played out across three years during desperate economic times, provided the political discourse in which New Yorkers contextualized social and cultural change. According to this context, the Tammany regime was giving way to reform. Political historians have echoed this interpretation ever since.

The social and cultural histories of this era of political turmoil, though, reveal many other facets. Seabury's inquiries largely did not concern nightlife, but his investigations, especially his first one, brought the treatment of women, the policing of "vice," and the place of prostitution in city life into new public perspective. Like popular trends in nightlife in the early 1930s, such as stock burlesque, transvestite shows, and high-volume, low-cost nightclub shows, Seabury's effort (through its very example) made interactions between the sexes in nightlife a cause for analysis and reform. Although by 1932 financial scandals and the issue of relief from the Depression had clearly overshadowed these social concerns, the impact of Seabury's early revelations about the official treatment of working-class women remained, and they would influence Fiorello H. La Guardia's imminent attempts to reform civic life in the contexts of social policy, leisure, and nightlife.

# CHAPTER 7
## Nightlife in the La Guardia Era

If Robert Moses could have had his way—and he always tried to—the nightclub was the symbol of the Tammany era that the new reform government in New York City, taking power in 1934, would toss most forcefully onto the ash heap of history. A veteran state bureaucrat and political infighter, now Mayor Fiorello H. La Guardia's commissioner of city parks, Moses marked the new era in city government by plotting the razing of the Central Park Casino. To him, the old Calvert Vaux building, renovated and decorated by Joseph Urban in the 1920s and leased and operated by the Broadway restauranteur Sidney Solomon, epitomized the corruption and lost opportunities of the Jimmy Walker years.

For Moses, Walker's carefree nights on the Casino's dance floor were the antithesis of his ideal of modern leisure. As the state parks commissioner in the 1920s Moses originated pioneering projects on Long Island that revealed the basic contours of his philosophy of leisure reform. In many ways Moses was an anti-urbanist who wanted to redirect city dwellers to meticulously engineered, high-volume recreation sites on the fringes of the metropolitan region. He planned the Northern and Southern State Parkways on Long Island to be conduits for automobile excursions from the city to his new outdoor parks at Jones Beach, Valley Stream, and Hempstead. Moses's love of the sea—his favorite pastime was open-water swimming—helped dictate an emphasis on beaches, while his progressivist faith in engineering led him to use bricks and mortar to improve on nature. Fresh air and ocean views were almost all that remained of nature once Moses was finished with his construction of paved roads and walkways, bathhouses, restaurants, playgrounds, zoos, and parking lots.[1]

In the 1930s, as Moses turned to reshaping recreation in New York City, he retained his goal of symbolically cleansing the masses out of doors. But the mission now was more urgent. Outdoor leisure, to Moses, was the antidote to densely packed city life. The facilities he built in the five boroughs were designed specifically to get New Yorkers out of doors and off of the streets. Moses despised the animal warmth and the decadent, multiethnic, walled-in artifice of urban leisure of the 1920s. During the opening of his new West Side Manhattan/Riverside Drive project in 1935 he mused, "I wonder sometimes whether our people, so obsessed with the seamy interior of Manhattan, deserve the Hudson [river]." Moses's onetime reform colleague Frances Perkins recalled that he considered the public "lousy, dirty people, throwing bottles all over Jones Beach. . . . It's a great amorphous mass to him; it needs to be bathed, it needs to be aired, it needs recreation, but not for personal reasons—just to make it a better public." As Robert Caro's biography has famously shown, Moses's contempt for street-level urban life led him in succeeding decades to wrench people, capital, and leisure out of the five boroughs and into the wider metropolitan region. His ruthless metropolitanism set him apart from more genteel champions of regional development. As Moses himself put it to George McAneny of the Regional Plan Association, "The chief difference today between the Regional Plan . . . and my crew is that we have to concentrate on immediate objectives, and are naturally wary of comprehensive schemes which are too remote from practical considerations to constitute a program for those who live in the tough world of politics and business in which everything is measured by results."[2]

In 1934, in the city itself, Moses's immediate objectives included the destruction of the dual symbol of nightlife and Tammany rule. His campaign to raze the Central Park Casino, in the opinion of a fellow reform official, was "revenge, pure and simple . . . for what [Jimmy] Walker had done to Governor [Al] Smith" in 1932, falling prey to a scandal that helped to ruin Smith's presidential campaign. (Although a Republican, Moses owed his career in state politics to Smith, who fervently admired his talents.) Whatever his basic motive might have been, Moses was morally indignant about the Casino, denouncing it as "a racket" that overcharged wealthy patrons in order to make huge profits for Sidney Solomon's concession and for Walker's friends. Mayor La Guardia and other city officials saw no urgency or political advantage in the demolition and avoided comment. Some citizens, though, were moved to outright opposition. Older New York natives recalled that in the 1890s they had ridden carriages to the building and stopped for ice cream. Various correspondents, including the *New York Times* doyenne Iphigene Ochs Sulzberger, challenged the need for the demolition, and restaurant owners offered to buy the site and renovate it for the general public. But Moses could not be moved. He labeled such protests "preposterous" and asserted blandly that "I am satisfied that no restaurant is required at this place, that none could be operated successfully, and that the proper use for this area is for a playground for children."[3]

In May 1934 Moses unilaterally terminated Solomon's concession, calling the Casino's exclusive clientele and high prices "entirely unsatisfactory to the [Parks] Commission" and citing the kitchen for sanitary violations. Solomon sued the city for breach of contract and sought to prevent the demolition. After a long delay the court hearing took place in February 1936. Solomon proved a poor chief witness for his case, admitting that he had earned hundreds of thousands of dollars as the Casino's manager and "failing" to remember the names of city officials he had fed at no charge. However, Solomon's attorney Charles H. Tuttle (the former federal prosecutor in Manhattan) called the commissioner to the stand and managed to embarrass him as well. Tuttle produced a menu from the Tavern on the Green, the new eatery Moses had built on the west side of Central Park, and showed that its lunch prices were about as high as the Casino's. Moses lost in the local supreme court but won his appeal in the state's highest court. (Victory was inevitable, since Moses had written the legislation for the parks commission that permitted him to raze any "incidental" building he chose.) The day after the decision in his favor, Moses's bulldozers began to demolish Vaux's facade and Urban's interiors of oak, mirrored glass, and floral wallpaper (see Fig. 7).[4]

Like nothing else, Robert Moses's vendetta against the Casino illustrated how political reform, coming to power with the election of La Guardia, might have allied itself with a campaign for a new nightlife in Manhattan. To discover if such a campaign actually was launched, we must largely bypass Moses—whose empire-building ambitions quickly lured him away from parks and back to bridges and highways—and turn to the philosophy and policies of Fiorello La Guardia himself.

La Guardia was a passionate and consistent advocate of clean and honest government, but he was also mercurial, opportunistic, and even demagogic at times. While the daunting task of instituting a reform regime in New York City might have caused any mayor to be inconsistent and contradictory in his policies, La Guardia's personal qualities helped to ensure a higher level of internal conflict. This son of an Italian American bandmaster often spoke of transforming the city through the arts and leisure, but he never proposed or put through a coherent plan to that effect. Throughout the first five years of his mayoralty (the focus of this chapter) nightlife was only a sporadic and minor issue. His highly publicized effort in 1937 to eliminate burlesque theater forever from the city—which largely succeeded—can hardly be considered a full-fledged campaign against prurience and frivolity, nor did other scattered municipal initiatives (against rackets in the restaurant waiters' union and in prostitution, for example) add up to a coherent policy.

Nevertheless, the sheer scope of the La Guardia administration's reform efforts—supplemented by the impact of the national New Deal on the city—changed the foundation of the urban context, physically

Figure 7. The demolition of the Central Park Casino in May 1936. The parks commissioner Robert Moses targeted the nightclub—renovated in 1929 by Joseph Urban for Jimmy Walker and his friends—as a symbol of Tammany Hall rule and morally degenerate nightclub leisure. Milstein Division of United States History, Local History, and Genealogy, The New York Public Library, Astor, Lenox, and Tilden Foundations.

and metaphorically, in which nightlife rested. Building projects either encouraged or funded by the city government gradually transformed the Manhattan cityscape, demolishing entire districts that were the scene of nightlife in the 1920s, and municipal planning initiatives caused further change. La Guardia, moreover, instituted a generation's worth of social reforms that pledged to revolutionize the government's role in city life. Many utopian aspects of these policies fell short, though. The expectations of women, African Americans, and labor unions were raised, only to be fulfilled in limited ways at best. Campaigns to eliminate organized crime and vice from the city's streets produced headlines and convictions but failed to usher in a utopia of law and order.

Civic life, in short, was altered by the replacement of the Tammany way and workforce with the clean code of reform, and by the introduction of new and effective programs that enhanced the reputation of the city government. For working-class New Yorkers and nightlife professionals, though, La Guardia's regime seemed to produce not a new utopia but merely new varieties of the hard-edged policing, regulation of female and gay sexuality, and suppression of nightlife "vices" such as prostitution and gambling that had been evident under Tammany rule. While civic life was transformed, the basic culture of nightlife—and the city government's basic attitude toward it—was largely unaltered by that transformation. As we will see in later chapters, unlike during the era of Prohibition, private rather than public actors predominantly reshaped Manhattan's nightlife.

Moments after midnight on 1 January 1934, Fiorello La Guardia took the oath of office as mayor, among family and associates gathered in the home of Samuel Seabury. The location of the ceremony was significant: without Seabury's support, La Guardia would never have been elected mayor. Jimmy Walker's resignation in September 1932 made Joseph V. McKee, the Democratic president of the Board of Alderman, acting mayor. Since McKee opposed Tammany Hall, the machine secured a court order for a special November election to fill the remaining year in Walker's term. Tammany leaders considered asking Walker to run for vindication, but instead they chose judge John P. O'Brien, who easily defeated a Republican and Mayor McKee, a write-in contender. McKee's last-minute campaign won a quarter of a million votes, though, and inspired an instant campaign by advocates of "good government" for a bipartisan "fusion" ticket to run in the regular election in 1933.[5]

Fiorello La Guardia had lost his seat in Congress in the Democratic landslide that elected Franklin D. Roosevelt president and John P. O'Brien mayor. Although he had also lost to Walker in 1929, La Guardia now angled for the fusion mayoral nomination. Old-line Protestant fusionists wanted to nominate Seabury, but he declined and endorsed La Guardia (who had shrewdly cultivated the judge's support). Fusion leaders blanched at the former congressman's bluntness and exotic ethnicity and offered the honor to a dozen other men, all of whom declined. Seabury then vetoed their sole willing choice, Robert Moses, because of his close relationship to Al Smith. La Guardia became fusion's sole option. As O'Brien faded, Joseph McKee mounted a third-party challenge, but La Guardia demagogically accused McKee of anti-Semitism and rode the charge to victory.

Coming near the nadir of the Great Depression, La Guardia's election hardly seemed like a decisive change of course. He won only 42 percent of the total vote, polling 300,000 votes less than the combined Democratic tally. His "crazy quilt" coalition, as one historian has called it, contained many Socialists—a fact that spelled the beginning of the end for Norman Thomas's party—and influential, like-minded liberal reformers in the City Affairs Committee, which Thomas had helped to found. La Guardia would offer important city offices to Thomas (who declined) and Paul Blanshard (who quit the Socialists and accepted), but he shunned the Communist Party and its labor allies. He could not appear to be too radical. The bulk of his votes came from Italian American voters—not all of whom voted for La Guardia—and better-off Jews and Protestants. About a third of the Irish voters also supported fusion. La Guardia faced the same problem that the reform mayors Seth Low and John Purroy Mitchel had confronted: trying to find sustainable common ground among these diverse anti-Tammany cohorts.[6]

Faced with an immediate budgetary crisis, La Guardia made large cuts in the city work rolls and restructured the city's debt. Despite his initial lack of funds, from the moment he was sworn in La Guardia characteristically sought to govern ambitiously. The promise of enormous relief assistance from the New Deal gave La Guardia the funds to act. His friend and fellow Republican iconoclast, Harold Ickes, the secretary of the interior, allowed him virtually to help design the Public Works Administration (PWA) and take an initial $92 million in relief aid—nearly a fifth of the national total. Thousands of unemployed men were immediately put to work building parks and playgrounds. Their master was Robert Moses, the new commissioner of city parks, who used his low-wage workforce to transform virtually every piece of open public land. The ruthlessness Moses displayed against the Central Park Casino typified his style. He retained his control of the Long Island state parks and the Triborough Bridge Authority and moonlighted in 1934 as an unsuccessful candidate for governor. (President Roosevelt, an old political enemy of Moses's, connived in vain to oust him from the parks job.) Earning the grudging admiration of La Guardia, Moses husbanded power and funds, and by 1936 the new Works Progress Administration (WPA) was dispensing over seven thousand New Deal jobs a day in the city. Washington's largesse funded Moses's Triborough Bridge, the West Side renewal, the razing of ten thousand tenement buildings, and the construction of Harlem Houses and Williamsburg Village.[7]

For his part, La Guardia dramatized himself as the antithesis of Jimmy Walker. He told reporters two days before becoming mayor that he would reward no friends with high-paying posts: "You simply can't be grateful to the people who would work for you." One Democrat later accused him of "making ingratitude a virtue." He made impressive headway in rooting out municipal corruption, emulating the investigative profile and methods of his mentor, Samuel Seabury. Paul Blanshard and the former Seabury aide Irving Ben Cooper excavated numerous subcultures of graft, bribery, and wasteful spending. New hospital and corrections commissioners led "raids" of their facilities to eradicate mismanagement and, in the latter's case, inmates' control of wings of the Welfare Island jail. New Deal funds allowed La Guardia to expand the civil service rolls, weakening Tammany's grip on municipal employ-ment. Irish dominance made way for a far more representative munici-pal workforce. Emboldened by his budgetary and reform successes, as well as by spending in Washington, La Guardia gloried in the role of all-purpose urban crusader. He launched campaigns against city noise, spoiled milk, and street organists. He repeatedly proposed to "demolish the jails [on Welfare Island] and make playgrounds instead." (The men's jail was soon moved to a new "scientific" site on Rikers Island, but hospitals and rest homes—not playgrounds—replaced it on Welfare Island.) Riding to city fires in a motorcycle sidecar, conducting youth bands, and smashing slot machines with a sledgehammer, La Guardia coupled substantial reforms with homely acts of showmanship.[8]

In this sense, then, La Guardia was a complex and revealing contrast to his Broadway-styled predecessor, Jimmy Walker. The two mayors shared a love of urban leisure and the performing arts. La Guardia was at least as convinced as Walker of the importance of entertainment in modern city life, and he philosophized about cultural policies far more often than his predecessor ever had. In 1921, as president of the Board of Aldermen, La Guardia advocated public housing, municipal milk sta-tions, and other progressive reforms. He also vowed, though, that if elected mayor "I would provide more music and beauty for the people, more parks and more light and air and all the things the framers . . . meant [by] 'life, liberty, and the pursuit of happiness.'" Partially reject-ing reform moralism, he opposed motion picture censorship, doubting that censors really cared "how long a kiss lasts or whether the villain uses a gun or an axe."[9]

These sentiments reflected La Guardia's rich life experiences in Italy, New York City, the American West, and Hungary, which nurtured inter-ests as diverse as aviation and the opera. His mercurial emotions, though, tended to overwhelm any cool judgments he might have made about cultural and moral issues. La Guardia's biographer Thomas Kess-ner observes that he "could not reason through the complex quagmire of the twenties on intellectual grounds alone." Even though he lived in Harlem and represented it for twelve years in Congress, he always favored the classics over jazz, which he considered "a primitive, unpleas-ant form of music." In the 1920s La Guardia wrote the draft of a novel, *Tony Goes to Congress*, in which the disillusioned wife of a Tammany boss rekindles an old romance with a more sensitive male acquaintance. Their passions included progressive politics—"They both knew the ten-ements. They both knew what unemployment meant"—but also the arts. "They were both cultured. They both loved music."[10] The awkward story, never published, reveals both La Guardia's sympathy with the relaxed personal morality of the nightclub era and his continuing attachment to traditional aesthetics.

During the 1933 mayoral campaign La Guardia rearticulated his vision of a city revivified by the arts. In his major speech on the topic of "social justice" he ticked off familiar urban issues—housing, playgrounds, hospitals, the courts—and then, "at the risk of seeming too romantic," he extolled a New Deal for musicians, who would play for the "millions of people who know good music, and like it . . . in every nook and cranny of New York." Months later, now in office, he drove across Manhattan in an open-air vehicle with a friend. He gazed up at the buildings and mused, "I am in the position of an artist or a sculptor. . . . I can see New York as it should be and as it can be. . . . But now I am like the man who has a conception that he wishes to carve or to paint, who has the model before him, but hasn't a chisel or a brush."[11]

In certain respects Robert Moses became La Guardia's "chisel," transforming the leisure landscape of the city with extensive public works. In the symbolic case of the Central Park Casino, though, Moses's reform goals were ambiguous at best. At worst, according to critics, he seemed to be replacing a Tammany Hall restaurant racket with one of his own. A correspondent who lamented the loss of the Casino disputed Moses's contention that it had been too exclusive. She argued that for "the 'inbetweens' who haven't the entré to smart clubs but who do enjoy gracious living[,] the Casino (once Claremont, alas!) provide[s] an 'escape' into that gracious world." The Claremont Inn cited in the letter was a 1780s tavern on Riverside Drive and 125th Street. Moses was "in entire agreement" with another correspondent who called the Claremont a "disgraceful political night-club," but Moses did not raze the Claremont; instead he installed a popularly priced concession that featured dancing. When that failed, though, Moses instituted a more high-priced (but not exclusive) menu. His restauranting tendencies suggested an elitism that hardly differed from that of the Central Park Casino. The Boardwalk Restaurant at Jones Beach was a high-priced "tony night club" with tuxedoed waiters and a parquet dance floor. In 1931 Moses haughtily defended the restaurant: "We promised the local people on Long Island who gave us their beach land that we would maintain certain standards. . . . It is a stupid and vicious thing, in our opinion, to advocate that great public parks in the suburbs shall be only for the poor." While Moses asserted that "we can do things at Jones Beach which cannot be done at Central and Prospect Parks," he did maintain exclusivity in Central Park by creating the Tavern on the Green restaurant.[12]

Moses personally directed the design of this restaurant in a sheep barn built in 1870 on the park's west side that cost $1.3 million in public money—more than triple the price of the Casino's privately funded renovation. The eatery's opening night cost each couple a twenty-five-dollar cover charge. Doormen in hunting regalia and concessionaires and band members in comic-opera costume greeted diners. Though not as high as the Casino's, dinner prices at the Tavern were still out of the reach of most city residents. Lunch rates were more reasonable, but as Moses himself testified, the Casino's had been as well. Moses, in short, replaced privately financed Central Park nightlife with a publicly funded restaurant of similar exclusivity. True, the Tavern was not a political clubhouse, as Moses accused the Casino of having been—but Moses's own office, in the Arsenal Building across Central Park, filled that function quite well.[13]

La Guardia, unlike Moses, never made any particular nightclub into a bête noir. In the early months of his term, in fact, he allowed the extension of the legal "curfew" or closing time for nightclubs. Clubowners, pleading for flexibility so they might revive their stagnant business after the repeal of Prohibition, found receptive ears in the municipal government. Also, since a court had recently declared that all state laws were governed by standard time, lawyers argued that nightclubs should be allowed to stay open all year until 3:00 AM eastern standard time—which daylight savings time disguised as 4:00 AM for half of the year. In the Board of Aldermen a 4:00 AM curfew bill was presented by Murray Stand, the Tammany stalwart who had been arrested in a venue during the "war on the nightclubs" in 1928. It passed easily. La Guardia signed the bill into law without protest, and in the future even stretched the curfew further on New Year's Eve, allowing clubs to stay open until 5:00 AM.[14]

The mayor, however, also appeased moral reformers critical of nightlife. In 1934 these individuals, led by the Society for the Suppression of Vice, endorsed a new wave of crackdowns on nightclubs, noting the persistence of such long-standing ills as the widespread overcharging of guests and the mingling of female entertainers and hostesses with customers. Male seducers, including gigolos who identified themselves to "lonely women" by wearing green carnations in their lapels, were also cited as a concern. The police commissioner John O'Ryan, whose office had been responsible for issuing cabaret licenses since 1931, responded with new rules that required menus with printed prices and forbade the employment of "hostesses, companions, or dance partners" in clubs. In dance halls, which O'Ryan also licensed, hostesses could remain employed, but a new rule ordered that dance floors be railed off from tables. In the same vein La Guardia began to zone clubs more strictly. Responding to similar complaints against clubs and dance halls, he instructed O'Ryan to deny operating licenses to establishments in "purely residential districts."[15]

These efforts indicated the perpetuation of Protestant moral reform efforts into the era of the Depression. More important, they also suggested how La Guardia proceeded to put his own stamp on New York's effort of two decades—then still unique among American cities—to govern building construction and use through a blend of zoning, curfews, and air-space restrictions. The attorney Paul Chevigny has noted that "the original [1926 cabaret] ordinance regulated only the licensing of the clubs themselves," but "over the years, it [took] on accretions of zoning and safety provisions."[16] Nightclubs, put in the spotlight by moralists, illustrated some of these regulatory trends. They were a small but well-publicized part of the huge and perplexing puzzle of how to manage demolition and renovation in old city areas and urban expansion into rural regions of the five boroughs.

Fusion reformers tried to gain control of the process by instituting comprehensive city planning. Taken together, Robert Moses's imperious transport authorities constituted one enormous planning initiative. Other members of La Guardia's team, though, sought a more deliberate and structured mechanism. Jimmy Walker had created a city planning department in 1930, but it had been ineffectual. Furthermore, according to one observer, a committee to revise the city charter, which had been devised by his successor John O'Brien, was "kept . . . in a state of turmoil" by its chairman, Alfred E. Smith. La Guardia created a new commission under the guidance of the preeminent New Dealer Rexford Guy Tugwell. In 1937 Tugwell's commission reported that "the present zoning of the city is not even reasonably in accord with existing living conditions," noting that some four million residents were crammed into dense neighborhoods in which manufacturing and commerce operated unchecked. A permanent planning commission became part of the new city charter passed by voters in late 1936. With Tugwell again at the head, the commission adjusted zoning and height criteria, but not without controversy. "Zoning was (and is) not planning," the historian Carol Willis has noted, and Tugwell's effort to pull the elements of urban planning together resulted in intense criticism from all sides, especially from business. In 1940 a *New York Times* editorial asked, "Does [Tugwell] find the public interest and private interest irreconcilable? . . . Yes." His struggles were compounded by Mayor La Guardia's own lack of interest in planning, except as a tool for keeping borough governments in line.[17]

The zoning and planning controversies were central examples of how La Guardia's reform administration initiated broad and important public debate about the nature, scope, and extent of reform. While they affected all city residents and businesses, zoning and planning especially caused well-publicized and influential changes in nightlife. In the 1920s, with the approval of a malleable Board of Estimate, nightclubs had expanded into traditional residential areas in Manhattan such as the west fifties. Public outcry against the clubs and gangsters, especially from neighborhood and business associations, led to their gradual enclosure along Broadway and its side streets in the theater district and strict regulation regarding the presence of music, dance, food, and drink. Fusion's interest in nightclub regulation reached its apex in 1940, when the city ordered the fingerprinting of all cabaret employees and required them to possess special identification cards.[18]

The years 1934 to 1939 also witnessed reform initiatives sponsored by La Guardia with respect to women, burlesque, prostitution, organized crime, and Harlem. As these initiatives were implemented—and as they stimulated controversy—they had a tangible impact on nightlife. The highly publicized new nightclub scene of the mid-1930s, in turn, shed more light on both the changes that reform had fostered and the social problems it continued to overlook. Pointing to nightlife, La Guardia could claim isolated successes, but he was generally stymied in his effort to eliminate "vice" and the power of racketeers in those industries. The mayor's utopian dreams, and his frustrations, became entwined in planning for the major leisure initiative of his administration in the late 1930s, the New York World's Fair at Flushing Meadows.

The issue of the treatment of women in the magistrates' courts, so vividly exposed by Samuel Seabury, had provided an emotional core to fusion's challenge to the Tammany government. However, La Guardia's attention to the suffering of working-class women was curiously inconsistent and produced few clear policy successes. As Thomas Kessner has noted, the mayor viewed women in traditional terms, accepting their recent inroads to jobs and careers but finding it difficult to shed nineteenth-century notions of female domesticity. He congratulated the League of Women Voters for bringing "house cleaning methods to public affairs," forbade his secretaries from wearing makeup, and expected his wife Marie to keep up—and to stay put in—their apartment in East Harlem. La Guardia relied almost entirely on male assistants and rarely focused on women's issues. Although women were central to the municipal court scandal, in 1933 La Guardia the candidate discussed it entirely in masculine terms: "A really shocking situation prevails. . . . A man is arrested, charged with some offence. If he is well off he gets a lawyer and works the machinery of justice without difficulty. But if he is poor, he has no such redress." La Guardia almost never mentioned endangered womanhood as a rationale for reform, as had his fellow fusionist and Episcopalian, Samuel Seabury. As we have seen, after Seabury exposed the framing ring the policing of prostitution declined drastically, but in his first months in office the preoccupied La Guardia devoted little time to diminishing New York's status as a "wide open town."[19]

La Guardia did largely continue the liberalization of policies toward the institutionalization of women that had begun under Tammany rule after the Seabury revelations. In the wake of these revelations and of the suffering of women in the Great Depression, what the WPA writer Henry Drimer labeled "a policy of charitable understanding and humane effort at rehabilitation" was pursued in city corrections. Echoing the defunct Committee of Fourteen, La Guardia's aides, such as the commissioner of hospitals, Sigismund S. Goldwater, advocated the "scientific" treatment of female inmates. In 1932 the city had begun to hire matrons to provide guidance to women in jails, halfway houses, and hospitals.[20]

The centerpiece of this policy was the new women's House of Detention on West 10th Street near the site of the old jail at Jefferson Market (the former hive of the prostitution framing ring, which continued to house the Manhattan Women's Court). While the exterior of the twelve-story building resembled a bland apartment house, the steel entryway featured a touch of nightclub decor from the 1920s, steel ornamental "leaves of the Egyptian lotus." The interior seemed to Drimer "more like an apartment hotel than a prison." The all-female staff helped the inmates provide "the feminine touch of pictures, doilies, and nicknacks" which made "each floor a compact little feminine community." The house's "modern equipment" included a rotating chapel floor (reminiscent of nightclub stages) with Catholic, Protestant, and Jewish altars. Despite such cosmetics, the new jail was still punitive. Women with venereal diseases wore brown uniforms instead of blue ones. The roof athletic field, Drimer noted, was "protected by a strong iron screen to prevent tennis balls from going over the wall, and incidentally, makes impossible any suicide attempt by jumping from the roof."[21]

More generally, La Guardia's administration displayed an ambivalence about replacing punitive law enforcement with compassion and rehabilitation. During the last years of the Tammany regime, especially during the tenure of the police commissioner Grover Whalen, the corruption of officers, the use of "third degree" tactics in questioning, the reckless searches for career criminals, and the violent suppression of radical groups' peaceful public gatherings had provoked controversy. La Guardia's first police commissioner, the retired army general John F. O'Ryan, maintained what he called a "militaristic" police stance against labor rallies in particular. The commissioner proposed a "rifle squad" to preserve public order against a major taxi drivers' strike and other picket lines. Union leaders condemned O'Ryan's "Fascist policies and inclinations," and the mayor, who in Congress had coauthored landmark labor legislation, soon clashed with the commissioner as well. O'Ryan's eventual replacement was Lewis J. Valentine, the head of the celebrated anti-Tammany police Confidential Squad in the 1920s.[22]

Valentine was more permissive toward radical marchers, noting that "Americans have a right to parade," but he too flaunted tough police tactics in the "war" against crimes such as gambling and prostitution. Valentine (and La Guardia) associated street-level perpetrators of vice with career criminals, "muscle men or racketeers," who allegedly made petty whoring or gambling into big business. In a controversial comment, Valentine pointed to suspects in a lineup at headquarters and exhorted officers not to "be afraid to muss them up . . . blood should be smeared all over that velvet collar." When a young armed robbery suspect died in custody after violent handling, Valentine blithely labeled him "just another dead criminal" and "a small loss." Police chiefs elsewhere criticized his comments but Valentine remained defiant, defending dragnet arrests for disorderly conduct and the use of stool pigeons and the third degree. " 'From information received,' more thieves have been captured than by crime laboratory detection methods," he claimed.[23]

Valentine received the full support of Mayor La Guardia, who yearned to appear as intolerant of street crime as he was of municipal corruption. In the first days of his term he famously shouted to parole officers, "I'm going to grab every tinhorn gambler in the city of New York by the scruff of the neck and throw him over into New Jersey!" At first La Guardia had little time or power to chase criminals, though, and he had to contend with a Tammany district attorney, William C. Dodge, who, while honest, used old and ineffective methods. The mayor made a great show of anti-crime initiatives. On one occasion, to announce a campaign against produce racketeers La Guardia stood in a vegetable market in the Bronx and recited an old city law that forbade the sale of artichokes. (Cold weather, however, stymied police buglers who were to provide fanfares to accompany the mayor's proclamation.) At the state level, governor Herbert Lehman proposed draconian crime-prevention reform that would have required the fingerprinting of all New York City residents, the creation of a "public enemy" classification, and strict registration of guns (as well as the admission of women to juries and other reforms). Lehman went too far, offending a wide array of interest groups, and his proposal was defeated.[24]

La Guardia and Lehman were upstaged by a dapper former federal attorney, barely over the age of thirty, who had used his connections in Republican legal circles to win an appointment as a special state prosecutor. Thomas E. Dewey was a native of rural Michigan who had grown up listening to his father's scathing denunciations of Tammany Hall. Dewey had come to New York to study classical singing before he turned to the law. Dewey owed his rapid rise to the former U.S. attorneys Emory Buckner and George Medalie, who cultivated young lawyers with political ambition. As Medalie's assistant, Dewey won income tax convictions of the bootlegger Waxey Gordon and the Harlem gambling chief Henry Miro. Appointed special prosecutor by Lehman in 1935, Dewey gained a sizable budget, a staff of sixty-five, and even a new court run by a sympathetic judge in which to try his cases. The ambitious and coldly efficient Dewey went about looking for rackets. His main targets were Dutch Schultz (who had escaped conviction in upstate New York) and the Tammany boss James Hines. Schultz was assassinated later that year, however, and Hines proved elusive. After convicting a group of loan sharks, Dewey stalked a little-known criminal, Charles "Lucky" Luciano, whom he accused publicly of being a ruler of the underworld.[25]

Dewey's celebrated prosecution of Luciano on brothel-keeping charges translated the anti-prostitution crusade of the 1920s into a new incarnation appropriate for the era of the Depression and municipal reform. Dewey had hoped to prosecute Luciano—or anyone, for that matter—for gambling or labor racketeering. To him prostitution seemed to be a small-time vice that the city, in the wake of the fallout from the framing ring, could not even regulate effectively. The Committee of Fourteen was gone.

In 1935, though, Police Commissioner Valentine, the Reverend George D. Egbert (the leader of the Society for the Prevention of Crime), and others sought a new campaign against "the social evil." Anti-prostitution laws had never stopped being a tool of social repression. Dozens of female suspects continued to be hauled nightly into the Women's Court. Three-quarters of all black women arrested in Harlem in the early 1930s were charged with vagrancy or prostitution, and more than half of the women in the House of Detention were African American. In Harlem pimps remained active largely because the protection money that Dutch Schultz paid to police officers sheltered prostitution as well as the numbers racket. Economic desperation continued to drive working-class women into the prostitution trade in Harlem. These included some white women, such as the one hired at this time by the seventeen-year-old John F. Kennedy and his friend Lem Billings for their first sexual experiences.[26]

By 1934—before Dewey began his work—La Guardia's hunt for Dutch Schultz brought the madam Polly Adler back into the limelight. The police suspected correctly that Adler's brothel was protected by Schultz. Adler later revealed that this "protection" was involuntary and came at a high and extorted price. The city planned an elaborate sting operation in the building that housed Adler's twelve-room brothel apartment in eastern Midtown. Her telephone was tapped and the building's elevator operator was paid to become a spy. A client of Adler's was persuaded by the district attorney to file an accusation, and the madam was arrested in March 1935. Adler gained some sympathy from a *New York Daily News* editorial that accused La Guardia of reviving a predecessor's methods of entrapment. "The Mayor would do well to remember, we think, that it was the vice cop frameup revelations which started the Walker Administration toward its ruin." Adler and four female employees were easily convicted, but the magistrate Jonah Goldstein (a former advisor to the Committee of Fourteen) ensured that male customers would not be named in public. The madam served thirty days at the House of Detention, tending to the suicide-proof roof garden and enduring the homilies of the Salvation Army major Agnes McKernan (another veteran of the Committee of Fourteen). In 1936 Adler was arrested again, a casualty of Thomas Dewey's dragnet through the remaining high-priced brothels in Manhattan.[27]

Dewey's attention had been turned to prostitution in 1935 by the attorney Eunice Hunton Carter. The only African American on Dewey's staff, Carter's contacts in Harlem told her that after the repeal of Prohibition, former bootleggers had moved into the call-girl business. She exhumed the records of the Committee of Fourteen to trace patterns of prostitution. Armed with new investigative powers granted by the state legislature, Dewey arrested over a hundred suspected pimps and prostitutes. The houses of Cokey Flo, Gas-house Lil, Frisco Jean, Silver-Tongued Elsie, and Adler's acquaintance "Diane B." were shuttered. Dewey's lawyers brought the suspects in for questioning at his offices in the Woolworth Building; one lawyer recalled "never [having] seen so many prostitutes before or since. The rooms were crawling with them." Once the trial began, cooperative female witnesses were allowed to leave jail for two movies a month and one "decent" meal a week. One of them was taken by Dewey's lawyers to a Chinese restaurant on Broadway, while another was escorted to the Paramount Theater "followed by dinner and martinis at the Oyster Bar restaurant."[28] Going far beyond Samuel Seabury's favorable treatment of Chile Acuna and other witnesses, Thomas Dewey seemed to accept the new nightlife and made it part of the fabric of enticement and rewards available to helpful witnesses.

After gaining Luciano's conviction on sixty-one counts of "compulsory prostitution," Dewey came to the rescue of restaurants, which had been preyed upon by an employees' union operated by Dutch Schultz and Jules Martin. As in the case of Luciano, Dewey exaggerated the extent of the criminality, but the union had extorted money from well-known establishments such as the Hollywood Restaurant and Jack Dempsey's and had forced them to hire certain waiters and concession-aires. Schultz and Martin were both dead, but Dewey was able to indict and convict thirteen of their associates. Afterward the Association of Restaurant Employees and Waiters became a legitimate organization, lifted by the groundswell of labor organizing nurtured by the Wagner Act of 1935. In this way, collective bargaining became a mainstay of Manhattan's nightlife. Dewey, meanwhile, rode his successes to election as the city's district attorney.[29]

Dewey's headline-grabbing exploits illustrated again how fragmentary investigations into social problems—often defined simplistically as "crimes"—and criminal convictions of questionable long-term effectiveness usually took the place of true social reform. Mayor La Guardia shared this eagerness to score high-profile victories against crime. In the first months of his administration he was preoccupied with capturing Dutch Schultz and shutting down his lucrative numbers or "policy" racket in Harlem. Police officers zealously pursued participants in the numbers game, arresting hoards of poor black players who dreamed of winning fortunes. In the early 1930s over half of all the arrests of African Americans in Harlem were for "possession of policy slips." In the first half of 1935, even though a major riot filled the jails with looting suspects, policy-slip arrests in Harlem were still triple the number of theft arrests. Before his violent death in November 1935, though, Dutch Schultz remained untouched for his policy activities, enjoying the political protection of the Tammany boss Jimmy Hines. (A decade earlier Hines had provided similar services to the nightclub pioneer Larry Fay.) In 1939 Thomas E. Dewey finally gained Hines's conviction, which he exploited the next year in a bid for the Republican presidential nomination. The Harlem policy racket lived on, though. As Dewey's former colleague Herbert Brownell noted decades later, urban racketeering was "a never-ending problem."[30]

In the broader social context beyond crime and punishment, the riot in Harlem of March 1935 was the chief evidence of the shortcomings of La Guardia's reform agenda. Part of the shortcomings were personal. La Guardia lived in East Harlem and appointed African Americans to important positions, but, as Thomas Kessner has argued, "their pain was strange to him, far more distant than that of the other ethnics with more familiar backgrounds." La Guardia, in short, had "no . . . shared experience with blacks." More important, the Depression had caused tremendous suffering among African Americans. To La Guardia, Kessner notes, "the problems seemed so intractable." Half of all adults were unemployed, and in 1935 43 percent of all families in Harlem were on public

relief, which was often ineffectively distributed. One winter the entertainers Bill Robinson and the Mills Brothers appeared at a benefit in the
midtown Hollywood Restaurant to raise funds for the purchase of coal
for Harlem's residents.[31] Leisure facilities in Harlem remained minimal.
Robert Moses, who earlier had encouraged racial segregation and the
discomfort of black visitors at Jones Beach State Park, now virtually
ignored Harlem in the city parks-building campaign. Only one playground was built there and in Brooklyn's black Stuyvesant Heights district, and the public pool in Harlem—like the one at Jones Beach—was
kept unheated because Moses believed that blacks avoided cold water.[32]

On 19 March 1935, the arrest in Harlem of a sixteen-year-old boy for
theft, followed by false rumors of a police beating, sparked an epidemic
of looting. Over one hundred Harlemites were arrested and three African Americans were killed by police fire. The event has since been called
the first classic "ghetto riot" in U.S. history, in which blacks targeted
outside business owners and the police in a "cleansing" of their community.[33]

The riot in Harlem put an end to whites' fantasies of the region as a
biracial playground, fantasies that nightlife had done much to perpetuate. African American residents sent city officials urgent pleas for action.
The labor leader A. Philip Randolph warned of "the people's . . . pent-
up wrath and resentment against conditions of oppression, exploitation
and discrimination." The insurance agent James Dickson wrote the
mayor, "even in darkest Africa the colored man has at least his own hut
and the enjoyment of his own family. . . . What in the name of common
sense could the colored folk of Harlem do? Do you know that many of
the Elevator Men on my Elevators received less than a dollar a day? Do
you know that Apartments in my houses reeked with filth through no
fault of the tenant?" In Dickson's view Harlem's sordid nightlife, "the
Gin Mills–Dope Dens–Stills–Apartments of ill repute and Saturday Night
Parties etc.," was an outgrowth of everyday injustice. Another correspondent noted "open Prostitution, Gambling on the streets [and] Dice
games." The initial official city report on the riot, drafted by a biracial
commission, also depicted nightlife as an environmental menace. It
noted that a public school on 135th Street stood within two blocks of
"18 beer gardens, 6 liquor saloons, 4 moving picture houses, and 2
hotels, alleged to be disreputable, as well as one SOLID BLOCK of
rooming houses, which are known to be the centre of vice."[34]

White fusion officials might be expected to take action against these
squalid conditions and harmful nightlife. Instead, like their counterparts in other riot-torn cities, they countered black anger by placing the
blame on Harlemites themselves. Police Commissioner Lewis Valentine
and others compelled the mayor to suppress the draft report of the may-

or's riot commission, which also scathingly attacked Harlem's inferior facilities. "The environment of Harlem would not be the sole cause of adult delinquency and criminal behavior," Valentine argued, claiming instead that "delinquency is high among the negro population of the United States as a whole." The people, not the place, caused crime. Valentine conceded that prostitution, specifically, "may be due to economic conditions and the like," but he put more emphasis on the dangers posed by prostitutes, who according to "health examinations by the Womens Court" spread venereal disease widely. Similarly, Mary Sullivan of the policewomen's bureau found Harlem overrun with odd deviants, such as a "pale, furtive-looking negro" man who bleached his face and hair and wrote "poison-pen letters" to well-known women in the city.[35]

The mayor's correspondence file reveals a strain of virulent racism among whites. "New York City simply cannot make room for all the coons that would like to come here to get more on relief," one man wrote. Another argued that "the colored people have gone to[o] far with their knives and razors and so forth. . . . [They] butcher one another and get off with it, by dodging around. . . ." The "negroe [is] running wild in Harlem," a writer warned, while a Mr. La Pointe predicted that "you are just inviting a race riot and possible lynching if you cater to these black things much longer."[36] Such hostility ensured that La Guardia could not launch an effective policy to improve Harlem. The mayor genuinely sympathized with his commission's findings, and his administration increased spending on facilities in Harlem, but the general oppression and inequality persisted.

In his first term as mayor, La Guardia achieved important structural changes, including a new city charter that abolished the Board of Aldermen and otherwise streamlined government. He also established a relationship with New Deal Washington that brought billions of dollars in public works funds into the city. As the stories of law enforcement, racket busting, and race relations show, though, despite fragmentary success and some innovation, the fusion administration generally failed to "clean up the city" and effect fundamental social reform. As in earlier decades, officials sought convenient targets and "solutions" that generated favorable headlines, and they bent to popular prejudices.

For nightlife, these trends meant that while the improving economy and employment situation reenergized business (as the following chapter shows), city officials also continued to pursue performers and patrons to score easy political points. Mayor La Guardia, with his sentimental attachment to morally healthful, street-level art and culture, eagerly led most of these efforts.

The repeal of Prohibition in late 1933, weeks before La Guardia became mayor, encouraged him and other officials to search for other newsworthy moralistic crusades. Repeal removed a cumbersome federal apparatus from city law enforcement and took the legal spotlight away from middle-class and elite lawbreaking, leaving the mayor free to dictate a new agenda for moral policing. Some historians have argued that the end of Prohibition initiated a more insidious and oppressive regime of intervention into private lives. The historian George Chauncey finds that repeal "inaugurated a more pervasive and more effective regime of surveillance and control" and "made it possible for the state to redraw the boundaries of acceptable sociability that seemed to have been obliterated in the twenties." Fiorello La Guardia, the city's self-styled "sculptor," launched a series of often petty crusades for the cultural betterment of New York. While he contravened city regulations that threatened to shut down "wholesome" circuses and movie houses and gloried in conducting bands and orchestras in impromptu appearances, he also railed against "indecent" magazines, slot machines, organ grinders (whom he banned, along with other "unnecessary" street noise), and burlesque.[37]

The campaign against burlesque was La Guardia's most sustained and revealing effort to regulate a nightlife institution, to push back modern tolerance and sexual license. Jimmy Walker's anti-burlesque campaign in 1932 had closed a few theaters in Midtown, but only temporarily. Desperate theater owners could not ignore the continuing profitability of "stock" burlesque in the middle of the Depression. In 1933 the Minsky brothers negotiated a deal with the O'Brien administration that allowed them to return to business; the deal permitted a retired founder of the "clean" Columbia circuit to screen and approve all burlesque acts. When La Guardia took office he named Paul Moss as the new commissioner of licenses. Moss was a lifelong veteran of show business. As a child in the 1890s he was part of a blackface vaudeville act, and he later became a motion picture producer, theater operator, and producer of stage hits such as *Subway Express*. As licensing commissioner Moss emulated the mayor's street-level activism, clearing Tammany patronage from newsstands in favor of disabled veterans, banishing obscene magazines, and placing new regulations on junk shops, sidewalk photographers, theater-booking agencies, and others. Moss continued the screening procedure for burlesque, curiously striving to make the theaters "family places instead of being largely only for men." Under Moss burlesque did come to resemble vaudeville in ways, featuring comic and dancing talent with general appeal and more modest striptease performers, such as the rising star Gypsy Rose Lee. Three Minsky-owned theaters and two other burlesque houses prospered in the theater district.[38]

In 1937, however, while seeking reelection, La Guardia ordered Moss to launch a crusade against burlesque. Once again, church groups— particularly Catholics this time—inspired city action. O. R. Miller of the New York Civic League opined that "any girl who would be part of such a show . . . deserves to be out of employment for a long, long time and to go hungry." A man wrote the mayor that his two sons had become addicted to burlesque: "Their passions were aroused and [they] began to go with prostitutes and bad company. . . . The politicians have fatted on graft that lets these sewers operate, and all by Jews." The city refused to renew licenses to fourteen burlesque theaters (nine in Manhattan, five in Brooklyn), and the term "burlesque" was forbidden in any licensed theater. This inspired theater owners and employees to counter Miller's condemnation with warnings to La Guardia about Depression-style suffering. "Give these unfortunates a chance to again earn a liveli-hood," Mollie Minsky wrote the mayor; "don't send them on Relief." A twenty-year-old performer at the Irving Place Theater, Vivian Rumer, insisted that "I am leading a respectable and moral life," as did "all the girls I am associated with," and she resented Moss's "vulgar epithets" about them. Musicians, doormen, and technicians sent in standardized letters to the mayor, arguing that "if burlesque theatres close we will be on the street again." One correspondent estimated that three thousand people worked in the fourteen theaters.[39]

La Guardia and Moss seemed to be motivated by a strong moral out-rage, stoked by provocative reports about the nature and impact of bur-lesque performances. A copy of a new dissertation by Daniel Dressler of New York University on "burlesque as a cultural phenomenon" made its way into the mayor's files. Visiting many burlesque performances, Dressler found that although "the casual attendee perhaps need undergo no lasting conflict," burlesque became an addiction for some men. In a darkened theater "an entire row of poorly riveted seats will vibrate with the masturbatory movement. Here and there a homosexual will make stealthy advances to a likely neighbor. One will touch the geni-tals of another." While Dressler noted that burlesque was hardly the only salacious urban temptation, and that only a small minority actually patronized the theaters, he concluded that "burlesque as an institution is a socially pathological phenomenon centering on a low moral level to appetites which ought to have more adequate means of satisfaction." La Guardia echoed this conclusion, attacking "commercialized filth," while Moss called burlesque employees "prostitutes" and "morons." The mayor also associated burlesque with a perceived recent rise in sex crimes. Correspondents deluged his office with opinions about the causes of rape and indecent exposure, and La Guardia endorsed the psychological observation of all convicted sex offenders as a partial solution.[40]

A legal counterattack by burlesque producers resulted in court orders that temporarily reopened some theaters. The mayor, though, felt that he had the discretion to supersede the orders. Burlesque producers negotiated a compromise, forming a carefully delineated new association, governed by a board of lawyers and ministers, that would oversee cleaner "follies" shows. Any obscene "motion, movement, gesture, or gesticulation . . . [or effort to] speak, recite, sing or otherwise render dialogue, songs, ballads, poetry, or prose" that was obscene would be forbidden. Moss banned the name "Minsky" from the brothers' shows as well. In 1938, after out-of-town striptease promoters descended on Manhattan with more salacious shows to satisfy customer demand, La Guardia and Moss launched an even noisier crackdown that closed even the "follies" theaters. The state courts upheld these rulings, effectively killing burlesque in New York City. Instead of creating "a reincarnation of old vaudeville in modern revue form," as the last active burlesque producers had hoped to do, La Guardia and Moss drove striptease into an isolated and disreputable entertainment underground.[41]

Some observers noted that burlesque was not the sole challenge to sexual rectitude. In his dissertation David Dressler noted that "burlesque, of course, is not the only institution that leads to . . . engag[ing] in a pursuit of which one is ashamed and which one hides from friends." The theater critic George Jean Nathan observed that with the ubiquity of female flesh on Broadway, visitors had difficulty telling if they were "in a night club or a nudist camp, a burlesque show or a girls' shower room." In particular it was widely observed that burlesque and nightclubs presented almost identical levels of public nudity. Noted strippers worked in clubs owned by Nils T. Granlund and Billy Rose. La Guardia's correspondent James McMahon observed that in nightclubs "strip-tease is glorified in an extensive form." Another writer castigated "every dance hall, cabaret, or other place . . . where 'strip teasers' were employed." Joseph Beha similarly put "burlesque theatres and night clubs" in one category and argued that "scores and scores" of the latter were "evil resorts." (Beha celebrated the "razing [of] the champagne Casino in Central Park and turning the grounds into a play-scape for the children.") Another correspondent, noting Police Commissioner Valentine's recent warning to nightclubs, claimed that they "have become lewd to the extreme." But Valentine never raided nightclubs. They were likely the beneficiaries, and burlesque the victim, of a double standard. James McMahon noted that "a woman who artisticly [sic] unclothes herself before an audience shall have the same effect on a person rich or poor, educated or un-educated[;] you can't change human nature with money or education." The city's "reform" government, though, seemed to have targeted selectively a leisure genre with a particularly vulnerable public image.[42]

Another vogue of the early 1930s, the transvestite or "pansy" show, had abated considerably by mid-decade, but a rash of reports of sex crimes and "perversions" also led La Guardia to launch an unprecedented dragnet against public homosexual behavior. These years witnessed a growing homophobia nationwide. As George Chauncey has put it, beginning in the mid-1930s a "powerful cultural reaction" against gay men and lesbians grew, supplanting the vogue for public displays of gay culture and the relative tolerance of the previous decade. "Gay life in New York," Chauncey writes, "was *less* tolerated, *less* visible to outsiders, and *more* rigidly segregated in the second third of the century than the first." The official repression of nightclub "pansy shows" and drag balls had begun in 1931. Police Commissioner Edward Mulrooney's campaign temporarily shut down all public transvestitism in Midtown and in Greenwich Village. After the repeal of Prohibition the New York State Liquor Authority (SLA) linked gay-themed speakeasies with "disorderly" saloons that flouted the new liquor-sale regulations. In 1938 the SLA explicitly forbade homosexual-themed bars and threatened tolerant establishments with closure. The police made highly publicized arrests of male transvestites. Gay-friendly establishments such as the Times Square Bar and Grill were shuttered and later lost their court appeals to reopen in the summers of 1939 and 1940, during the time of the world's fair. Cruising sites such as Bryant Park were now strictly policed, and policewomen raided lesbian tea rooms and sent their proprietors to city hospitals for psychiatric evaluation. The city raised little objection, though, when gangsters began to underwrite a new network of clandestine and unpretentious gay bars. In general, as Chauncey concludes, gay life became "more hidden and more segregated from the rest of city life than it had been before."[43]

By the time it entered its last year in 1937, Fiorello La Guardia's first term in office had created virulent opposition and many controversies—usually generated by La Guardia himself—as well as successful reform. That year, however, the mayor's formidable campaigning, coupled with his progress in cleaning up city government and creating Depression relief programs, easily won him a second term. By then, though, the fusion movement had suffered reverses; it had lost its majority on the Board of Estimate and filled only three of the sixty-five seats on the Board of Aldermen. Tammany Hall was making a strong comeback, and reform's future was in doubt.[44]

After his reelection La Guardia threw his energies into planning what he considered both a symbolic and tangible step toward a better city: the New York World's Fair. The idea for the fair had an impeccable reform pedigree, coming in 1935 from George McAneny, a banker and the president of the Regional Plan Association. It quickly gained the support of Robert Moses, who had already begun to clean up the ash heaps in Flushing Meadows, Queens, and now proposed the site for the fair and a subsequent park (which would be the city's largest). In a bipartisan spirit, Grover Whalen was named president of the fair corporation. Tammany Hall-style celebrity greeting, New Deal-style public works achievement, and faith in technology and the future thus came together in planning for the fair. La Guardia's chosen theme, the World of Tomorrow, guided the planners. The mayor's vision of "tomorrow" reflected his long-held attitudes toward urban leisure. It was both gleaming and futuristic and redolent of street life in an idealized city, featuring "bands of strolling players—singers, dancers, musicians, acrobats, clowns . . . roam[ing] about the Fair . . . strumming banjoes, singing popular songs, giving out swing music."[45]

The fair, which was held in the warmer months of 1939 and 1940, became a summation of the La Guardia administration's diffuse policies and positions on urban leisure. The 1938 crackdown on homosexual bars took place in advance of the arrival of millions of visitors to the fair. Organizers also hoped to monitor carefully the content of the exposition. The fair would have its own exclusive leisure venue, the Terrace Club, which was reserved for major sponsors. Whalen and La Guardia initially hoped that the fair would present a vision of a well-organized city that banished the salaciousness that often characterized urban nightlife and leisure.[46]

Disreputable sex attractions, though, had dominated the unofficial "midways" at past fairs in other cities. Even the vigilant organizers of New York's fair could not keep the seedy, rough-edged spirit of Coney Island or Times Square from invading the World of Tomorrow. When the turnstiles failed to produce the expected profits, the fair's organizers grudgingly began to allow sideshow attractions on the outskirts of Flushing Meadow. Attractions such as Strange As It Seems, Seminole Village, Sun Worshippers, and Nature's Mistakes filled the commercial strip outside the fairgrounds. Crystal Lasses, whose publicity at the door promised "real" naked women inside, was operated by the industrial designer Norman Bel Geddes (who had also created the Futurama exhibit inside the fair). The police inspected the Congress of Beauty, which was operated by the nightclub impresario Nils T. Granlund. They found that one dancer hid her nakedness with a fan, another had her costume undraped by a trained parrot, and a third, dressed and coiffed as half male and half female, did a solo "Dance of the Lovers." Salvador Dalí's anatomically suggestive funhouse, The Dream of Venus, featured topless women in a diving tank. The Reverend George Egbert complained to Paul Moss about "orgies" and "filthy numbers" at the Cuban Village cabaret. Moss and La Guardia ordered the police to raid the Cuban Village during its "Miss Nude of 1939" contest, and its three operators were put in jail.[47]

The fair's dual nature testified to the limited impact of fusion reform on public morals and the limits of La Guardia's ability to reshape the city along the lines of his high-minded expressive ideals. Along with his firing of the philosopher Bertrand Russell from the City College of New York for his advocacy of free love, the mayor's sputtering attacks on indecency at the fair marked an end to his six-year campaign to resculpt urban morals and leisure. The gathering of war clouds across the world only underlined the changing cultural landscape.[48] While La Guardia, Robert Moses, Thomas E. Dewey, and others had remade the city's government and economy and had prosecuted many alleged threats to public safety and morals, they never came close to eradicating the tolerance and experimentation that had marked the new behavior and nightlife of the 1920s. Instead they created a new variation of the ineffective moralism that had guided Tammany governments in the previous decade. Club entrepreneurs, meanwhile, adapted to these political conditions, and using new economic strategies they strove to remake Manhattan's nightlife in the late 1930s.

# CHAPTER 8
# A New Deal for Nightclubs

The year 1933 had brought the nadir of the nightclub era. However, if customers had left Manhattan that year and spent the subsequent half decade cut off from the city, they would have found a markedly different scene upon their return in 1938.

In that year virtually the only surviving club from the 1920s was the El Chico in Greenwich Village. Desirable locations had hosted numerous clubs in succession, while other buildings were converted to other uses or even demolished to make way for new construction. Nevertheless, by 1938 nightclubs were back in vogue. Liquor again flowed legally. There were fewer clubs, but some of them were enormous, and the profits and decorating budgets of popular sites far outpaced those of the late 1920s. That year the Stork Club, seating a thousand well-heeled customers on two floors in streamlined luxury, celebrated Walter Winchell's return from a long "sabbatical" in Hollywood. The leading Broadway columnist was now a nationally known radio and film star who covered major crime stories and European diplomatic crises as well as celebrity gossip. Winchell made Table 50 in the Cub Room of the Stork Club his base of operations, where he welcomed show business royalty and corporate and political leaders. The former vaudeville dancer had risen far, and so had the once illicit and disreputable nightlife that cradled his urban celebrity milieu. Federal agents no longer raided nightclubs; now the nation's top crime investigator, the FBI director J. Edgar Hoover, was a frequent dining partner of Winchell's at Table 50.[1]

The high-flying fortunes of Winchell and the Stork Club suggest a few of the trends that shaped the revival of nightclubs after 1933. The high-volume concept pioneered by Nils T. Granlund and the Hollywood Restaurant was widely copied. After an emphasis on low costs and unpretentiousness in the early 1930s, though, conspicuous consumption again was championed in nightlife, and celebrity performers and wealthy customers were again presented as paragons. To an extent, the flush new nightlife expressed the greater confidence in civic life, owing to the perceived progress that the La Guardia administration had made in improving employment opportunities, cleaning up government, and launching new building projects. In addition, the repeal of Prohibition brought about a new governance of alcoholic consumption and, more importantly, a new culture of drinking that emphasized personal self-control. Moreover, the animal passions that were explored and celebrated in nightlife in the 1920s were also more regulated, as exoticism and female nudity were now presented in more carefully defined, professionally polished, and often safely nostalgic contexts.

Nostalgia and revived prosperity in nightlife may have indicated the successes of the La Guardia administration, but the shortcomings of reform in the era of the New Deal were also evident in the field of leisure. Social and economic inequality remained in New York City, and events such as the riot in Harlem and the dragnets against transvestites indicated the limits of harmony and tolerance in the "new" city. Despite the revelations and public debate of the late 1920s and the early 1930s, nightclubs continued to objectify women and portray nonwhites in a derogatory fashion. Although the New Deal promoted egalitarianism, Manhattan's clubs continued to market their wares to different classes. Continuing debates about status, inclusion, and the nature of public behavior and amusements still deeply influenced the content of nightlife and the discourse about it. In short, it might be said that the class-based labor and political struggles of the New Deal era were reproduced in the basic bifurcation of Manhattan's nightlife between elite-minded nightclubs—occupying an environment that came to be called "café society"—and networks of plain and inconspicuous bars and dance halls for poor and socially stigmatized New Yorkers. Adding ideological critique to the latter networks were a handful of significant new leftist venues that promoted social democracy and racial equality.

In 1933 Broadway theaters led the general economic revival of Midtown. After keeping their houses shuttered for months, even years, some owners were now able to buy their way out of receivership at low prices. In October *Variety* claimed that "Broadway is in the throes of a big comeback." Seven critical and popular stage successes had opened within nine days, including *As Thousands Cheer, Murder at the Vanities*, and *Double Door.* Hollywood studios' purchase of film rights to stage plays became a fortuitous new source of substantial investment capital (amounting to over $1 million annually by 1936). In addition, although talking pictures kept driving theatrical companies across the nation out of business, the appearance of film stars such as Katharine Hepburn and Walter Huston in Broadway productions helped to revive some of the larger theaters in Manhattan. Fine new works by George S. Kaufman, George and Ira Gershwin, Irving Berlin, Maxwell Anderson, and Thornton Wilder, along with the occasional oddity such as the revue *Hellzapoppin*, ensured a thin but steady stream of durable hit shows. Lee and J. J. Shubert emerged from their period in bankruptcy more dominant on Broadway than ever before, and they achieved a virtual monopoly in theater ownership.[2] Notable assistance also came from the New Deal. A National Recovery Administration (NRA) code was drafted for Broadway theaters, and for two years the National Association of the Legitimate Theater administered the code to the owners' benefit. In 1935 the Federal One initiative of the Works Progress Administration (WPA) fostered the Federal Theatre Project, which reopened more theaters and allowed hundreds of unemployed actors and technicians to return to work.[3]

Despite these gains, Midtown's theatrical revival was limited in nature. Traveling and stock productions that had previously nurtured Broadway were not revived. On the street smaller and older theaters remained shuttered or were converted into the burlesque houses that generated public controversy. The street itself did not regain its former cachet as a pleasant promenade. The Federal Writers Project's *WPA Guide to New York City*, based on reporting from 1937 and 1938, portrayed the "outer shell" of the theater district as a crust of "bars and restaurants, electric signs, movie palaces, taxi dance halls, cabarets, chop suey places, and side shows of every description," while Times Square itself suffered from "scores" of "fruit juice stands garlanded with artificial palm leaves, theater ticket offices, cheap lunch counters, cut-rate haberdasheries, burlesque houses, and novelty concessions." Until the city government closed down burlesque in 1939, the creations of Irving Berlin and Thornton Wilder played alongside the Minskys' stock-burlesque spectacles. Broadway's reliance on largesse from Hollywood and Washington attested to the central fragility of the theatrical revival; neither was a guaranteed long-term endowment. Finally, vaudeville—an essential pillar of New York's theater industry—had been drastically diminished by talking pictures. By the end of the decade it would be virtually extinct. Theater, in short, revived itself along a few carefully calibrated and rationalized lines of development, and now lacked the depth and variety it had possessed before the Depression.[4]

The theater revival nevertheless aided the general recovery of Manhattan's nightlife. Nearby hotels, largely moribund as nightlife centers during Prohibition, rebounded. The passage in December 1933 of the Twenty-first Amendment, which repealed Prohibition and nullified the Volstead Act, proved to be the most significant factor in the revival of nightlife in the 1930s. After repeal, for example, theatrical ticket brokers moved their operations from various speakeasies—where their businesses had been illegal—into hotel lobbies. Only two months after repeal a *New York Times* reporter noted that "theatregoing [has] taken a big jump" and "begun to resume its old air of gayety." Ticket brokers told him that "last-minute orders pour in from these offices around late cocktail time and dinner time." Hotel box offices thrived because, in addition, repeal ensured that "the good old custom of dining in hotels has prodigiously revived."[5]

Thanks to the new legitimacy of the liquor trade, establishments that had gone bankrupt during Prohibition and the Depression were bought up and renovated by entrepreneurs. A *Times* reporter noted that by early 1934 large hotels were "spending thousands of dollars [an average of $14,000 each] to make their places more attractive," dispensing money "for bars, for lighting, for dance floors; money for gadgets that go with drinking, such as buckets for champagne, cradles for other wines; money for silver and glassware and kitchenware; money for noisemakers, rattles, balloons, paper caps and favors." The lavish spending was accompanied by the revival of elite pretenses among nightlife participants. Even though fewer dress codes were now in effect, a trend in favor of formal dress swept hotels and restaurants. "More men are in tails than . . . since the dinner jacket sneaked into favor . . . just before the World War," while "long frocks for the girls—however bare their backs" also gained popularity. Hotels and wealthy patrons conspired to make outward manifestations of class differentiation, common in nightlife in the 1920s, the fashion once again.[6]

In the 1930s, elitism still included an element of racism. As prosperity returned some venues changed their public profiles by banishing nonwhite customers and employees. Connie's Inn in Harlem somewhat incongruously converted itself into a German beer garden, and Chinese restaurants around Times Square were bought up, often without the consent of owners, and converted into more exclusive and Caucasian-themed eateries and nightclubs. The Palais Royal and the Churchill Restaurant (later Yeong's) were now being "reclaimed" from what *Variety* termed the "Yellow Peril" of the late 1920s, and white investors planned to re-Westernize the old premises of Rector's and Reisenweber's restaurants as well.[7]

As in the hotels, the impact of repeal on restaurants and smaller gathering places was profound. Predictably, repeal caused thousands of speakeasy locations to become vacant within weeks. A few speakeasy operators, particularly Sherman Billingsley of the Stork Club and John Perona of El Morocco, were able quickly to join the ranks of legitimate nightclub owners. The King Beer Company of Brooklyn, a legal business that was owned by the ex-bootlegging Steinberg brothers, underwrote the large new Casino de Paree, which was managed by Billy Rose. Despite the persistence of some speakeasy personnel, though, the vast networks of closeted drinking establishments that had arisen during Prohibition disappeared. Observers predicted that the leisure scene would revert to its pre-1920 appearance, exchanging speakeasies for a vast new population of revived saloons.[8]

But the old-time saloon did not make a comeback. The impact of both the Volstead Act and the general urban rebellion against it ensured that neither the laws nor the culture of drinking would resemble that of the pre-Prohibition era. The Twenty-first Amendment replaced the failed shared federal-state sovereignty over liquor enforcement with one of the strongest expressions of states' power in constitutional history. In New York City after repeal, Police Commissioner Edward Mulrooney instituted a municipal liquor code that conformed to the state's new regulation standards. All establishments were required to apply for licenses to serve liquor or wine; successful applicants paid $500 for the former and $66.67 for the latter. Sales on credit were banned, as were "screens, blinds or curtains" on windows facing the street. (This last requirement, a reporter noted, ensured that drinking would now "be used as window dressing in the [hotel] lobbies.") Doorways to adjoining premises were banned, as well as gambling, to ensure that no licensee became a host to illegal activity. Attempting to squelch the dangerous and "unhealthful" overcrowding that had been found in some speakeasies, the code banned alcoholic consumption by persons standing at bars. As the *Times* noted, this ensured that "the set-up of little tables still characteristic of the café" would dominate, and waiters would still manage commerce between the bar and the tables.[9]

This new physical configuration of drinking establishments immediately conferred a shrine-like quality to the bar. As the *New York Times* reporter Henry Brock argued, "so completely has prohibition at home and [drinkers'] going abroad to escape prohibition lifted the curse from the bar that the bar itself is exhibit A of the new order." "Coquette or metallically resplendent bars . . . had got to be the chief attraction of the speakeasies," and now hotels were installing "even more grand-scale bars." At the new Colonnades room at the Essex House a massive old oak bartop was exhumed and restored with great fanfare. After repeal, New Yorkers did not refer to legal drinking establishments as "saloons," but rather gave them a revealing new designation. The *bar* now lent its name to the entire surrounding venue.[10]

By February 1934 Henry Brock could also detect that post-repeal public drinking was now both more democratic and more disciplined. During Prohibition, barside drinking largely "for men only" had been replaced by semiprivate liquor consumption by mixed couples and groups sitting at tables. Repeal now made such table drinking truly public once again, encouraging (along with the new laws) a new restraint in behavior. "Unreconstructed speakeasy hounds," Brock noted, "confess a feeling akin to nakedness about this drinking in public." According to one such veteran of the 1920s, while "some people still get drunk at parties under repeal . . . they do not emit warwhoops or fall down and fold up on the floor. Instead, they freeze themselves stiffly upright. . . . *Control is the word, no longer abandon*." "A group that is crowding the drinks makes itself too conspicuous for comfort" in most establishments. Owing both to "a revolt of youth against slackness" and to "the retirement [from heavy drinking] of many elders," bars after 1933 welcomed "a cheerful, unhurried lot of men and women . . . with few symptoms of feverish thirst." Perhaps as a result of this change, heavy drinkers became eager to overcome the obsessive alcoholic consumption they had pursued during Prohibition. It was a New York stockbroker named Bill Wilson who in 1935 founded Alcoholics Anonymous, the organization that encouraged compulsive drinkers to confront their addiction— significantly, in tightly controlled semipublic group settings—and which became, in Ann Douglas's words, "the most important self-help group therapy in the world."[11]

In New York and across urban America, this new regime of alcoholic self-discipline greatly facilitated the revival of hotels, restaurants, and bars, and it was instrumental in conferring a respectable new status to nightclubs. More than any other urban institution, nightclubs seemed to be making the most surprising and diversified comeback. By November 1934, according to Henry Brock, there were "night clubs of every degree, night clubs for every complexion, night clubs for everybody." Repeal allowed for the flowering of clubs "in the back rooms of the old-time saloons," in neighborhoods, and in cavernous midtown venues such as the Hollywood Restaurant. Most of these sites featured "the thoughtful provision of hired entertainers . . . the floor show, with extra thrills for ringside tables." Three years later another *New York Times* writer observed that the nightclub business was booming "as has not been enjoyed hereabouts since the whoopee wild days of the late 1920s." While speakeasies had numbered in the thousands in New York City, *Variety*'s Abel Green argued in 1937 that "there are more niteries, pubs, taverns, roadside inns, large and small cafes, hotels and nite spots offering entertainment today than there were speakeasies during the Great Drought."[12]

In the first season of repeal, in late 1933, the new wave of nightclubs already fell into a few distinct categories. Since the economy was still weak, caution and conformity dictated the owners' strategies. As in the 1920s, some clubowners almost slavishly copied French models. Abel Green reported in *Variety* on "the Gallicizing of America": "Fol-de-rol that obtained in Paris, before Wall Street laid an egg, can be had right here at home." Within two months the Café de Paree, the Palais Royal, the Chez Paree, the Montmartre, the Montparnasse, and the Petit Palais all opened in Midtown. Later came the Bal Musette, which like the Montparnasse was located in the forties near Eighth Avenue, where the more genuine cafés attracted actual French customers. Establishments such as the enormous Casino de Paree or the brownstone-housed Petit Palais, though, were only cosmetically French, and provided only minor touches such as whipped cream on pancakes.[13]

Perpetuating a strategy pioneered by Florenz Ziegfeld (who had died in 1932), nightclubs used French precedents to justify their increased display of female nudity. The huge successes of stock burlesque and Nils T. Granlund's undraped productions at the Hollywood Restaurant inevitably encouraged copying by other clubs, but continental pretenses helped to smooth the introduction of ample nudity to a mass audience (and also to fend off the official persecution that plagued burlesque). In about 1934, for example, the Club Frivolity advertised a "Parisian Nights" revue, featuring twenty female dancers in Spanish dress who stripped down to their waists. A comic routine (perhaps inspired by *King Kong*) featured a man in a gorilla suit carrying a woman in rags, her breasts exposed.[14] In 1936 the sprawling and heavily promoted French Casino intensified the Gallic influence on Broadway—and its use to promote public nudity—by importing an entire show from the original Folies Bergères.

The vogue for French trappings was part of another post-repeal trend in nightclubs, as well as in hotels and restaurants that also featured entertainment: the revival of "class" or elite pretenses. Instead of sprouting along Broadway on the forties blocks as they had in the 1920s, higher-priced nightclubs now appeared in the east fifties, closer to the expensive hotels and apart from the now highly democratic and often disreputable theater district. In the 1920s very few clubs had been located in this neighborhood, except Don Dickerman's snobbish (and anti-Semitic) Heigh-Ho club and the Trocadero at the same site. These clubs, along with a few Russian tea rooms, had lured wealthier customers into this district of handsome but increasingly vacant brownstone mansions, and after repeal club operators with pretensions made it their center of operations. An early venture was a new House of Morgan on 54th Street and Madison Avenue, where the nightclub veteran Helen Morgan held forth amid white leather walls, gold mirrors, chrome trim, and an immense cocktail lounge featuring a circular bar.[15]

By the mid-1930s the Stork Club and the El Morocco epitomized the elitist trend in the east fifties. Sherman Billingsley, an Oklahoma native and the youngest in a family of veteran bootleggers, rebounded from a federal prison term for smuggling to become a prosperous real estate developer in the Bronx. In 1928 Billingsley acquired a speakeasy on the West Side he named the Stork Club. Three years later he moved it to

East 51st Street, and just after repeal he relocated to 53rd Street near Fifth Avenue. Billingsley pondered how to promote his costly new enterprise, rejecting "this or that Frenchy and fancified title," until his gimmick of awarding expensive gifts to customers finally paid off.[16]

Billingsley's close affiliation with the Bronx's Tammany Hall boss, Edward Flynn, had ensured his survival during Prohibition, and now Flynn's close ties to the Roosevelt administration helped to make the Stork Club a celebrated destination for government officials and prominent Democrats. Billingsley formed a notable friendship with the FBI director J. Edgar Hoover, who frequented the Stork whenever he was in town (accompanied by his ubiquitous assistant Clyde Tolson). Hoover recruited the clubowner as an informant on alleged radicals in Manhattan's nightlife. Billingsley, who had close ties to the theatrical community and had married a Ziegfeld dancer, also cultivated a stable of entertainers as regular customers. Walter Winchell became the Stork's most welcome guest, and Winchell turned the club's nightly goings-on into gossip that was consumed nationally through his syndicated column and radio broadcasts.[17]

Viewed in the context of nightclub history, the Stork Club's elite pretenses were mitigated by its embrace of the high-volume, no-cover charge business plan embraced by the more democratic clubs of the 1930s. The club was housed in a very large venue, two floors of an eight-story office building (which Billingsley owned in its entirety) that accommodated nearly a thousand patrons. Drink prices were high, beginning at one dollar, but a dollar also covered each individual's entry into the club. Billingsley cleverly adapted the Hollywood Restaurant's high-volume concept to a "class" club by lavishing attention on celebrities and carefully controlling the admission of average customers. His haughty focus on celebrity contrasted with more straightforward interest of nightclubs in the 1920s in having customers spend a great deal. Billingsley enforced an unwritten policy of admitting only white customers, which he relaxed only reluctantly a decade and a half later (after a celebrated conflict with the entertainer Josephine Baker). "The clean cut young American type is the type of customer Billingsley most wants," Robert Sylvester wrote. "He despises the erotic, the exotic and the foreign types." The huge sunken main room, the prominently placed numbered tables to which particular celebrities had special claim, the caricatures of these same luminaries hanging on the walls, and the altar-like, U-shaped bar were highly publicized. The club featured entertainment and dancing largely as appendages to the more prominent social pageantry. Vocalists who "headlined" at the Stork usually were celebrities themselves, such as Lita Grey Chaplin, the former wife of the film star.[18]

El Morocco, located a block north and east of the Stork Club, was run by John Perona, who had formerly operated a speakeasy for a gang of bootleggers. Like Billingsley, as *Fortune* magazine noted in 1936, Perona discriminated in admitting customers, using an "elastic cover charge . . . to separate the chic from the goats." While the Stork Club sought performers, writers, and politicians, El Morocco built a following of affluent college students. The club was smaller than the Stork, seating about four hundred, and it featured no floor show. Perona notably updated the condescending exoticism of nightlife in the 1920s with subtle new lighting techniques, an attention to color and textures, and a somewhat less crude resort to African and Saharan stereotypes. An artificial night sky, masked by palm trees, contrasted with the brightly lit glitter of the Stork's interior, while the zebra pattern on El Morocco's walls (easy to identify in newspaper photographs) became its trademark. A black man known as "Maraschino," draped in North African robes, served as the greeter and doorman. The El Morocco was adopted as a base by rival columnists of Walter Winchell, and these writers stoked a well-publicized competition with the Stork Club that sealed the east fifties' reputation as the site for carefully constructed, highly publicized leisure involving celebrities and other seekers of fame.[19]

Different in so many ways from the big business-oriented exclusivity that characterized the "society" of the Social Register in the Gilded Age, the nightlife in the east fifties during the mid-1930s nevertheless promoted social artifice and hierarchy in a way that earned it the nickname "café society." The origins of the term are unclear. The columnist Maury Paul, writing as Cholly Knickerbocker, had used it beginning in 1919, but its application to the nightclub scene of the mid-1930s was credited to either of two *Vanity Fair* editors, Clare Boothe Brokaw or Helen Lawrenson. In 1937 an article in *Fortune* magazine (which was published by Brokaw's new husband, Henry Luce) broadcast the label and encouraged its general use. Besides the main centers—the Stork, El Morocco, and Jack and Charlie's (known as "21")—café society could be found in the revived Montmartre (a longtime "snooty" locale, in *Variety*'s view), the Petit Palais (in a brownstone), and Barney Gallant's (the Greenwich Village promoter's new club on East 54th Street). There were also refurbished dining room-cabarets in hotels, such as the Plaza's Persian Room, the Pennsylvania's Madhattan Room, the St. Regis's Iridium Room, the Park Central's Cocoanut Grove, the Sherry-Netherland's Russian Eagle, and the Hotel New Yorker's club. Under murals created by artists such as Ralph Hitz and the late Joseph Urban's assistants (now operating as Urban Associates), guests paid cover charges averaging two to three dollars a person and at least one dollar per drink.[20] While more private than the large "class" clubs, the Stork and the El Morocco, the hotel rooms also gained heavy coverage in the newspaper columns, which incorporated them into the perceived network of café-society nightlife.

Café society's pretensions were exemplified by the vogue of the debutante cabaret singer. In 1938 a feature article in *Life* magazine traced this trend. The article claimed that it had been initiated in 1934 by Eve Symington. The daughter of a former U.S. senator—and the wife of a future senator as well—Symington became a nightclub singer because her family "felt they needed money" during the Depression. Thriving during the hotel cabaret revival, Symington was earning $1,000 a week by 1937, when she retired from the trade. The erstwhile society matron Cobina Wright, "no longer rich," "now makes money singing and coaching singers" such as her daughter Cobina, Jr., who made $300 a week performing at the Waldorf-Astoria's room. Alice Marble, the reigning national women's tennis champion, succeeded young Cobina Wright at the Waldorf. Adelaide Moffett, the daughter of a bankrupt former oil company executive, was scheduled to begin a residency at the new Delmonico's restaurant. Sigrid Lassen, the daughter of an exiled Russian princess who herself had worked as a Ziegfeld dancer and perfume saleswoman, sang at a club called Armando's.[21]

The debutante singers were more fortunate counterparts of the Committee of Fourteen's "charity cases," the working-class women in New York who had been forced into prostitution by hard times. The singers' significance to contemporary observers, though, lay in their perceived social pedigrees and graces; economically benighted as they might have been, they proved to be valuable assets for a nightlife subculture that turned away patrons of modest means and defined itself in opposition to the democratic nightlife on Broadway. A brittle note of caution sounded in the pronouncements of café society in the 1930s; notably absent were statements resembling those of the debutante Ellin Mackay in 1925, which praised nightclubs for their mingling of classes and sensibilities.[22]

The vogue of the debutante singer suggested undercurrents of defensiveness and insecurity in the ranks of café society. Young men from newly rich families with little social standing embraced the glamour that debutante singers were said to symbolize. The Stork Club, for example, decisively shaped the tastes and behavior of young Jack Kennedy, who followed the lead of his father, a New Deal official who was a frequent customer. The *Life* article of 1938 had derided the scene from without. Its anonymous author argued that "socialite singers take jobs away from poor girls," and was amused to claim that debutante talent searches unintentionally aped disreputable theatrical agencies' exploitation of poor women. An amateur singing contest at La Coq Rouge restaurant was "open only to debs or post-debs of good social standing," including the niece of the duchess of Marlborough and Winston Churchill, but *Life* concluded that "most of them were much more at home in the Social Register than in any musical register." In fact, the author went on, the singers (by implication, like all of the strivers who shaped café society) were liminal, even alienated figures in the city's social structure. "None of them tries the tougher Broadway night clubs where their names would mean little. Staid society, already aghast at the publicity appetite of today's debutantes, thinks the trend is deplorable."[23]

Similarly, the exclusivity of the Stork Club was designed to hide Sherman Billingsley's anxiety about real and imagined dangers to his standing and livelihood. Nightclubs had always been an uncertain business, sometimes even a dangerous one, and cautious owners did not forget this lesson during the club revival of the mid-1930s. Billingsley feared the restaurant union's influence on his employees in the wake of the New Deal—initially because of the union's ties to organized crime, but later on because of its perceived threat to his profit margin. The possible infiltration of his club by nonwhite and left-wing customers, as well as theft by competitors of his formula for success, also gave Billingsley concern.[24] While the New Deal introduced to America the concept of "social security"—the idea that all citizens might always rely on a dignified minimum status and income—the self-consciously hierarchical entrepreneurs of café society found reasons to feel less secure during a time of striking success.

Such anxieties were scarce at the most unapologetically lavish new venue for café society. The Rainbow Room had the benefit of being underwritten by the world's wealthiest family. Opening in late 1934 on the sixty-fifth floor of the new RCA Building in Rockefeller Center, the Rainbow Room blended the models of the roof-garden restaurant and the exclusive "nest" club and took them, literally and figuratively, to new heights. The Room blended the executive-nest concept of the Chrysler Building's Cloud Club with that of the east-fifties nightclub, creating a glittering new synthesis of wealth and leisure. The Rockefeller family itself—especially John Jr. and his most showmanlike son, Nelson—took an interest and a lead in developing the Rainbow Room. Backed by the family's bottomless resources, the Room could lose hundreds of thousands of dollars a year—as, inevitably, it did—and still survive. In an indication of this confidence, the club's manager, John Roy, carried the debutante-employee trend to new lengths. *Fortune* magazine noted that even "one of the telephone girls is a Social Registerite."[25]

Constructed by the firm of Todd, Robertson, and Todd and decorated by Elena, "the Rainbow Room," in *Fortune*'s words, "is one of the few night resorts in the world that really looks like a tank-town movie fan's idea of the elegant life." The club gained its name from a "color organ," operated by an employee from an elaborate electrical switchboard, that bounced countless hues off of a mirrored ceiling dome and a chandelier. Mirrors and chrome lined the terraced emerald-green room, which housed both a restaurant and a revolving dance floor. The Ray Noble Orchestra serenaded dancers, who modeled their steps on those of the resident professionals Ramon and Renita. At $3.50 the Rainbow Room's *prix fixe* dinner was one of the most expensive in the city. More welcoming to middle-class patrons was the Rainbow Grill on the opposing (western) side of the building's floor, which served dinners for $2.50 and eschewed the Room's stiff dress code. "A good-sized delegation of out-of-town celebrants" might have helped the rooms to achieve solvency, but as *Fortune* reported "the Rockefeller interests can be relied on to remedy the [deficit] sooner or later." The result was a club that operated independently of the rules of economic scarcity by which its competitors had to play, and that provided its customers with the opportunity to inhabit Hollywood's version of Manhattan's nightlife. Within a year, in turn, the MGM movie studio memorialized the Rainbow Room in an even more iconic vision, the Club Raymond, in the 1935 musical *Swing Time.*[26]

The construction and design of Rockefeller Center, in which the Rainbow Room was housed, indicate the general spatial and stylistic forces at work in Manhattan that directly and indirectly reshaped late nightlife in the 1930s. Looming like jagged granite peaks in a brand-new mountain range, the towers of the center (eventually twelve in number) were the most dramatic new addition to the Manhattan skyline since the Depression halted skyscraper construction. The site of the center, between Fifth and Sixth Avenues and 48th and 51st Streets, had been a disreputable area of tenements and speakeasies. (Columbia University, which owned most of the land, had been a negligent landlord.) As the Rockefeller-funded Committee of Fourteen had found in 1928, these blocks held speakeasies such as the Aquarium, Quigley's, and the Spirit of Paris Society. The Green Room nightclub, Maxine's basement club, Tony's speakeasy, and "furnished rooms" used for prostitution graced West 49th Street, fathoms below the space in the air that would later be occupied by the Rainbow Room. In 1928 persons standing at the location of the future entrance to the Radio City Music Hall, looking across Sixth Avenue toward Broadway, could glimpse the Charm Club, the Knight Club, Pete's Blue Hour Restaurant, the Rose Room Club, the Greenwich Club, and Tommy Guinan's Chez Florence—many of which were shut down that year by the federal government's "war on the nightclubs."[27]

Also in 1928, Otto Kahn had approached Columbia University with the idea of razing one of these blocks to construct a new building for the

Metropolitan Opera. The Rockefellers became involved as a potential financial backer. When the Opera withdrew from the project, John D. Rockefeller, Jr. took the lead and expanded it into a skyscraper development that would cover three entire blocks. "Metropolitan Square" became "Radio City" when the General Electric Company (the owner of NBC) signed on as the main tenant, but John Jr. renamed the center in honor of his ancient father. (John Sr. lived long enough conceivably to learn that his teetotaling, devoutly religious son had opened a nightclub.) The architect Raymond Hood's design derived from the German notion of the *Stadtkrone*, a city under one roof, featuring tall office buildings with diverse open spaces in between. Internationally themed skyscrapers encouraged a monumental sort of stylistic eclecticism and a lavish public art program. In 1933 the Mexican artist Diego Rivera contributed his mural, *Men at the Crossroads*, to the east lobby of the RCA Building. The left half of the mural included a decadent nightclub scene—perhaps a foreshadowing of the Rainbow Room?—amid other vignettes of the war- and disease-ridden capitalist present, while the right half depicted Lenin leading the workers toward communism and liberation. Nelson Rockefeller paid off Rivera and ordered the mural destroyed.[28]

The Rivera affair was one of many controversies surrounding the new complex. Some criticisms were savage; Lewis Mumford called the entire project "the sorriest failure of imagination and intelligence in modern American architecture." Even Mumford, though, was delighted by the RKO Roxy Theater in the Radio City Music Hall, an early component of the center that opened in 1932. The world's largest indoor theater, with 6,200 seats, a 210-foot stage containing three movable sections, and the most spacious orchestra pit yet seen, the Radio City Music Hall (as the theater also came to be called) was also lavishly decorated with contemporary art. Even the restrooms awed patrons with their murals and sculptures. The enormous expense, however, collided with the economic realities of 1932, as well as the rapid extinction of the vaudeville that was to have been the theater's mainstay. After Samuel "Roxy" Rothafel was fired as manager and RKO went into receivership, John D. Rockefeller, Jr. took over the theater's operations. The name of the Rockettes, an enormous, sanitized incarnation of the Ziegfeld girl show, now suggested Rockefeller instead of Roxy. As one history of Radio City notes, "worried earlier that he would be forced to run the Metropolitan Opera, [John Jr.] now found himself patron of the Rockettes." Even more than the Rainbow Room, the Radio City Music Hall showed how the wealthiest "legitimate" economic forces helped to pull New York's nightlife out of the throes of the Great Depression. While still incomplete by 1938, Rockefeller Center loomed for Mumford and others as a portent of the possible future demolition of more vital and valuable old Manhattan neighborhoods. The Rainbow Room, at worst, took the publicly funded elitism of Robert Moses's Tavern on the Green a step further, suggesting a future of privately constructed and policed nightlife for the benefit of only the most affluent city residents.[29]

Elite trends tell only a part of the story. Rockefellers and debutantes still shared nightclub ownership with former bootleggers and other speakeasy veterans. In 1935, Abel Green of *Variety* reported a "renaissance" of less exclusive nightclubs, even though venues such as Barney Gallant's club had recently failed. The murder of a gangster at the Paradise Restaurant served as a pretext for the firing of Nils T. Granlund, while the owners of Granlund's former establishment, the Hollywood Restaurant, sold half of their interest to the resident bandleader, Abe Lyman. While clubs featuring female impersonators had been banned from official licensing by Commissioner Paul Moss, "the saucy lyric songsters continued in the smaller joints, [a] heritage of the hideaway speaks." Clubs in Greenwich Village such as Jimmy Kelly's and Sully's Show Boat exhibited both the pretensions and the pandering that took place in the district, where strippers plied their trade in cellars next to clubs with interiors designed by Joseph Urban.[30]

Green also argued that "Harlem is doing a valiant comeback, flourishing on the psychology of slumming in the black-and-tans." Popular uptown sites now included the Savoy Ballroom, Dickie Wells's Shim Sham Club, the Ubangi Club, Pod's and Jerry's, the renowned Cotton Club, and Small's Paradise (recovering from near-ruin during the Depression). However, Connie's Inn—once the staple of black-themed entertainment in Harlem, but now a beer hall—had relocated to 48th Street. Within weeks after the riot in Harlem of March 1935, the district's nightlife renaissance came to a halt. The Cotton Club found its all-white clientele shunning visits to uptown. In February 1936 the famous site on Lenox Avenue and 142nd Street was closed. (Later in 1936, though, a successful new cabaret, the Plantation Club, was launched in this venue.) The next fall a new Cotton Club opened at 200 West 48th Street, the former site of the Palais Royale and the second Connie's Inn, which had recently failed.[31] The midtown Cotton Club survived for the rest of the decade on the strength of its main attraction, Cab Calloway's orchestra. Meanwhile, though, African American performers suffered from a dearth of roles in the Broadway theater and the decline of black vaudeville touring circuits.

Cab Calloway's success at the Cotton Club reflected the fact that the African American presence in nightlife after 1935 was almost wholly dependent on the new vogue of big-band jazz, or "swing" music. Before that year most white customers had shown little inclination for the blues-inflected, rough-timbred instrumental improvisation of King Oliver, Jelly Roll Morton, Louis Armstrong, and their heirs—the founders of the great mainstream jazz tradition. "Hot" jazz was popular with black audiences but enjoyed only a small following among white musicians and fans. In August 1935, though, Benny Goodman's orchestra caused a sudden popular sensation during its residency at Los Angeles's Palomar Ballroom, which led to national success and heavy promotion of a new "swing era." That fall, *Variety* dropped its regular "Nite Clubs" section and added a new column on "Swing Stuff." The shift in white Americans' listening tastes was led by a new generation of adolescent consumers that had been profoundly shaped by the disruptions of the Depression and was now eager for a music it could call its own and look to for reassurance and fun. The "jitterbug" generation—especially its intense, stylishly dressed, multiethnic New York City contingent—gained considerable attention from the press and from adults concerned about its alleged contribution to juvenile delinquency. African American counterparts to the white jitterbugs—some arrayed in a costume of protest, the zoot suit—graced the Savoy Ballroom and other venues in Harlem with spectacular dance steps.[32]

Swing music quickly dominated the live music scene of midtown Manhattan. As befitted the white domination of the big-band era, black musicians were definitely unequal partners, featured and regularly employed far less often in theater engagements and long-running club dates. Large venues such as the Paramount Theater played host to the Benny Goodman, Artie Shaw, and Glen Gray big bands, as well as Ray Noble's more traditional "sweet" group from the Rainbow Room; a rarer African American band was the Cab Calloway orchestra, making the short trip from the midtown Cotton Club. More significantly, by 1935 West 52nd Street had became the location for a string of swing-jazz clubs. In microcosm, the scene on West 52nd, or "Swing Street," represented both the marginalization of black performers and the possibilities for a culturally radical alternative to mainstream nightlife in the 1930s.

The block of the street between Fifth and Sixth Avenues featured rows of brownstones that the city and developers had long targeted for demolition. These sites had been filled with speakeasies. In the early 1930s wrecking balls and rivet guns a block away heralded the construction of Rockefeller Center and the demolition of the Eighth Avenue elevated track. In 1935 a row of brownstones on 52nd Street itself was razed, but the surviving structures soon became filled with low-rent clubs, often in basements. Swing Street amounted to one of the most creative renovations of emptied speakeasy space in Manhattan. Anomalies included "21," at that address on the block, a rival to the exclusive clubs found in the east fifties, and Jack White's Club 18, which mostly updated Texas Guinan's raucous revues and humiliations of elite customers (waiters screamed abuse at Alfred Vanderbilt and gave a Chinese diplomat a bag of dirty laundry). Generally, though, 52nd Street featured sites dedicated to swing music. These included the Onyx, which opened in 1927 as the street's pioneer music club. It was now joined by the Famous Door (in the Onyx's old location at number 35), the Yacht Club, Tillie's of Harlem, and Club 18. The Three Deuces and Jimmy Ryan's followed later in the decade. Just across Sixth Avenue on the street were the Hickory House and the Harlem Uproar House, while Kelly's Stable sat behind them on 51st Street. For at least a decade, Swing Street presented a kind of working-class, stylistically unpretentious rebuff to the values and ideology represented by the Rockefeller Center complex abutting it to the south.[33]

The Famous Door became the best known of these sites, in part because its owners included the popular radio bandleader Lenny Hayton. Hayton's manager, Jack Colt, also oversaw the club's affairs. Other investors, chipping in a total of $2,800, included swing musicians on the cusp of fame such as Jimmy Dorsey and Glenn Miller. The club was intended to provide a reliable venue for swing musicians and a place where they could gather, but other customers were attracted by the door inside (autographed by visiting celebrities) which gave the club its name, the fine music, and drinks that started at fifty cents. Financial problems forced the club to move down the street in 1936, but its popularity at the new site was soon ensured. Colt employed black pianists such as Teddy Wilson and Art Tatum to perform during intermissions, and the club also provided the first midtown exposure for Bessie Smith (near the end of her career) and Billie Holiday (at the beginning of hers). Generally, though, the Famous Door was a white musicians' club.[34]

Swing Street as a whole was a white domain in which black musicians found little encouragement and employment. In her autobiography Billie Holiday lodged a famous indictment against the district, noting that "white musicians were 'swinging' from one end of 52nd Street to the other, but there wasn't a black face in sight on the street except Teddy Wilson. . . . There was no cotton to be picked between Leon and Eddie's and the East River, but man, it was a plantation any way you looked at it." At the Famous Door Holiday and Wilson "were not allowed to mingle any kind of way. The minute we were finished with our intermission stint we had to scoot out back to the alley or go out and sit in the street." She and Wilson were eventually fired for mingling with a white customer, the bandleader Charlie Barnet. (Holiday had to wait until the 1940s to make a return to Swing Street, when she spent two successful years at Kelly's Stable.)[35] The racial predicament was bad enough to inspire a crusade of sorts among sympathetic white participants, which ultimately resulted in the founding in 1939 of the color-blind Greenwich Village nightclub mockingly named Café Society.

Surprisingly, it was only in the closing months of the decade that radical left-wing politics in Manhattan thrust the cultural phalanx of its activity into nightlife. Especially in light of the fact that Europe had played host to a vital political cabaret culture for decades, the leftist New York night-club was very late in coming.

However, in Manhattan it grew out of fertile soil. During the early 1930s the city's Communist Party, targeting African American support in Harlem, had used the district's heralded nightlife as a base for recruit-ment. In 1931, most notably, the party held what the mainstream press called "the first Soviet-style show trial in America" in the Harlem Casino. Two thousand spectators filled the dance hall to witness the cas-tigation of August Yokinen, a party member and janitor at the Finnish Workers' Educational Club in Harlem who had failed to react when three black patrons were ejected from a club dance. (Yokinen dutifully pled guilty and was ordered to hold rallies and demonstrations for racial equality in Harlem.) Most New Yorkers, though, associated communism in the city with bloody labor clashes and police repression. By mid-decade some leftist rhetoric and much voter support had been co-opted by the La Guardia administration and the Labor Party, the new anti-Communist organization it nurtured. This co-optation had cultural effects as well. Commentators on swing music began to ally it with the populistic but pro-capitalist sentiments of the New Deal consensus—a consensus that rejected political radicalism, often was insensitive to racial inequality, and only reluctantly empowered the working classes.[36]

Despite their political setbacks, leftists in New York City retained con-siderable cultural influence. Responding to continuing racial inequality in Manhattan, as well as to the growing international threat of fascism, politically radical musicians, theatrical artists, and promoters launched a few articulate and forceful alternatives to regular nightlife institutions. What the historian Michael Denning has called the "cultural front"—a large, diverse, and well-defined alternative to the traditional capitalistic concept of America—was forming. The cultural apparatus of movies, radio, and the WPA Federal One programs for creative professionals, Denning argues, achieved a critical mass by the mid-1930s. The Group Theatre challenged the safe formulas and conventions of Broadway; the Newspaper Guild, led by Heywood Broun, fostered critical journalism; and the *Partisan Review* brought a Marxist perspective to its championing of modern art and its critique of mass culture. Other elements of this movement learned to embrace popular entertainment. The Communist Party itself sought to incorporate swing music into its advocacy of the proletariat, hiring young black musicians for Young Communist League dances and for its upstate summer gathering, Camp Unity.[37] A multiethnic wave of young people from the jitterbug generation supplied much of the energy and the idealism behind this movement.

An important figure on the New York scene, perhaps the only creative figure with the ambition, audacity, and talent to bring a radical artistic vanguard together, was Orson Welles. Like many innovators in the city's nightlife, Welles was a midwesterner who shunned bourgeois conventions to indulge in urban culture. By 1936, not yet twenty-one, Welles brought his precocious theatrical gift to the Federal Theatre Negro Unit in Harlem. He provocatively staged an all-black, Haitian-themed version of *Macbeth* in the Lafayette Theatre and advocated equal opportunity for African American performers. While some Harlemites criticized *Macbeth*'s supervision by white men—Welles and the producer John Houseman—the production was a popular sensation, filling the theater and the surrounding streets with crowds of enthusiastic African Americans. The next year Welles's and Houseman's production of the labor-themed opera *The Cradle Will Rock* seemed to herald a radical theatrical alternative to Broadway, but the Federal Theatre Project, facing conservative criticism, halted its presentation. (That criticism escalated until Federal One's funding was terminated in 1939.) In addition, Welles's frenetic work pace, traveling between jobs in speeding ambulances and toiling without sleep for days—fueled by prodigious eating, drinking, and amphetamines—diverted him from a coherent radical artistic agenda. Welles remained committed to social progress—for example, in 1941, after completing *Citizen Kane*, he staged Richard Wright's *Native Son* in New York—but he was an increasingly distracted advocate.[38]

Although his showmanship and love of nightclubs qualified him superbly for the task, Welles—unlike another theatrical impresario, Billy Rose—never tried to create a club. This fact epitomizes the Left's surprising reluctance during most of the 1930s to found its own nightclubs, despite the creative and communitarian promise of such venues that had recommended them to European activists, and that seemed to be easily translatable to the New York scene. Signs of experimentation soon emerged, though. Greenwich Village had lost a great deal of its political cachet and had suffered from the rise, fall, and revival of tourist-oriented nightlife. The Cuban-themed El Chico and the burlesque-themed Jimmy Kelly's did not quite turn the Village into a second Times Square, but before 1935 the district also could not create an alternative to mainstream nightlife. Still, a handful of bohemian entrepreneurs gradually nurtured a self-consciously radical leisure scene. Max Gordon, for example, ran the Village Vanguard in a succession of former speakeasy venues, finally settling in a basement on Seventh Avenue. More avant-garde than radical, the Vanguard at first featured poetry as often as swing music. While the Vanguard attracted an audience and some favorable press, its fame as a jazz club—and its wave of imitators in the Village—lay decades in the future.[39]

The radical café finally made appearances in New York in 1939. The previous December the Theatre Arts Committee for Peace and Democracy (TAC), an organization of the Communist Party, had sponsored a concert at Carnegie Hall called "From Spirituals to Swing" which promoted the musical traditions of proletarian African Americans. The next year the TAC, while fending off attacks from hostile theater unions, formed Cabaret TAC at the midtown YMHA on Lexington Avenue. In Abel Green's opinion, it was "the first American nightclub that appealed to the politically-minded trade." Featuring a swing trio as well as the folk singer Aunt Molly Jackson, a racially mixed chorus, and politically minded music such as Earl Robinson's "Ballad for Americans," Cabaret TAC was an eclectic and high-minded effort to transplant the European cabaret concept to America in the face of the commercialized entertainment that New York had produced. However, the cabaret operated only sporadically, and it gave its last presentations in 1940.[40]

More typically Manhattan in style was Café Society, which was founded in January 1939 on Greenwich Village's Sheridan Square by a footwear wholesaler named Barney Josephson. Urged on by his brother, an active Communist, Josephson established the mockingly named café as "the right place for the wrong people," a proudly color-blind club that would present black musicians and social critiques without restraint. Showcasing Billie Holiday, who famously introduced the anti-lynching ballad "Strange Fruit" at the club, as well as political comedians such as Zero Mostel, Café Society brought a unique critical perspective to nightlife just as the 1930s were ending. Popular Front activists such as Teddy Wilson, Lena Horne, Orson Welles, and Canada Lee (later the star of Welles's *Native Son*) showed up as performers and customers. In 1940 Josephson opened another club, Café Society Uptown, on East 58th Street. The concept proved so popular that it attracted the attention of J. Edgar Hoover, who put the clubs under the surveillance of the FBI. While the two venues ironically attracted some of the café-society elites they satirized, they also provided a durable and influential radical perspective that served as a model for alternative nightlife in the 1940s.[41]

In the long view provided by the historian Michael Denning, we perceive the cultural Left gaining some ascendency during World War II, but then facing erosion and suppression during the conservative revival of the postwar era.[42] Through the history of nightlife especially, though, we can see that already in the late 1930s radical cultural politics had been pushed to the fringe, both nationally by moderates such as Franklin Roosevelt and by conservatives such as J. Edgar Hoover and in New York City by the shrewd and calculating Fiorello La Guardia. Instead of a decentralized worker's paradise, La Guardia and Roosevelt had helped to create a socially moderate but bureaucratically massive welfare state that was adept at gaining support from unions and interest groups by means of limited legal protections and piecemeal entitlement programs. As the story of Robert Moses particularly attests, this meant that power now flowed into new bureaucracies that could be as undemocratic and autocratic as the capitalist monopolies of old.

In the late 1930s, as war approached on the world scene, the city's nightlife reflected this new bureaucratic tendency, a reordering of capital and venues to serve masses of customers as efficiently as possible, offering titillation and inebriation without threatening the social status quo. For the sake of profitability and a form of social order, the social and sexual experimentation of the 1920s had been subsumed into a highly rationalized nightlife industry. This was, perhaps, the ironic result of the waves of investigation and regulation that had washed over Manhattan's nightlife in the decade and a half since the advent of the Fay-Guinan nightclub.

We turn now to the career of the most successful nightlife entrepreneur of the 1930s, Billy Rose, whose innovations in his clubs particularly illustrate the evolution of attitudes toward city life itself. As Rose took his own path to the city government's culminating leisure enterprise of the decade—the New York World's Fair—he reshaped concepts of the nightclub in ways that seemed to indicate the closing of the institution's definitive era in Manhattan.

# CHAPTER 9
# Billy Rose and Nightclubs for the Masses

New York City's nightlife in 1938 or 1939 featured entrepreneurs as colorful and varied as Barney Josephson, Sherman Billingsley, Max Gordon, and John Perona. In those years, however, they all stood in the shadow of the diminutive Billy Rose. In a familiar fashion for nightclub promoters, the former William Rosenberg had risen from obscurity to the peak of the business in less than a decade. At the end of the 1930s Rose's reputation rested on the unprecedented success of his two large clubs in midtown Manhattan, the Casa Mañana and the Diamond Horseshoe.

The Casa Mañana, which opened in December 1937, was situated in the old Earl Carroll Theatre at Seventh Avenue and 50th Street. It seated eleven hundred customers. The Diamond Horseshoe (on 46th Street, west of Broadway), which opened exactly a year later, held seven hundred. The Casa was decorated in the popular streamlined or *moderne* style, with a revolving stage and a "Palm Beach Bar," complete with sun lamps, in the rear of the room. The Horseshoe was an elaborate updating of an opulent saloon, inspired by nostalgic tales of the lobster palaces and revues of the 1890s and 1900s. Art Nouveau flourishes wound their way down staircases and up the basement pillars, deep burgundy tones, chandeliers, and beveled mirrors dominated the room, and display cases held reproductions of Diamond Jim Brady's jeweled stickpins and other evocative artifacts. The Silver Dollar Bar was upholstered by the eponymous currency embedded in its acrylic floor. Entertainment in both clubs featured Rose's trademark blend of vaudeville, burlesque, and popular talent—what *Variety* called "corn, schmaltz, and cheesecake" (see Fig. 8).[1] The Casa's opening revue featured the Irish American tenor Morton Downey, the fan dancer Sally Rand, and the comedian Doc Rockwell, and later also headlined the actress Lupe Velez, the singer Peggy Fears, the comedians Shaw and Lee, and the dancing 12 Aristocrats. The Diamond Horseshoe's opening featured "the comic waiter" Frank Libuse, old-time ballad singers Fritzie Scheff and Joe E. Howard, Tom Patricola and his dancing shoes, bell ringers, fire eaters,

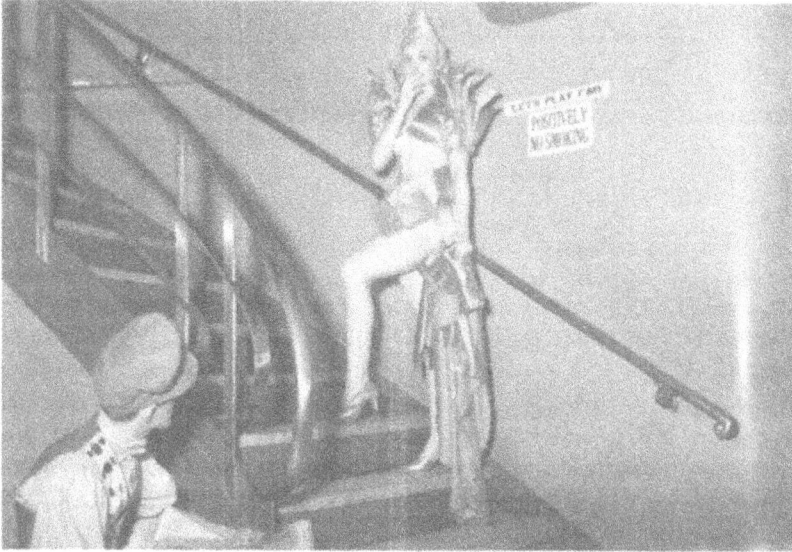

Figure 8.  A dancer in typical costume for a nightclub revue, 1938, backstage at Billy Rose's Casa Mañana. Billy Rose Theatre Collection, The New York Public Library for the Performing Arts, Astor, Lenox, and Tilden Foundations.

and a reenactment of the Ziegfeld icon Anna Held's famous milk bath (atop the bar, behind a scrim veil).[2]

Rose's two clubs admitted capacity audiences almost every night and proved to be the most consistently profitable high-volume nightclubs in New York City. As the historian Lewis Erenberg has shown, they became models for similar establishments in New York and in cities across North America. Their success and influence indicated important transformations in leisure and in American culture during the Great Depression. Erenberg, for example, has argued that Billy Rose's smoothly run, mass-oriented nightclubs represented a kind of "vision in miniature of a smoothly operating futuristic world."[3]

This futuristic vision derived its success from Rose's canny study of the nightclub business in the 1920s and early 1930s. His clubs were complex cultural productions that blended the wild, primitivist tendencies of the inaugural Fay-Guinan clubs with the pretensions of the "class" establishments of the late 1920s. Rose also carefully shaped his business ventures to conform to the contours of policing and regulation that had been carved out by reform groups and municipal governments of the Prohibition and Depression eras. Rose took great care with his expenditures, bookkeeping, and marketing methods and brought a new element of economic predictability to the nightclub business.

The content of Rose's entertainment showed the most significant innovation, however. While his clubs pushed female nudity to new levels of prominence, they also stressed vaudeville and circus themes, nostalgic motifs that reassured and comforted a chastened and cautious Depression-era clientele. More than any other clubowner Rose drew on America's small-town entertainment roots to reconceive the nature of the city's amusements. In doing so, Rose consciously embraced the egalitarian ideology of the New Deal and the Democratic Party and brought a new political undercurrent to the content of nightlife.

Rose also worked to break down the walls that separated the nightclub from the fresh air of the outdoors. His most dramatic departure from nightclub traditions did not come in his clubs themselves but rather at world's fairs and other large-scale, open-air expositions. Rose's unusual professional odyssey in the 1930s—from Broadway to the circus, to Fort Worth, Texas and the Cleveland lakeshore, back to Broadway, and then to the highly successful Aquacade at the 1939–40 New York World's Fair—also showed mass taste evolving (and being steered) away from the modernistic, urban identity that nightlife had symbolized in the 1920s. Nightclubs and the mass audience, now poised between the Depression and war, pursued both titillation and nostalgia within a new context of self-discipline and careful municipal regulation, but they also increasingly moved out of urban settings and took the first steps toward a suburban or posturban concept of leisure fantasy and fulfillment. Billy Rose's success story thus can be considered both a final chapter of the story of the nightclub era and a prologue to the new leisure trends of mid-twentieth-century America.

The slow pace of economic recovery and the repeal of Prohibition both ensured that the one nightclub success story of the Depression-ridden early 1930s—the high-volume, no cover-charge restaurant—would thrive even more in the immediate future. The Hollywood Restaurant had pioneered the formula in 1929 by banishing cover charges, instituting low dinner prices, and offering an elaborate vaudeville-style show and a scantily dressed female chorus line at no extra cost. Operating in a huge room, the Hollywood's economy of scale allowed it to make a greater profit per customer, despite its low prices. On the eve of repeal, though, the Hollywood's owners, Joe Moss and Jake Amron, faced strong new competition from the Paradise Restaurant, which they could glimpse through the door of their establishment across the intersection of Broadway and 49th Street (see Fig. 9). The Paradise's success occurred largely because its owners, Nicky Blair and Jack Adler, lured their producer and master of ceremonies, Nils T. Granlund, away from

Figure 9. The façade of the Paradise Restaurant, at Broadway and 49th Street, in 1935. "NTG" was Nils Thor Granlund, the impresario who earlier had originated the high-volume, low-cost nightclub, complete with dinner and variety show, at the nearby Hollywood Restaurant. New York Public Library.

the Hollywood. Each venue packed in thousands of customers weekly. Both occasionally featured "headline" acts; in October 1933, for example, the Hollywood employed Rudy Vallée's orchestra and the Paradise featured Paul Whiteman. Gross earnings totaled at least $20,000 a week for each club. At the Paradise Granlund recreated his famous chorus line, whose "girls," in *Variety*'s opinion, "were unquestionably the beaut champs extant."[4]

Another new high-volume club, the Casino de Paree on West 54th Street, had also opened in 1933, in anticipation of the end of Prohibition. The Casino was owned by the Steinberg brothers, bootleggers who were now the legitimate owners of the Kings Beer brewery in Brooklyn. One of their limited partners was Billy Rose, who had been hired to produce the Casino's shows. In the 1920s Rose had operated two speakeasies, the Backstage and the Fifth Avenue Clubs. The former closed because of violent gangland interference in the liquor trade, while the latter failed because Rose refused to serve any liquor at all. While he was uneasy about working again for underworld veterans, Rose brought experience and a brazen self-confidence to bear on the task of applying the Hollywood Restaurant's formula for success to the Casino.

Occupying the former Gallo Theater, the Casino de Paree allowed hundreds of diners to watch shows and to dance (see Figs. 10a and b). Like the Hollywood and the Paradise, the Casino charged no cover fee and set low rates for dinner (from $1.00 to $2.50). For his show, Rose

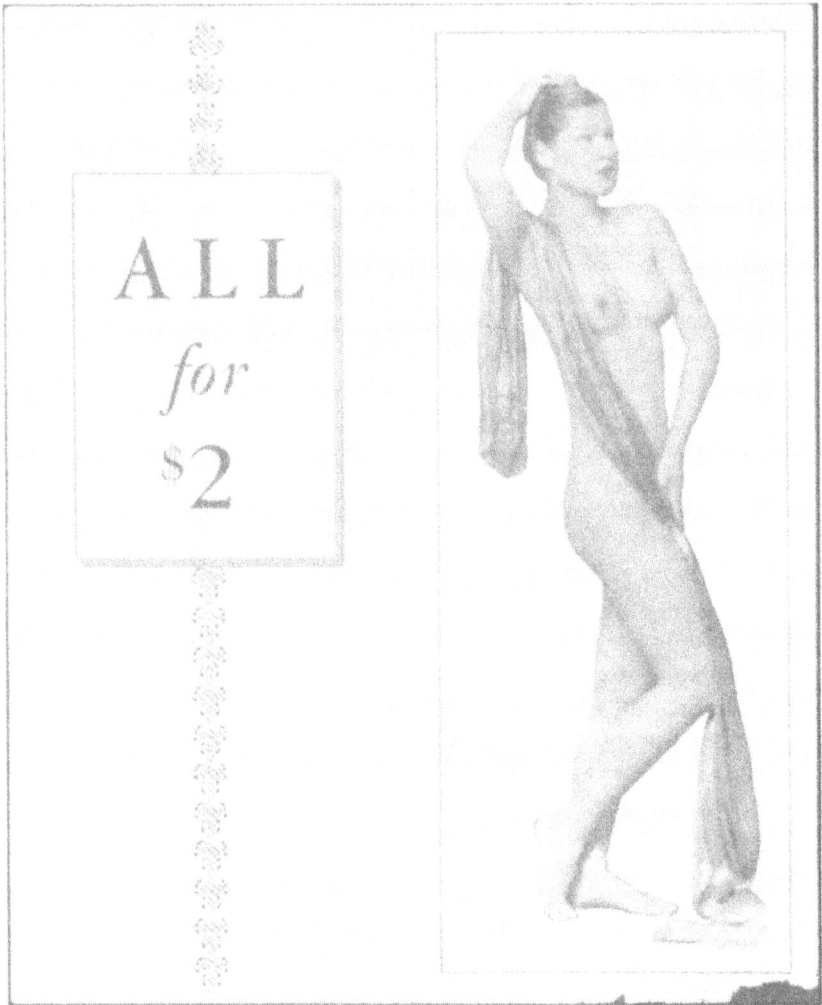

Figure 10a and b. A handbill advertising the Casino de Paree, which opened in 1933 under the management of Billy Rose. Like other clubs of the era, this one emphasized low prices, newspaper publicity, and the undraped female form. Billy Rose Theatre Collection, The New York Public Library for the Performing Arts, Astor, Lenox, and Tilden Foundations.

drew on lessons he had learned in the previous two years as the producer of a continually evolving revue variously entitled *Corned Beef and Roses*, *Sweet and Low*, and *Crazy Quilt* (its final designation). Underwritten by the wealthy bandleader and former clubowner Roger Wolfe Kahn, starring Rose's wife, the comedienne Fanny Brice, and George Jessel,

WHAT IS IT?

**IS IT A THEATRE . . . NO!!**
though on a STAGE we present a full length
musical extravaganza produced by BILLY ROSE.

**IS IT A RESTAURANT . NO!!**
though you eat and drink what you will (thanks to
Liquor License No. RL-733).

**IS IT A DANCE HALL . NO!!**
though there is continuous dancing to the music
of two of America's great orchestras.

**IS IT A SIDE SHOW . . NO!!**
though in an ordinary size FISH BOWL you see a
completely nude LIVING little lady.

WHAT IS IT?

**It's the Most Sensational
Bargain in the history of
New York Night Life!!!**

BELIEVE IT OR NOT! FOR $2
you get the Revue, the Dinner, the Dancing, The Girl
in the Fish Bowl, and a hundred other novelties—

*Casino de Paree*

54th Street              Opens at 6 P.M.
West of Broadway         Tel. Cir. 7-2686

*What the Critics Say—*

WALTER WINCHELL in the
                    *Daily Mirror* . . .
    "New York has a smash—not for just a night,
    not for just a year—but ALL WAYS."

PERCY HAMMOND in the
                    *Herald-Tribune* . . .

ED SULLIVAN in the *Daily News* . . .
    "The best sound show in New York."

ROBERT GARLAND in the
                    *World-Telegram* . . .

BERNARD SOBEL in the *Daily Mirror* . .

ABEL in *Variety* . . .

WHITNEY BOLTON in the *Telegraph* .

GEORGE ROSS in the *World-Telegram* .

Figure 10b

and enlisting the talents of Busby Berkeley and Ring Lardner, the show
featured salacious burlesque skits, animal acts, and first-class songs. Like
Nils T. Granlund at the Hollywood Restaurant, Rose both emulated the
Ziegfeld concept of the feminine chorus line and literally stripped it of
artistic pretensions. In *Variety*'s words, in a late edition of *Crazy Quilt* the
women's performances consisted of "a mirror number, rhumbas, har-
lemania, Hawaiian [music], and a black art stunt."[5]

Even more aggressively than Granlund, Rose recruited aging, low-cost
vaudeville talent—comedians, singers, dancers, animal acts, "flash acts,

bell-ringers, even fire-eaters." Rose's agent Jack Lewis scoured the nation for the best inexpensive talent. Such acts were recruited for the Casino de Paree's "Small-Time Cavalcade," which performed along with a "Fat Girl Ballet" and the young Benny Goodman's jazz band. The cavalcade and ballet revealed a penchant for nostalgia that later became Rose's trademark. Rose obscured his reliance on vaudeville has-beens by advertising the Casino's production as "the Ziegfeld show of cabaret entertainment." Having spent $125,000 on the theater's renovation and $20,000 on Rose's show, the Steinbergs needed a hit, and Rose gave them one. By the end of 1933 the Casino was grossing $40,000 a week. *Variety* noted that over one thousand customers packed into each show to watch the vaudevillians and the celebrity headliner, the boxer Max Baer. The chorus line's costumes did not "eclipse the out-and-out nudist trends of the Paradise and Hollywood cabaret-restaurants," but "achieve the same pulchritudinous intrigue" and are "plenty bullish on the optics." (A bar in the building was named "The Nudist," perhaps to convey the same impression.)[6]

In 1934 the success of Rose's show encouraged the Steinbergs to underwrite Billy Rose's Music Hall, at the former Hammerstein Theatre at Broadway and 53rd Street. Here Rose embraced nostalgia to the fullest, painting the interior red, white, and gold and hiring what Rose's sister, Polly Gottlieb, later called "corny but wonderful" circus and vaudeville performers. During sing-alongs with the audience, "the customers got dewy-eyed with 'Sweet Adeline.'" All clubowners valued good publicity, but Rose took ballyhoo to new extremes. The most notable innovation at the Music Hall was a forty-foot-high electric sign, stretching down the front of the building, that emblazoned his name above Broadway.[7]

The sign announced a moment of triumph in Rose's intense and lifelong campaign of self-advancement. Born in 1899, Billy Rosenberg grew up in poverty on the Lower East Side, but in high school he found success as a track runner and a competitive stenographer. Billy caught the attention of the shorthand-writing entrepreneur John Robert Gregg, who taught Rose his new method and groomed him to become the national amateur champion. Billy failed to win the title, but in 1918 he was hired as the stenographer for the War Industries Board in Washington. Here he began his long and significant relationship with the board's chairman, the financier Bernard Baruch. Billy would seek to emulate Baruch's Democratic politics, financial acumen, love of the good life, and womanizing. Owing to his continuing friendship with Baruch, Rose was the rare clubowner of working-class origins who had close ties to the financial and political establishment.

After the war Billy traveled the country; on his return to New York he rejected a secretarial career and fell in with the Broadway theatrical community. His young adult years resembled those of Jimmy Walker a generation earlier. Shortening his name to Billy Rose, he became a song lyricist and quickly found success. His best-known credits remain "Me and My Shadow" and "Barney Google with the Goo-Goo-Googly Eyes." He also was credited with the lyrics for Texas Guinan's revue *Padlocks of 1927*. During the decade he also agitated for more ample royalty payments for songwriters, and as we have seen he spent two years pursuing his first short-lived ventures in nightclub management, the Backstage and the Fifth Avenue Clubs.[8]

In the course of these activities Rose became an expert self-publicist. He was a favorite of Walter Winchell and other newspaper columnists in search of colorful copy. In 1929 Rose and Fanny Brice, an established vaudeville star, were married at City Hall by Mayor Jimmy Walker. As a lyricist Rose generated controversy. His authorship of lyrics to "Me and My Shadow," "I Found a Million Dollar Baby (In a Five and Ten Cent Store)," "It's Only a Paper Moon," and other hits was hotly disputed. The composer Harry Warren concluded that Rose mostly "stimulated the real lyricists to produce" good work, for which he then took full or partial credit. When he moved into stage producing in 1931 with *Crazy Quilt*, his promotional efforts were enhanced by the hiring of the publicist Ned Alvord. Alvord was a circus promoter who specialized in luring parsimonious small-town folk to the big top. He encouraged Rose to advertise *Crazy Quilt* (and later the Casino de Paree and the Music Hall) in the same blunt, gaudy, and nearly delirious manner that had made circuses a success. Alvord's first posters for *Crazy Quilt* used a black and yellow color scheme, about which Rose commented "you couldn't look at it without smoked glasses."

With his giant sign over the Music Hall in 1934, Rose, unlike most other clubowners, made himself the central object of publicity. Journalists, biographers, and even Rose himself gave crude psychological explanations for this, arguing that his height (five feet, three inches) instilled a permanent sense of inferiority that he was driven to overcome. It was also reported that he resented his taller wife's fame and loathed the label of "Mr. Fanny Brice." In fact, though, Brice had helped his career far more than she had hurt it, and Rose would continue to promote himself frenetically long after his marriage to Brice had ended. Rose recognized that his name could be a signifier and a trademark, a referent for the chaotic blend of entertainment that his productions and venues provided.[9]

Besides the quantity and brazen quality of his publicity, Rose also made a trademark of his verbal facility, speed, and emphasis. In shorthand competitions in the 1910s Rose had been able to take dictation on a chalkboard with both hands at a speed of 250 words a minute, read the text back verbatim at the same pace, and then reread the text backwards for good measure. As a lyricist and a show business producer Rose used words as tools of his trades, not as simple signifiers but as building blocks for cacophonous avalanches of publicity. He trained himself to be a songwriter by copying hit lyrics in the New York Public Library, studying them, and charting their rhyming patterns on a blackboard. Rose conscientiously applied shorthand rules of speed and economy. His accomplishments in lyric writing, while disputed, were genuine, and they lay in his ability to pare down others' lines into punchy, saleable snippets. He determined that an entire class of popular favorites were "songs built around a silly syllable." Rose supplied the undisciplined songwriters Al Dubin and Mort Dixon with "titles, phrases, and ideas" (as well as liquor) and took cowriting credit. He was the only lyricist to become a successful nightclub owner, probably because he was the only *kind* of lyricist who could have done so—one who perceived words almost solely as assets in a money-making endeavor.[10]

Like Walter Winchell, Damon Runyon, and other Broadway stylists, Rose used words to shock and punctuate, and like advertisers, he used them to sell products. Alliteration was a favorite lyrical device—his song titles included "I've Got a Feeling I'm Falling," "There's a Rainbow 'Round My Shoulder," and "He Looks at Her, Then He Goes Ha, Ha, Ha"—and he took to advertising himself as "Broadway Billy," the "Basement Belasco," and the "Bantam Barnum." He made endless puns on his last name, most notably to weld his identity to that of his dancers; the tall ones became his "Long-Stemmed Roses," his troupe of heavy dancers "the Rosebuds." In these and many other ways—for example, in his newspaper column of the 1940s, "Pitching Horseshoes"—Rose used words to punctuate bluntly a selling point or an idea. Even though he employed some of the circumlocution that Runyon made a hallmark of Broadwayese, Rose's prose above all contained a hard-boiled punch, such as when he recalled, "I invested some of this [songwriting] loot in the nightclub business—principally, I think, because I wanted to wear a black hat and meet some girls." Or, regarding gangsters: "It wasn't until 1933 that I again got mixed up with the broken-fingernails set."[11]

A year later, in 1934, the Steinberg brothers, the veterans of organized crime who employed Rose during his first period of nightclub success, forced him to leave the business for some months. Rose had become familiar with underworld management during his initial clubowning stints in the 1920s; Arnold Rothstein had given him some helpful business advice, but otherwise Rose found gangsters to be talentless predators. Now, while taking a working vacation in Europe in 1934, Rose left the management of the Casino de Paree and the Music Hall to his employers. Their missteps caused prices to rise and the quality of the entertainment to fall, as key talents such as Benny Goodman were encouraged to leave. After Rose returned from Europe the Steinbergs threatened him with violence if he interfered. A series of lawsuits ensued, including one filed by Billy Rose (the individual) against Billy Rose Music Hall, Inc. (which the Steinbergs controlled). (Rose also had to contend with the city licensing commissioner Paul Moss, who ordered the Music Hall to obtain a theater license because it showed short movies. Rose halted the screenings because theaters were not permitted to sell liquor.) The parties eventually settled out of court, but Rose still feared for his safety. His friend Bernard Baruch contacted the attorney general, Homer Cummings, who persuaded J. Edgar Hoover to provide unique FBI protection for Rose. For four years the producer avoided working in the New York nightclub scene. In the wake of the litigation the Steinbergs' two clubs failed, but the high-volume concept to which Rose contributed continued to be the main engine behind the resurgence of nightclubs around Broadway in the mid-1930s. In 1934, while Rose was out of the business, the opening of the French Casino redefined the high-volume formula for the rest of the decade.[12]

The French Casino was the most lavish high-volume club New York City had yet seen (see Fig. 11). This enterprise was developed by the owners of the Earl Carroll Theatre at 50th Street and Seventh Avenue, just above where Broadway crossed Seventh Avenue. Louis F. Blumenthal, Jack Shapiro, and Charles Haring needed to fill the theater after the demise of Carroll's revues and a failed effort to show films. (Carroll, meanwhile, relocated to California, where he opened a successful new nightclub.) The scale of the French Casino was unprecedented. The partners spent over $200,000 in an effort to create a restaurant-cabaret for fifteen hundred customers. Clifford Fischer, who was hired to manage the club, took the French cabaret theme to a new level and spent $60,000 to hire an actual troupe from Paris's Folies Bergères. The Casino's scarlet and silver paneling and Art Nouveau murals overlooked terraced floors and a balcony for the diners. A large dance floor bordered the old theater stage. Here a company of acrobats, comics, and dancers put on revues, interspersed with the Folies show, to the accompaniment of the Jack Denny and Vincent Travers orchestras. Musical revues sometimes featured the popular ocean-liner motif, but evocations of continental Europe predominated. Tableaux mimicked compositions by Picasso and Matisse and dance numbers made use of both traditional and modernist materials and styles, for example juxtaposing a flamenco dance with Renita Kramer's startling pantomime (in which, costumed as half man and half woman, she made love to herself in an expressionistic

Figure 11. A busy night at the French Casino, Manhattan's most profitable nightclub in 1935. Waiters and concessions salespersons were important members of the nightclub workforce. Billy Rose Theatre Collection, The New York Public Library for the Performing Arts, Astor, Lenox, and Tilden Foundations.

moonlit scene). Female nudity was also prominently featured. All of this, and a five-course dinner, was offered by the French Casino for $2.50 per customer.[13]

The Casino's opening weeks did not go smoothly. A jealous rival threw stink bombs into the lobby one evening and forced the club to close early, and the police arrested the managers Carl Snyder and Charles Haring for running an indecent show. (The charge was later dismissed in court.) The French Casino nevertheless became the rage of Midtown. Liquor sales at the club's Marionette Bar provided enough income for Fischer to pay his four hundred employees their weekly salaries in excess of $20,000. Taking part in a general business trend during the Depression, Blumenthal and Shapiro announced plans to open the first nationwide chain of high-volume nightclubs, creating a brand name that would rationalize and standardize nightlife across America. The chain eventually became international, opening clubs in London and Paris as well as Chicago and Miami and earning $5 million in 1936. Later that year, in an act of hubris, Carl Snyder set up a business that booked the club's "girl shows" in high-priced East Side hotel cabarets frequented by café society. As *Variety* put it, "Where heretofore the east side bunch visited the French Casino as a lark and a 'slumming' gag, the idea is to keep 'em on the east side and give 'em the same Broadway atmosphere, albeit with refinement and class."[14]

The French Casino dominated the high-volume club business for three years. As a result, earnings at the pioneering Hollywood and Paradise restaurants declined drastically. In 1937, though, the experienced team of the entrepreneur Louis Brecker and the bandleader George Olsen mounted a challenge to the French Casino's supremacy. They raised and spent $500,000 to create the International Casino within the walls of the old Criterion Theater on Times Square (see Fig. 12). The architect Thomas Lamb and the designer Donald Deskey concocted a mammoth supper club for 2,500 patrons arrayed on three technologically innovative floors. The first nightclub to feature an escalator as well as the capacity to freeze an ice rink on the dance floor, the International eschewed the lush and cluttered Art Nouveau design of the French Casino. Instead, it epitomized the streamlined moderne style of the 1930s. Influenced in part by the movies' recent portrayals of sleek club decor, Deskey also tastefully paid tribute to Joseph Urban, whose later theater designs foreshadowed the International's flowing, functional curves, as well as to newly popular South American design trends. The state liquor code required that each club could contain only one customer bar, so Deskey wound a forty-foot-long spiral table from the second-floor "bar room" down to the "cocktail room" on the first floor. A staircase took customers down to the cavernous dining room amphitheater, which was lined with beige, rose, and chrome panels. Meals were brought by dumbwaiter from the third-floor kitchen to the terraced tables below. The dance floor at the vortex of the main floor could serve as a stage when platforms and stairs were lowered mechanically from the

Figure 12.  Times Square at night, 1939. The International Casino, New York's most lavish nightclub, dominates the scene, but huge deficits would soon force it to go dark. Milstein Division of United States History, Local History, and Genealogy, The New York Public Library, Astor, Lenox, and Tilden Foundations.

ceiling, as well as an ice rink. Two orchestras played in the wings, often behind screens.[15]

Despite its modernist trappings the International Casino's floor show remained rooted in the conventional formula of the 1930s, featuring chorus-line nudity and the Granlund-Rose synthesis of Ziegfeld and burlesque. The chorus masters Pierre Sandrini and Jacques Charles, providing the proper Gallic influence, made highly publicized statements about their philosophy of dancer selection in articles published months before the club's opening. Sandrini used various "tests" for applicants, carefully rating how each woman made an "approach" in a swimsuit, "danc[ed] for personality," lit a cigarette, "flirt[ed] over the shoulder," fondled a teddy bear, and "stroll[ed] in cool austerity." Charles emphasized the paramount importance of the woman's legs, and he and Sandrini remarked on how "the Hollywood influence" had made the

American ideal of female beauty taller and slimmer. Photos from the International's revue indeed indicate that the classic "leg show" predominated on the floor—and that male customers leered at the dancers. One of them, Maria Domeney, was photographed with a giant man's hand grabbing her around the waist (suggesting the persistent influence of *King Kong*). Photos of individual International Casino dancers, topless but covered strategically by objects they held, appeared widely in such publications as the *National Police Gazette* and the *Men's Apparel Reporter.* An article in 1938 on the International's dancers stressed that they shed their clothes but "not [their] wits" and resisted the advances of all male customers except "the m[e]n of their dreams," but this image of "today's super-showgirls" with long legs perpetuated the stereotype of the narrow-minded gold-digger that was prevalent in the 1920s.[16]

The International Casino's opening in September 1937 heralded what one journalist called "the most titanic struggle in night club history," between the club and the French Casino five blocks to the north. Like its rival the new contender ran into trouble on opening night, when the stage mechanisms failed to work properly. More trouble ensued in later months, as Brecker and Olsen faced mounting debts. In March 1938 they declared bankruptcy, but they also hired Robert Christenberry, who had just modernized the Astor Hotel across Times Square, to manage the International. Business improved for a while, and the International's trademark Cuban band sounds made the club's Conga dance the rage of 1938. (Many nightclubs of this era sought a trademark dance. Iridium at the St. Regis Hotel promoted the "Lambeth walk," La Conga featured the "danzonette"—a "cross between the rhumba and conga"—and the Rainbow Room displayed the "sambixe"—the samba mixed with the Brazilian *maxine.*) Most notably, the Casino's revival siphoned away enough customers from the Hollywood Restaurant and the French Casino to force those clubs into receivership as well. Unlike Brecker and Olsen, though, Joe Moss and the team of Blumenthal, Fischer, Shapiro, and Haring could not restructure their way out of bankruptcy.[17] The International Casino had triumphed in a brutal Darwinian struggle. But Billy Rose had returned to the nightclub business and was becoming its dominant force.

The giant nightclubs that served as Rose's models were representative of larger economic forces at work. Structural changes in the city and its economy, reflecting the impact of the Depression on the nation as a whole, had become evident by the late 1930s. In many businesses, these years were an era of consolidation. Dozens of automobile companies and other big businesses, as well as thousands of independent grocers, department stores, and dry-goods retailers, had fallen victim to the slump, and in the ensuing recovery economies of scale developed—not, as the New Deal envisioned, with existing businesses planning their revivals, but with the most aggressive and opportunistic entities absorbing or eliminating their weaker competition.[18]

In entertainment, this process allowed record companies such as Columbia and RCA to absorb numerous smaller disk manufacturers, led musical bookings to be nearly monopolized by the Music Corporation of America (MCA), enabled Irving Mills to begin cornering ownership rights to thousands of songs, and reinforced the Shubert organization's chokehold on theater ownership and the Hollywood studios' oligarchy of movie houses and celluloid "product." This process also hastened business's pursuit of market research, to define "the public" in the clearest and most manipulable terms so that the "average" consumer's demands could be abstracted out of billions of purchasing decisions and met with lines of carefully crafted and pretested products. The movie studios' sophisticated test-screening method, featuring viewer questionnaires that pinpointed potential strengths and weaknesses in films, was one example of the new market research.[19]

Similarly, New York City's government found in the Depression the impetus to increase efficiency and rationalize financial and administrative processes that, during the slump, had fallen into chaos. Under Fiorello La Guardia, for example, the city in 1936 scrapped its cumbersome old charter, which was encrusted with 2,400 pages of addenda. The new charter replaced the Board of Aldermen with a City Council and created fairer voting procedures for city and borough offices. In 1939 La Guardia also engineered the biggest municipal takeover of private businesses in history, the consolidation of the city's entire transit system, purchased for $326 million. But business also took aggressive new initiatives in improving its own prospects—initiatives that often invaded the public sphere (as progressive reformers had defined it). The building of Rockefeller Center was an important example of business's new role in planning. So, too, was the founding in 1934 of the New York City Convention and Visitors Bureau by the private Merchants Association; it was designed to stimulate the placement of international, national, and regional meetings in the city. The hope, of course, was that many more tourists would come to New York and spend their money. "Enlisting the backing of hotel men, merchants and other business interests likely to benefit from an increase in convention business," the Bureau hoped to bring an additional 400,000 visitors to the city in its first year of existence. By 1939 its goals had been surpassed.[20]

At the same time, though, the city was struggling with a new threat to its solvency: an acceleration of suburbanization and the diffusion of urban society across a broad metropolitan region. Other American cities

had experienced this as well. Some, especially Chicago, had already witnessed the most dramatic expansion of their suburban and "exurban"
regions. New York's suburban diffusion, though, inevitably had the
largest and most dramatic consequences. Despite Jimmy Walker's occasional lip service to regional planning, Tammany Hall had largely
shunned any consideration of people or business beyond the city limits.
Reformers such as Fiorello La Guardia and Robert Moses, though, took
regional planning as an article of faith. The controversial, visionary
study published in 1931 by the private Regional Plan Association (RPA)
foresaw development along the railroads and highways radiating fifty
miles out of the city, in a three-state area. Populations and industries,
the RPA study predicted, would spread out into existing farmlands and
marshes. In the 1930s Radburn, New Jersey became the region's first
planned suburb.

The RPA and other planning advocates also foresaw the deindustrial-
ization of New York City itself. As the chairman of La Guardia's new city
planning committee, Rexford Guy Tugwell advocated and began to
implement the relocation of Manhattan garment workers to Hights-
town, New Jersey. While Tugwell's committee had little success in imple-
menting its ideas, Robert Moses—the commissioner of city parks, the
chairman of the Triborough Authority, and the ruler of a half-dozen
other bureaucratic fiefdoms—kept building parkways and bridges across
Long Island, through Westchester County, and between the boroughs,
creating massive neighborhood dislocations and, surprisingly, ever
worse traffic snarls. While contemporaries still viewed Moses as the mira-
cle worker of the public sector, his projects became increasingly reckless
and ill-considered—becoming, in Robert Caro's words, "not ends but
means . . . of obtaining more and more power." Nevertheless, in their
inefficient and ugly way, the expressways and bridges hastened the
arrival of the metropolitan area that regionalists were predicting. By
1939, as one study of New York planning has put it, "the new megalopo-
lis was visible to all."[21]

Moses's interborough bridges also hastened Manhattan's decline in
relation to the rest of the city. In the 1910s the island had begun to give
up large numbers of residents, especially Jewish immigrants, to new
housing developments in the Bronx. In the 1920s the pace accelerated
and also witnessed considerable movement to Brooklyn as well. In the
next decade Brooklyn became the most populous borough and Queens
became the next residential boom region. By 1939 *Fortune* magazine
could call the two eastern boroughs the "bedrooms of Manhattan."
Moses's proposal that year for a bridge between Brooklyn and Manhattan's Battery Park was a rare failure, but the Brooklyn Battery Tunnel
was successfully recommended by planners as its substitute, showing the

urgency of the interborough commuting problem. That issue, more than any other, allowed La Guardia to push through his grand consolidation of public transit. Thus, owing to changes in infrastructure, the growing role of the automobile, and various hues of regional utopianism among influential planners, the focus of New York City's identity in Manhattan was being altered.[22]

These trends formed part of the context that helps to explain the significance of the triumph of Billy Rose's nightclubs and Aquacades in the late 1930s. These venues served both as a culmination of the classic nightclub era and as a harbinger of the post-urban, post-nightclub era that would dominate American leisure in later decades.

After the demise of his Music Hall in 1934, Billy Rose might have concluded that his foray into vaudevillian nostalgia, redolent of the country and the small town, had been misguided. In fact, though, over the next two years Rose's attachment to nostalgic entertainment only deepened. He was perhaps the first entrepreneur to realize that the profitability of Manhattan's nightclubs was limited by the clubowners' and regulars' own city-bound provincialism. While migrants such as the Coloradans Damon Runyon and Harold Ross and the Oklahoman Sherman Billingsley were creating idealized concepts of life in Manhattan in print and in nightclubs, the native New Yorker Billy Rose (aided by Ned Alvord) had learned from the success of his national tour of *Crazy Quilt* in 1932 that nostalgic promotion worked the best. "It was Ned who taught me that the short cut to the customer's poke is by way of the roadside fence— that 'bill it like a circus' sells more tickets than 'to be or not be.'" Rose proudly noted that his success with a vaudeville lineup at the Music Hall "was my first meeting with the pretty lady called 'Nostalgia' and we've been big buddies ever since."[23]

After leaving the Steinberg brothers' nightclubs Rose toured Europe, where he witnessed circus performances before mass audiences. Returning home, Rose pursued a new project for promotion on Broadway. He gained financial backing from the Whitney family, Bernard Baruch, and other elites for a huge circus show to be produced at the vacant New York Hippodrome. Rose also enlisted prime talent to create *Jumbo*—the writers Ben Hecht and Charles MacArthur, the musical comedy-writing team of Richard Rodgers and Lorenz Hart, the directors George Abbott and John Murray Anderson, and the comedian Jimmy Durante, as well as dozens of circus performers, actors, and animal acts. Jumbo had been the name of Phineas T. Barnum's most famous elephant, and the show allowed Rose to cement his identification with the master promoter of the nineteenth century. (Rose ordered his staff to locate circus memorabilia from the estate of Charles Stratton, "General Tom Thumb," so that he might purchase them for a planned "Museum of Broadway.") Featuring a single large circus ring, complicated sets, improbable musical numbers and a plot that replayed the Montague-Capulet feud under the bigtop, *Jumbo* was delayed for months by logistical problems. When it opened it drew huge crowds (including famous customers whom Rose exploited for publicity). The show could not recoup its enormous cost, but its undeniable popularity confirmed Rose's suspicion that large-scale, primary-color popular entertainment that broke down genre boundaries and evoked the past was a big draw in New York City in the 1930s.[24]

Before he returned to nightclubs, Rose struck gold in "the territory" beyond the city limits, developing highly profitable ventures that further confirmed his perception of the contemporary popular taste for nostalgia. In 1936, on the strength of *Jumbo*, he was hired by business leaders in Fort Worth to produce the Texas Centennial Exposition. His employers wanted him to create a spectacle of pure entertainment to lure customers away from the more sober and educational centennial fair to be held in Dallas, the perennial rival of Fort Worth. Led by the newspaper publisher Amon T. Carter and later assisted by the banker Jesse Jones (undoubtedly at the urging of Jones's friend Bernard Baruch), the sponsors accepted Rose's $100,000 fee and his plan for the large-scale outdoor attraction. The promoter quickly traded his P. T. Barnum persona for that of Buffalo Bill Cody, and he posed for the cameras in a cowboy outfit.

The Fort Worth Exposition realized Rose's ideas on a vast and airy scale. The "Last Frontier" was an enormous updating of the Buffalo Bill Wild West show (with music and dance added), featuring a thousand performers and a herd of bison. The Sunset Trail replicated an Old West town. *Jumbo* was brought to Fort Worth as well. Most significantly, Rose transmuted his nostalgic nightclub revue into an outdoor fair attraction. The Hispanic flavor and premonitions of tomorrow expressed in its title—Casa Mañana—were misleading. According to Rose's publicity, the attraction's claim to modernity was its massive rotating stage, "3½ times larger than that of Radio City Music Hall." "Two 450 horsepower Motors [were] required to Operate this Leviathan of Rostrums, with its 4,264,000 Pounds of actual deadweight plus its Lovely Freight of 250 Eye-bedeviling Coryphees over a pool of Limpid Crystal containing 617,000 Gallons of Real Water." The Casa was the Casino de Paree placed in a huge amphitheater, which seated four thousand diners at tables and thirty-five hundred others on benches. The revue theme nostalgically evoked world's fairs past and present, and featured Rose's usual eclectic blend of entertainers. Like the Casino de Paree, the Casa Mañana featured a striptease show in the basement. The "Nude Ranch" starred the fan dancer Sally Rand, a veteran of exposition in multiple senses of the term, who first gained fame at the 1933 Chicago world's fair.[25]

A big success, the Fort Worth Exposition converted Rose into an aficionado of large-scale fairs and won him over to the use of large outdoor facilities to attract crowds. Lincoln Dickey had been the first director of the New York City Convention and Visitors Bureau. He now managed Cleveland's lackluster Great Lakes Exposition, and in 1937 he hired Rose, an old acquaintance, to overhaul the fair. Promising Dickey "I'll build you a Casa Mañana right on . . . Lake [Erie]," Rose came up with a big water show. He coined the term "Aquacade" and proceeded to hire hundreds of swimmers, entertainers, boat pilots, and other participants. The headliners were the Olympic swimming champions turned film stars Johnny Weissmuller and Eleanor Holm. Rose became infatuated with Holm, and although they were both married, they conducted a highly public affair. In 1939 Rose divorced Fannie Brice and married Holm, appearing to turn from his urban Jewish past toward the suburban, middle-American identity that Holm's celebrity persona evoked (although in reality she also was a native of New York City).[26]

In late 1937, flush from the success of his fairs, Rose returned to New York to launch his new pair of nightclubs, the Broadway version of the Casa Mañana and the Diamond Horseshoe. To Rose's satisfaction the first club was housed in the old Earl Carroll Theatre, the site of the now defunct French Casino, which years earlier had helped to drive Rose out of the nightclub business. Now he relocated his outdoor attraction in Fort Worth to this sprawling room and found instant success with his blend of Latin American decor and eclectic vaudeville-style entertainment. The Diamond Horseshoe, four blocks to the south, opened a year later.

Both clubs were immensely profitable. The Casa Mañana gave Rose a net return of $120,000 in its first year, an unprecedented annual earning in the nightlife business. The Diamond Horseshoe was even more successful, becoming the highest-grossing club ever to open in New York City. In its first ten weeks of operation it earned Rose a profit of $76,000 on a gross take of $260,000. (By 1943 it would serve seventy-five hundred customers a week and make a $1.25 million profit for the year.) The two clubs' successes inspired imitations across the nation. In Detroit and Baltimore the owners of old theaters with capacities of up to two thousand seats copied the Rose formula, as did operations in Philadelphia, Chicago, Los Angeles, and Cleveland. All tried to repeat Rose's mix of dinner, alcohol, vaudeville, and female dancers—as well as his very low drink and food minimums and lack of any cover charge.[27]

Few of them, though, could equal Rose's peculiar ability to maximize

his profits. Rose was as systematic a businessman as he had been a stenographer and songwriter, carefully applying all of the lessons he had
learned in his earlier enterprises. While he sometimes spent lavishly on
star talent, on a daily basis he kept his supply and staff budgets at a minimum. As *Fortune* magazine noted in 1939, Rose "had a encyclopedic
knowledge of what things cost": "He will decree, in one scene, that the
little dancing girls shall have no more than six balloons each to throw at
the guests, and he once vetoed the use of confetti in an act after adding
the cost of cleaning to the cost of the confetti." Rose had his large staff
under careful management (divided between restaurant and show workers). Charles Orenstein, the manager of the Paramount Hotel above the
Casa Mañana, supervised accounting. Orenstein tailored concessions
contracts to exact the maximum profit from them, amounting to about
$65,000 annually from the two clubs. Determining the frequency with
which diners asked to be moved to better tables, Rose instituted a "location change" charge; few customers resented it, and it brought in $1,200
a week. To increase customer volume Rose mastered the city's new tour-
ist-promotion mechanism. He hired publicists to comb the bulletins of
the Convention and Visitors Bureau, obtain contact information for
convention organizers, and aggressively offer each of them special low
rates and fringe benefits. Twenty percent of Rose's huge clientele came
from this convention trade.[28]

Rose, like other clubowners, had to accommodate a new reality of the
post-New Deal era: the power of New York City's combative service-
worker unions. Workers in few other cities took so much advantage of
the National Labor Relations Act of 1935 and of the more liberal legislation passed in New York State. The opening of the Casa Mañana was
marred by a threatened picket by Chorus Equity. In the industry as a
whole, 1938 was marked by a struggle over union representation for
nightclub dancers—a struggle between competing unions as well as
between labor and management. An American Federation of Labor
affiliate, the American Federation of Actors, succeeded in wresting bargaining rights for chorus dancers away from Chorus Equity, which the
former group accused of ineptitude (even though it had won a contract
for the dancers at the International Casino). An even more colorful
struggle was waged by the Hotel and Restaurant Workers' Union—the
erstwhile racket of Dutch Schultz, which had been cleaned up by
Thomas E. Dewey's prosecutions. The union kept up running battles
with hotels and eateries. For example, it successfully appealed the firing
of nine waiters at the Stork Club all the way up to the state's highest
court. Demands for wage increases by the waiters' group, as well as by
the Cooks, Pastry Chefs, and Assistants' Union, also led Billy Rose to
threaten to close the Casa Mañana.[29]

It was Billy Rose's ability to craft a unique clubgoing experience, how-ever, not his acumen in dealing with accounting books and unions, that captivated customers and observers. The club's nostalgic decor and entertainment did not just grow out of Rose's earlier experiments; they also evoked significant cultural preferences in Depression-era America. His "nostalgia" was actually a melding of mass-market business acumen, promotional ballyhoo, and the lesson that the mass public had come to cherish old-time content. In his Wild West, aquatic, and Gay Nineties acts, Rose found a common ground between the urbane nightclub and the back-to-the-land, populistic spirit of the New Deal era.[30]

In the 1930s Rose identified strongly with Democratic politics and New Deal policies. As Lewis Erenberg first noted, Rose's success owed something to the renewed confidence of Americans in the first flush of the New Deal. Rose was not blind to that. Like other Democrats on Broadway, he praised Franklin D. Roosevelt onstage, first in a Music Hall revue entitled "Here's to Broadway" which portrayed the street's transi-tion from the murky speakeasies of the 1920s to colorful present-day confidence. Rose also identified his efforts with the government's. His clubs' low prices were promoted as a New Deal for consumers. Rose described the Cleveland Aquacade, admission one dollar, as "a $10 show scaled down to fit the purse of the times." Noting that this Aquacade employed 5,000 people, Rose boasted that "the WPA and I will solve this unemployment situation." At the Casa Mañana the next year, Rose echoed Roosevelt's rhetoric in an advertisement that flattered "Mr. For-gotten Man (the guy who pays the check)." "I don't think a table is worth a $5 tip," he argued.[31] Repeal and recovery thus also enhanced consumer rights and product value. Through his early war work with Baruch, Rose developed a sense of civic involvement unusual for a night-club owner; it was inspired in part by his desire to mingle with the rich and powerful, but it was also genuine enough to lead him to philan-thropy and outspoken opposition to bigotry in his later years.

The era of the New Deal also saw a more general move away from 1920s-style urbanism toward a sentimental attachment to rural America. New York natives such as the composer Aaron Copland became champi-ons of the "common man," a man usually depicted as a farmer or a sharecropper tied to the soil. Possibly when he shifted his frame of refer-ence from the northeastern Democratic Party elite around Baruch to its counterpart in Fort Worth, Billy Rose embraced a variety of this com-mon-man ideology as well as a more specific attachment to old-time rural music. Even back in New York, Rose found that migrants from the hinterland, so set on becoming urbanites, covertly retained their old tastes: "Turn the average customer at El Morocco upside down and acorns will fall out of his pocket."[32] Despite this, curiously, Rose's nightclubs in the late 1930s featured an almost entirely urban nostalgia, focusing on New York at the turn of the century, perhaps because Rose himself could not stray far from his own roots.

Just like his business and accounting methods, though, Rose's nostalgic club atmosphere had distinctly modern elements. Rejecting Nils T. Granlund's somewhat perverse fondness for amateurish acts, he picked his vaudeville talent with great care. Entertainment, Rose argued, "must be strange, it must be wonderful, but above all, it must be professional." Also, unlike the intimate clubs of the 1920s, which encouraged the mingling of performers with customers, the Horseshoe and the Casa Mañana (like his earlier theater-restaurants) presented spectacles set apart by footlights, kept at a distance from the passive onlookers. Like movie theaters and baseball stadiums, the functioning of the modern large nightclub relied on a disciplined and restrained mass audience.[33] As in the theater and the opera house, America's club audiences were becoming more passive consumers of spectacles, and like the scrim in front of Anna Held's milk bath, the shows' nostalgic orientation provided them with a veneer of safety and comfort.

Described this way, of course, Rose's clubs would not have seemed very appealing to customers in the 1930s. But the contradictions between modernity and nostalgia in the clubs were not merely embodied in their design and in the nature of their entertainment. Beneath the somewhat bland surfaces of Rose's shows, persistent, dark cultural themes that flourished in the 1920s—alcoholism, sexuality, illicit behavior, the subversion of social taboos—remained vital.[34] For example, while Rose rejoiced in the decline of Prohibition-era bootlegging and courted a presumably sober-minded "family man," repeal gave him the chance to make liquor the legitimate center of his profit engine. In the Music Hall's Barbary Coast Bar a sign told the customer to "pour your drink down the well," in order to look at a "miniature" nude woman at the bottom (by means of trick mirrors). In this interesting procedure, liquor became a medium of exchange within a miniaturized economy, in which the male gaze and sexuality were constricted to the dimensions of a peepshow. Here, at least, Rose emulated the old-time carnivals he usually denigrated.

Liquor ruled in other ways. Gilbert Seldes, generally an admirer of Rose's, had noted that "the atmosphere" at the old Casino de Paree had been "liquorish if not downright boozy." As other owners in the 1930s knew, liquor revenue subsidized the cheap dinners and cover-free entertainment. "The profit is in the bottle," Rose was fond of saying, "and the bottle goes on the table." At the Diamond Horseshoe, *two* bottles— one bourbon, one scotch—actually were placed before customers the moment they took their seats. As Rose's sister Polly Gottlieb recalled,

"On each bottle a strip was pasted along the side with numbers from one to eighteen to mark the number of drinks. The waiter was instructed to be quick with the ice setups, and Noble Sissle and the band . . . were told to play loud and louder. . . . 'When the music's high, the customers want to get higher,' Billy said."[35] Rose hoped that the customers' drunkenness would not make them unruly but rather cause a fog to set in. This alcoholic daze was perhaps an essential precondition of the nostalgic illusion that he sought to create.

So was sex. Nightclubs in the 1920s played host to a volatile combination of crime and the near-seduction of male customers by female performers that sometimes skirted the edges of prostitution. In those years, as a novice songwriter and clubowner, Billy Rose himself seduced countless chorus members, and, as his sister noted, "sex with the single girl became his favorite indoor sport for the next forty years." In the 1930s, however, since burlesque-style explicitness was under attack by the La Guardia administration, overt allusions to the sex act and the aggressive promotion of nudity fell out of fashion. Like some of his successful competitors, Rose shrewdly used sex both to promote his clubs and to help define the new line between the acceptable and the unacceptable. Many of his publicity materials contained nude or nearly nude female performers, with their genitalia artfully concealed. For his shows in Fort Worth, Cleveland, and New York, he hired Sally Rand, the dancer famous for her evasion of anti-burlesque laws with carefully placed fans and bubbles. For all of his promotion of Rand's Nude Ranch and the like and his frequent disparagement of peepshows, though, Rose's fleshiest attractions were rather attenuated, like the "girl in a fishbowl" at the Music Hall. His opening show at the Casa Mañana featured the striptease performer Hinda Wassau (formerly of Minsky's), whose topless dance was quickly suppressed by the police.[36]

Most strikingly, in his nightclubs Rose translated his voracious sexual appetite, as well as his shows' burlesque tendencies, into a fetish for oversized chorus women. The Diamond Horseshoe's Rosebuds troupe harkened back to the day of eroticized female heftiness, but his main feminine archetype was the "Long-Stemmed Rose": the streamlined, exaggerated female form, even more elongated than the ideal favored by Pierre Sandrini at the International Casino. The minimum height requirement for Rose's dancers was 5 feet 6 inches, and he gave special billing to such tall women as Mary "Stuttering Sam" Dowell (brought up from Texas, like many of his discoveries), who stood at 6 feet, $2^{1}/_{2}$ inches. Rose's obsession reached its apex in 1946, when "Siri," a Swedish woman 6 feet, 6 inches tall, was featured at the Diamond Horseshoe. Rose typically promoted the *concept* of height with his own unique, typically fierce promotion. As many noted at the time, his fascination with

Figure 13.  The producer Billy Rose inspecting female performers at an audition in Cleveland in 1937 during the creation of the first Aquacade. Billy Rose Theatre Collection, The New York Public Library for the Performing Arts, Astor, Lenox, and Tilden Foundations.

height may have reflected his dislike of his own short stature, but it also meshed with American culture's growing tendency to distort and fetishize the female form (which, historians have determined, were among the strategies used to limit and demonize female sexuality). Rose's Broadway depictions thus helped to pave the way for the fetishized feminine images of the 1940s (which replaced height with bust size as the focus of attention).[37]

Rose had a cruel side. His sister noted that even with his friends and family, Rose "wasn't secure enough to stop hurting people" and often ridiculed their claims and boasts. He exhibited this tendency in his highly publicized judging of his female "talent." Promotional photographs showed him measuring his chorines' legs with a tape and marching militarily among lines of auditioners standing at attention, his eyes at their chest level (see Fig. 13). When he spoke of his standards for his chorus line, he harkened back to his embrace of nostalgia. "I glorify wholesomeness. I often pass up a pretty girl because she looks a little tired, a little blasé. I like girls to whom the theater is still a novelty, exciting. Of course, I observe the regular things—straight features, good teeth, good limbs, a ready smile. But if a girl looks tired and uninteresting, she's not interesting to me. I have found there are dividends in wholesomeness."[38]

Nevertheless, Rose hoped that the impact of his chorines on male customers would be somewhat less than wholesome. More subtly and successfully than his competitors, Rose subsumed and reworked the stock-burlesque striptease that the city banned in 1938. Counting on the effect of alcohol to elicit sexual stimulation from the sight of his high-kicking, "wholesome" dancers, Rose claimed that "every time a customer with two drinks inside of him gets a flash of their white panties, he gets an idea he's seeing more than he's seeing."[39]

Just as Rose carefully managed the sexual energy in his shows, he also reined in the bestial fury found in *Jumbo* and the "Last Frontier" spectacle in Fort Worth. The producer often alluded to the theme of danger in entertainment, which had been overt in nightlife in the 1920s but was generally less popular during the Depression. He was fond of saying that "the biggest box-office attraction is death." He exploited this attraction in the opening show at the Casa Mañana, "Let's Play Fair," in which a startling act featuring six Bengal tigers was incongruously inserted. Rose planned a 1939 World's Fair attraction (which was never mounted) called Killers of the Deep, featuring "Captain Bradford Craswell in a death-challenging fight with a Man-Eating Shark" and "the most terrifying collection of sea monsters ever assembled." Simultaneously Rose began a friendship with Salvador Dalí, who notably shared Rose's affinity for entertainment with latent sexuality and violence. Dalí's funhouse attraction at the New York World's Fair, The Dream of Venus, was mounted with Rose's help, and the artist later contributed sketches to Rose's autobiography.[40] On a more overtly wholesome note, Eleanor Holm, who starred in the Cleveland and New York Aquacades, merged the circus-animal athleticism with the long-stemmed feminine ideal that Rose simultaneously promoted.

Billy Rose's nightclubs, therefore, created sites and productions that finely balanced nostalgia, a distorted and fetishized femininity, and intimations of danger. A fourth ingredient of his showmanship was his embrace of large open spaces. Under Rose's tutelage, the smoky nightclub of the city was opening up into larger settings for public interaction, in big halls and even in the outdoors. His climactic success of the 1930s showcased this trend *in extremis*.

Figure 14. The club of the future? The Billy Rose Aquacade at the New York World's Fair, 1939. Billy Rose Theatre Collection, The New York Public Library for the Performing Arts, Astor, Lenox, and Tilden Foundations.

The most profitable and popular exhibit at the New York World's Fair of 1939–40 had little to do with the fair's stated theme, the "World of Tomorrow." Billy Rose's Aquacade was an enormous exhibition of swimming gymnastics, accompanied by music, presenting nostalgic odes to the beach resorts and world's fairs of earlier decades (see Fig. 14).

The show fulfilled the terms of the contract that Rose signed with the World's Fair Corporation in June 1938. Rose had won the right to produce the entertainment centerpiece at the fair by beating out such competitors as Jake Shubert and the Music Corporation of America, each of whom had proposed an ice-skating extravaganza. In the agreements of 1938, the fair corporation pledged to build an amphitheater for Rose that would hold ten thousand customers. In turn Gotham Productions (later renamed Billy Rose's Exposition Spectacles) agreed to build two large revolving stages that would be paid for with $160,000 of the gate receipts, and it promised to provide $100,000 in production costs. Rose would pay rent from 10 percent of the gate receipts and 12 percent of the grosses from concessions (ranging from "boutonnieres and corsages and perfumes" to "toilets," which Rose also controlled). All of the other earnings, after taxes, would be Rose's to keep. The fair corporation, in addition, agreed to prohibit from the grounds any other musical venue holding more than fifteen hundred spectators. Rose had to present two shows daily in May and October and four shows each day from June through September. Billy Rose and Grover Whalen, the president of the fair corporation, personally signed the agreements.[41]

The show was initially entitled "My Country 'Tis of Thee," but it was soon renamed "Billy Rose's Aquacade." In 1939 it starred the tenor Morton Downey and the swimming stars Johnny Weissmuller, Eleanor Holm, and Gertrude Ederle, who were assisted by the Vincent Lopez Orchestra, the Fred Waring Glee Club, and dozens of "Aquafemmes," "Aqua-Gals," and "Aquadudes." That year the show evoked the beaches of the world in song and aquatic ballet: Miami, Coney Island (in 1905), Venice's Lido, and the Aquacade itself. In 1940 another Olympic champion and movie Tarzan, Buster Crabbe, replaced Weissmuller as "Adonis" and joined the rest of the previous year's cast. This edition of the show celebrated world's fairs past and present: San Francisco in 1915, Paris in 1925, Chicago in 1933–34, and New York in 1940. Motorboats streamed across the four-hundred-foot-wide pool and fountains shot water through colored lights, creating a vibrant spectacle that entertained over five million spectators in each of the fair's years. Other vital and influential productions at the fair, such as Mike Todd's stage show *The Hot Mikado*, stood in the shadow of the Aquacade.[42]

Some characteristics of Rose's earlier nightclub ventures also applied to this vast outdoor venue. The publicity campaign for the Aquacade lifted the promoter's techniques to a new plateau of shrillness. The decibel level of Rose's loudspeakers at Flushing Meadows drew protests from other exhibitors at the fair and from the parks commissioner Robert Moses, who forced Rose to reduce the volume. The crowds kept coming, though, and the profits mounted. As in Rose's smoke-filled indoor venues, sexuality was barely contained beneath the smiles and skintight swimsuits at the Aquacade. While one journalist's fondest memory of the fair was "perhaps the goose flesh on a pretty swimmer's thigh," Rose also received many complaints about the performers' scanty costumes. Sexual urges that had been so overtly expressed in nightclubs in the 1920s simmered beneath the surface of the show and the crowds' good behavior, but occasionally they emerged. One customer phoned Rose's office to complain about "a man and a woman . . . carrying on in the water having either a necking party in water or a fun fest, kissing and ducking each other and apparently not taken very seriously by one of the uniformed employees of the Aquacade, leaving the impression that these antics are a daily occurrence." Rose himself indulged in similar impulses. As Esther Williams has recalled, while she was performing as a teenager at Rose's Aquacade at the other world's fair in San Francisco, she fought off the combined advances of Rose, Johnny Weissmuller, and Morton Downey.[43]

In two years the New York Aquacade grossed more than $43 million. Under the contract Rose was entitled to perhaps half of that amount, and thus easily became the wealthiest entrepreneur in the history of New York's nightlife. These profits were testimony to the potency of Rose's careful reworking of the nightclub and world's fair formulae. He brought the suggestiveness and sexual experimentation of the smoky nightclub into the open, in the fresh air of a newly eroticized and post-urban—but also a highly nostalgic—public entertainment space. In 1940, with the world at war and their deficits mounting, the fair's organizers embraced Rose's nostalgic strategy, marketing the second season as a "super country fair," whose mascot was "Elmer," a folksy farmer played by an actor, who greeted customers at the front gate.[44] In the shadow of Manhattan's skyscrapers and the fair's gleaming Trylon tower, therefore, foreshadowings of a life and leisure beyond the city, in distant fields even beyond the existing metropolitan region, could be detected. The consequences for nightlife and human interaction in metropolitan America would be momentous, and they drew the interwar nightclub era to a close.

# CONCLUSION
## The Nightclub Era in Retrospect

Billy Rose's turn to outdoor mass entertainment on the urban fringes was not the only possible indication that, in 1940, a distinct "nightclub era" was coming to an end. War in Europe brought both a palpable stream of refugee nightclub talent from Vienna and other cities and a less tangible sense that the culture as a whole was changing.[1] New financial pressures forced many clubs to close, and the *New York Times* noted that spectacles in the style of Billy Rose were "disappearing" from the nightclub scene. Nils T. Granlund left the city for Hollywood, where he opened a new club. Escalating demands by employees' unions cut into the managers' profit margins but also renewed the fear of labor racketeering by organized crime. These concerns led the police commissioner, Lewis J. Valentine, to order the compulsory fingerprinting of all waiters, bartenders, and cooks in city establishments. Critics of nightclubs once again attacked their alleged immorality and venality. Federal investigations led to the indictment of half a dozen clubowners for income tax fraud. The owner of El Toreador, among others, was jailed.[2]

These trends persisted. After America's entry into the war the federal government imposed a 30 percent "nightclub tax" as part of the general effort to raise revenue from leisure consumption. Later reduced by a third, the tax nevertheless drove up prices and reduced profits and forced new waves of closings. In 1944 another moralistic crusade by Mayor Fiorello La Guardia resulted in more tax investigations and jailings of clubowners.[3]

Nationally, a knell was sounded on 28 November 1942, when the Cocoanut Grove nightclub in Boston was destroyed by fire. Said to have been caused when a busboy lit a match next to a paper palm tree on the ground level, the fire in the club consumed more highly flammable decorations and raced upstairs to the main level. On the dance floor the flames sucked in the room's oxygen and created a fireball. Only half of the one thousand people in the club—twice its legal capacity—managed to escape through the single available exit, the revolving door at the ground-floor entrance. Four hundred ninety-two people were killed in the deadliest building fire in U.S. history. While the disaster did not directly lead to a boycott or movement against nightclubs, it reinforced less tangible attitudes that had been building among many urbanites for years: against densely packed indoor entertainment, closeted interiors, and heavily developed urban space. Such attitudes eventually produced obituaries for the nightclub. In 1950 the writer Robert Sylvester blamed massive urban construction, the flight of customers to the suburbs, and "spiraling 'costs of operation'" for the clubs' decline, but he also argued that "the night club . . . was an anachronism which, by some stroke of luck, lasted thirty years before the public caught up with its faults and frailties. . . . The 'special dinner' steaks which required a hacksaw, the bad whisk[e]y in the trick glasses, the intrusive or insulting cigarette girl, the backache chairs, the knee-cramping tables . . . so quickly and so completely without warning, become obsolete and unwanted."[4]

The larger context of global violence drew some nightlife figures away from their parochial prewar interests. Not surprisingly Billy Rose offers a particularly striking example. Rose's early work with Bernard Baruch during World War I gave him a sense of involvement with the world scene, and more than any other nightclub figure, his interwar career seemed to acquire international connotations (some of which, oddly enough, were not of his devising). During the 1930s the German Nazi newspaper *Der Angriff* ran a publicity photograph of Rose inspecting a line of scantily dressed female chorus applicants and misidentified the scene with the caption, "guidance of the expert white slaver, La Guardia." In 1941 Rose wrote to Lord Halifax after the capture of Rudolf Hess: "May I suggest that your Government let me put him on exhibit—all receipts to go to the British war charities?" The clubowner publicized his letter, which drew Nazi criticism. During the fall of Berlin in 1945, Adolf Hitler chose to commit suicide because he vowed that "I will not fall into the hands of an enemy who requires a new spectacle, exhibited by the Jews, to divert his hysterical masses." Weeks later, while on a tour of U.S. Army recreation facilities, Rose visited Dachau and Berlin, where he slept in Heinrich Himmler's bed. In later years the "Bantam Barnum" became an articulate and major benefactor of the state of Israel.[5]

However, signs of decline in the New York nightclub business, owing to global cataclysm or local conditions, do not tell the entire story. In New York, Billy Rose's Casa Mañana and Diamond Horseshoe continued to earn huge profits, while the Latin Quarter, opening in 1942 at the former site of the Palais Royale, soon outpaced the business in Rose's clubs. Run by the former vaudeville booker Lou Walters and a staff of 250, the Latin Quarter grossed over $3 million a year, of which Walters and his partners kept about $210,000. Travel agencies across the nation booked parties at the Latin Quarter for tourist and convention groups, often months in advance. The Stork, "21," El Morocco, and hotel piano rooms continued to attract more status-conscious elites.[6]

The World War II era, in short, offered neither a distinct end to the nightclub industry in New York nor a smooth continuation. Nevertheless, it is appropriate to conclude this study in 1940. In that year the United States began to mobilize for war. As numerous historians have noted, World War II transformed almost all cultural institutions.[7] Especially after the attack on Pearl Harbor, New York City reverted to a fortress footing that exceeded its effort during World War I. The nightclub business and clubgoing as a recreation, while still vital, were subordinated in many ways to the war effort.

As a result, after 1940 nightclubs displayed less freshness and innovation than in the preceding two decades. Stylistic motifs generally recycled those of clubs of the 1930s, while a number of jazz venues embraced nostalgia fully and commemorated "Dixieland" music of the 1920s. The large-volume, tourist-friendly restaurant club, pioneered at the Hollywood Restaurant in 1929, remained the dominant business model, as the continuing successes of Rose and Walters indicated. In addition, the municipal regulatory regime developed in the 1920s and modified by the reform government in the 1930s remained in place (as it does today). In the 1930s the dichotomy between well-financed nightclubs, appealing to middle-class or elite clienteles, and modest venues for socially marginalized groups had been established. This dichotomy was continued in the 1940s, as working-class African Americans and Puerto Ricans, and homosexuals—under intense surveillance from the police—maintained their own nightclubs mostly in storefronts, back rooms, and other simple locales.

In other words, while changes in ownership, locales, and personalities persisted, the New York City nightclub—formerly a highly dynamic cultural institution—had become static. It might be said to have entered a kind of "postmodern" condition of unoriginality. Nostalgia, not innovation, kept clubs such as Jimmy Ryan's and the Diamond Horseshoe operating through the decade. The freshest new trend, growing to an extent out of the example of Barney Josephson's Café Society, was New York's version of "cabaret," hotel clubs and other small sites that lured more educated patrons with clever satire. Songs and skits of the Revuers and other groups, along with the nascent urban folk movement, laid the groundwork for the sophisticated critique of McCarthyite America in the 1950s by stand-up comedians and singer-songwriters. Cabaret, though, was largely a departure from and a rejection of the nightclub model as it had come to be defined, which suggested that younger urbanites were seeking other forms of intimate nightlife. The stagnation of the classic nightclub model gradually doomed even the most vital venues of the 1940s to eventual obsolescence. The Stork Club was one of the few establishments that hung on until the 1960s. El Morocco was able to revive itself periodically on waves of nostalgia. The Rainbow Room at Rockefeller Center—never strictly a nightclub—hung on until the 1980s and then modernized its facilities, becoming a very expensive yet vital shrine of the *moderne* style of the 1930s.[8]

The classic nightclub era ending in 1940 had exerted a profound influence on the cultural history and civic life of the city. The nightclub had been born in 1914 in response to municipal regulators' new one o'clock closing law. That "curfew" was the response of Victorian-minded reformers to the growth of intimate nighttime leisure establishments. These venues, in the reformers' view, synthesized the brothel, the working-class dance hall, and the morally questionable after-theater restaurants of the rich into a disturbing new locale for sexual promiscuity. Cabaret owners responded to the new law by purchasing existing club charters, issued by the state government, to evade the closing time. Well before 1920, in other words, the cabaret-cum-nightclub had been branded by opponents as a site of morally dangerous modernity.

The coming of Prohibition and the illegal liquor trade, leading to the promotion of nightclubs by Larry Fay and other bootleggers as outlets for their wares, only deepened this identification of nightclubs with corrosive modernity. Meanwhile, female and male customers found the clubs to be sites of sexual and social experimentation and ethnic and racial mixing. The personal clocks of nightlife's participants were readjusted as they partook of clubs until dawn and slept into the afternoon. The affluence of most clienteles in the clubs in Midtown and Harlem in the 1920s ensured that these sites lacked subversive political content, but the irrationality, sexual titillation, and class and ethnic mixing that took place encouraged pre-political subversions of the rational and hierarchical bases of everyday urban life. Similarly, while capitalism reigned supreme in the nightclub business, its fun-house distortion of conspicuous consumption drove prices and expenditures to outlandish heights, and its liquor trade blurred the boundaries between legitimate and illegitimate economic activity in the city. The participation of Slavic, Jewish, Italian, Latin American, and African American performers, promoters, and customers made nightclubs a site of social experimentation. White Americans' obsession in the 1920s with national racial identity and bloodlines caused the entertainment, decor, and motifs of the clubs to represent both their fears and their latent desires. Broadway publicists, newspaper columnists, magazine writers, and others quickly promoted the nightclub's image as an incubator of rollicking and subversive modern trends.

Widespread perception of the nightclub as the locus of modernity put it at the center of cultural-political debate in the 1920s. Nocturnal leisure's longtime association in the public mind with career criminals, gambling, prostitution, and racial amalgamation received new elaboration and emphasis. The Committee of Fourteen viewed nightclubs through the lens of past moral judgments and thus misperceived many of the new male-female interactions in nightlife as evidence of prostitution. Similarly, the city government's recent regulatory innovations— including zoning, licensing, and "scientific" police methods—were brought to bear on the infiltration and prosecution of nightclubs, mainly through the licensing and three o'clock closing law of 1926. The moralistic tenor of municipal regulation was significantly undercut by Tammany Hall's and Mayor Jimmy Walker's long social and business involvement in nightlife. Nightclubs, from the beginning, were part of the political culture that regulated them. Reformers outside the government such as the City Affairs Committee thus could sum up their indictment against Walker by labeling him "the nightclub mayor"—a shorthand reference that Walker and his supporters accepted and often encouraged. In the 1920s, then, a new synergy between urban political identities and show business was established. In the case of Tammany Hall and nightclubs, business affiliations and a common interest in promoting "stars" in the mass media helped to make a celebrity out of Walker, a modern version of the charismatic leader type identified by Max Weber.[9] This synergy conflated personality and celebrity with the mundane responsibilities of bureaucratic government. Animated by the new concept of "public opinion," political players—much like Broadway publicists—grasped at promotional gimmicks to capture the fancy of the largely faceless mass electorate to which they appealed.[10] For good or for ill, as the mass media grew more pervasive in succeeding decades, this dynamic became even more central to American civic life.

Reformers who took aim at nightclubs (such as Grover Whalen and Emory Buckner), Tammany Hall (Samuel Seabury), or both (Mabel Walker Willebrandt) also cultivated their personal celebrity as a tool. They produced voluminous headlines but were only partly successful in achieving their reform goals. The general failure of reform and regulation was due in part to the conflicting governmental jurisdictions that overlaid New York's civic life. City, state, and nation had different interests in the Manhattan cultural landscape. The city nightclub law of 1926 reflected Tammany Hall's peculiar brand of moralistic policing, which placated Irish Catholic sensibilities at the same time that it continued to provide a haven for the police graft and clubhouse gambling that profited Tammany's members. Washington, D.C.'s interest in New York's nightlife was largely driven by the national stereotype of the city

as the prime violator of Prohibition. And Albany, through its sponsor-
ship of the Seabury investigations and various new laws, acted upon the
upstate populace's traditional disdain for the metropolis. These differing motivations ensured that the nightclub would be blamed for varied
social ills and prescribed different administrative remedies. The Walker
administration regulated nightclubs as part of a general campaign
against public indecency. Federal Prohibition enforcers such as Buckner
and Willebrandt used the padlock to turn the nightclub into a symbol
of the illegal liquor trade. Seabury, echoing the Committee of Fourteen,
found the clubs, in collusion with the police, facilitating the abuse of
women in the city.

Seabury's crusade led directly to the fusion government of Fiorello La
Guardia, whose sweeping reform agenda included a vague but passionate, and intensely personal, commitment to the purification of the city's
amusements. The new parks commissioner, Robert Moses, brought his
own special zeal to bear on the issue, razing the Central Park Casino
and promoting outdoor amusements and his concept of the wholesome
restaurant (exemplified by the Tavern on the Green and the Claremont
Inn). La Guardia's efforts included the promotion of circuses and children's attendance of movies and an attack on slot-machine gambling,
but they reached their sharpest definition in his campaigns against burlesque theaters in Midtown and striptease at the New York World's Fair.

The fact that La Guardia generally did not take action against nightclubs per se—and that even Moses lost interest in them—suggests how
the Great Depression and other changes had redefined the cultural significance of the clubs since the 1920s. During the years of Prohibition
and the Depression many clubs and their denizens had adapted to regulatory and economic pressures and had entered the civic mainstream.
The difficult early years of the Great Depression winnowed their numbers dramatically and required that surviving clubs adopt the high-
volume, no-cover-charge formula to appeal to a broad middle-class
clientele. The repeal of Prohibition encouraged clubs to conform carefully to new liquor laws. As La Guardia's obsessive campaign to eliminate
burlesque indicates, successful nightclubs obeyed the liquor code and
other regulations so fully that the mayor was willing to overlook (to the
consternation of some citizens) the clubs' displays of female nudity. Billy
Rose's highly popular embrace of nostalgic themes in his clubs, meanwhile, showed that these locales were making a major cultural accommo-
dation. Even the revival of elite clubs in the realm of "café society" had
the scent of nostalgia, not innovation, attached to it. Clubs in the 1930s
gave up some of the mantle of modernity to ensure a more stable and
reassuring existence for themselves in difficult times.

The accommodations made by these nightclubs helped to ensure their profitability, but they also made the clubs less relevant to the important cultural concerns of New York in the mid-1930s. An analogy can be found in the increasing failure of the La Guardia regime to address crises in the city's social fabric. Reformers congratulated themselves on having slain perceived civic beasts of the 1920s, especially by ousting Tammany Hall, repealing Prohibition, and putting liquor under lawful regulation. However, they responded much less effectively to new long-term threats to civic health that emerged in the 1930s from the same corners of the urban jungle. The end of the underworld alcohol trade channeled experienced and ruthless entrepreneurs into other areas of endeavor—labor racketeering, prostitution, narcotics, and gambling—which expanded during the 1930s. (Arnold Rothstein had foreseen and pioneered this diversification of organized crime in the previous decade.) Thomas E. Dewey's highly publicized prosecutions shed light on this new phenomenon, but like Willebrandt and Seabury before him, Dewey's political opportunism, cult of celebrity, and limited powers curtailed his ability to reduce organized crime effectively. Dewey inflated the notoriety of his main prey, Lucky Luciano, and gained the conviction of the Tammany boss Jimmy Hines long after his most active years. Meanwhile, Frank Costello's careful bookkeeping and management largely went unnoticed, and Costello proceeded to construct an organized crime network on a scale that Rothstein would have envied.

Most ominously, Costello bankrolled Tammany Hall to an electoral comeback in the late 1930s. La Guardia kept Tammany's candidates out of the mayor's chair until 1946, but by then virtually all of the city's other government offices had been reclaimed by the Democratic machine, and the peripatetic mayor—distracted by his nationwide wartime duties—saw the popularity of reform government undercut by the renascent machine.[11] In this era, though, there was little association of nightclubs with the evolution of politics and organized crime. While Walter Winchell and J. Edgar Hoover kept the Stork Club in the headlines as a somewhat dubious bulwark against fascism and communism, nightclubs generally were situated within a well-defined commercial nexus that had very little role to play in the prime political struggles of the 1940s.

Since the 1920s nightclubs had proved most potent as sites of a new, open sexuality and racial and ethnic mixing. While the clubs of the 1920s had indulged in stereotyping and the exploitation of female and nonwhite employees, they had also acknowledged and provocatively displayed the city's heretofore hidden social and sexual experimentation and ethnic variety. By the late 1930s, though, the most commercially successful clubs promoted toothless and nostalgic representations of social differences. The travel and interracial contact that Harlem's nightclubs of the 1920s especially had encouraged—superficial as that contact usually might have been—had ceased with the decline of the uptown club scene. The vogue for female impersonators, similarly, which had indicated a tentative exploration by mainstream clubgoers of homosexuality, had also vanished by 1937.

The depiction of the "new woman" in nightclubs by the late 1930s was more complex and problematic. In the 1920s, the bootleggers' clubs essentially played with the paradox that had been presented to nightlife by Florenz Ziegfeld's chorus line. Ziegfeld had "glorified the American girl" and her corn-fed Anglo-Saxon innocence while he also removed her clothing and provided her with the mature sexual awareness of a Folies Bergères dancer. Generally speaking, middle-class America's various negotiations of the paradox of the Ziegfeld Girl produced a general tension about the nature of white womanhood in the 1920s. This tension is evident in the confused findings of the Committee of Fourteen, which misinterpreted much of the new social behavior as evidence of prostitution. The declining age of nightclub chorus dancers and the more salacious alternatives offered by stock burlesque lessened the perception that increased nudity in clubs posed a moral threat.

Another factor that weakened the cultural impact of nightclubs was the increased passivity of the audience. The "action environment" of clubs in the 1920s, in which Texas Guinan's chorines popped cherries into male customers' mouths, had given way to carefully managed spectacles that strictly regulated contact between performers and patrons and encouraged the patrons' self-regulation. This behavior was representative of the Great Depression's general encouragement of personal self-discipline. As a result of this, much of the benefit of nightclubs for female customers—who had found self-expression and a form of social freedom in the smoky rooms of the 1920s—seemed to have disappeared. Nightclubs of the 1930s, led by Billy Rose, offered the passive consumption of carefully crafted presentations of female nudity instead of any new vision of women's assertiveness and independence. Although Rose, as well as the striptease performer Gypsy Rose Lee, claimed that female dancers pursued intellectual interests offstage, the ample display of flesh could hardly be considered a recognition of the dancers' nonphysical attributes. In the long run, ironically, the clubs would suffer from their idealized version of the passive striptease experience. In the 1940s, in a move that might be interpreted as a partial revival of the animal intimacy and grotesquerie that had been found in clubs of the 1920s and early 1930s, "strip clubs" originated in small venues across the city, especially in dilapidated spaces on Times Square that had once housed nightclubs.[12]

The larger urban context shows a similar lack of advancement for women in civic life. Based on its investigations of nightlife, the Committee of Fourteen's calls in the 1920s for attention to the social roots of prostitution and a policy of crime prevention—widely echoed by criminologists and social workers—suggested a holistic approach to the difficulties faced by women in the city. Samuel Seabury's exposure of the police framing ring and limited excursions into the affairs of the unfairly sentenced minors, Vivian Gordon, and Polly Adler inspired some calls for a similar new agenda. The Depression, though, deepened the plight of working-class women and limited the government's ability to launch a comprehensive program for their benefit. Subsequently, under the La Guardia administration, the city did increase its attention to women's problems, putting female social workers and police officers in greater positions of responsibility and reforming various city departments, most notably women's corrections. However, like many of the mayor's initiatives, programs for women were often piecemeal and driven by headlines. New York City offered only a limited vision of the improvement of women's lives. The story of the status of women in the interwar era thus indicates a series of missed opportunities. In a similar vein, La Guardia's opportunistic dragnet against transvestites indicated that civic tolerance toward homosexuals was actually in decline.

Despite La Guardia's liberal principles and policies, the late 1930s brought about a more intense social and cultural segregation of whites and African Americans. The riot in Harlem in 1935 not only curtailed biracial nightlife there; it also ensured that white fears and hostility toward Manhattan's growing black population would be heightened. General capital flight from Harlem increased, de facto residential segregation worsened, and, in a crowning blow, the police and the city government tacitly permitted the increased pollution of the ghetto with organized crime, narcotics, and gambling. While nightlife paid a cultural tribute to Harlem's growing Latin American population by adopting dance steps, musical rhythms, and design motifs from south of the border, that population also fell prey to the city's new abandonment of its nonwhite residents.

Finally, the nightclub era shows how leisure trends denoted the growth of an important American urge to abandon urban life. Millions of Americans, of course, remained enticed by the lure of city living, and after the 1930s New York City remained by far the most powerful magnet that attracted them. By this time the *New Yorker*, which had been founded by the Colorado native Harold Ross, had shed its early identity as a humor magazine and now romanticized Manhattan as a city of liveable neighborhoods that were seasoned with risk, intellectual stimulation, and adventure.[13] Self-styled sophisticates from the hinterlands first subscribed to the magazine and then moved to the city themselves. The dense concentration of finance and business contacts, as well as a growing fascination with the skyscraper as the site of corporate headquarters, helped to ensure that Manhattan remained the nation's most important business center. Even before World War II, though, native Manhattanites were leaving the island to live in other boroughs, and residents of the entire city were fleeing to the suburbs and points beyond. Robert Moses's expressways and parkways channeled them there, and Billy Rose's Aquacade at the World's Fair presented a vision of what leisure, sexuality, and nocturnality might look like on the suburban frontier.

Historians have shown that many factors—including federal mortgage policies, wartime migration, and ghettoization—contributed to the largely white post-World War II flight from cities to the suburbs.[14] The story of the New York nightclub, though, shows how this major historical trend partly had its roots in urbanites' growing disaffection with leisure in the city. The nightclub was a symbol of urban consumerism, density, and modernity, as well as of the individual's desire to dissolve into a crowd, pursue a nocturnal existence, and experience city diversity and experimentation to the fullest. Owing to regulation, scandal, and demonization, nightclubs became a symbol of an intensely urban modernity. Even before the end of the 1920s, as we have seen, champions of nightlife such as the *New Yorker* expressed ambivalence about what the clubs represented. After 1930 the clubs themselves, responding in part to customers' preferences, pursued a new spaciousness and featured anti-urban and nostalgic themes. Billy Rose took this trend the furthest, promoting a circus in the cavernous Hippodrome and then taking his concepts outdoors, into sprawling waterside amphitheaters.

Rose, of course, was a native New Yorker and as authentic a veteran of the nightclub of the 1920s as one might wish to find. Many other such veterans, such as Nils Granlund, Earl Carroll, and others who relocated to southern California, or Harry Richman, who gravitated to Florida, could be found stepping outside for fresh air in the 1930s. In the 1940s Emil Perona used some of the profits from his brother John's El Morocco club to create the 400-acre Perona Farms in rural Andover, New Jersey, complete with a dairy barn, hayrides, a swimming lake, and a dining pavilion.[15] Acting on their preferences, the modernist cohort of the 1920s and 1930s helped to lead a good portion of the white American majority to leisure and life in suburbia, as well as to what would later be called the Sunbelt states.

In the decades after World War II New York City often witnessed recapitulations of the civic and social crises that occurred in the 1920s and 1930s. Ghettoization and ethnic fragmentation worsened. The city's finances, caught in a vise between the flight of business tax revenue and escalating union contracts and social service expenses, decayed progressively until 1975, when the city was brought to the brink of default for the first time in forty-three years. Still, with so much money moving through government coffers and with machine politics revived after 1945, cyclical patterns of corruption emerged more strongly than ever, mocking the declarations of victory by the Seabury-La Guardia forces in 1933. Police misconduct also emerged repeatedly. An NYPD scandal was a major factor in the forced resignation of the Tammany mayor William O'Dwyer in 1950, and revelations poured forth in later decades, from Frank Serpico's testimony in 1970 to the brutality allegations of the 1990s. The exploitation of women by the police force persisted as well. In 1998, for example, twenty city police officers were charged with having permitted the operation of a brothel for a decade in return for free sexual favors from prostitutes.[16]

Such degradation of civic life was accompanied by stark contrasts in the physical development of Manhattan, which had a major impact on leisure. World War II made the island the world's financial center, and with the arrival of the United Nations it became the diplomatic center as well. The U.N. Secretariat building typified the dramatic new construction that quickly dwarfed much of prewar midtown Manhattan— rectangular glass-and-steel skyscrapers in the postwar "international" style of Ludwig Mies van der Rohe and others. This large-scale capital investment symbolized the new priorities in the ordering of space, as well as leisure, on the island. Fiorello La Guardia's dream of intimate, street-level entertainment for diverse clienteles—which he had struggled to realize in the 1930s—evaporated.

Allusions in nightlife to ethnic motifs, authentic or ersatz, largely disappeared in the era of the sleek new international style. After World War II Billy Rose even transformed his Diamond Horseshoe, eliminating nostalgic trappings in favor of "romantic décor in red and black . . . a feminine singing chorus . . . and an orchestra with twenty violins." Fifty-second Street's swing clubs lost their charm and their jazz-loving clientele, and as Robert Sylvester put it, these venues "decayed into strip tease clip joints and worthless sucker traps with carnival barkers, broads hustling tables, finger men on the prowl, lookouts for blackmail mobs on steady duty, badger game victims and various other dregs." In the 1960s all of those venues were razed for the construction of skyscrapers. The sensuality and intimacy celebrated in nightlife in the 1920s also went fully underground in the conspicuously seedy environment of Times Square, the re-closeted gay subculture, and in the bohemian arts colonies of Greenwich Village and SoHo. Black Harlem, notably, became a "gilded ghetto" (as sociologists described black Chicago in the 1950s), containing a substantial middle class but dominated by a majority of poor, persecuted, and trapped African Americans.[17] New clubs such as Count Basie's could not last more than a few years in such an environment.

Such conditions eventually did stimulate a thoughtful and increasingly effective rebellion in favor of a revival of small-scale city life. In 1956 the "new urbanist" movement was launched when well-heeled residents of the upper West Side campaigned to stop Robert Moses's plan to tear down a playground in Central Park to build a parking lot for his Tavern on the Green. The movement received its definitive statement in Jane Jacobs's manifesto of 1961, *The Death and Life of Great American Cities*, and crystallized under her leadership against Moses's efforts to raze entire blocks of Greenwich Village for an expressway across Manhattan. Jacobs and the new urbanism stressed the need for overall urban safety and livability, for children as well as adults, propagating a more domesticated version of the urban-neighborhood romanticism found in the *New Yorker*.[18] City living, in their view, held inevitable risk but also could feature far more neighborliness and order if the ruthlessness of current urban development were curbed.

Vestiges of romanticism shaped Jacobs's and the *New Yorker*'s visions of life in New York City after World War II. As the sociologist Elizabeth Wilson has pointed out, new urbanists such as Jacobs took for granted the presence of populations with stable incomes and access to jobs and education, and ignored the flight of capital that enveloped Harlem and other districts in deeper blight.[19] It might be added that in the 1950s, despite the return of Tammany Hall to municipal rule, Jacobs and other middle-class women enjoyed protections in certain neighborhoods, enabled by policies dating from the La Guardia era, that many working-class and nonwhite women still had not received. As Wilson also notes, the artist, gay, and "yuppie" gentrifications that inspired neighborhood revivals after 1970 did little to solve the general decay and anomie of the post-World War II city.

Similarly, the new urbanism and gentrification also did not generate the level of social mixing in nightlife and the diverse geography of leisure that had been seen in the 1920s and early 1930s. Cabarets and cutting-edge jazz clubs such as the Village Vanguard mainly attracted aficionados and the self-styled intelligentsia, while hotel piano rooms appealed to a nostalgic (and wealthy) older generation. Since the revival of immigration in the 1960s the traditional neighborhood clubhouse—legally chartered or otherwise—has enjoyed a revival in New York City in dozens of national flavors. Most recently, highly commercialized tourist attractions that pass for middle-class urban nightlife, such as Planet Hollywood and the House of Blues, have become the successors to the nightclubs of Don Dickerman and other exploiters of the form. New musical developments such as the folk revival, rock, reggae, and soul have stimulated more vital club genres. The most widely chronicled clubs have been the highly publicized large dance establishments that prospered during the era of nascent gay rights and high drug use in the 1970s and 1980s, such as Steve Rubell's Studio 54 (at the old location of Billy Rose's Casino de Paree) and Peter Gatien's Limelight and Club USA.[20] Occasionally, as in the police raid and ensuing riot at the Stonewall Bar in 1969, the story of club leisure intersects starkly with the broader history of social struggle in the city. All of these stories, I would argue, constitute newer chapters in New York City's leisure history, rather than continuations of the interwar nightclub era.

By contrast, though, the regulation of nightlife in New York has shown a remarkable continuity with the interwar decades. The 1926 cabaret licensing law remains on the books, and for generations it has been amended to strengthen the city's ability to close down establishments. The revision in 1940 that brought the fingerprinting of employees also introduced the notorious "cabaret card," which denied employment to performers ever convicted of an offense (a group that eventually included Frank Sinatra, Thelonious Monk, and many others). Disasters such as the fatal fire at the Blue Angel club in 1975 encouraged the city to pass stringent and expensive requirements for sprinklers, fire alarms, and exits. Many clubs subsequently remained unlicensed to avoid these expenses. Some court challenges to the law succeeded. The attorney Maxwell Cohen led the battle that struck down the cabaret card, while Paul Chevigny has helped to liberalize the restrictions on the size of musical ensembles in restaurants.[21]

Regulation of nightlife has increased in other ways, though. In 1990 the city was rezoned to ban cabarets in recently gentrified sections of Manhattan such as TriBeCa. When a fire the same year at the Happy Land, an unlicensed social club in the Bronx, killed eighty-seven Dominican immigrants, a new wave of club raids was launched. Since 1994 the administrations of Rudolph Giuliani and Michael Bloomberg have used the cabaret law even more broadly, in the words of the *Village Voice*, "to combat quality-of-life complaints and troublesome clubs." In 2002 the police under Bloomberg launched raids on unlicensed dance clubs, on the pretext of possible safety violations. Neither the city department of consumer affairs (which now licenses cabarets) nor the New York Nightlife Association, an organization of licensed nightclubs, finds a reason to eliminate or even to soften the cabaret law. The club owner David Baxley, though, considers the law "totalitarian. Two years ago the only places it was illegal to dance were Manhattan and Afghanistan. And now you can dance in Afghanistan."[22]

From the perspective of the twenty-first century, in many ways the Manhattan of the 1920s may seem as distant as Afghanistan. Nevertheless, despite dramatic social and cultural changes and the persistence of stringent municipal regulation, the attraction, even the romance, of the 1920s' nightclub's dark walls, intimate tables, potentially explosive spontaneous revelry, and celebration of ethnic and class diversity have lingered in our largely anti-urban national culture. The clubs represented a dream of sorts, a modernistic fantasy of community, diversity, consumption, and free experimentation—human desires that withstand the passing of institutions and eras. Although a majority in the United States may resist urban living, cities live on, and the number of municipalities with more than a million residents grows every decade. Urban life also continues to exert a strong fascination, especially for the young and the nonwhite. Rock music clubs, discotheques, and techno and rave dancing clubs, as well as nostalgic evocations of the 1950s cocktail lounge, testify to the enduring appeal of risk-filled, sexually charged behavior in close quarters—controlled risk that maintains social order while allowing patrons to experiment with sex, extravagance, wagering, and other forms of personal heedlessness.[23] As always, these nightlife experiments reflect the political and economic contexts of their time and help to define gender and ethnic identities for discrete subcultures, and on occasion for American culture as a whole. In such ways, these venues add new chapters to the chronicle of individual and collective self-definition through leisure in the world's great, diverse, and imperfect democracy.

# Notes

Sources frequently cited in the notes are identified by the following abbreviations:

BRTC Billy Rose Theatre Collection, Performing Arts Library, New York Public Library
C14 Committee of Fourteen papers, Rare Books and Manuscripts, New York Public Library
JJW James J. Walker mayoral papers, New York City Municipal Archives

*Preface*

1. Stephen Graham, *New York Nights* (New York: George H. Doran, 1927), 89–96; also Louise Berliner, *Texas Guinan: Queen of the Night Clubs* (Austin: University of Texas Press, 1993), 111–12.

2. *New York Times*, 4 July 1926, 3.

3. This study concerns itself with Manhattan (New York borough in the city of Greater New York and New York County in the state of New York) because its nightclubs were clearly the city's most influential. However, as these pages show, leisure and civic life in the other boroughs and across the metropolitan area also were significant, and helped to shape the Manhattan experience in many ways.

4. Nathan Huggins, *Harlem Renaissance* (New York: Oxford University Press, 1973); David Levering Lewis, *When Harlem Was in Vogue* (New York: Knopf, 1981); Kevin J. Mumford, *Interzones: Black/White Sex Districts in Chicago and New York in the Early Twentieth Century* (New York: Columbia University Press, 1997); Lewis A. Erenberg, *Steppin' Out: New York Nightlife and the Transformation of American Culture* (Westport, Conn.: Greenwood Press, 1981); Hazel V. Carby, "Policing the Black Woman's Body in an Urban Context," *Critical Inquiry* 18 (summer 1992), 738–55; and Ann Douglas, *Terrible Honesty: Mongrel Manhattan in the 1920s* (New York: Farrar Straus Giroux, 1995). See also William R. Taylor, *In Pursuit of Gotham: Culture and Commerce in New York* (New York: Oxford University Press, 1992).

5. Warren Susman, "The Culture of the 1930s," in *Culture as History: The Transformation of American Society in the Twentieth Century* (New York: Pantheon Books, 1984), 150–83; Lawrence W. Levine, "American Culture and the Great Depression," in *The Unpredictable Past: Explorations in American Cultural History* (New York: Oxford University Press, 1993), 206–30; and Richard Pells, *Radical Visions and American Dreams: Culture and Social Thought in the Depression Years* (1973; reprint, Urbana: University of Illinois Press, 1998), esp. parts 3 and 5.

6. Besides Douglas and Carby see also Huggins, *Harlem Renaissance*, esp. chap. 3; Günter H. Lenz, "Symbolic Space, Communal Rituals, and the Surreality of the Urban Ghetto: Harlem in Black Literature from the 1920s to the 1960s,"

*Callaloo* 35 (spring 1988), 309–45; and Robert F. Worth, "*Nigger Heaven* and the Harlem Renaissance," *African American Review* 29 (autumn 1995), 461–73.

7. Explorations of civic life in American urban history include Francis E. Rourke, "Urbanism and American Democracy," *Ethics* 74:4 (1964), 255–68; David L. Westby, "The Civic Sphere in the American City," *Social Forces* 45:2 (1966), 161–69; and Thomas Bender, *New York Intellect* (New York: Knopf, 1987), esp. the prologue, 191–204, 279–86. Mary Ryan's scholarship is the most important recent contribution; see *Civic Wars: Democracy in Public Life in the American City During the Nineteenth Century* (Berkeley: University of California Press, 1997), and "Civil Society as Democratic Practice: North American Cities during the Nineteenth Century," *Journal of Interdisciplinary History* 29:4 (1999), 559–84. See also Reed Ueda, "Second-Generation Civic America: Education, Citizenship, and the Children of Immigrants," ibid., 661–82.

8. Ryan, *Civic Wars*, esp. chap. 7; also Sean Wilentz, *Chants Democratic: New York City and the Rise of the American Working Class, 1788–1850* (New York: Oxford University Press, 1986), chap. 5.

9. Walter Lippmann, *The Phantom Public* (New York: Harcourt, Brace, 1925) and *A Preface to Morals* (New York: Macmillan, 1929); John Dewey, *The Public and Its Problems* (New York: Henry Holt, 1927); and Robert B. Westbrook, *John Dewey and American Democracy* (Ithaca, N.Y.: Cornell University Press, 1991), esp. 294–316.

10. Johan Huizinga, *Homo Ludens: A Study of the Play Element in Culture* (New York: Beacon, 1955), esp. 12, 205. See also Roger Caillois, *Man, Play, and Games*, trans. Meyer Barash (New York: Free Press, 1961), 58; Brian Sutton-Smith, *The Ambiguity of Play* (Cambridge, Mass.: Harvard University Press, 1997), esp. chap. 11; Enid Welsford, *The Fool* (1935; reprint, Garden City, N.Y.: Doubleday, 1961); and Mihai I. Spariosu, *Dionysus Reborn: Play and the Aesthetic Dimension in Modern Philosophical and Scientific Discourse* (Ithaca, N.Y.: Cornell University Press, 1989).

11. Representative of the British scholarship is John Clarke and Chas Critcher, *The Devil Makes Work: Leisure in Capitalist Britain* (Urbana: University of Illinois Press, 1985), and Paul Chatterton and Robert Hollands, *Urban Nightscapes: Youth Cultures, Pleasure Spaces, and Corporate Power* (London: Routledge, 2003). Early American scholarship includes Weaver Pangburn, "The Worker's Leisure and His Individuality," *American Journal of Sociology* 27 (1922), 433–41; Clarence E. Rainwater, "Socialized Leisure," *Journal of Applied Sociology* 28 (1923), 258–64; and L. C. Walker, *Distributed Leisure* (New York: Century, 1931). More recent work includes Erenberg, *Steppin' Out*; Roy Rosenzweig, *Eight Hours for What We Will: Workers and Leisure in an Industrial City, 1870–1920* (New York: Cambridge University Press, 1983); Kathy Peiss, *Cheap Amusements: Working Women and Leisure in Turn-of-the-Century New York* (Philadelphia: Temple University Press, 1986); Lizabeth Cohen, *Making a New Deal: Industrial Workers in Chicago, 1919–1939* (Cambridge, U.K.: Cambridge University Press, 1991), esp. chap. 3; and Steven M. Gelber, *Hobbies: Leisure and the Culture of Work in America* (New York: Columbia University Press, 1999).

I do not systematically explore the relation of nightclub leisure to industrial labor. Since nightclubs often were expensive play sites for the middle and wealthy classes, they perhaps offer an unusual case study in the relationship of leisure to work. Nevertheless, issues regarding wage labor in Manhattan—involving nightclub employees as well as workers in associated fields in nightlife—repeatedly surface in the history of the clubs. I have folded these labor issues into my general examination of the state of civic life in Manhattan.

12. See, for example, Jürgen Habermas, *The Structural Transformation of the*

*Public Sphere*, trans. Thomas Burger and Frederick Lawrence (Cambridge, Mass.: Polity Press, 1989); Amitai Etzioni, "A Moderate Communitarian Proposal," *Political Theory* 24:2 (1996), 155–71; Harry Brighouse, "Civic Education and Liberal Legitimacy," *Ethics* 108:4 (1998), 719–45; and Robert D. Putnam, *Bowling Alone: The Collapse and Revival of American Community* (New York: Simon and Schuster, 2001), esp. 187–203, 402–17. A fascinating historiographical debate that explores the ties between leisure and civic life in early modern English towns can be found in Angus McInnes, "The Emergence of a Leisure Town: Shrewsbury, 1660–1760," *Past and Present* 120 (August 1988), 53–87, and Peter Borsay, "The Emergence of a Leisure Town: Or an Urban Renaissance?" *Past and Present* 126 (February 1990), 189–96.

13. Neal Gabler, *Life: The Movie: How Entertainment Conquered Reality* (New York: Vintage, 2000), esp. 99–117.

14. Douglas, *Terrible Honesty*, 18–21; Westbrook, *John Dewey and American Democracy*, 294–301; see also the fascinating discussion of the interwar press in Paula S. Fass, *Kidnapped: Child Abduction in America* (Cambridge, Mass.: Harvard University Press, 1999), chaps. 2 and 3.

15. See, for example, George Chauncey, *Gay New York: Gender, Urban Culture, and the Making of the Gay Male World 1890–1940* (New York: Basic Books, 1994), 5; Robin D. G. Kelley, *Race Rebels: Culture, Politics, and the Black Working Class* (New York: Basic Books, 1994), 8; and David W. Stowe, "The Politics of Café Society," *Journal of American History* 84 (1998), 1385. All have been influenced by James C. Scott, *Weapons of the Weak: Everyday Forms of Peasant Resistance* (New Haven, Conn.: Yale University Press, 1985) and *Domination and the Arts of Resistance: Hidden Transcripts* (New Haven, Conn.: Yale University Press, 1990).

*Chapter 1*

1. Thomas M. Coffey, *The Long Thirst: Prohibition in America, 1920–1933* (New York: Norton, 1975), 21–23, 122; Nils Thor Granlund with Sid Feder and Ralph Hancock, *Blondes, Brunettes, and Bullets* (New York: David McKay Co., 1957), 117.

2. Additional information on Larry Fay is found in Morris Markey, "Fear, Inc.," *New Yorker*, 28 September 1929, 42–47; clippings in Texas Guinan scrapbook, BRTC; *New York Times*, 2 January 1933, 1, 3; and Leo Katcher, *The Big Bankroll: The Life and Times of Arnold Rothstein* (New Rochelle, N.Y.: Arlington House, 1959), 238–51. On Guinan and Fay, see O. O. McIntyre letter to Texas Guinan, ca. March 1933, Guinan scrapbook; Granlund, Feder, and Hancock, *Blondes, Brunettes, and Bullets*, 119, 122; and Louise Berliner, *Texas Guinan: Queen of the Night Clubs* (Austin: University of Texas Press, 1993), chap. 3.

3. Coffey, *The Long Thirst*, 21–23; Granlund, Feder, and Hancock, *Blondes, Brunettes, and Bullets*, 94, 119, 126, 129; Jimmy Durante and Jack Kofoed, *Night Clubs* (New York: Knopf, 1931), 67; clippings on Fay in Guinan scrapbook, BRTC; *New York Times*, 2 January 1933, 1, 3.

4. Department of Commerce, *Statistical Abstract of the United States, 43rd Number* (Washington, D.C., 1920), 426, 599, 602, 604; Thomas Kessner, *Fiorello H. La Guardia and the Making of Modern New York* (New York: McGraw-Hill, 1989), 202–4.

5. General surveys of New York leisure after 1870 include David Nasaw, *Going Out: The Rise and Fall of Public Amusements* (New York: Basic Books, 1993), chaps. 1–2, and "Cities of Light, Landscapes of Pleasure," in David Ward and Olivier Zunz, eds., *The Landscape of Modernity: Essays on New York City, 1900–1940* (New York: Russell Sage Foundation, 1992), 273–86. Focused studies include Randy

D. McBee, *Dance Hall Days: Intimacy and Leisure among Working-Class Immigrants in the United States* (New York: New York University Press, 2000); Brooks Atkinson, *Broadway* (New York: Macmillan, 1970), 53–80; Robert W. Snyder, *The Voice of the City: Vaudeville and Popular Culture in New York* (New York: Oxford University Press, 1989); Robert C. Allen, *Horrible Prettiness: Burlesque and American Culture* (Chapel Hill: University of North Carolina Press, 1991), chaps. 3–4; John F. Kasson, *Amusing the Million: Coney Island at the Turn of the Century* (New York: Hill and Wang, 1978); and Woody Register, *The Kid of Coney Island: Fred Thompson and the Rise of American Amusements* (New York: Oxford University Press, 2001).

6. On the origins of the nightclub, see Lewis A. Erenberg, *Steppin' Out: New York Nightlife and the Transformation of American Culture* (Westport, Conn.: Greenwood Press, 1981), chaps. 2–4, esp. 129–30. See also Abel Green and Joe Laurie Jr., *Show Biz: From Vaude to Video* (New York: Henry Holt, 1951), esp. chaps. 5, 7, 9. On Ziegfeld, see Susan A. Glenn, *Female Spectacle: The Theatrical Roots of Modern Feminism* (Cambridge, Mass.: Harvard University Press, 2000), chap. 5; Richard Ziegfeld and Paulette Ziegfeld, *The Ziegfeld Touch: The Life and Times of Florenz Ziegfeld, Jr.* (New York: Harry N. Abrams, 1993); and Linda Mizejewski, *Ziegfeld Girl: Image and Icon in Culture and Cinema* (Durham, N.C.: Duke University Press, 1999).

7. On the general effect of Prohibition, see Richard F. Hamm, *Shaping the Eighteenth Amendment* (Chapel Hill: University of North Carolina Press, 1995), esp. 251–55; and John J. Rumbarger, *Profits, Power, and Prohibition: Alcohol Reform and the Industrializing of America, 1800–1930* (Albany: SUNY Press, 1989), chap. 10. Prohibition's impact on nightlife is related in Erenberg, *Steppin' Out*, chap. 6; Robert A. M. Stern, Gregory Gilmartin, and Thomas Mellis, *New York 1930: Architecture and Urbanism Between the Two World Wars* (New York: Rizzoli, 1987), 271–72; Frank Case, *Tales of a Wayward Inn* (New York: Frederick A. Stokes, 1938), 172–73; and Herbert Asbury, *The Great Illusion: An Informal History of Prohibition* (1950; rep. New York: Greenwood, 1968), 150–53, 192–93.

8. On gangsters in nightclubs, see Granlund, Feder, and Hancock, *Blondes, Brunettes, and Bullets*, 137–40, 168; Durante and Kofoed, *Night Clubs*, 145, 154, 163–67, 194; Lewis J. Valentine, *Night Stick: The Autobiography of Lewis J. Valentine* (New York: Dial Press, 1947), 41–43, 49, 55–60; Robert Sylvester, *No Cover Charge: A Backward Look at the Night Clubs* (New York: Dial Press, 1956), 2–4, 201; and Markey, "Fear, Inc.," 42.

9. Billy Rose, *Wine, Women, and Words* (New York: Simon and Schuster, 1948), 11–12; Durante and Kofoed, *Night Clubs*, 117–23; and Harry Richman with Richard Gehman, *A Hell of a Life* (New York: Duell, Sloan and Pearce, 1966), 105ff. Employment statistics are in *New York Times*, 20 November 1926, 19; 2 January 1927, VIII, 6. On Salvin-Thompson, see *New York Times*, 15 May 1924, 1, and Durante and Kofoed, *Night Clubs*, 216–17. On Dickerman, see Steven Watson, *Strange Bedfellows: The First American Avant-Garde* (New York: Abbeville Press, 1991), 214; Allen Churchill, *The Improper Bohemians: A Re-creation of Greenwich Village in Its Heyday* (New York: E. P. Dutton, 1959), 150–64; and Erenberg, *Steppin' Out*, 254. On elite clubs, see the *New Yorker*, for example 20 February 1926, 69; 6 November 1926, 71–73; 11 December 1926, 71; 30 April 1927, 93; 10 December 1927, 106; and 24 December 1927, 4.

10. Durante and Kofoed, *Night Clubs*, 205; Berliner, *Texas Guinan*, 44 and passim; and Lewis Erenberg, "Impresarios of Broadway Nightlife," in William R. Taylor, ed., *Inventing Times Square: Culture and Commerce at the Crossroads of the World* (New York: Russell Sage Foundation, 1991), 167.

11. Bryan D. Palmer, *Cultures of Darkness: Night Travels in the Histories of Transgression (Medieval to Modern)* (New York: Monthly Review Press, 2000), 13. On O'Keeffe and New York City, see Roxana Robinson, *Georgia O'Keeffe: A Life* (Hanover, N.H.: University Press of New England, 1998), 203–9, 293. The thesis presented in this paragraph challenges Lewis Erenberg's assertion that nightlife in the 1920s largely perpetuated cultural concerns that had originated in the lobster palaces of the 1900s and the cabarets of the 1910s. See Erenberg, *Steppin' Out,* chap. 8.

12. Cabaret listings in the *New Yorker,* 12 November 1927, 10; also 12 February 1927, 8.

13. Caroline F. Ware, *Greenwich Village 1920–1930: A Comment on American Civilization in the Post-War Years* (Boston: Houghton Mifflin, 1935), 54; see also 55, 95–96. On Greenwich Village nightlife in the 1920s also see the *New Yorker,* 24 August 1929, 2; Charles G. Shaw, *Nightlife: Vanity Fair's Intimate Guide to New York after Dark* (New York: John Day Co., 1931), n.p.; and Lewis Erenberg, "Greenwich Village Nightlife," in Rick Beard and Leslie Cohen Berlowitz eds., *Greenwich Village: Culture and Counterculture* (New Brunswick, N.J.: Rutgers University Press, 1993), 356–70.

14. Ware, *Greenwich Village 1920–1930,* 54; *Variety,* 16 October 1929, quoted in David Levering Lewis, *When Harlem Was in Vogue* (New York: Knopf, 1981), 208; also 106, 208–11.

15. *New Yorker,* 18 December 1926, 76.

16. Edmund Wilson, "Night Clubs," *New Republic* 44 (9 September 1925), 71; Stephen Graham, *New York Nights* (New York: George H. Doran, 1927), 96; *New York Times,* 30 June 1926, 10; and Carl Van Vechten diary, entries for 5 November 1924 and 3 January, 28 February, 4 March, and 3 April 1925, box 111, Carl Van Vechten papers, Rare Books and Manuscripts Room, New York Public Library.

17. Luc Sante, *Low Life: Lures and Snares of Old New York* (New York: Farrar Straus and Giroux, 1991), esp. 278–86; Stern, Gilmartin, and Mellis, *New York 1930,* 271, 275; H. I. Brock, "Nightlife: New York's Vast Monopoly," *New York Times Magazine,* 2 March 1930, 9; *New Yorker,* 9 April 1927, 25–28, and 29 December 1928, 9; and George Chauncey, *Gay New York: Gender, Urban Culture, and the Making of the Gay Male World 1890–1940* (New York: Basic Books, 1994), 164–65.

18. Palmer, *Cultures of Darkness,* 17. See also Murray Melbin, *Night as Frontier: Colonizing the World after Dark* (New York: Free Press, 1987); and Joachim Schlör, *Nights in the Big City: Paris, Berlin, London, 1840–1930,* trans. Pierre Gottfried Imhof and Dafydd Rees Roberts (London: Reaktion Books, 1998).

19. On European cabaret, see Lisa Appignanesi, *The Cabaret* (New York: Universe, 1976); Stan Shipley, *Club Life and Socialism in Mid-Victorian London* (Oxford: History Workshop, 1983); Harold B. Segal, *Turn-of-the-Century Cabaret* (New York: Columbia University Press, 1987), esp. xiii, chap. 4; Peter Jelavich, *Berlin Cabaret* (Cambridge, Mass.: Harvard University Press, 1993); and W. Scott Haine, *The World of the Paris Café: Sociability among the French Working Class* (Baltimore: Johns Hopkins University Press, 1996).

20. For the history of Manhattan nocturnality, see Sante, *Low Life,* 152–76, 186. Stanley Walker, *The Night Club Era* (New York: Frederick A. Stokes, 1933), 218–23.

21. John O'Connor, *Broadway Racketeers* (New York: Horace Liveright, 1928), viii, x, 72–76, 188–99 (originally serialized in the *New Yorker,* 12 November 1927, 105–7, and 26 November, 101–3). See also Emile C. Schnurmacher [*sic*], "Bunco," *New Yorker,* 8 May 1926, 32–33.

22. Irving Lewis Allen, *The City in Slang: New York Life and Popular Speech* (New York: Oxford University Press, 1993), chap. 10.

23. *New Yorker*, 13 March 1926, 24; 6 November 1926, 23; 23 July 1927, 24–25; 6 August 1927, 10–11; and 8 February 1930, 60.

24. *New Yorker*, 25 December 1926, 35; Schnurmacher, "Bunco," 32; and *New Yorker*, 11 December 1926, 71. See also Theodore Pratt, "Panhandler," *New Yorker*, 9 July 1927, 50.

25. Wilson, "Night Clubs," 71; Graham, *New York Nights*, 88; and Berliner, *Texas Guinan*, 111.

26. An example of the *New Yorker*'s speakeasy series is Niven Busch, Jr., "Speak-easy Nights," *New Yorker*, 7 May 1927, 19. Estimates of the speakeasy population are found in Asbury, *The Great Illusion*, 210; and Edward Hope [Coffey], *Manhattan Cocktail* (New York: Lincoln MacVeagh/Dial Press, 1929), xi.

27. Brock, "Night Life," 8–9. On entry into speakeasies, see Asbury, *The Great Illusion*, 228; Graham, *New York Nights*, 63; and Committee of Fourteen, 25 June 1924 meeting minutes, box 35, C14.

28. Charles G. Shaw, *Nightlife: Vanity Fair's Intimate Guide to New York after Dark* (New York: John Day Co., 1931), 18–20. The variety of speakeasies is best conveyed in the series by Niven Busch, Jr., "Speak-easy Nights," in the *New Yorker*, 7 May 1927, 18; 2 July 1927, 14–15; 6 August 1927, 14–15; 10 December 1927, 104–5; 18 February 1928, 17–18; 5 January 1929, 27; 2 February 1929, 22; and 8 February 1930, 60. See also Graham, *New York Nights*, 69; Al Hirschfeld, *Manhattan Oases: New York's 1932 Speakeasies* (New York: Dutton, 1932); Walker, *The Night Club Era*, 40–46; Morris Markey, *That's New York!* (New York: Macy-Masius, 1927), 165–72, and *Manhattan Reporter* (New York: Dodge, 1935), 51–52; and Durante and Kofoed, *Night Clubs*, 32–33.

29. Michael A. Lerner, "Dry Manhattan: Class, Culture, and Politics in Prohibition-Era New York City, 1919–1933" (Ph.D. diss., New York University, 1998), chap. 5.

30. Frank Ward O'Malley, "The Fatty Degeneration of Broadway," *New Yorker*, 24 August 1929, 24; Josie Turner, "The Decline of Leering," *New Yorker*, 30 July 1927, 39; One Drinker, "Notes on Drinking," *New Yorker*, 30 April 1927, 30–31; Ford Madox Ford, *New York Is Not America: Being a Mirror to the States* (New York: Albert and Charles Boni, 1927), 34; and [Lois Long], "Tables for Two," *New Yorker*, 12 January 1929, 36.

31. Wilson, "Night Clubs," 71; Graham, *New York Nights*, 89–96.

32. Thorstein Veblen, *The Theory of the Leisure Class: An Economic Study in the Evolution of Institutions* (New York: Macmillan, 1899); Paula S. Fass, *The Damned and the Beautiful: American Youth in the 1920s* (New York: Oxford University Press, 1979), chap. 1. Mackay is quoted in Erenberg, *Steppin' Out*, x (the original article appeared in *New Yorker*, 28 November 1925, 7–8, and 12 December 1925, 15–16). See also Thomas Kunkel, *Genius in Disguise: Harold Ross of the New Yorker* (New York: Random House, 1995), 129; and Laurence Bergreen, *As Thousands Cheer: The Life of Irving Berlin* (New York: Da Capo, 1996), chaps. 10–11. On Kahn, see Roger Wolfe Kahn, clippings file, BRTC.

33. Rube Goldberg, "Are There More Than One Otto Kahn?" *New Yorker*, 9 April 1927, 22–23; Granlund, Feder, and Hancock, *Blondes, Brunettes, and Bullets*, 207. On Kahn, see also *New Yorker*, 20 February 1926, 23–24; 19 November 1927, 23; Robert A. Caro, *The Power Broker: Robert Moses and the Fall of New York* (New York: Knopf, 1974), 185–203, 277; and Theresa M. Collins, *Otto Kahn: Art, Money, and Modern Time* (Chapel Hill: University of North Carolina Press, 2002). For more on the Hollywood Restaurant, see Chapter 5.

34. *New Yorker*, 6 November 1926, 71–73, and 11 December 1926, 71; Katcher, *The Big Bankroll*, 168.

35. Various listings in the *New Yorker*, including 20 February 1926, 69; 17 April 1926, 12; 6 November 1926, 71–73; 25 December 1926, 12; 30 April 1927, 93; 10 December 1927, 106; and 24 December 1927, 4; Erenberg, *Steppin' Out*, 242–43; *New York Times*, 15 October 1927, 5, and 27 December 1927, 12; Durante and Kofoed, *Night Clubs*, 149–51; and Roger Wolfe Kahn clippings file, BRTC.

36. Long quoted in *New Yorker*, 18 June 1927, 73. See also *New Yorker*, 21 August 1926, 3; 30 April 1927, 93; 12 January 1929, 36; 8 June 1929, 78; 28 September 1929, 18; 1 December 1928, 120; Stern, Gilmartin, and Mellis, *New York 1930*, 607–10; and Gregory F. Gilmartin, "Joseph Urban," in Taylor, ed., *Inventing Times Square*, 273, 275, 282.

37. *New Yorker*, 5 February 1927, 55. See also *New Yorker*, 3 April 1926, 42; 4 May 1929, 40; 8 June 1929, 78; and 8 February 1930, 60. See Lois Long, memo to Harold Ross, n.d. [1929], *New Yorker* papers, box 6, Rare Books and Manuscripts, New York Public Library, for Long's insight into the magazine's dress symbols.

38. Durante and Kofoed, *Night Clubs*, 148. See also *New Yorker*, 6 March 1926, 8; Hirschfeld, *Manhattan Oases*, 78. On performing waiters, see *New Yorker*, 13 March 1926, 5; 20 March 1926, 47; 20 November 1926, 72; 7 May 1927, 88–89; and 30 June 1928, 45; and Erenberg, *Steppin' Out*, 249.

39. On waiters, see *New Yorker*, February 1926, 44; 21 August 1926, 20; 11 September 1926, 22; 25 September 1926, 16; 25 December 1926, 42–43; and 13 July 1929, 14–15; 20; A. J. Liebling, *The Telephone Booth Indian* (Garden City, N.Y.: Doubleday, 1942), 120–22; John Armstrong, "Serving the Gentry," *American Mercury*, August 1928, 394–95, 398; and Shaw, *Nightlife*, 12–13. On concessions, see, for example, Liebling, *The Telephone Booth Indian*, 113–23; and Richman and Gehman, *A Hell of a Life*, 104.

40. On Dickerman, see Walker, *The Night Club Era*, 83; and *New Yorker*, 16 October 1926, 58–60. See also *New Yorker*, 20 March 1926, 46; and Harold Ross memo to Lois Long, 28 February 1927, *New Yorker* papers.

41. *New Yorker*, 27 November 1926, 69; 11 December 1926, 70; 18 December 1926, 76; 1 January 1927, 36; 12 January 1929, 36; and 4 May 1929, 40.

42. Gilbert Seldes, "A Civilized Metropolis," *New Yorker*, 16 October 1926, 29. The *New York Sun* report is reprinted in *New Yorker*, 27 November 1926, 68. See also *New Yorker*, 6 November 1926, 69; and 12 January 1929, 36.

43. Graham, *New York Nights*, 14, 18–19, 20–21, 24.

44. Wilson, "Night Clubs," 71. On Dickerman clubs, see *New Yorker*, 11 December 1926, 72; 1 January 1927, 36; 4 May 1929, 40, 42; 14 December 1929, 12, 14; and 8 February 1930, 60–61.

45. Jackson Lears, *Fables of Abundance: A Cultural History of Advertising in America* (New York: Basic Books, 1994), 163; and Neil Harris, *Humbug: The Art of P. T. Barnum* (Boston: Little, Brown, 1973). On immigrants in New York, see, for example, Thomas Kessner, *The Golden Door: Italian and Jewish Immigrant Mobility in New York City* (New York: Oxford University Press, 1977).

46. On telephone book listings, see *New Yorker*, 1 January 1927, 41. Ford, *New York Is Not America*, 96–97, 118, 127–29. On views regarding ethnicity and assimilation in the 1920s, see Macdonald Smith Moore, *Yankee Blues: Musical Culture and American Identity* (Bloomington: Indiana University Press, 1985); and Walter Benn Michaels, *Our America: Nativism, Modernism, and Pluralism* (Durham, N.C.: Duke University Press, 1995).

47. Stern, Gilmartin, and Mellis, *New York 1930*, 25–27.

48. On the Russian vogue in France in the 1910s, see Peter Wollen, *Raiding the Ice Box: Reflections on Twentieth-Century Culture* (London: Verso, 1993), chap. 1; and Gilbert Seldes, *The Seven Lively Arts* (New York: Harper, 1924), 260–62. Russian nightclub listings in the *New Yorker* include 20 February 1926, 12–13; and 6 March 1926, 47.

49. See Katcher, *The Big Bankroll*, 46, 303; Konrad Bercovici, *Manhattan Side-Show* (New York: Century, 1931), 77, 94; Neal Gabler, *Winchell: Gossip, Power, and the Culture of Celebrity* (New York: Knopf, 1994), chaps. 1–2; and Bergreen, *As Thousands Cheer*, 245–62. Harry Richman is quoted in Richman and Gehman, *A Hell of a Life*, 94.

50. *New Yorker*, 16 October 1926, 58–60 (italics in original); 26 February 1927, 68; 4 December 1926, 90; and 7 June 1930, 70.

51. *New Yorker*, 14 September 1929, 22. See also 21 September 1929, 19; and Moore, *Yankee Blues*, chap. 5.

52. On exoticism and U.S. consumerism, see Lears, *Fables of Abundance*, 115, 118–20; and William Leach, *Land of Desire: Merchants, Money, and the Rise of a New American Culture* (New York: Pantheon, 1993). *New York American* clipping, 29 December 1932, in Fay Marbe scrapbooks, volume 866, BRTC. *New Yorker*, 6 November 1926, 69; Stern, Gilmartin, and Mellis, *New York 1930*, 262–63; and Graham, *New York Nights*, 25. See also descriptions in *New Yorker*, 13 July 1929, 56; 13 July 1929, 60; 13 March 1926, 27, 39; and 20 March 1926, 64; and *New York Times*, 15 April 1928, X, 5.

53. Markey, *Manhattan Reporter*, 258–65; Parker quoted in *New Yorker*, 23 November 1929, 128. See also Ruth Glasser, *My Music Is My Flag: Puerto Rican Musicians and Their New York Communities, 1917–1940* (Berkeley: University of California Press, 1995), chap. 1.

54. See, for example, Gilbert Osofsky, *Harlem: The Making of a Ghetto* (New York: Harper and Row, 1971); Nathan Irvin Huggins, *Harlem Renaissance* (New York: Oxford University Press, 1971); and Ann Douglas, *Terrible Honesty: Mongrel Manhattan in the 1920s* (New York: Farrar Straus Giroux, 1995), part 3.

55. M. P., "The Art Galleries," *New Yorker*, 19 February 1927, 70–72; and Ben Hecht, "The Caliph Complex," *New Yorker*, 4 December 1926, 30–31. See also *New Yorker*, 11 August 1928, 4; and 8 February 1930, 61.

56. Lewis, *When Harlem Was in Vogue*, 130, 229–30. On jazz in New York, see Samuel B. Charters and Leonard Kunstadt, *Jazz: A History of the New York Scene* (Garden City, N.Y.: Doubleday, 1962), chaps. 2–4; Gunther Schuller, *Early Jazz: Its Roots and Musical Development* (New York: Oxford University Press, 1968), chaps. 6, 7; Mark Tucker, *Ellington: The Early Years* (Urbana: University of Illinois Press, 1991); and Joshua Berrett, *Louis Armstrong and Paul Whiteman: Two Kings of Jazz* (New Haven, Conn.: Yale University Press, 2004).

57. Graham, *New York Nights*, 24.

58. Rudolph Fisher, "The Caucasian Storms Harlem," *American Mercury* 11 (August 1927), quoted in Lewis, *When Harlem Was in Vogue*, 165. See also Lewis, *When Harlem Was in Vogue*, 208–11; and Sylvester, *No Cover Charge*, 58.

59. Graham, *New York Nights*, 24; *New Yorker*, 20 November 1926, 72; and 23 July 1927, 36–37.

60. *Chicago Herald-Examiner*, 10 February 1933, clipping in Guinan scrapbook. See also Berliner, *Texas Guinan*, 129 and passim.

61. Glenn, *Female Spectacle*, 45; Wilson, "Night Clubs," 71; and Graham, *New York Nights*, 87–93.

62. Reginald Marsh, "Texas Guinan" (1931), reprinted in Norman Sasowsky, *The Prints of Reginald Marsh* (New York: Clarkson N. Potter, 1976), 160.

63. See Peter Bailey, "Parasexuality and Glamour: The Victorian Barmaid as Cultural Prototype," *Gender and History* 2 (summer 1990), 148–72; Billie Melman, ed., *Borderlines: Genders and Identities in War and Peace, 1870–1930* (New York: Routledge, 1998); and M. Alison Kibler, *Rank Ladies: Gender and Cultural Hierarchy in American Vaudeville* (Chapel Hill: University of North Carolina Press, 1999).

64. Erenberg, *Steppin' Out*, chap. 7; Glenn, *Female Spectacle*, chap. 5; Ziegfeld and Ziegfeld, *The Ziegfeld Touch*, passim; and Mizejewski, *Ziegfeld Girl*, esp. chaps. 2 and 4.

65. Granlund, Feder, and Hancock, *Blondes, Brunettes, and Bullets*, 127; Jelavich, *Berlin Cabaret*, 175–85; Wollen, *Raiding the Ice Box*, 54–60; and Frank Sullivan, "Tiller Traditions," *New Yorker*, 19 February 1927, 22–23. Glenn, *Female Spectacle*, 170; see also 170–74.

66. See, for example, Kunkel, *Genius in Disguise*, 107; and Long-Ross memos, 1925–29, box 6, *New Yorker* papers.

67. See various articles in the *New Yorker*: 7 June 1930, 70; Josie Turner, "The Decline of Leering," 30 July 1927, 39; Baron Ireland, "Night Club," 30 October 1926, 73; and cartoon, 11 August 1928, 20.

68. Theodore Pratt, "Cornet," *New Yorker*, 30 April 1927, 87; and Frederick Lewis Allen, "Those Fifth-Avenue Girls," *New Yorker*, 8 February 1930, 19–20. On date rating, see Beth Bailey, *From Front Porch to Back Seat: Courtship in Twentieth-Century America* (Baltimore: Johns Hopkins University Press, 1988), chaps. 1–2.

69. Sylvester, *No Cover Charge*, 200; Granlund, Feder, and Hancock, *Blondes, Brunettes, and Bullets*, 127–28. See also Durante and Kofoed, *Night Clubs*, 136–37. The Poole case is described in *New York Evening Graphic*, 9 October 1928, clipping in box 36, C14.

70. Richman and Gehman, *A Hell of a Life*, 4, 90–93, 110–11, 117; and newspaper clipping, 3 April 1938, Harry Richman clippings folder, BRTC. The Broadway gossip columnist Mark Hellinger and his wife were also injured in the yacht explosion.

71. *New Yorker*, 30 April 1927, 31; 27 November 1926, 74–76, 78.

72. *New Yorker*, 20 July 1929, 26; 22 January 1927, 14; Erenberg, *Steppin' Out*, chap. 4.

73. Max Page, *The Creative Destruction of Manhattan, 1900–1940* (Chicago: University of Chicago Press, 1999), esp. chaps. 1–2. For articles on gardening and roof farming, see *New Yorker*, 2 April 1927, 96–101; 30 April 1927, 22; Babette Deutsch, "A New York Childhood," 15 December 1928, 31–34; and 23 April 1927, 28–29. See also the Peter Arno cartoon, 22 December 1928, 10. For Hokinson and Held, see *New Yorker*, 25 December 1926, 22; and 11 June 1927, 12.

74. *New Yorker*, 22 December 1928, 42; and 15 December 1928, 95. Other *New Yorker* items alluding to leisure in Florida and other tropical climes are found in 15 December 1928, 92; 2 February 1929, 21; 16 February 1929, 16–17; 22 June 1929, 49; 14 September 1929, 23; 23 November 1929, 21; and 15 February 1930, 15.

75. Commissioner of Licenses, *1927 Report of the Department of Licenses* (New York, 1928), 29; *1929 Report* (New York, 1930), 31.

*Chapter 2*

1. 25 October 1928 meeting minutes, box 86, C14. On Guinan's reputation, see Louise Berliner, *Texas Guinan: Queen of the Night Clubs* (Austin: University of Texas Press, 1993), esp. chap. 1.

2. See Timothy J. Gilfoyle, "Prostitutes in History: From Parables of Pornography to Metaphors of Modernity," *The American Historical Review* 104:1 (1999), 117–41; Judith R. Walkowitz, *City of Dreadful Delight: Narratives of Sexual Danger in Late Victorian London* (Chicago: University of Chicago Press, 1992); Christine Stansell, *City of Women: Sex and Class in New York, 1789–1860* (Urbana: University of Illinois Press, 1987), 180–84; Ruth Rosen, *The Lost Sisterhood: Prostitution in America, 1900–1918* (Baltimore: Johns Hopkins University Press, 1982), chap. 1; Sarah Deutsch, *Women in the City: Gender, Space, and Power in Boston, 1870–1940* (New York: Oxford University Press, 2000), chaps. 1–2; and Mary E. Odem, *Delinquent Daughters: Protecting and Policing Adolescent Female Sexuality in the United States, 1885–1920* (Chapel Hill: University of North Carolina Press, 1995), chap. 4.

3. Walter Lippmann, *A Preface to Politics* (1914; reprint, New York: Macmillan, 1933), 125, 127, 129, 152.

4. Timothy J. Gilfoyle, *City of Eros: New York, Prostitution, and the Commercialization of Sex, 1790–1920* (New York: Norton, 1992), 298–300, 302–3; Robert E. Riegel, "Changing American Attitudes Toward Prostitution (1800–1920)," *Journal of the History of Ideas* 29:3 (1968), 449–52; Mark Thomas Connelly, *The Response to Prostitution in the Progressive Era* (Chapel Hill: University of North Carolina Press, 1980), 13–14; Rosen, *The Lost Sisterhood*, 28; and Richard O'Connor, *Courtroom Warrior: The Combative Career of William Travers Jerome* (Boston: Little, Brown, 1963).

5. Gilfoyle, *City of Eros*, 303–6; Martin Mayer, *Emory Buckner* (New York: Harper and Row, 1968), 86–88; Kevin J. Mumford, *Interzones: Black/White Sex Districts in Chicago and New York in the Early Twentieth Century* (New York: Columbia University Press, 1997), chap. 1; Committee of Fourteen, *1919–20 Annual Report* (New York, 1920), 27 (cited hereafter as *Annual Report*, by year); *1929 Annual Report*, 35; 25 May 1922 meeting minutes, box 86, C14.

6. Gilfoyle, *City of Eros*, 304; *1924 Annual Report*, 12; George Worthington to Bascom Johnson, 20 June 1927, box 7, C14; and R. L. Duffus, "Now the Night Clubs Are Under Fire," *New York Times*, 15 July 1928, XI, 8.

7. 5 June 1930 press release, box 7, C14; 1928 folder, box 7. Mary Simkhovitch's Committee of Fourteen correspondence is located in the Greenwich House papers, Robert Wagner Labor Collection, Tamiment Library, New York University, boxes 21 and 29. On Katharine Bement Davis, see Kenneth Finegold, *Experts and Politicians: Reform Challenges to Machine Politics in New York, Cleveland, and Chicago* (Princeton, N.J.: Princeton University Press, 1995), 59.

8. George Worthington letters to Lawrence Dunham (Bureau of Social Hygiene), 2 December, 4 December 1930, box 7, C14; *1926 Annual Report*, 33; and assorted correspondence with other anti-prostitution groups, box 7.

9. *1919–20 Annual Report*, 6, 45–46; *1921 Annual Report*, 8–9, 18; *Brooklyn Eagle* clipping, 28 March 1921, in box 86, C14; and *1922 Annual Report*, 14.

10. *1922 Annual Report*, 3, 11; *1919–20 Annual Report*, 7–8; *1921 Annual Report*, 27; 21 April 1921, 20 February 1922, 23 March 1922 meeting minutes, box 86, C14.

11. In New York state, prostitution enforcement relied on section 887 of the

criminal code (vagrancy), subdivision 4A, solicitation, and various sections of the penal law that forbade disorderly houses, disorderly conduct in public, pimping, husbands forcing their wives into prostitution, and transport across state lines. Correspondence from 1931, box 7, C14.

12. *New York American* clipping, 9 April 1923; 22 March 1923 meeting minutes; 26 February 1924 meeting minutes, 2; 1924 *Annual Report*, 23, box 86. See also *Annual Reports:* 1919–20, 8; 1921, 13; 1922, 6–7; 1923, 8–9; and 1925, 6, 21. On attitudes toward male customers in prostitution, see John C. Burnham, "The Progressive Era Revolution in American Attitudes Toward Sex," *Journal of American History* 59:4 (1973), 885–908; Connelly, *Response to Prostitution in the Progressive Era*, 77; and Rosen, *The Lost Sisterhood*, 50–55, 168.

13. *1924 Annual Report*, 9; *Times Square Daily* clipping, 26 June 1924, 1924 file, box 35, C14.

14. Convention reports, 21–24 June, 29 June 1924; see also 25–26 June, 7 July 1924 reports, box 35, C14. Committee papers still forbid the release of names of individuals mentioned therein. I use pseudonyms here, except for persons such as "Jew Bessie" who were identified in the press and in the court.

15. *Annual Reports:* 1925, 4, 33; 1926, 4, 30–31, 39; and 7 January 1926 meeting minutes, box 86, C14.

16. Street-by-street data from a 1928 survey by Committee of Fourteen, box 36, C14.

17. *1927 Annual Report*, 18–19; Duffus, "Now the Night Clubs Are Under Fire," 1, 3.

18. Information in this paragraph and the following one is from the street-by-street Midtown survey, box 36, C14.

19. Five years after John D. Rockefeller, Jr. financed most of this investigation of prostitution in the West Fifties, he razed these blocks to build the complex that bore his family's name.

20. *1925 Annual Report*, 30–32; 1 December 1927 meeting minutes, 1; 24 January 1929 meeting minutes, box 86, C14.

21. The Harlem street survey is in various reports, 24 February–18 July 1928, box 35, C14.

22. 1928 Harlem reports, box 35; George Worthington memo, n.d. (April 1929), box 7, C14; and 26 April 1929 meeting, minutes, box 86, C14. See also Mumford, *Interzones*, esp. chaps. 6 and 8.

23. Reisner and Krass quoted in *New York American*, 19 October 1928, 1; Mrs. George J. Anderson letter to George Worthington, 11 January 1929; George Worthington letter to New England Watch and Ward Society, 16 October 1929, box 7, C14.

24. Polly Adler, *A House Is Not a Home* (New York: Rinehart, 1953), 65; investigator reports: 3 January 1927; 22 September 1926; 2 December 1926; 23 June 1924, box 35, C14. The voluminous references to cab drivers, elevator operators, and waiters include the following *Annual Reports:* 1921, 8–9; 1924, 10; 1928, 12; and investigator reports: 12 November 1924; 17 November 1924; 19 January 1926; 20 September 1926; 4 May 1928; 18 April 1929; 9 January 1930; 21 May 1930; and 14 August 1930, box 35, C14.

25. 1 December 1927 meeting minutes, 2, box 86, C14; 26 October 1922 meeting minutes, 6, box 86; *Annual Reports:* 1927, 21; 1928, 13–15.

26. Duffus, "Now the Night Clubs Are Under Fire," 3, 8; 1928 *Annual Report*, 10–12, 26–27, 31–34. The activities of Mademoiselle Fifi can be traced in investigator reports from 13 October 1926; 2 December 1926; and 18 December 1927, box 35, C14; and Adler, *A House Is Not a Home*, 36–47.

27. Investigator reports: 15 January 1927; 24 October 1925; 10 December 1926; 10 April 1930; 19 January 1929; 10 December 1926; and 24 June 1924, box 35, C14.

28. *New York American* clipping, 23? October 1928, box 96; investigator reports: 20 January 1926; 11 January 1927; and 17 October 1926, box 35, C14.

29. 26 October 1922 meeting minutes, 6, box 86; *1928 Annual Report*, 13–15; investigator reports: 15 January 1927, 24 January 1929, 9 January 1930, and 18 May 1928, box 35, C14. Princeton Grill information and street-by-street data are in box 36. On the coatchecking "bouncer," see 15 January 1927 report, box 35.

30. Elizabeth Butler letter to George Worthington, 11 November 1930, 1929 folder, box 7, C14; Whalen quoted in Berliner, *Texas Guinan*, 147. See Chapter 4 of this book for Whalen's nightclub campaign.

31. On theatrical booking agencies, see *1928 Annual Report*, 15–18, 23; George Worthington letter to Grover Whalen (forwarding the 1928 report), 6 April 1929, box 7; *New York Graphic* clipping, 22 October 1929, "Hostesses" clippings file, box 96; and 22 March 1929 meeting minutes, 2, box 86, C14. On use of women to sell real estate, see 4 May 1928 investigator report, box 35, C14.

32. For correspondence from citizens, see, for example, 1924 folder, box 35. Evidence of fruitless investigations of citizen complaints can be found in 1925 folder, box 35, and passim; and 1928, 1929 correspondence folders, box 7, C14. The reference to the Club El Fey is in 15 December 1924 investigator's report, box 35. A committee investigator was able to infiltrate one high-priced call flat, where sex acts were sold for $200, and to cause the arrest of one female employee; see *1927 Annual Report*, 28. For a description of Polly Adler's early career, see Adler, *A House Is Not a Home*, 44, 65, 101.

33. An example of an investigation leading to a police arrest is found in 25 June 1923 report, box 35, C14. Copies of the green sheet, "Statement of Arresting Officer in Prostitution Case," are in 1923–25 folder, box 35.

34. 1928 street report, box 36; 12? October 1923 letter to Committee of Fourteen, 1923 folder, box 35, C14; and 15 January and 20 January 1927 investigator reports, box 35.

35. *Annual Reports:* 1921, 8–9; 1925, 4.

36. Lewis A. Erenberg, *Steppin' Out: New York Nightlife and the Transformation of American Culture* (Westport, Conn.: Greenwood Press, 1981), chap. 7; Harry Kahan letters to George Worthington, 19 July, 18 August, 21 August 1928, 1928–1931 correspondence folder, box 7; 1927–28 folder (1929 report misfiled); and 1927–30 folder, box 35, C14. On prostitution in Europe, see also Joachim Schlör, *Nights in the Big City: Paris, Berlin, London, 1840–1930*, trans. Pierre Gottfried Imhof and Dafydd Rees Roberts (London: Reaktion Books, 1998), 185–96.

37. *1922 Annual Report*, 6; 25 October 1928 meeting minutes, box 86, C14. For the committee's comment on the automobile, see *1924 Annual Report*, 11.

38. 1931 folder, box 7; 1927–30 folder; 1924 folder, box 35; and 24 October 1925 investigator report, box 35, C14.

39. 1923–25 folder; 29 May 1924 report, box 35, C14. On the masquerade, see 8 February 1926 report, box 35.

40. *Annual Reports:* 1925, 15; 1924, 41; "Memorandum of Rules of Evidence Governing Investigators of the Committee of Fourteen," circa May 1930, box 7; and Bascom Johnson letter to George Worthington, 18 September 1929. See also Worthington letter to Johnson, 28 September 1929, box 7, C14.

41. Investigator reports: 5 January 1931, 1–6; April 1932, box 35, C14.

42. Investigator reports: 25 July 1928; 27 January 1931, box 35, C14.

43. *1919–20 Annual Report,* 7–8.

44. On the Red Light Abatement Act, see *1926 Annual Report,* 26–27. On the committee's future plans, see William H. Baldwin letter to James Pederson, 8 January 1929; and "Broadening the Committee's Work" (emphasis in original), confidential memo (circa March 1930), box 7, C14.

45. George Worthington letter to Mrs. L. F. Fitch, 19 April 1930; memo draft, n.d. (1930); "The Crime Prevention Bureau," n.d. (1930); clippings from *New York Times,* 17 June 1931, 27; *New York Daily News,* 31 December 1931, n.p., box 7, C14. Contemporary accounts of the theory and practice of crime prevention include Emory S. Bogardus, "Exploring for the Causes of Crime," *Journal of Social Forces* 3:3 (1925), 464–66; C. E. Gehlke, "Crime," *The American Journal of Sociology* 34:1 (1928), 157–71; Frederic M. Thrasher, "The Study of the Total Situation," *Journal of Educational Sociology,* 10 (1928), 599–612, esp. 608–9; Arthur Evans Wood, "Crime," *American Journal of Sociology* 35:6 (1930), 1027–41; and Harry M. Shulman, "Crime Prevention and the Public Schools," *Journal of Educational Sociology* 4:2 (1930), 69–81. Shulman was the head of the Causes of Crime subcommittee of the Baumes Committee.

46. Sarah Schuyler Butler letter to George Worthington, 14 January 1930; Worthington quoted in *New York World,* 27 February 1930; Schneiderman quoted in *New York Times,* 27 February 1930, clippings in box 7, C14. See also Belle Moskowitz letter to George Worthington, 24 February 1930, box 7.

47. *Annual Reports:*1925, 34; 1927, 34; 1928, 36; 24 May 1929 meeting minutes, 2, box 86; and memo, "Suggestions by Committee of 14 for Recommendations to Mayor Walker and His Cabinet," n.d. (1931), box 7, C14. Worthington hoped to become a judge himself. In 1930 he notified the mayor of "my candidacy for the position of city magistrate." Worthington's references included Percy Straus and W. E. B. Du Bois. He was not appointed. George Worthington letter to James J. Walker, 30 October 1930, Courts subject file, box 239, JJW.

48. See Chapter 6 of this book.

49. On the committee and the ASHA, see George Worthington letter to Bascom Johnson, 27 March 1929; Johnson letter to Worthington, 18 September 1929; James Pederson letter to William F. Snow, 27 November 1929, box 7; Edward McGuire letters to George Worthington, 3 July 1929, 24 April 1930, box 7; and meeting minutes: 22 March 1929, 1 and 22 March 1929, 1, box 86, C14. *New York Mirror,* 22 December 1931, clipping, box 96; E. Rosen (Office Workers Union) letter to Worthington, 21 December 1931, box 7; and Worthington memo, 2 December 1932, box 8.

50. *1926 Annual Report,* 49; *New York Times* editorial, 16 July 1927, box 86; investigator report, n.d., 1926 folder, box 35; 22 November 1928 meeting minutes, box 86, C14.

51. References to homosexuality include *1928 Annual Report,* 12, and 1928 Harlem reports, box 35. Violence citations include investigator reports of 13 July 1925, 1 January 1931 and 10 January 1931, box 35, C14.

52. Arrest records, reel 1, New York Society for the Suppression of Vice papers, Manuscript Division, Library of Congress; Jay A. Gertzman, *Bookleggers and Smuthounds: The Trade in Erotica, 1920–1940* (Philadelphia: University of Pennsylvania Press, 1999), chap. 3; and Jonah Goldstein, oral history, Oral History Research Center, Columbia University, 65.

*Chapter 3*

1. Statements about Walker are from Edward J. Flynn, *You're the Boss* (New York: Viking, 1947), 52; and Gene Fowler, *Beau James: The Life and Times of Jimmy Walker* (New York: Viking, 1949), 91. Biographies of Walker are found in Fowler, *Beau James*, 34–46, and Thomas Kessner, *Fiorello H. La Guardia and the Making of Modern New York* (New York: McGraw-Hill, 1989), 157.

2. *New York Times*, 3 July 1925, 2. That same day, at City Hall, credentials for a second mayoral hopeful (William T. Collins) were presented by another Broadway actor, Andrew Mack.

3. On the banquet, see George Walsh, *Gentleman Jimmy Walker: Mayor of the Jazz Age* (New York: Praeger, 1974), 69. On Walker and the stage, see *New York Times*, 7 August 1927, II, 13; 28 September, 3. The date Walker was filmed at the Ziegfeld Follies was probably 10 January 1928; see Richard Ziegfeld and Paulette Ziegfeld, *The Ziegfeld Touch: The Life and Times of Florenz Ziegfeld, Jr.* (New York: Harry N. Abrams, 1993), 63.

4. Fowler, *Beau James*, 70–71, 166; *New York Times*, 2 October 1927, VIII, 22; and *New Yorker*, "Talk of the Town," 2 June 1928, 20–21.

5. Fowler, *Beau James*, 86–90, 91; Leo Katcher, *The Big Bankroll: The Life and Times of Arnold Rothstein* (New Rochelle, N.Y.: Arlington House, 1959), 215.

6. Transcript of Walker interview with journalist (a "Mr. Thackery"), n.d. (circa June 1931), Speeches subject file, box 273, JJW. The classic study of self-presentation is Erving Goffman, *The Presentation of Self in Everyday Life* (New York: Anchor, 1959). On the *flâneur*, see Walter Benjamin, *The Arcades Project*, trans. Howard Eiland and Kevin McLaughlin (Cambridge, Mass.: Harvard University Press, 1999), 21–22, 416ff; and Keith Tester, ed., *The Flâneur* (London: Routledge, 1994).

7. Fowler, *Beau James*, 109.

8. Stanley Walker, *City Editor* (New York: Frederick A. Stokes, 1934), 63; *New York Times*, 15 July 1929, quoted in "Items and Abstracts," *American City* 41 (August 1929), 3.

9. Grover A. Whalen, *Mr. New York: The Autobiography of Grover A. Whalen* (New York: Putnam, 1955), 88–100; John K. Winkler, "Profile [Queen Marie]," *New Yorker*, 23 October 1926, 26; *New York Times*, 19 October 1926, 1, 3; and Walsh, *Gentleman Jimmy Walker*, 95. On Queen Marie, see also Roland Marchand, *Advertising the American Dream: Making Way for Modernity, 1920–1940* (Berkeley: University of California Press, 1985), 97.

10. *New York Times*, 18 December 1926, 36; 23 December 1926, 3.

11. Classic accounts include Gustavus Myers, *The History of Tammany Hall*, rev. ed. (New York: Boni and Liveright, 1917), 311, 315–18; and M. R. Werner, *Tammany Hall* (Garden City, N.Y.: Doubleday, 1928), chap. 4. More recent studies are Nancy J. Weiss, *Charles Francis Murphy, 1858–1924: Respectability and Responsibility in Tammany Politics* (Northampton, Mass.: Smith College, 1969); Chris McNickle, *To Be Mayor of New York: Ethnic Politics in the City* (New York: Columbia University Press, 1993), 8; and Steven P. Erie, *Rainbow's End: Irish-Americans and the Dilemmas of Urban Machine Politics, 1840–1985* (Berkeley: University of California Press, 1988), 87.

12. Norman Thomas and Paul Blanshard, *What's the Matter with New York* (New York: Macmillan, 1932), 44, 230. For an opposing view, see Flynn, *You're the Boss*, 24–25.

13. Kenneth Finegold, *Experts and Politicians: Reform Challenges to Machine Poli-*

*tics in New York, Cleveland, and Chicago* (Princeton, N.J.: Princeton University Press, 1995), 8, 30, 34, 50–52, 61.

14. Erie, *Rainbow's End*, 98, 107.

15. For an overview of traditional analyses of Tammany Hall, see Jon Teaford, "Finis for Tweed and Steffens: Rewriting the History of Urban Rule," *Reviews in American History* 10 (December 1982), 133–36. See also Erie, *Rainbow's End*, 98, 107; Finegold, *Experts and Politicians*, 11.

16. Alva Johnston, "Profile [John Voorhis]," *New Yorker*, 22 June 1929, 23–26; Eddie Dowling, oral history, Columbia Oral History Research Center, 325–26; and Jonah J. Goldstein, oral history, Columbia Oral History Research Center, 28.

17. Daniel Czitrom, "Underworlds and Underdogs: Big Tim Sullivan and Metropolitan Politics in New York, 1889–1913," *Journal of American History* 78 (September 1991), 552; Robert A. Caro, *The Power Broker: Robert Moses and the Fall of New York* (New York: Knopf, 1974), 117; Neal Gabler, *An Empire of Their Own: How the Jews Invented Hollywood* (New York: Crown, 1988), chap. 2; Flynn, *You're the Boss*, 62–63; and Mary Sullivan, *My Double Life* (New York: Farrar and Rinehart, 1938), 9.

18. *New York Times*, 17 December 1925, 1; and Lowell M. Limpus, *Honest Cop: Lewis J. Valentine* (New York: E. P. Dutton, 1939), 113, 118–21.

19. Limpus, *Honest Cop*, 118–21; New York Joint Legislative Committee to Investigate the Administration of the Various Departments of the Government of the City of New York, *Final Report* (Albany, N.Y., 1931), 1:308–32 and passim.

20. For the preceding two paragraphs: *New York Times*, 31 August 1927, 21; and New York Joint Legislative Committee, *Final Report*, 2:424–77 and passim.

21. Limpus, *Honest Cop*, 144–48; New York Joint Legislative Committee, *Final Report*, 2:572, 607; and *New York Times*, 13 March 1927, 1, 3, and 14 March, 1.

22. See, for example, "Minutes of Conference Held at the Office of the Mayor, July 20, 1926, with a Committee of Strikers of the IRT Company," Transit subject file, box 280, JJW; "Conference, February 26, 1931, with Mid-Town Business Men," minutes, Transit subject file, box 280, JJW; *New York Times* clipping, November 1928, Housing subject file, box 242, JJW; and Fowler, *Beau James*, 182, 220–21, 240–43.

23. See miscellaneous correspondence between the Committee of Fourteen and city government officials, 1928–31 and 1930 correspondence folders, box 7, C14.

24. Arrest records, reel 1, New York Society for the Suppression of Vice papers, Manuscript Division, Library of Congress; Thomas H. Cowan, oral history, Columbia Oral History Center, 35; and *New York Times*, 11 May 1926, 18.

25. *New York Times*, 8 January 1927, 36; Mae West play typescripts, reel 1, Manuscript Division, Library of Congress; clippings from *New York Daily Mirror*, 21 March 1930; *New York Herald-Tribune*, 17 March, 29 March, 4 April 1930; *New York Sun*, 2 April 1930, in Censorship—Stage—U.S.—1930 scrapbook, BRTC; Department of Licenses, *1926 Report* (New York, 1926), 9–10, 13; and Leslie Taylor, "New York Theater Raids, 1926–1927" (paper delivered at the annual meeting of the American Studies Association, Kansas City, 3 November 1996). The Wales Law remained in effect until 1970.

26. Editor's comment from *New York Telegraph*, 15 October 1927, clipping in district attorney scrapbooks, microfilm reel 47, New York Municipal Archives. On Walker and magazines, see *New York Times*, 12 January 1927, 26. On Chaplin, see *New York Times*, 13 January, 27. On the play jury, see also 30 December 1926, 18, 22.

27. Fred Austin, "Night Clubs' Curfew Enters Another Cycle," *New York Times*, 2 January 1927, VIII, 6. An international perspective on city curfews is in Joachim Schlör, *Nights in the Big City: Paris, Berlin, London, 1840–1930*, trans. Pierre Gottfried Imhof and Dafydd Rees Roberts (London: Reaktion Books, 1998), 112. On New York dance halls, see Randy D. McBee, *Dance Hall Days: Intimacy and Leisure among Working-Class Immigrants in the United States* (New York: New York University Press, 2000).

28. Department of Licenses, *1925 Report* (draft), 3 (all reports in box 32, JJW); *1927 Report*, 27.

29. Department of Licenses, *1925 Report* (draft), 13–17.

30. Department of Licenses, *1927 Report* (draft), 3–4.

31. *New York Times*, 9 February 1926, 27; 20 February, 19; and "Talk of the Town," *New Yorker*, 20 February 1926, 19.

32. *New York Times*, 4 April 1926, IX, 5; 15 April, 17; 8 June, 1; and 11 June, 23.

33. "A Local Law to Regulate Dance Halls and Cabarets and Providing for Licensing the Same," *Proceedings of the Board of Aldermen* (New York, 1926), 138–40.

34. Latham C. Squire, *Zoning in New York* (New York: Home Title Guaranty Co., 1948), 6–7, 12; Gerald E. Fitzgerald, "A History of Zoning in New York City" (M.P.A. thesis, City College of New York, 1955), 8–18, 29; S. J. Makielski, Jr., *The Politics of Zoning: The New York Experience* (New York: Columbia University Press, 1966), 40–44; and Todd W. Bressi, ed., *Planning and Zoning New York City: Yesterday, Today, and Tomorrow* (New Brunswick, N.J.: Center for Urban Policy Research, 1993), esp. Carol Willis, "A 3D CBD: How the 1916 Zoning Law Shaped Manhattan's Central Business District," 3–26, and Richard A. Plunz, "Zoning and the New Horizontal City," 27–47. The zoning law divided the city's territory in three ways: height, area, and use districts. My discussion focuses on the latter classification.

35. Fitzgerald, "A History of Zoning in New York City," 75; Makielski, *The Politics of Zoning*, 44; *New York Times*, 28 November 1926, XI, 1; 3 December, 23; 10 December, 16; and "List of Places by Street, With Occasional Notes," typescript [1928], box 36, C14.

36. *New York Times*, 30 June 1926, 1, 10.

37. *New York Times*, 30 June 1926, 10.

38. Stone quote is in *New York Times*, 20 November 1926, 19. Stand quote is in *New York Herald-Tribune*, 8 December 1926, 1. *Proceedings of the Board of Aldermen*, 572.

39. Pratt and Stand quotes in *New York Herald-Tribune*, 8 December 1926, 1; McGuinness quote in *New York Daily News*, 8 December 1926, 9; *Proceedings of the Board of Aldermen*, 572–75. See also *New York Times*, 8 December 1926, 1, and 23 December 1926, 3.

40. Paul Chevigny, *Gigs: Jazz and the Cabaret Laws in New York City* (New York: Routledge, 1991), 55; generally see 54–57.

41. Department of Licenses, *1927 Report*, 8–9. In March 1927 the district attorney declared nightclubs to be covered by the Wales Law banning objectionable theatrical performances; in April he found all nightclubs to be in compliance. *New York Times*, 12 April 1927, 17.

42. *New York Times*, 6 January 1927, 10; 11 January, 21; 1 March 1927, 19. See also *New York Times*, 2 January 1927, 3; 3 January, 1; 9 January, 22; 23 February, 25; 5 March, 32; and 16 April, 7.

43. Walker quoted in *New York Times,* 4 October 1927, 1. See also *New York Times,* 6 October 1927, 27; 9 October 1927, 13; 11 October, 48; 22 November, 17; 26 November, 31; and 7 December, 9. The Salon Royale ad was in the *New Yorker,* 26 May 1928, 91.

*Chapter 4*

1. Louise Berliner, *Texas Guinan: Queen of the Nightclubs* (Austin: University of Texas Press, 1993), 44 and passim.
2. The quotation is from Mabel Walker Willebrandt, *The Inside of Prohibition* (Indianapolis: Bobbs-Merrill, 1929), 111. General information on the crafting and enforcement of Prohibition is in Richard F. Hamm, *Shaping the Eighteenth Amendment* (Chapel Hill: University of North Carolina Press, 1995), 251–55; Thomas M. Coffey, *The Long Thirst: Prohibition in America, 1920–1933* (New York: Norton, 1975), 82–85, 137–39, 156–57, 175–77; Dorothy M. Brown, *Mabel Walker Willebrandt: A Study in Power, Loyalty, and Law* (Knoxville: University of Tennessee Press, 1984), 66; Michael A. Lerner, "Dry Manhattan: Class, Culture, and Politics in Prohibition-Era New York City, 1919–1933" (Ph.D. diss., New York University, 1998), chap. 1, 47–49, chap. 4; and Isidor Einstein, *Prohibition Agent #1* (New York: Frederick A. Stokes, 1932).
3. Quotation in *New York Times,* 13 October 1922, 16. See also *New York Times,* 8 October 1922, 17; 12 October, 3; 16 October, 19; 18 October, 21; 19 October, 14; and *United States v. John Reisenweber et al.,* federal Equity Court docket, 27 February 1922, file 23-014-51, Mail and Files Division, Department of Justice, Record Group 60, National Archives at College Park, College Park, Md. (henceforth "DOJ file 23-014-51").
4. *New York Times,* 19 October 1922, 14.
5. Smith quoted in *New York Times,* 2 June 1923, 1–2; Coffey, *The Long Thirst,* 111–15; Willebrandt, *The Inside of Prohibition,* 177, 307; Lerner, "Dry Manhattan," 184–87; and Hamm, *Shaping the Eighteenth Amendment,* 271.
6. Quotations from *New York Times,* 15 May 1924, 1; and 16 May, 1. For this paragraph and the following one: *New York Times,* 27 March 1924, 6; 18 April, 21; 17 May, 17; 23 May, 6; 10 June, 11; and 11 June, 24. The Palais Royale later struck a deal with the government which allowed it to reopen as a restaurant; *New York Times,* 20 July 1924, 8.
7. John Holley Clark memo to Mabel Walker Willebrandt, 10 March 1924; J. J. Byrne memo to Willebrandt, 22 December 1924, DOJ file 23-014-51; and Lerner, "Dry Manhattan," chap. 4.
8. Lyman Ward memo to Willebrandt, n.d. [dictated by telephone early December 1924], DOJ file 23-014-51.
9. *New York Times,* 2 July 1927, 19; and Edward Behr, *Prohibition: Thirteen Years That Changed America* (New York: Arcade, 1996), 167.
10. The federal judicial Southern District of New York contained the counties of New York and the Bronx and nine other counties to the north, up to but not including the county of Albany.
11. The comment about padlock cases is in Ward memo to Willebrandt, n.d. [December 1924]. The marshal's comment is in William C. Hecht to Rush L. Holland, 16 January 1925, DOJ file 23-014-51. See also *United States v. John Reisenweber;* William Hayward memo to Willebrandt, 12 November 1923; Ward memo to the attorney general, 14 February 1925, DOJ file 23-014-51.
12. Regarding purchase of padlocks, see Ira K. Wells letter to Comptroller

General, 2 April 1924, DOJ file 23-014-51. For this paragraph and the next: William Hayward memo to Rush L. Holland, 19 November 1923; Holland to William C. Hecht, 13 March 1924; Emory R. Buckner to Attorney General, 24 April 1925, and response, n.d.; and receipts for screw eyes (1926), padlocks (1928); DOJ file 23-014-51.

13. Buckner memo to Attorney General, 24 April 1925.

14. Morris Markey, "Mr. Buckner Explains," *New Yorker*, 14 November 1925, 7–8.

15. Fisher quoted in Sigmund Diamond, "Surveillance in the Academy: Harry B. Fisher and Yale University, 1927–1952," *American Quarterly* 36 (1984), 11–12. See also Martin Mayer, *Emory Buckner* (New York: Harper and Row, 1968), 72–75, 183–84, 188–90; [New York Civic League], *Reform Bulletin* 17 (March 1926).

16. Emory R. Buckner testimony, U.S. Congress, Senate Committee on the Judiciary, *The National Prohibition Law: Hearings before the Subcommittee*, 69th Cong., 1st sess., 7 April 1926, 96, 99–100, 111–15. On the issue of the lack of dependable agents, see also Buckner memo to the attorney general, 24 April 1925.

17. Buckner testimony, U.S. Congress, 97–99, 107–9, 113. Discussions of federal difficulties are in *Emory Buckner*, 185–87; and Lerner, "Dry Manhattan," 184.

18. Buckner testimony, U.S. Congress, 102, 108–9. Equity court procedure is described in Mayer, *Emory Buckner*, 187; Robert B. Watts memo to Willebrandt, 29 September 1927, DOJ file 23-014-51; Peter Charles Hoffer, *The Law's Conscience: Equitable Constitutionalism in America* (Chapel Hill: University of North Carolina Press, 1990); and William T. Quillen and Michael Hanrahan, "A Short History of the Delaware Court of Chancery, 1792–1992," in *Court of Chancery of the State of Delaware, 1792–1992* (Dover: Historical Society for the Court of Chancery of the State of Delaware, 1992).

19. For club closings, see summary lists of padlock cases, May 1926 and April–August 1927, DOJ file 23-014-51; and *New York Times*, 4 July 1926, 3.

20. On Buckner's resignation, see *New York Times*, 30 March 1927, 1, 6; and Morris Markey, "Reporter at Large," *New Yorker*, 9 April 1927, 38. On the city regulation, see Chapter 3 in this book; E. B. White, "The Summer Theatre," *New Yorker*, 23 July 1927, 34; *Padlocks of 1927* program, BRTC. On Guinan in 1927, see Ann Douglas, *Terrible Honesty: Mongrel Manhattan in the 1920s* (New York: Farrar Straus Giroux, 1995), 38; and Berliner, *Texas Guinan*, 123.

21. E. C. Rankin memo to Willebrandt, 23 January 1927, DOJ file 23-014-51.

22. "Maurice Campbell," *Internet Movie Database*, http://www.imdb.com/name/nm0132720/ (20 October 2004); *New York Times*, 2 July 1927, 19; and 17 October 1942, 15 (Campbell's obituary).

23. *New York Times*, 9 February 1928, 27; 1 March, 27; and 22 March, 27.

24. *New York Times*, 1 January 1928, 1, 16; 6 January, 48; 18 February, 19; 29 February, 8; 1 July, 1; 1 August, 1; and 2 August, 1.

25. The main source here is the *New York Times*, 29 June 1928, 27; 30 June, 1; and 1 July, 1. See also *New York Daily News*, 29 June 1928, 1; 30 June, 1; and "1930" folder, n.d. (but dealing with 1928 padlockings), box 7, C14. Specific padlockings are listed in Equity minutes, United States Superior Court of the Southern District of New York, 16 June–31 July 1928, National Archives Northeast Division, New York City. Out-of-town agents are discussed in Willebrandt to J. M. Doran, 25 February 1929, DOJ file 23-014-51.

When Guinan and Morgan surrendered themselves the next morning, the government was unprepared. Prohibition officials could find no paperwork that charged them. The women then drove to the U.S. Attorney's office, which reluctantly drew up some indictments. *New York Times*, 1 July 1928, 1.

26. *New York Times*, 1 July 1928, 1, 13. A discussion of Democratic Party politics in connection with the raid is in Lerner, "Dry Manhattan," 374–79.

27. Quotations and details of Willebrandt's life in this paragraph and the next three paragraphs are from Mabel Walker Willebrandt diary (1922–23) and letter to parents, 20 June 1925, in box 5, Mabel Walker Willebrandt papers, Manuscript Division, Library of Congress. Other information is in Brown, *Mabel Walker Willebrandt*, chaps. 1–2. A Prohibition case from New York City argued by Willebrandt was United States Supreme Court, *Lambert v. Yellowley*, 272 U.S. 581 (1926). Willebrandt's file on the George Remus case is in folder 2, formerly classified correspondence, DOJ file 23-1907. On Willebrandt and Remus, see also Behr, *Prohibition*, introduction, 160–66.

28. Newspaper and magazine article clippings, box 5, Willebrandt papers; and John S. Martin, "Profile [Mabel Willebrandt]," *New Yorker*, 16 February 1929, 25. A similar article is E. J. Woolf, "The Woman Behind the Night Club Raids," *New York Times*, 2 September 1928, IV, 3. Al Smith's use of the term "Prohibition Portia" is mentioned in Willebrandt's obituary, *New York Times*, 9 April 1963, 31.

29. Willebrandt telegram to Charles Tuttle, 17 July 1928; and Willebrandt telegrams to U.S. Marshal William C. Hecht, 31 July and 1 August 1928. Concerning income tax returns, see A. R. Brindley letters to Willebrandt, 15 and 17 August 1928; Andrew Mellon letter to Willebrandt, 14 September 1928; and acting secretary of the Treasury letter to Willebrandt, 28 November 1928. On the Committee of Fourteen subpoenas, see C. B. Carter memos to William D. Moss, 15 August 1928, DOJ file 23-014-51.

30. Tuttle's reactions to the June raid are described in *New York Times*, 2 August 1928, 1, 6; and 3 August 1928, 16. His subsequent protest is described in *New York Times*, 8 August 1928, III, 1; 19 August, 1; and 21 August, 1.

31. Willebrandt telegram to John G. Sargent, n.d. (ca. 22 August 1928), DOJ file 23-014-51.

32. *New York Times*, 23 August 1928, 1; 25 August, 17; 26 August, 13; Willebrandt telegram to Tuttle, 26 August 1928; DOJ file 23-014-51.

33. Willebrandt telegram to Nathan Morrison, 29 August 1928, DOJ file 23-014-51. Excerpts from the Springfield speech are in Willebrandt, *The Inside of Prohibition*, 304–5. Willebrandt letters to supporters include letters to Lucy Lloyd, 4 September 1928, and to Rachel H. Perry, 3 September 1928, in DOJ file 23-014-51. See also Willebrandt campaign speech, 3 November 1928, box 4, Willebrandt papers. The Talburt cartoon is reprinted in Brown, *Mabel Walker Willebrandt*, 162.

34. *New York Times*, 7 August 1928, 23; 8 August, 4; 14 August, 9; 11 September, 1; 12 September, 1; 26 January 1929, 19; 6 February, 29; 17 April, 29; and 27 April, 6.

35. List of Judge Goddard's equity padlock cases, November 1928. Thacher decision and Willebrandt's reaction are discussed in Marna S. Poulson letter to Willebrandt, 15 September 1928; Willebrandt letter to Marna S. Poulson, 4 October 1928; and unidentified news clipping attached to latter. On Stone, see Maurice Campbell memo to Willebrandt, 9 March 1929; and Charles Tuttle memo to Leslie Salter, 14 March 1929. On the Furnace Club, see Willebrandt memo to Attorney General, 29 March 1929, DOJ file 23-014-51.

36. Letters to Willebrandt, 1929: Joseph A. Gray, 19 April; Agnes McKernan, 13 April; John McInall, 10 April; Victor McEleny, 12 April, DOJ file 23-014-51; and "Talk of the Town," *New Yorker,* 27 April 1929, 13. For Willebrandt's resignation and later activities, see various 1929 clippings, box 5, Willebrandt papers; and Brown, *Mabel Walker Willebrandt,* 109–16.

37. *New York Times,* 18 October 1928, 31; 17 November, 21; 28 November, 29; 29 November, 29; and 17 October 1942, 15.

38. President's Research Committee on Social Trends, *Recent Social Trends in the United States: Report of the President's Research Committee on Social Trends* (New York: McGraw-Hill, 1933); National Commission on Law Observance and Enforcement [Wickersham Commission], *Report on the Enforcement of the Prohibition Laws of the United States* (Washington, 1931), http://www.drugtext.org/library/reports/wick/ (October 2004).

39. For this paragraph and the next: the Rothstein murder and investigation are covered in Lowell M. Limpus, *Honest Cop: Lewis J. Valentine* (New York: E. P. Dutton, 1939), 16, 136; and Lewis J. Valentine, *Night Stick: The Autobiography of Lewis J. Valentine* (New York: Dial Press, 1947), 111–15. Whalen describes his time as police commissioner in *Mr. New York: The Autobiography of Grover A. Whalen* (New York: G. P. Putnam's Sons, 1955), 134–64; see also James Lardner and Thomas Reppetto, *NYPD: A City and Its Police* (New York: Henry Holt, 2000), 205–7. On Whalen joining the Committee of Fourteen, see press release, 5 June 1930, 1930 folder, box 7, C14.

40. *New York Times,* 6 January 1929, 1, 21.

41. Whalen, *Mr. New York,* 156; among many relevant *New York Times* articles, see 30 December 1928, 1, 6; 26 January, 19; 19 April 1929, 1; and 20 July, 1.

42. Department of Licenses, *Report of the Department of Licenses, 1929* (New York, 1929), 7–8, 11–12.

43. Robert A. Caro, *The Power Broker: Robert Moses and the Fall of New York* (New York: Knopf, 1974), 338. See also correspondence on Central Park Casino leases, 1918–28, box 97, Robert Moses papers, Rare Books and Manuscripts, New York Public Library.

44. Robert A. M. Stern, Gregory Gilmartin, and Thomas Mellis, *New York 1930: Architecture and Urbanism Between the Two World Wars* (New York: Rizzoli, 1987), 288; Gregory F. Gilmartin, "Joseph Urban," in William R. Taylor, ed., *Inventing Times Square: Commerce and Culture at the Crossroads of the World* (New York: Russell Sage Foundation, 1991), 283–84; Joseph Urban, Central Park Casino design book and correspondence, box 31, series III, Joseph Urban papers, Rare Books and Manuscripts, Columbia University; Gene Fowler, *Beau James: The Life and Times of Jimmy Walker* (New York: Viking, 1949), 248–50; Caro, *The Power Broker,* 339; and Roy Rosenzweig and Elizabeth Blackmar, *The Park and the People: A History of Central Park* (Ithaca, N.Y.: Cornell University Press, 1992), 200, 202–3.

45. Trial briefs by Prohibition agents, May 1931 [Hollywood Restaurant], 11 November 1931 [Central Park Casino], DOJ file 23-014-51. For general coverage of the arrests, see *New York Times,* 26 April 1930, 1, 8; and 25 June, 1, 18. See also Lerner, "Dry Manhattan," 401–2.

46. *New York Times,* 27 April 1930, 1, 2; 25 June, 1, 18; and 2 July, 1, 2; Lerner, "Dry Manhattan," 405.

47. *New York Times,* 2 July 1930, 2; Jackson Morris memo to "Major Shaw," 8 November 1931; Nathan Morrisson memo to G. A. Youngquist [assistant attorney general], 7 January 1932. See also Amos W. Woodcock [Prohibition adminis-

trator] letter to Youngquist, 20 November 1931; George Z. Medalie memo to Youngquist, 7 December 1931; and Morrisson memo to Medalie, 16 February 1932, DOJ file 23-014-51.

48. For information on Medalie, see Thomas E. Dewey, oral history, Oral History Research Office, Columbia University, 296–98; Mary M. Stolberg, *Fighting Organized Crime: Politics, Justice, and the Legacy of Thomas E. Dewey* (Boston: Northeastern University Press, 1995), 67–68. For prosecution strategy, see Morrisson memo to Medalie, 16 February 1932; Medalie memo to Youngquist, 27 February 1932, DOJ file 23-014-51. For trial results, see *New York Times*, 22 June 1932, 1–2, and 30 December, 19.

49. George Z. Medalie memo to Nathan Morrisson, 14 June 1933; Morrisson memo to Medalie, 21 June 1933; Thomas E. Dewey memo to Morrisson, 11 December 1933; Morrisson memo, n.d., DOJ file 23-014-51. On shifts in American culture that led to the repeal of Prohibition, see Hamm, *Shaping the Eighteenth Amendment*, 268–71; Paul L. Murphy, "Societal Morality and Individual Freedom," in David E. Kyvig, ed., *Law, Alcohol, and Order: Perspectives on National Prohibition* (Westport, Conn.: Greenwood, 1985), 67–80; and John J. Rumbarger, *Profits, Power, and Prohibition: Alcohol Reform and the Industrializing of America, 1800–1930* (Albany: SUNY Press, 1989), chap. 10.

*Chapter 5*

1. Fitzgerald quoted in Ann Douglas, *Terrible Honesty: Mongrel Manhattan in the 1920s* (New York: Farrar Straus Giroux, 1995), 464.

2. On the cult of the skyscraper in the 1920s, see Hugh Ferriss, *The Metropolis of Tomorrow* (New York: Ives Washburn, 1929); Rem Koolhaas, *Delirious New York*, 2d ed. (New York: Monacelli Press, 1994), 110–25; and Robert A. M. Stern, Gregory Gilmartin, and Thomas Mellis, *New York 1930: Architecture and Urbanism Between the Two World Wars* (New York: Rizzoli, 1987), 32–33.

3. Merian C. Cooper and Ernest B. Schoedsack (directors and producers), *King Kong* (1933). See also Andrew Bergman, *We're in the Money: Depression America and Its Films* (1970; reprint, Chicago: Ivan R. Dee, 1992), chap. 6; Orville Goldner and George E. Turner, *The Making of King Kong: The Story Behind a Film Classic* (South Brunswick, N.J.: A. S. Barnes, 1975); Michael H. Price and Douglas Turner, eds., *Spawn of Skull Island* (reprint; n.p.: Luminary Press, 2002); and Cynthia Erb, *Tracking King Kong: A Hollywood Icon in World Culture* (Detroit: Wayne State University Press, 1998).

4. General coverage of motion pictures about Manhattan in the 1920s is found in Richard Barrios, *A Song in the Dark: The Birth of the Musical Film* (New York: Oxford University Press, 1995), esp. 196–97; and Ethan Mordden, *The Hollywood Studios: House Style in the Golden Age of the Movies* (New York: Knopf, 1988), 44–45. See also *Nightlife of New York*, film copyright record #21695, Moving Picture Division, Library of Congress; and Burton W. Peretti, "*Glorifying the American Girl*: Translating Broadway to the Motion Picture Screen" (paper presented at the annual meeting of the Mid-Atlantic Popular Culture Association, Albany, N.Y., November 2000).

5. Abel Green and Joe Laurie, Jr., *Show Biz: From Vaude to Video* (New York: Henry Holt, 1951), 327. Atkinson is quoted in Brooks McNamara, "The Entertainment District at the End of the 1930s," in William R. Taylor, ed., *Inventing Times Square: Culture and Commerce at the Crossroads of the World* (New York: Russell Sage Foundation, 1991), 179.

6. Niven Busch, "The Yellow Bowery," *New Yorker,* 13 July 1929, 26–28; *New York Times,* 15 April 1928, X, 5; Department of Licenses, *1929 Report* (New York, 1929), 11, box 32, JJW; *Variety,* 27 October 1931, 1. See also Arthur Bonner, *Alas! What Brought Thee Hither? The Chinese in New York, 1800–1950* (Madison, N.J.: Fairleigh-Dickinson University Press, 1997); and H. I. Brock, "Night Life: New York's Vast Monopoly," *New York Times Magazine,* 2 March 1930, 9.

7. *Variety,* 8 January 1930, 121; 29 January 1930, 1; 2 April 1930, 72; and 6 August 1930, 67.

8. On club closings, see *Variety,* 10 September 1930, 64. On Chinese restaurants, see *Variety,* 27 October 1931, 1. See also Louise Berliner, *Texas Guinan: Queen of the Night Clubs* (Austin: University of Texas Press, 1993), 164; and Stanley Walker, *The Night Club Era* (New York: Frederick A. Stokes, 1933), 90, 96. On Harlem, see David Levering Lewis, *When Harlem Was in Vogue* (New York: Knopf, 1981), 242; Gilbert Osofsky, *Harlem: The Making of a Ghetto* (New York: Harper and Row, 1971); and Cheryl Lynn Greenberg, *"Or Does It Explode?": Black Harlem in the Great Depression* (New York: Oxford University Press, 1991), chaps. 1–3.

9. Thomas Kessner, *Fiorello H. La Guardia and the Making of Modern New York* (New York: McGraw-Hill, 1989), 165–71; Robert A. Caro, *The Power Broker: Robert Moses and the Fall of New York* (New York: Knopf, 1974), 323–27; Beth S. Wenger, *New York Jews and the Great Depression: Uncertain Promise* (New Haven, Conn.: Yale University Press, 1996), chap. 1; Jacqueline Jones, *Labor of Love, Labor of Sorrow: Black Women, Work, and the Family from Slavery to the Present* (New York: Basic Books, 1985), 215–16; and Greenberg, *"Or Does It Explode?,"* 56–86.

10. Walter Winchell, "The Real Broadway," *The Bookman* 66 (December 1927), 378, 381–82; *Brooklyn Eagle* clipping, 29 December 1932, in Texas Guinan scrapbook (compiled by her publicist, John Stein), BRTC.

11. Charles G. Shaw, *Nightlife: Vanity Fair's Intimate Guide to New York after Dark* (New York: John Day Co., 1931), 23; Walker, *The Night Club Era,* 199, 201, 203–4.

12. Walker, *The Night Club Era,* 205. On Marsh, see Norman Sasowsky, *The Prints of Reginald Marsh* (New York: Clarkson N. Potter, 1976). Background on American perceptions of crowds may be found in Mary Esteve, *The Aesthetics and Politics of the Crowd in American Literature* (Cambridge, U.K.: Cambridge University Press, 2003), which concludes in the 1930s.

13. Konrad Bercovici, *Manhattan Side-Show* (New York: Century, 1931), 254, 257, 279.

14. Bercovici, *Manhattan Side-Show,* 258, 261, 263, 269–72. On Hubert's Museum, see Green and Laurie, *Show Biz,* 325. See also licensing commission hearing on burlesque shows transcript (1932), Indecent Shows folder, box 242, JJW, 71, 331. For cultural context, see Robert Bogdan, *Freak Show: Presenting Human Oddities for Amusement and Profit* (Chicago: University of Chicago Press, 1990), 35–38; Rachel Adams, *Sideshow U.S.A.: Freaks and the American Cultural Imagination* (Chicago: University of Chicago Press, 2001), esp. epilogue; and Anthony Bianco, *Ghosts of 42nd Street: A History of America's Most Infamous Block* (New York: HarperCollins, 2004), 86–96.

15. General coverage of nightclub gangland violence is in Walker, *The Night Club Era,* 172; and Lewis J. Valentine, *Night Stick: The Autobiography of Lewis J. Valentine* (New York: Dial Press, 1947), 31–32. On Schultz, see Paul Sann, *Kill the Dutchman! The Story of Dutch Schultz* (1971; reprint, New York: Da Capo, 1991), chaps. 1, 12; and Greenberg, *"Or Does It Explode?,"* 102. On Guinan, see Berliner, *Texas Guinan,* 178, 180. On Winchell, see Neal Gabler, *Winchell: Gossip, Power and the Culture of Celebrity* (New York: Knopf, 1994), 155.

16. *New York Evening Journal*, 3 January 1933. On Fay's milk racket, see Morris Markey, "Fear, Inc.," *New Yorker*, 28 September 1929, 42–45. On Fay's death, see *New York Times*, 2 January 1933, 1, 3; *New York City Mirror*, 2 January 1933; and *New York City Journal*, 15 May 1933, clippings in Texas Guinan scrapbook.

17. On Fay's decline, see Thomas M. Coffey, *The Long Thirst: Prohibition in America, 1920–1933* (New York: Norton, 1975), 313–15. The circumstances of Fay's death are given in *New York City News*, 2 January 1933, clipping in Texas Guinan scrapbook.

18. *New York Daily Mirror*, 3 January 1933; *London Daily Express*, 3 January 1933, clippings in Texas Guinan scrapbook.

19. *New York Daily News*, 15 December 1932; *Philadelphia Record*, 16 December 1932, clippings in Texas Guinan scrapbook.

20. *Houston Chronicle*, 13 March 1933, clipping in Texas Guinan scrapbook.

21. Berliner, *Texas Guinan*, 181–85; various funeral clippings can be found in Texas Guinan scrapbook.

22. Fay Marbe scrapbooks, BRTC.

23. On Richman's career in the 1930s, see Harry Richman clippings folder, BRTC. Details of his aviation and union activities are found in *New York Times*, 15 September 1936, 1; and *New York Post*, 15 August 1939. The Richman quote is in Harry Richman and Richard Gehman, *A Hell of a Life* (New York: Duell, Sloan and Pearce, 1966), 4.

24. Nils Thor Granlund with Sid Feder and Ralph Hancock, *Blondes, Brunettes, and Bullets* (New York: David McKay Co., 1957), 147–56, 205–6.

25. Granlund, Feder, and Hancock, *Blondes, Brunettes, and Bullets*, 203, 206. On the Hollywood Restaurant raid, see Chapter 4 in this book; and *New York Times*, 26 April 1930, 1.

26. Granlund, Feder, and Hancock, *Blondes, Brunettes, and Bullets*, 202–5; *Variety*, 8 January 1930, 121.

27. For this and the following paragraph: *Variety*, 23 April 1930, 73.

28. *Variety*, 6 November 1929, 66; Granlund, Feder, and Hancock, *Blondes, Brunettes, and Bullets*, 124, 207, 211.

29. See Chapter 3 in this book. See also *New York American*, 23? October 1928 clipping, box 96, C14.

30. *Variety*, 23 April 1930, 73. See also Allen Brandt, *No Magic Bullet: A Social History of Venereal Disease in the United States Since 1880*, 2d ed. (New York: Oxford University Press, 1987), chap. 4; John D'Emilio and Estelle B. Freedman, *Intimate Matters: A History of Sexuality in America* (New York: Harper and Row, 1988), 241–47; Francis G. Couvares, "Hollywood, Main Street, and the Church: Trying to Censor the Movies Before the Production Code"; and Marybeth Hamilton, "Goodness Had Nothing to Do with It: Censoring Mae West," in Francis G. Couvares, ed., *Movie Censorship and American Culture* (Washington, D.C.: Smithsonian Institution Press, 1996), 129–58, 187–211.

31. *Variety*, 23 April 1930, 73. See also Daniel Horowitz, *The Morality of Spending: Attitudes Toward the Consumer Society in America, 1875–1940* (Baltimore: Johns Hopkins University Press, 1985), chap. 8; Andrew R. Heinze, *Adapting to Abundance: Jewish Immigrants, Mass Consumption, and the Search for American Identity* (New York: Columbia University Press, 1990), chaps. 11, 13; and David Nasaw, *Going Out: The Rise and Fall of Public Amusements* (New York: Basic Books, 1993), chap. 16.

32. Warren Susman, *Culture as History: The Transformation of American Society in the Twentieth Century* (New York: Pantheon, 1985), 150–83. See also Couvares, ed., *Movie Censorship and American Culture*.

33. Walker, *The Night Club Era*, 205.

34. Robert C. Allen, *Horrible Prettiness: Burlesque and American Culture* (Chapel Hill: University of North Carolina Press, 1991), chaps. 5–7; and Rachel Shteir, *Striptease: The Untold History of the Girlie Show* (New York: Oxford University Press, 2004), 4–6, 46–70.

35. Allen, *Horrible Prettiness*, 243–51; Shteir, *Striptease*, 128, also 92–109.

36. Bercovici, *Manhattan Side-Show*, 258–60; 1932 licensing commission hearing on burlesque shows, 13–14, 28, 142.

37. Licensing commission hearing in 1932 on burlesque shows, 20, 173, 680, 960–63, 977 (Atkinson), 1035–36, 1040; Shteir, *Striptease*, 142–45.

38. Licensing Commission hearing, 50–53 (Moskowitz), 857–58 (Feldheim), 977 (Atkinson); Shteir, *Striptease*, 144. See also Bianco, *Ghosts of 42nd Street*, 112–17.

39. Allen, *Horrible Prettiness*, 253–55.

40. *Variety*, 4 February 1931, 84; 10 December 1930, 1; George Chauncey, *Gay New York: Gender, Urban Culture, and the Making of the Gay Male World, 1890–1940* (New York: Basic Books, 1994), 200.

41. See Chauncey, *Gay New York*, 190, 236, 244–58, 303; Kevin J. Mumford, *Interzones: Black/White Sex Districts in Chicago and New York in the Early Twentieth Century* (New York: Columbia University Press, 1997), chap. 8; Bryan D. Palmer, *Cultures of Darkness: Night Travels in the Histories of Transgression (Medieval to Modern)* (New York: Monthly Review Press, 2000), chap. 13; Caroline F. Ware, *Greenwich Village 1920–1930: A Comment on American Civilization in the Post-War Years* (Boston: Houghton Mifflin, 1935), 55; and Eric Garber, "A Spectacle in Color: The Lesbian and Gay Subculture of Jazz Age Harlem," in Martin B. Duberman, Martha Vicinus, and George Chauncey, Jr., eds., *Hidden from History: Reclaiming the Gay and Lesbian Past* (New York: New American Library, 1989), 318–31.

42. Mumford, *Interzones*, 82, chap. 8.

43. Chauncey, *Gay New York*, 13; Committee of Fourteen, *Annual Report* (New York: 1928), 12. Kevin Mumford erroneously calls the committee's statistic a tally of sightings of homosexuals in clubs in Harlem only; *Interzones*, 80. For a general discussion of attitudes in the 1930s toward gay men, see John D'Emilio, *Sexual Politics, Sexual Communities: The Making of a Homosexual Minority in the United States, 1940–1970*, 2d ed. (Chicago: University of Chicago Press, 1998), chap. 1.

44. Chauncey, *Gay New York*, 117; Mae West play typescripts, reel 1, Manuscript Division, Library of Congress.

45. Chauncey, *Gay New York*, 170–73. This conclusion, though, conflicts somewhat with Chauncey's earlier statement that the 1920s were a time of "relative tolerance" toward gays (9). See also Adams, *Sideshow U.S.A.*, chap. 4.

*Chapter 6*

1. On the Rothstein murder, see *New York Times*, 4 November 1928, 1; 7 November, 1; 9 November, 24; Carolyn Rothstein, *Now I'll Tell* (New York: Vanguard Press, 1934), 233–44; Donald Henderson Clarke, *The Reign of Rothstein* (New York: Vanguard Press, 1929), 300–314; and Leo Katcher, *The Big Bankroll: The Life and Times of Arnold Rothstein* (New Rochelle, N.Y.: Arlington House, 1959), 1–7.

2. Details of the magistrates' cases are given in William B. Northrop and John B. Northrop, *The Insolence of Office: The Story of the Seabury Investigations* (New York: Putnam, 1932), 3–6, 123; Walter Chambers, *Samuel Seabury: A Challenge* (New

York: Century, 1932), 215, 227. See also Norman Thomas and Paul Blanshard, *What's the Matter with New York* (New York: Macmillan, 1932), 103–4; and Thomas Kessner, *Fiorello H. La Guardia and the Making of Modern New York* (New York: Viking, 1989), 162–63, 221. The Magistrates' Courts are described thoroughly in Raymond Moley, *Tribunes of the People: The Past and Future of the New York Magistrates' Courts* (New Haven, Conn.: Yale University Press, 1932), esp. chap. 2.

3. Biographical information on Seabury is found in Herbert Mitgang, *The Man Who Rode the Tiger: The Life and Times of Judge Samuel Seabury* (Philadelphia: Lippincott, 1963), chaps. 2–4, 7–8.

4. Morris Markey, "The Vanished Judge," *New Yorker*, 11 October 1930, 43–46.

5. An Associated Press report in 2005 alleged that a letter had surfaced that included hearsay about a plot to kill Crater, which resulted in his burial at "the current site of the New York Aquarium." "New Lead Surfaces in Missing Judge Case," *Danbury News-Times*, 28 August 2005, 3. See also Richard J. Tofel, *Vanishing Point: The Disappearance of Judge Crater, and the New York He Left Behind* (Chicago: Ivan R. Dee, 2004).

6. [Samuel Seabury,] Supreme Court, Appellate Division, First Judicial Department, "*In re* Lewis Brodsky" (Albany, 1931), 8–9; [Seabury,] Supreme Court, "*In re* Jesse Silbermann" (Albany, 1931), 4, 6. Regarding Dreyer, see Thomas and Blanshard, *What's the Matter with New York*, 112–14. On Goodman, see 7, 14 January 1931 investigator reports, box 35, C14. The two Goodmans were found not to be relations.

7. *New York Times*, 25 February 1931, 1, 18; Chambers, *Samuel Seabury*, 265, 274.

8. Chambers, *Samuel Seabury*, 265.

9. On the accountant and the alleged brothel keeper, see Northrop and Northrop, *The Insolence of Office*, 44–47, 86–87. On the witness testimony and the alleged brothel keeper, see [Seabury,] Supreme Court, "*In re* Jean H. Norris" (Albany, 1931), 14–15, 18–19, 29. On the "wayward minor," see Chambers, *Samuel Seabury*, 270–71.

10. Women's Court docket, New York City, 1931, 215, microfilm, New York Municipal Archives; Billie Holiday and William Dufty, *Lady Sings the Blues* (New York: Doubleday, 1956), 26–27. I came across Holiday's docket entry by chance. To my knowledge no other scholar had previously located or referred to it.

11. [Seabury,] Supreme Court, *In the Matter of the Magistrates' Courts in the 1st Judicial District and the Magistrates Thereof, and of Attorneys at Law Practicing in Said Courts* (Albany, 1931), 17. On the Fleischmann company, see Thomas Kunkel, *Genius in Disguise: Harold Ross of the New Yorker* (New York: Random House, 1995), 92, 112; and Roland Marchand, *Advertising the American Dream: Making Way for Modernity 1920–1940* (Berkeley: University of California Press, 1985), 16–18.

12. Chambers, *Samuel Seabury*, 269, 272, 274, 301. On the reformers' descriptions of Tammany politicians, see Thomas and Blanshard, *What's the Matter with New York*, 77; and Chambers, *Samuel Seabury*, 301.

13. Chambers, *Samuel Seabury*, 275.

14. Northrop and Northrop, *The Insolence of Office*, 41. On Corrigan, see Lowell M. Limpus, *Honest Cop: Lewis J. Valentine* (New York: Dutton, 1939), 142. For a general discussion of Seabury's rhetoric, see Gloria Marie Boone, "The Reform Rhetoric of Samuel Seabury of New York: The Battle against Tammany Hall and Municipal Corruption" (Ph.D. diss., Ohio University, 1982).

15. Mary M. Stolberg, *Fighting Organized Crime: Politics, Justice, and the Legacy*

*of Thomas E. Dewey* (Boston: Northeastern University Press, 1995), 23–25; Jonah Goldstein, oral history, Columbia Oral History Research Center, 481–82.

16. Thomas and Blanshard, *What's the Matter with New York*, 56; Chambers, *Samuel Seabury*, 218; Northrop and Northrop, *The Insolence of Office*, 72–77 (quote on 76).

17. The most influential essays comparing American culture in the 1920s and 1930s are found in Warren I. Susman, *Culture as History: The Transformation of American Society in the Twentieth Century* (New York: Pantheon, 1984), chaps. 3–4.

18. Northrop and Northrop, *The Insolence of Office*, 18.

19. Northrop and Northrop, *The Insolence of Office*, 19; Thomas and Blanshard, *What's the Matter with New York*, 119–20; and Committee of Fourteen, 26 May 1927 meeting minutes, 2, box 86, C14.

20. Northrop and Northrop, *The Insolence of Office*, 20; Thomas and Blanshard, *What's the Matter with New York*, 147.

21. [Seabury,] Supreme Court, "*In re* Jesse Silbermann," 2–5; and Joint Legislative Committee to Investigate the Administration of the Various Departments of the Government of the City of New York, *Intermediate Report of Counsel* (Albany, 1932), "Re: Abraham Karp," n.p. On the Brooklyn women's court, see *New York Times*, 14 January 1931, 2; 30 January, 13; 16 February, 1; 18 February, 11; 24 March, 16; and 7 April 1931, 2.

22. Northrop and Northrop, *The Insolence of Office*, 21; and Thomas and Blanshard, *What's the Matter with New York*, 21, 150. Police framing of innocent women on prostitution charges occurred in European cities as well; see Joachim Schlör, *Nights in the Big City: Paris, Berlin, London, 1840–1930*, trans. Pierre Gottfried Imhof and Dafydd Rees Roberts (London: Reaktion Books, 1998), 191–92.

23. Chambers, *Samuel Seabury*, 243; *New York Times*, 21 January 1931, 17; 22 January, 17; 8 February, 1; and 30 September, 3.

24. The preceding three paragraphs are based on Northrop and Northrop, *The Insolence of Office*, 27–30; Chambers, *Samuel Seabury*, 237–42; and Mitgang, *The Man Who Rode the Tiger*, 181–85.

25. Northrop and Northrop, *The Insolence of Office*, 30–32.

26. Northrop and Northrop, *The Insolence of Office*, 41; *New York Times*, 19 February 1931, 14.

27. [Seabury,] Supreme Court, "*In re* Jean H. Norris" (Albany, 1931), Exhibit D.

28. *New York Times*, 21 January 1931, 17; Northrop and Northrop, *The Insolence of Office*, 47–49. Women in another city who both fell prey to these same vulnerabilities and found some solutions are discussed in Sarah Deutsch, *Women and the City: Gender, Space, and Power in Boston, 1870–1940* (New York: Oxford University Press, 2000), esp. chaps. 2–3.

29. On the case involving the elevator operator, see Northrop and Northrop, *The Insolence of Office*, 42–44; and Chambers, *Samuel Seabury*, 246–47. On the framers' ineptitude, see Northrop and Northrop, *The Insolence of Office*, 50–51.

30. On Brady, see Chambers, *Samuel Seabury*, 249. Seabury's report on Potocki is reprinted in Thomas and Blanshard, *What's the Matter with New York*, 148–49. On Potocki, see also Northrop and Northrop, *The Insolence of Office*, 51.

31. *New York Times*, 9 January 1931, 2.

32. *New York Times*, 21 February 1931, 2; 23 March, 11; and 16 June, 2.

33. *New York Times*, 9 January 1931, 1–2.

34. *New York Times*, 9 January 1931, 1; 20 January, 1; and 22 January, 1, 17; Northrop and Northrop, *The Insolence of Office*, 65–66; and *New York Daily News*, 22 January 1931, 1–2. On Corrigan's report, see *New York Times*, 20 January 1931, 1.

35. *New York Times*, 22 January 1931, 1, 17; 23 January, 1; and 8 April, 2. The *New York Evening Post*, 22 January 1931, 2, features fine reporting by Ruth Seinfel on this story.

36. *New York Times*, 22 January, 1931, 22.

37. *New York Times*, 1 March 1931, 1–2; 2 March, 1; and Lewis J. Valentine, *Night Stick: The Autobiography of Lewis J. Valentine* (New York: Dial Press, 1947), 115–16.

38. *New York Times*, 7 May 1931, 2.

39. Polly Adler, *A House Is Not a Home* (New York: Rinehart, 1953), 181–82; *New York Times*, 7 March 1931, 2.

40. Adler, *A House Is Not a Home*, 183–86.

41. Adler, *A House Is Not a Home*, 173, 188–97. See also Herbert Mitgang, *Once Upon a Time in New York: Jimmy Walker, Franklin Roosevelt, and the Last Great Battle of the Jazz Age* (New York: Free Press, 2000), 120. Adler disguised the name of her attorney, but Jonah Goldstein identified him as Samuel J. Siegel; Goldstein oral history, 493.

42. Adler, *A House Is Not a Home*, 189–97. On the litigation resulting from the Adler testimony, see *New York Times*, 14 July 1931, 6; 23 July, 4; 6 August, 4; 8 August, 14; 15 August, 30; and 16 December, 1.

43. *New York Times*, 6 May 1931, 2; Adler, *A House Is Not a Home*, 199; and Limpus, *Honest Cop*, 195.

44. Northrop and Northrop, *The Insolence of Office*, 110–14.

45. On Tait, see Chambers, *Samuel Seabury*, 254. On Quinlivan, see Northrop and Northrop, *The Insolence of Office*, 30–33. On officers' tales of generosity, see Northrop and Northrop, *The Insolence of Office*, 35, 40. On lawyers and disbarment, see Thomas and Blanshard, *What's the Matter with New York*, 147–49; and *New York Times*, 25 February 1931, 18; 28 February, 2; 17 September, 7; and 25 December, 27.

46. On Walker's counsel, see *New York Times*, 21 February 1931, 2. On the conflict with the mayor over immunity, see Northrop and Northrop, *The Insolence of Office*, 64; and *New York Times*, 1 January 1931, 1–2; 4 January, 1; 14 January, 2; 21 January, 1; and 11 February, 1.

47. Stenographic report of City Affairs Committee "Mass Meeting" at Carnegie Hall, 30 March 1931, "City Affairs Committee Charges" subject file, JJW. Holmes was even more passionate in his criticism of militarists, writing to a friend that he wanted to "put them in a lethal chamber, and turn on the gas"; John Haynes Holmes letter to Devere Allen, 2 June 1932, box 4, John Haynes Holmes papers, Manuscript Division, Library of Congress.

48. New York Joint Legislative Committee to Investigate the Administration of the Various Departments of the Government of the City of New York, *Transcript of Testimony* (Albany, 1932), 1:89; Northrop and Northrop, *The Insolence of Office*, 178; and Thomas and Blanshard, *What's the Matter with New York*, 47, 301.

49. The main sources on Seabury's investigation of Tammany leaders' corruption are Northrop and Northrop, *The Insolence of Office*, 168–69, 194–97, 204–8, 211–15, 219–24, 236–48; and Mitgang, *The Man Who Rode the Tiger*, 218–20, 230–32. See also New York Joint Legislative Committee, *Transcript*, 1:59–109, 14:6179–6493; Thomas and Blanshard, *What's the Matter with New York*, 41, 52, 54; John Dewey, ed., *New York and the Seabury Investigation: A Digest and Interpretation* (New York: City Affairs Committee, 1933), 14–16, 18; Chambers, *Samuel Seabury*, 347–42; and Limpus, *Honest Cop*, 127, 129.

50. Valentine, *Nightstick*, 113–14. Details of Valentine's and Keller's testimo-

nies are related above, in Chapter 3. New York Joint Legislative Committee, *Transcript*, 2:949.

51. Blanshard quote from a speech at a City Affairs Committee meeting, 30 March 1931, in "City Affairs Committee Charges" subject file, box 230, JJW. Thomas quoted in Thomas and Blanshard, *What's the Matter with New York*, 156. See also their general coverage, 155–57.

52. New York Joint Legislative Committee, *Transcript*, 19:8344–777, 20:8848, 8930, 8948, 9036–41. For a general summary, see Mitgang, *Once Upon a Time in New York*, 143–50.

53. Mitgang, *Once Upon a Time in New York*, 160–61.

54. Mitgang, *Once Upon a Time in New York*, chap. 11; Kenneth S. Davis, *FDR: The New York Years, 1928–1933* (New York: Random House, 1985), 301–5, 353–55.

*Chapter 7*

1. Robert A. Caro, *The Power Broker: Robert Moses and the Fall of New York* (New York: Knopf, 1974), 494, 545.

2. Caro, *The Power Broker*, 318–19, 554; and Robert Moses letter to George McAneny, 15 September 1937, box 97, Robert Moses papers, Rare Books and Manuscripts, New York Public Library.

3. Marion M. McIntosh letter to Robert Moses, 3 March 1936; Iphigene Ochs Sulzberger letter to Moses, 14 May 1936; Leonard S. Gans letter to Moses, 9 April 1936; Moses letter to McIntosh, 10 March 1936; and Moses letter to Sulzberger, 24 December 1935, box 97, Moses papers.

4. Robert Moses to Sidney Solomon, 21 May 1934, box 97, Moses papers. See also Caro, *The Power Broker*, 397–401; and Roy Rosenzweig and Elizabeth Blackmar, *The Park and the People: A History of Central Park* (Ithaca, N.Y.: Cornell University Press, 1992), 451, 454–55.

5. For this paragraph and the following: On the fusion movement and the La Guardia campaign, see Thomas Kessner, *Fiorello H. La Guardia and the Making of Modern New York* (New York: McGraw-Hill, 1989), chap. 7; Chris McNickle, *To Be Mayor of New York: Ethnic Politics in the City* (New York: Columbia University Press, 1993), 34–35; Ronald H. Bayor, *Neighbors in Conflict: The Irish, Germans, Jews, and Italians of New York City, 1929–1941* (Urbana: University of Illinois Press, 1988), chap. 3; and August Heckscher and Phyllis Robinson, *When La Guardia Was Mayor: New York's Legendary Years* (New York: Norton, 1978), chap. 1.

6. On the "crazy quilt" coalition, see Steven P. Erie, *Rainbow's End: Irish-Americans and the Dilemmas of Urban Machine Politics, 1840–1985* (Berkeley: University of California Press, 1988), 121. On Thomas and Blanshard, see W. A. Swanberg, *Norman Thomas: The Last Idealist* (New York: Scribner's, 1976), 145. See also Bayor, *Neighbors in Conflict*, 136–39.

7. See especially Kessner, *Fiorello H. La Guardia*, chaps. 8–9. See also Heckscher and Robinson, *When La Guardia Was Mayor*, chap. 2; and Caro, *The Power Broker*, 360–73.

8. On La Guardia and ingratitude, see Kessner, *Fiorello H. La Guardia*, 259; and Jonah Goldstein, oral history, Columbia Oral History Research Center, 146. More generally on La Guardia and municipal reform, see Kessner, *Fiorello H. La Guardia*, 279–80, 287–89, 324–30. Edward J. Flynn offered a critical view of the new municipal workforce, claiming that La Guardia replaced Tammany Hall with "one the best political machines that ever functioned in New York."

Edward J. Flynn, *You're the Boss* (New York: Viking, 1947), 138. On the city's island jails, see *The WPA Guide to New York City* (1939; reprint, New York: New Press, 1992), 423–24, 426.

9. Kessner, *Fiorello H. La Guardia*, 83.

10. Kessner, *Fiorello H. La Guardia*, 107–9.

11. "Memorandum for Address for F. H. La Guardia on Social Justice," n.d. (October 1933), box 4095, La Guardia mayoral papers, New York Municipal Archives; Kessner, *Fiorello H. La Guardia*, 299–300.

12. On the Claremont Inn, see Marion M. McIntosh to Robert Moses, 3 March 1936. See also James H. Shipley letter to Moses, 19 March 1936; and Moses letter to Shipley, 21 March 1936. 1931 quote is from Sidney Solomon court affidavit, 23 November 1934, box 97, Moses papers.

13. Caro, *The Power Broker*, 374, 383. See also Rosenzweig and Blackmar, *The Park and the People*, 454–55. Moses always used lavish buffets at the Boardwalk Restaurant and the Tavern on the Green, paid for by tolls and city taxes, to woo political and business supporters; see Caro, *The Power Broker*, 824–26.

14. *New York Times*, 2 March 1934, 22; 9 March, 12; 18 April, 1; 8 June, 3; 17 September, 38; and 25 December 1935, 25.

15. *New York Times*, 1 September 1934, 15; 5 September, 23; and 6 September, 21.

16. Paul Chevigny, *Gigs: Jazz and the Cabaret Laws in New York City* (New York: Routledge, 1991), 57.

17. On Al Smith, see Richard A. Childs, oral history, Columbia Oral History Research Center, 65. Tugwell commission quote is from Gerald E. Fitzgerald, "A History of Zoning in New York City," (M.P.A. thesis, City College of New York, 1955), 35. Carol Willis, "A 3D CBD: How the 1916 Zoning Law Shaped Manhattan's Central Business Districts," in Todd W. Bressi, ed., *Planning and Zoning New York City: Yesterday, Today, and Tomorrow* (New Brunswick, N.J.: Center for Urban Policy Research, 1993), 22. *New York Times* is quoted in S. J. Makielski, Jr., *The Politics of Zoning: The New York Experience* (New York: Columbia University Press, 1966), 60–61. See also Fitzgerald, "A History of Zoning in New York City," 27–28; Willis, "A 3D CBD," 20–22; and Makielski, *The Politics of Zoning*, 47, 50–54, 58, and 119.

18. Chevigny, *Gigs*, 57–60.

19. Kessner, *Fiorello H. La Guardia*, 108–9. Quotation is from "Memorandum for Address for F. H. La Guardia on Social Justice," 5. On Seabury, see Chapter 6 in this book.

20. Henry Drimer, "House of Detention (Women)," WPA Writers Project draft, n.d. (circa 1938), microfilm roll 20, WPA Guide project collection, New York Municipal Archives, 1. See also Kessner, *Fiorello H. La Guardia*, 276–80.

21. Drimer, "House of Detention (Women)," 1–4. Other descriptions of the House of Detention are in *WPA Guide to New York City*, 138; Mary Sullivan, *My Double Life* (New York: Farrar and Rinehart, 1938), 278; and Polly Adler, *A House Is Not a Home* (New York: Rinehart, 1953), 272.

22. All quotations from Kessner, *Fiorello H. La Guardia*, 353–55. See also Heckscher and Robinson, *When La Guardia Was Mayor*, 56–59. On the third degree controversy, see Emanuel H. Lavine, *The Third Degree: A Detailed and Appalling Exposé of Police Brutality* (Garden City, N.Y.: Garden City Publishing, 1930); Michael Fiaschetti and Prosper Buranelli, *You Gotta Be Rough* (New York: Doubleday, Doran, 1930); and Zechariah Chafee, Jr., Walter H. Pollak, and Carl S. Stern, *The Third Degree* (1931; reprint: New York: Arno Press, 1969).

23. Quotations from Lowell M. Limpus, *Honest Cop: Lewis J. Valentine* (New York: E. P. Dutton, 1939), 201; and Kessner, *Fiorello H. La Guardia*, 356–57. See also Limpus, *Honest Cop*, 178, 195; and Lewis J. Valentine, *Night Stick: The Autobiography of Lewis J. Valentine* (New York: Dial Press, 1947), 204. On the NYPD suspect lineup, see Irving Crump and John H. Newton, *Our Police* (New York: Dodd, Mead, 1935), 114.

24. La Guardia quoted in Mary M. Stolberg, *Fighting Organized Crime: Politics, Justice, and the Legacy of Thomas E. Dewey* (Boston: Northeastern University Press, 1995), 47. Kessner, *Fiorello H. La Guardia*, 361–62. See also Stolberg, *Fighting Organized Crime*, 50–61, 109–13.

25. For this paragraph and the following: Stolberg, *Fighting Organized Crime*, 61–72ff., 90–98.

26. On Egbert, see Stolberg, *Fighting Organized Crime*, 52–53; and Adler, *A House Is Not a Home*, 246. On Harlem, see Cheryl Lynn Greenberg, *"Or Does It Explode?": Black Harlem in the Great Depression* (New York: Oxford University Press, 1991), 177. On Kennedy, see Geoffrey Perret, *Jack: A Life Like No Other* (New York: Random House, 2001), 37.

27. *New York Daily News* quotation is in Adler, *A House Is Not a Home*, 255. See also Adler, *A House Is Not a Home*, 233–37, 250–75; and Goldstein, oral history, 490–93. Once free, Adler began another brothel, but nightclub owners and other employers of young women turned her away. Adler left for California but returned in the 1940s to attempt another comeback. See her obituary, *New York Times*, 11 June 1962, 22.

28. Stolberg, *Fighting Organized Crime*, chaps. 6–7, esp. 121–22, 134–39.

29. Stolberg, *Fighting Organized Crime*, chap. 8; see also Adler, *A House Is Not a Home*, 288–97. Regarding Schultz, see also Paul Sann, *Kill the Dutchman!: The Story of Dutch Schultz* (1971; reprint, New York: Da Capo, 1991), 291–93.

30. Greenberg, *"Or Does It Explode?"*, 177, 192; Sann, *Kill the Dutchman!*, 170–84, 212–18ff.

31. Kessner, *Fiorello H. La Guardia*, 371–72. On the Hollywood Restaurant, see Nils Thor Granlund with Sid Feder and Ralph Hancock, *Blondes, Brunettes, and Bullets* (New York: David McKay Co., 1957), 221–22. On Harlem in the Depression, see State of New York, *Report of the New York State Temporary Commission on the Condition of the Urban Colored Population* (Albany, 1938), 13–15, 62ff.; Greenberg, *"Or Does It Explode?,"* 32–39; and Jacqueline Jones, *Labor of Love, Labor of Sorrow: Black Women, Work, and the Family, From Slavery to the Present* (New York: Vintage, 1986), 212–15.

32. Caro, *The Power Broker*, 318–19, 491–93, 510. See also Lawrence R. Chenault, "The Puerto Rican Migrant in New York City" (Ph.D. diss., Columbia University, 1938), esp. 52–61; and Greenberg, *"Or Does It Explode?,"* chap. 5.

33. Kessner, *Fiorello H. La Guardia*, 368–76. The taxonomy of U.S. race riots is explored in Anthony Platt, ed., *Politics of Riot Commissions, 1917–1970* (New York: Macmillan, 1971), introduction.

34. James Dickson letter to Eunice Hunton Carter, 26 March 1935; A. Philip Randolph letter to Eunice Hunter Carter, 19 May 1935; Dickson letter to Fiorello H. La Guardia, 26 March 1935 (spelling corrected); anonymous letter to La Guardia, 2 October 1941, microfilm roll 76, La Guardia papers, New York Municipal Archives; 1935 riot commission report draft, n.d., roll 76, La Guardia papers, 8.

35. Quotations from Lewis J. Valentine letter to Fiorello H. La Guardia, 30 April 1935; Sullivan, *My Double Life*, 205. Other officials' responses to La Guardia

are Edmond B. Butler, 7 May 1936; Charlotte Carr, 14 May 1936; and Sigismund Goldwater, May 1936, microfilm roll 76, La Guardia papers. See also Kessner, *Fiorello H. La Guardia*, 375–76. Examinations for venereal diseases of arrested prostitutes first began in the 1930s; see Adler, *A House Is Not a Home*, 199.

36. Letters to Fiorello H. La Guardia: anonymous, n.d.; anonymous, November 1941; "A true American," n.d.; and T. La Pointe, 27 June 1942, microfilm roll 76, La Guardia papers.

37. George Chauncey, *Gay New York: Gender, Urban Culture, and the Making of the Gay Male World, 1890–1940* (New York: Basic Books, 1994), 334; Kessner, *Fiorello H. La Guardia*, 344–47; and Heckscher and Robinson, *When La Guardia Was Mayor*, 147–51.

38. Abel Green and Joe Laurie, Jr., *Show Biz: From Vaude to Video* (New York: Henry Holt, 1951), 447–50; "The Business of Burlesque," *Fortune*, February 1935, 67–73; and Gypsy Rose Lee, *Gypsy: A Memoir* (New York: Harper and Brothers, 1957), esp. chaps. 1, 7–8. On Moss, see *New York Times*, 2 May 1937, 27, and 26 February 1950, 76 (Moss's obituary). See also Rachel Shteir, *Striptease: The Untold History of the Girlie Show* (New York: Oxford University Press, 2004), 179–93.

39. Letters to La Guardia: O. R. Miller, 3 May 1937; Horace Smith, 3 May 1937; Mollie Minsky, 3 June 1937, burlesque subject file, microfilm roll 14, La Guardia papers; Vivian Rumer, 30 April 1937. Standardized appeals from theater employees are found in Lu Bass telegram, 30 April 1937; Meyer Harris, n.d., licensing commission files, roll 512, La Guardia papers. See also Shteir, *Striptease*, 157, 171–75.

40. David Dressler, "Burlesque as a Cultural Phenomenon" (Ph.D. diss., New York University, 1937), 161, 185, 209, in roll 14, La Guardia papers; see also Shteir, *Striptease*, 199–200. Henry A. Ritter letter to La Guardia (quoting the mayor), 2 May 1937, roll 512; and La Guardia letter to Austin MacCormick (corrections director), 9 August 1937. See also miscellaneous correspondence, sex crimes subject file, roll 223, La Guardia papers.

41. Variety Revue Theatre Association of New York constitution and bylaws [July 1937]; Variety Revue Theatre Association of New York, press release, 11 July 1937, roll 14, La Guardia papers; and Robert C. Allen, *Horrible Prettiness: Burlesque and American Culture* (Chapel Hill: University of North Carolina Press, 1991), 258. For the burlesque controversy of 1937, see *New York Times*, 29 April 1937, 1; 1 May 1937, 1; and 2 May 1937, 1, 27; Green and Laurie, *Show Biz*, 449–53; and Allen, *Horrible Prettiness*, 252–58.

42. Dressler, "Burlesque as a Cultural Phenomenon," 202. Nathan quoted in Shteir, *Striptease*, 169. Letters to La Guardia: James W. McMahon, 3 May 1937; T. H. Rose, 3 May 1937; Joseph L. Beha, 17 April 1937; and Lawrence E. McAllister, 13 June 1937, roll 512, La Guardia papers.

43. Chauncey, *Gay New York*, 332–34, 337–48. On lesbians in New York in the 1930s, see Sullivan, *My Double Life*, 207–10. The notable case study of lesbian life in the 1930s (in Buffalo, New York) is Elizabeth Lapovsky Kennedy and Madeline D. Davis, *Boots of Leather, Slippers of Gold: The History of a Lesbian Community* (London: Routledge, 1992), chaps. 1–2. For a general discussion of gay repression in this decade, see John D'Emilio and Estelle B. Freedman, *Intimate Matters: A History of Sexuality in America* (New York: Harper & Row, 1988), 288.

44. Bayor, *Neighbors in Conflict*, 42–46, 126–33; Limpus, *Honest Cop*, 257–58; Kessner, *Fiorello H. La Guardia*, 415–17.

45. La Guardia quoted in Kessner, *Fiorello H. La Guardia*, 437. See also Kes-

sner, *Fiorello H. La Guardia*, 435–37; Caro, *The Power Broker*, 333n, 654, 1083–92; and Michael Mullen, "1939–1940 New York World's Fair," in John E. Findling and Kimberly D. Pelle, eds., *Historical Dictionary of World's Fairs and Expositions, 1851–1988* (New York: Greenwood Press, 1990), 293–300.

46. David Gelernter, *1939: The Lost World of the Fair* (New York: Free Press, 1995), 343.

47. Sideshow attractions are listed in Commercial Spectacles and Amusements file, New York World's Fair, 1939–40 papers, box 182, Rare Books and Manuscripts, New York Public Library; and Mullen, "1939–1940 New York World's Fair," 298. On Bel Geddes and Dalí, see Gelernter, *1939*, 125–30. See also Shteir, *Striptease*, 207–13.

48. On the Russell affair, see Kessner, *Fiorello H. La Guardia*, 474–75; and Heckscher and Robinson, *When La Guardia Was Mayor*, 269–75.

*Chapter 8*

1. Robert Sylvester, *No Cover Charge: A Backward Look at the Night Clubs* (New York: Dial Press, 1956), 243; and Neal Gabler, *Winchell: Gossip, Power, and the Culture of Celebrity* (New York: Knopf, 1994), 264–69.

2. *Variety*, 17 October 1933, 1; Abel Green and Joe Laurie, Jr., *Show Biz: From Vaude to Video* (New York: Henry Holt, 1951), 425–27; Brooks McNamara, "The Entertainment District at the End of the 1930s," in William R. Taylor, ed., *Inventing Times Square: Culture and Commerce at the Crossroads of the World* (New York: Russell Sage Foundation, 1991), 178–84; and Jack Poggi, *Theater in America: The Impact of Economic Forces, 1870–1967* (Ithaca, N.Y.: Cornell University Press, 1968), 25–26.

3. *Variety*, 2 January 1934, 116; and 1 January 1936, 210. On the Federal Theatre Project, see Jane S. De Hart, *The Federal Theatre, 1935–1939: Plays, Relief, and Politics* (Princeton, N.J.: Princeton University Press, 1967).

4. *The WPA Guide to New York City* (1939; reprint, New York: New Press, 1992), 167–70, quoted in McNamara, "The Entertainment District at the End of the 1930s," 182–83; Poggi, *Theater in America*, chaps. 2–3; and James Traub, *The Devil's Playground: A Century of Pleasure and Profit in Times Square* (New York: Random House, 2004), chap. 7.

5. Regarding repeal, see David E. Kyvig, *Repealing National Prohibition* (Chicago: University of Chicago Press, 1979); H. I. Brock, "Now Our Nightlife Glows Anew," *New York Times*, 11 February 1934, VI, 10.

6. Rose C. Feld, "Tinkling Joy Returns to Tin Pan Alley," *New York Times*, 18 February 1934, VI, 11; and Brock, "Now Our Nightlife Glows Anew," 10.

7. *Variety*, 26 September 1933, 43; and 10 October 1933, 1.

8. Green and Laurie, *Show Biz*, 391.

9. *Variety*, 14 November 1933, 39; Brock, "Now Our Nightlife Glows Anew," 10; and Richard F. Hamm, *Shaping the Eighteenth Amendment* (Chapel Hill: University of North Carolina Press, 1995), 271.

10. Brock, "Now Our Nightlife Glows Anew," 10; and *Variety*, 24 October 1933, 46. For historical context, see Madelon Powers, *Faces Along the Bar: Lore and Order in the Workingman's Saloon, 1870–1920* (Chicago: University of Chicago Press, 1998), 235–37.

11. Brock, "Now Our Nightlife Glows Anew," 10 (italics added), 19; and Ann Douglas, *Terrible Honesty: Mongrel Manhattan in the 1920s* (New York: Farrar Straus Giroux, 1995), 139.

12. H. I. Brock, "Running the Gamut of the Night Club," *New York Times Magazine*, 18 November 1934, 8. See also Brock, "Now Our Nightlife Glows Anew," 10; Bosley Crowther, "Hi-De-Ho! The Night Clubs Turn 'Em Away," *New York Times Magazine*, 21 March 1937, 14; and Abel Green, "Niteries on Road Back," *Variety*, 6 January 1937, 195. A somewhat different argument, with a national scope, is in Lewis A. Erenberg, "From New York to Middletown: Repeal and the Legitimization of Nightlife in the Great Depression," *American Quarterly* 38 (winter 1986), 761–78.

13. Green is quoted in a *Variety* newspaper clipping, n.d. (circa 1936), New York Night Clubs file, BRTC; *Variety*, 10 October 1933, 1, 40; 7 November 1933, 46; and 21 November 1933, 44.

14. Club Frivolity program, n.d. (Texas Guinan's endorsement dates the show before late 1933), New York Night Clubs 1930–1939 file, BRTC.

15. On the House of Morgan, see Robert A. M. Stern, Gregory Gilmartin, and Thomas Mellis, *New York 1930: Architecture and Urbanism Between the Two World Wars* (New York: Rizzoli, 1987), 291. On the Heigh-Ho club, see Chapter 1 of this book. On French design influences, see Stern, Gilmartin, and Mellis, *New York 1930*, 288–91; and *Variety*, 27 November 1935, 46.

16. Sylvester, *No Cover Charge*, 99–100; and Ralph Blumenthal, *Stork Club: America's Most Famous Nightspot and the Lost World of Café Society* (Boston: Little, Brown, 2000), 95–114.

17. Blumenthal, *Stork Club*, 16–17, 42–47, 102–3, 242–43.

18. Sylvester, *No Cover Charge*, 125. See also Blumenthal, *Stork Club*, 159–74, 176–79; and *Variety*, 18 December 1934, 46. On celebrity caricature, see Wendy Reaves, *Celebrity Caricature in America* (New Haven, Conn.: Yale University Press, 1998).

19. "Manhattan Night Life," *Fortune, March 1936*, 102–3, 162. On Perona and El Morocco, see also Sylvester, *No Cover Charge*, 98, 103–10.

20. On origins of the term, see David W. Stowe, "The Politics of Café Society," *Journal of American History* 84 (1998), 1387. For descriptions of café society clubs, see also 1933–35 *Variety* articles cited above, as well as 21 November 1933, 44; 19 December 1933, 46; and 2 October 1935, 48; and Stern, Gilmartin, and Mellis, *New York 1930*, 288.

21. "Society Girls Sing for Their Champagne Supper in Smart Manhattan Cafes," *Life*, 5 December 1938, 55–58.

22. Ellin Mackay, "Why We Go to Cabarets," *New Yorker*, 28 November 1925, 7–8, and 12 December 1925, 15–16. See also Chapter 1 in this book.

23. Geoffrey Perret, *Jack: A Life Like No Other* (New York: Random House, 2001), 68; "Society Girls Sing for Their Champagne Supper," 58. See also Green and Laurie, *Show Biz*, 445.

24. *New York Times*, 27 October 1938, 11; 24 November 1938, 33; 20 May 1939, 1; and 6 March 1940, 25; and Blumenthal, *Stork Club*, 42–45, 174–83.

25. "Manhattan Night Life," 101.

26. *Variety*, 16 October 1935, 53; 27 November 1935, 46; "Manhattan Night Life," 100–101, 104; *WPA Guide to New York City*, 337; and Stern, Gilmartin, and Mellis, *New York 1930*, 291.

27. Club information is from the street-by-street survey of Midtown by the Committee of Fourteen (1928), box 36, C14. See Chapters 2 and 4 in this book. See also *New York Times*, 31 July 1928, 1.

28. On the history of Rockefeller Center, see *WPA Guide to New York City*, 333–41; Stern, Gilmartin, and Mellis, *New York 1930*, 618–39; and Daniel Okrent,

*Great Fortune: The Epic of Rockefeller Center* (New York: Viking, 2003). On Rivera, see Hayden Herrera, *Frida: A Biography of Frida Kahlo* (New York: Harper and Row, 1983), 164–66.

29. Stern, Gilmartin, and Mellis, *New York 1930*, 636–56. The Mumford quote is on 644, and the Rockette statement is on 656. See also "Manhattan Night Life," 104.

30. Nils Thor Granlund with Sid Feder and Ralph Hancock, *Blondes, Brunettes, and Bullets* (New York: David McKay Co., 1957), 245–50; Abel Green, "Renaissance of Nite Clubs," *Variety* clipping (circa 1935), "New York Night Clubs 1930–39" folder, BRTC; and *Variety*, 11 December 1935, 55.

31. Green, "Renaissance of Nite Clubs"; and "Nightclubs and Other Venues," in Barry Kernfeld, ed., *The New Grove Dictionary of Jazz*, one-volume ed. (New York: St. Martin's, 1994), esp. 892.

32. See, for example, David W. Stowe, *Swing Changes: Big-Band Jazz in New Deal America* (Cambridge: Harvard University Press, 1996), introduction, chap. 2; Joel Dinerstein, *Swinging the Machine: Modernity, Technology, and African American Culture between the World Wars* (Amherst: University of Massachusetts Press, 2003), chap. 5; and Lewis A. Erenberg, *Swingin' the Dream: Big Band Jazz and the Rebirth of American Culture* (Chicago: University of Chicago, 1998), chaps. 1, 3.

33. For the preceding two paragraphs: "Nightclubs and Other Venues," 890–99; Sylvester, *No Cover Charge*, 181–83. On the symbolism of Swing Street, see, for example, Erenberg, *Swingin' the Dream*, 157–59.

34. Sylvester, *No Cover Charge*, 72–73; "Nightclubs and Other Venues," 894; and "Manhattan Night Life," 101–2.

35. Billie Holiday and William Dufty, *Lady Sings the Blues* (New York: Doubleday, 1956), 97, 99.

36. *New York Times*, 28 February 1931, 22; 2 March 1931, 1–2. On New Deal ideology, see Stowe, *Swing Changes*, esp. chaps. 1–2; Barbara Melosh, *Engendering Culture: Manhood and Womanhood in New Deal Public Art and Theater* (Washington, D.C.: Smithsonian Institution Press, 1991), esp. chaps. 3, 9; and David M. Kennedy, *Freedom from Fear: The American People in Depression and War, 1929–1945* (New York: Oxford University Press, 2000), esp. 256–57, chap. 9.

37. On Camp Unity, see Alyn Shipton, *Groovin' High: The Life of Dizzy Gillespie* (New York: Oxford University Press, 1999), 44; and George Torrece interview with author, 24 March 1988. On the Left in the 1930s, see Michael Denning, *The Cultural Front: The Laboring of American Culture in the Twentieth Century* (New York: Verso, 1998), 14–15; Paul R. Gorman, *Left Intellectuals and Popular Culture in Twentieth-Century America* (Chapel Hill: University of North Carolina Press, 1996), chap. 5; and Richard H. Pells, *Radical Visions and American Dreams: Culture and Social Thought in the Depression Years*, rep. ed. (Urbana: University of Illinois Press, 1998), 252–328.

38. Simon Callow, *Orson Welles: The Road to Xanadu* (New York: Viking, 1995), esp. chaps. 9, 11. See also Glenda E. Gill, *White Grease Paint on Black Performers: A Study of the Federal Theatre of 1935–1939* (New York: Peter Lang, 1988).

39. Max Gordon, *Live at the Village Vanguard* (New York: St. Martin's, 1980), chaps. 1–2.

40. Green and Laurie, *Show Biz*, 446. See also *New York Times*, 3 December 1939, IX, 11; 16 February 1940, 23; Denning, *The Cultural Front*, 14–15; and Stowe, *Swing Changes*, 56–68.

41. Stowe, "The Politics of Café Society," 1384–1406; Erenberg, *Swingin' the Dream*, chap. 5; and David Margolick, *Strange Fruit: Billie Holiday, Café Society, and an Early Cry for Civil Rights* (New York: Running Press, 2000).

42. Denning, *The Cultural Front*, 29.

*Chapter 9*

1. *Variety*, 30 November 1949, n.p., clipping in Billy Rose scrapbooks, BRTC.
2. *Variety*, 3 December, 24 December 1938, n.p., clipping in Billy Rose scrapbooks, BRTC.
3. Lewis A. Erenberg, "From New York to Middletown: Repeal and the Legitimization of Nightlife in the Great Depression," *American Quarterly* 38 (winter 1986), 762, 770. See also Jeffrey L. Meikle, *Twentieth Century Limited: Industrial Design in America, 1925–1939*, 2d ed. (Philadelphia: Temple University Press, 2001), esp. chap. 8.
4. *Variety*, 17 November 1933, 47.
5. *Variety*, 10 October 1933, 15. See also Polly Gottlieb, *The Nine Lives of Billy Rose* (New York: Crown, 1968), 86.
6. Gottlieb, *Nine Lives of Billy Rose*, 94; and *Variety*, 19 December 1933, 46. Regarding Rose's clubs of the early 1930s, see Stephen Nelson, *"Only a Paper Moon": The Theater of Billy Rose* (Ann Arbor, Mich.: UMI Research Press, 1987), chap. 2.
7. "Stage," *Newsweek*, 29 June 1935, 23; and Gottlieb, *Nine Lives of Billy Rose*, 94. Decades later the site of Billy Rose's Music Hall was renamed the Ed Sullivan Theater, and it is now the home of television's *The Late Show with David Letterman*.
8. For biographical information on Rose, see Billy Rose, *Wine, Women, and Words* (New York: Simon and Schuster, 1948); Gottlieb, *Nine Lives of Billy Rose*; Nelson, *"Only a Paper Moon"*; and Earl Conrad, *Billy Rose: American Primitive* (Cleveland: World Publishing, 1968). See also *Padlocks of 1927* program, BRTC.
9. For the preceding two paragraphs: Nelson, *"Only a Paper Moon,"* 7, 16–20; and Rose, *Wine, Women, and Words*, 14.
10. On Rose's study of songs, see "Flowering Rose," *Time*, 2 June 1947, 47–48. On Dubin and Dixon, see Nelson, *"Only a Paper Moon,"* 6–7.
11. Rose, *Wine, Women, and Words*, 11, 90. On Runyon, see Daniel R. Schwartz, *Broadway Boogie-Woogie: Damon Runyon and the Making of New York Culture* (New York: Palgrave Macmillan, 2003), esp. chap. 4.
12. On Rose and the Steinberg brothers, see *Variety*, 11 December 1934, 47; and Rose, *Wine, Women, and Words*, 91–92. On Rose and Moss, see *New York Times*, 19 September 1934, 15.
13. "Manhattan Night Life," *Fortune*, March 1936, 104–5. On Carroll, see Susan Waggoner, *Nightclub Nights: Art, Legend, and Style, 1920–1960* (New York: Rizzoli, 2001), 55.
14. On Blumenthal and Shapiro, see *St. Louis Post-Dispatch*, 5 September 1937. On acts in East Side hotels, see *Variety*, 23 October 1935, 47. Clippings in International Casino scrapbook, BRTC; *Variety*, 18 November 1936, 56.
15. Robert A. M. Stern, Gregory Gilmartin, and Thomas Mellis, *New York 1930: Architecture and Urbanism Between the Two World Wars* (New York: Rizzoli, 1987), 289–91; "International Casino, New York City," *Architectural Forum* 67 (September 1937), 385–88; and *St. Louis Post-Dispatch*, 5 September 1937, and King Features Syndicate article, n.d. (1938), clippings in International Casino Scrapbook, BRTC.
16. On Sandrini and Charles, see newspaper story, n.d. (circa July 1937); and *New York World-Telegram*, 11 September 1937. On International dancers, see King Features Syndicate article, n.d. (1938). Clippings in International Casino Scrapbook, BRTC.
17. On the club rivalry, see *St. Louis Post-Dispatch*, 5 September 1937. On the

International's struggles, see *New York World-Telegram*, 11 September 1937; and *New York Herald-Tribune*, 24 March 1938. Clippings in International Casino Scrapbook, BRTC. On nightclub dances, see Abel Green, "Too Many Class Joints?," *Variety*, 2 November 1938, 1.

18. On chain stores, see Lizabeth Cohen, *Making a New Deal: Industrial Workers in Chicago, 1919–1939* (Cambridge, U.K.: Cambridge University Press, 1991), 106–20, and *A Consumers' Republic: The Politics of Mass Consumption in Postwar America* (New York: Vintage, 2003), chap. 1, 301–2; and William R. Leach, *Land of Desire: Merchants, Power, and the Rise of a New American Culture* (New York: Vintage, 1994), 373–82.

19. See, for example, Russell Sanjek, *American Popular Music and Its Business: The First Four Hundred Years: Volume 3, 1900–1984* (New York: Oxford University Press, 1988), 123–27 passim; Thomas Schatz, *The Genius of the System* (New York: Pantheon, 1989), chaps. 2–3; and Andrew Bergman, *We're in the Money: Depression America and Its Films* (1971; reprint, New York: Ivan R. Dee, 1992).

20. Quotation in *New York Times*, 21 January 1934, II 6. On the city charter, see Thomas Kessner, *Fiorello H. La Guardia and the Making of Modern New York* (New York: McGraw-Hill, 1989), 404–6, 459–60; and August Heckscher and Phyllis Robinson, *When La Guardia Was Mayor: New York's Legendary Years* (New York: Norton, 1978), 128–30.

21. For the preceding two paragraphs: On New York and regional planning, see Stern, Gilmartin, and Mellis, *New York 1930*, 29, 41–48; and [Thomas Adams, Harold M. Lewis, and Lawrence M. Orton,] *New York: Regional Plan of New York and Its Environs, 1929–1931*, 2 vols. (New York: Regional Plan Association, 1931). On Moses, see Robert A. Caro, *The Power Broker: Robert Moses and the Fall of New York* (New York: Knopf, 1974), 19, 519–59 and passim. For national trends in regional planning, see Jon C. Teaford, *City and Suburb: The Political Fragmentation of Metropolitan America, 1850–1970* (Baltimore: Johns Hopkins University Press, 1979), 4, 110–21.

22. "Bedrooms of Manhattan," *Fortune*, July 1939, 145–46; and Heckscher and Robinson, *When La Guardia Was Mayor*, 223–33.

23. Rose, *Wine, Women, and Words*, 14, 15.

24. Nelson, *"Only a Paper Moon,"* chap. 3; and "Barnum Items, and Circus Items," list, n.d., Billy Rose scrapbooks, box 464, BRTC.

25. For the preceding two paragraphs: Nelson, *"Only a Paper Moon,"* chap. 4. For statistics on the Fort Worth attractions, see Texas Centennial Exposition publicity brochure, 1936, Billy Rose scrapbooks, box 464, BRTC.

26. Newspaper clippings, Billy Rose publicity file, BRTC; and Rose, *Wine, Women, and Words*, 24–26.

27. On Rose's profits, see "Girls Girls Girls," *Fortune*, July 1939, 121. On Rose's national influence, see Erenberg, "From New York to Middletown," 770.

28. "Girls Girls Girls," 180. On Rose and conventioneers, see also Lewis Erenberg, "Impresarios of Broadway Nightlife," in William R. Taylor, ed., *Inventing Times Square: Culture and Commerce at the Crossroads of the World* (New York: Russell Sage Foundation, 1991), 175.

29. "Girls Girls Girls," 120; *New York Mirror*, 21 January 1938; and *Billboard*, 29 January 1938, clippings, box 464, BRTC. Labor conflict in nightlife is chronicled in the *New York Times*, 18 December 1937, 6; 15 January 1938, 19; 18 January 1938, 26; 3 March 1938, 17; 27 October 1938, 11; 6 December 1938, 27; 12 December 1938, 25; 20 May 1939, 1; 20 January 1940, 2; and 6 March 1940, 25. For a general view of the Hotel and Restaurant Workers' Union, see also Jay

Rubin and M. J. Obermeier, *Growth of a Union: The Life and Times of Edward Flore* (New York: The Historical Union Association, 1943).

30. On 1930s populism, see Barbara Melosh, *Engendering Culture: Manhood and Womanhood in New Deal Public Art and Theater* (Washington: Smithsonian Institution Press, 1991), chaps. 2–3; Kenneth J. Bindas, *All of This Music Belongs to the Nation: The WPA's Federal Music Project and American Society* (Knoxville: University of Tennessee Press, 1996); Benjamin Filene, *Romancing the Folk: Public Memory and American Roots Music* (Chapel Hill: University of North Carolina Press, 2000), chap. 2; and Richard H. Pells, *Radical Visions and American Dreams: Culture and Social Thought in the Depression Years*, rep. ed. (Urbana: University of Illinois Press, 1998), esp. 202–18.

31. *New York Post*, 6 February 1937, 1; and Nelson, *"Only a Paper Moon,"* 83.

32. Nelson, *"Only a Paper Moon,"* chap. 5 and p. 76. Rose quote is from Rose, *Wine, Women, and Words*, 183.

33. Billy Rose, "World's Fairs," 20 August 1946 ("Pitching Horseshoes" column manuscript), Billy Rose scrapbooks, BRTC. On the disciplined audience, see Russell Lynes, *The Lively Audience* (New York: Harper and Row, 1985), esp. 128–30, and Lawrence W. Levine, *Highbrow/Lowbrow: The Emergence of Cultural Hierarchy in America* (Cambridge, Mass.: Harvard University Press, 1988), chap. 3.

34. See Chapter 1 in this book. See also Ann Douglas, *Terrible Honesty: Mongrel Manhattan in the 1920s* (New York: Farrar Straus Giroux, 1995), esp. 47–52; and Donna Haraway, *Primate Visions: Gender, Race and Nature in the World of Modern Science* (London: Routledge, 1990), esp. chap. 2.

35. For the preceding two paragraphs: "Vaudeville for Dinner," *Vogue*, 1 September 1934, 31; Gilbert Seldes, "Stage-Door Johnny, Pro-Tem," *Esquire*, September 1934, 137; and Gottlieb, *Nine Lives of Billy Rose*, 149.

36. Gottlieb, *Nine Lives of Billy Rose*, 44. On burlesque in the 1930s, Rand, and Wassau, see Chapters 5 and 7; Robert C. Allen, *Horrible Prettiness: Burlesque and American Culture* (Chapel Hill: University of North Carolina Press, 1991), esp. 248–58; and Rachel Shteir, *Striptease: The Untold History of the Girlie Show* (New York: Oxford, 2004), esp. 109–13, 149, 207. Reviews of Wassau's performances at the Casa Mañana include *New York Times*, 19 January 1938; *New York World Telegram*, 27 and 29 January 1938; and *New York Daily News*, 29 January, scrapbook clippings, box 490, BRTC.

37. *New York Sun* clipping, 1 December 1940, Billy Rose scrapbooks, BRTC; 1946 program, n.p., Diamond Horseshoe scrapbook, BRTC. Publicity photos of Long-Stemmed Roses can be found in "Billy Rose Clubs and Productions" box and box 464, programs and clippings collection, BRTC. On images of women, see Lois Banner, *American Beauty* (Chicago: University of Chicago Press, 1984), esp. 283–85; John D'Emilio and Estelle Freedman, *Intimate Matters: A History of Sexuality in America* (New York: Harper and Row, 1988), 302; and Elaine Tyler May, *Homeward Bound: American Families in the Cold War Era* (New York: Basic Books, 1990), 81–99.

38. Gottlieb, *Nine Lives of Billy Rose*, 120. Rose quotation is in *San Diego Evening-Tribune* (Associated Press story), 20 January 1938, clippings, box 490, BRTC. See also Conrad, *Billy Rose: American Primitive*, 96.

39. Gottlieb, *Nine Lives of Billy Rose*, 148.

40. "Death" quotation is in Gottlieb, *Nine Lives of Billy Rose*, 96. The Craswell attraction, anticipated for the forthcoming Aquacade, is described in Diamond Horseshoe program, 1939, Diamond Horseshoe scrapbook, BRTC. See also Nelson, *"Only a Paper Moon,"* 112.

41. 16 June 1938 agreement with 23 January 1939 addendum, box 383, New York World's Fair 1939–1940 papers, Rare Books and Manuscripts, New York Public Library.

42. 1939 and 1940 programs, "Billy Rose's Aquacade" folder, Edward Massey Collection, BRTC.

43. "Talk of the Town," *New Yorker*, 26 October 1940, 13; memo, 15 September 1939, New York World's Fair 1939–40 papers, box 383, Rare Books and Manuscripts, New York Public Library; and Esther Williams and Digby Diehl, *The Million Dollar Mermaid: An Autobiography* (New York: Simon and Schuster, 1999), 46–55.

44. Stern, Gilmartin, and Mellis, *New York 1930*, 754; and David Gelernter, *1939: The Lost World of the Fair* (New York: Free Press, 1995), 295, 307–8. Rose's wealth was not a record for U.S. show business before 1940. In 1927, for example, *Variety* estimated the circus owner John Ringling's fortune at $60 million; Abel Green and Joe Laurie, Jr., *Show Biz: From Vaude to Video* (New York: Henry Holt, 1951), 350.

*Conclusion*

1. On Viennese refugees, see Christian Klösch and Regina Thumser, *"From Vienna": Exilkabarett in New York 1938 bis 1950* (Vienna: Picus, 2002).

2. Regarding tax fraud, see *New York Times*, 2 February 1939, 13; 9 March 1939, 4; 26 May 1939, 18; 15 July 1939, 32; 19 September 1939, 28; and 27 October 1939, 27. On fingerprinting, see *New York Times*, 15 August 1940, 1; 21 August 1940, 22; 4 October 1940, 12; and 29 December 1940, 27. More generally see *New York Times*, 13 August 1939, IX, 8; 31 December 1939, VII, 6; and 11 February 1940, IX, 3; Nils Thor Granlund with Sid Feder and Ralph Hancock, *Blondes, Brunettes, and Bullets* (New York: David McKay Co., 1957), 277.

3. Thomas Kessner, *Fiorello H. La Guardia and the Making of Modern New York* (New York: McGraw-Hill, 1989), 551–52; and Susan Waggoner, *Nightclub Nights: Art, Legend, and Style, 1920–1960* (New York: Rizzoli, 2001), 98–99.

4. See John C. Esposito, *Fire in the Grove: The Cocoanut Grove Tragedy and Its Aftermath* (Cambridge, Mass.: Da Capo, 2005); Edward Keyes, *Cocoanut Grove* (New York: Atheneum, 1984); and Robert Sylvester, *No Cover Charge: A Backward Look at the Night Clubs* (New York: Dial Press, 1956), 292–97.

5. *Der Angriff* clipping with translation in Billy Rose publicity file, BRTC; Billy Rose, *Wine, Women, and Words* (New York: Simon and Schuster, 1948), 133–34, 288; and Hugh Trevor-Roper, *The Last Days of Hitler* (1947; reprint, Chicago: University of Chicago Press, 1992), 210 (quoting Hitler's last political will and testament).

6. Sylvester, *No Cover Charge*, 25–38.

7. See, for example, John Morton Blum, *V Was for Victory: Politics and American Culture During World War II* (New York: Harcourt Brace Jovanovich, 1976), esp. chap. 1; Geoffrey Perret, *Days of Sadness, Years of Triumph: The American People, 1939–1945* (New York: Coward, McCann and Geoghegan, 1973), esp. part 3; and William M. Tuttle, Jr., *"Daddy's Gone to War": The Second World War in the Lives of America's Children* (New York: Oxford University Press, 1993), esp. chaps. 6 and 14. On changes in wartime New York, see Robert A. M. Stern, Thomas Mellins, and David Fishman, *New York 1960: Architecture and Urbanism Between the Second World War and the Bicentennial* (New York: Monacelli, 1995), 13–18; and Edward

Robb Ellis, *The Epic of New York City: A Narrative History*, rep. ed. (New York: Carroll and Graf, 2005), chap. 47.

8. James Gavin, *Intimate Nights: The Golden Age of New York Cabaret* (New York: Grove Weidenfeld, 1991); Angelo Zuccotti (El Morocco doorman), obituary, *New York Times*, 12 August 1998, A17; Joseph Giovannini, "Rainbow Room," *New York Times*, 7 August 1987, A20; and Dennis Hevesi, "Ah, Yes, Isn't It Romantic?," *New York Times*, 7 December 1987, B1–2.

9. See, for example, S. N. Eisenstadt, ed., *Max Weber on Charisma and Institution Building: Selected Papers* (Chicago: University of Chicago Press, 1968).

10. The concept of public opinion was developed most influentially by Walter Lippmann in *The Phantom Public* (New York: Harcourt, Brace, 1925). See also Robert B. Westbrook, *John Dewey and American Democracy* (Ithaca, N.Y.: Cornell University Press, 1991), 294–316.

11. Kessner, *Fiorello H. La Guardia*, 570–73; Chris McNickle, *To Be Mayor of New York: Ethnic Politics in the City* (New York: Columbia University Press, 1993), 52–57; and Robert Caro, *The Power Broker: Robert Moses and the Fall of New York* (New York: Knopf, 1974), 683–92.

12. Rachel Shteir, *Striptease: The Untold History of the Girlie Show* (New York: Oxford, 2004), 179–93, 235–42.

13. See Thomas Kunkel, *Genius in Disguise: Harold Ross of the New Yorker* (New York: Random House, 1995), 322–46; Mary F. Corey, *The World Through a Monocle: The New Yorker at Midcentury* (Cambridge, Mass.: Harvard University Press, 1999), chap. 1, conclusion; and Ben Yagoda, *About Town: The New Yorker and the World It Made* (New York: Scribner, 2000), chaps. 4, 5.

14. Kenneth T. Jackson, *Crabgrass Frontier: The Suburbanization of the United States* (New York: Oxford University Press, 1987), chaps. 11–12; and Thomas J. Sugrue, *Origins of the Urban Crisis: Race and Inequality in Postwar Detroit* (Princeton, N.J.: Princeton University Press, 1998), chaps. 2, 3.

15. On Perona Farms, see Lawton Mackall, *Knife and Fork in New York* (New York: Robert McBride, 1948), 238.

16. James Lardner and Thomas Reppetto, *NYPD: A City and Its Police* (New York: Henry Holt, 2000), chap. 13; *Washington Post*, 18 July 1998, 2.

17. Quotation is from Mackall, *Knife and Fork in New York*, 197. The standard work on postwar New York architecture and planning is Stern, Mellins, and Fishman, *New York 1960*, esp. 19–23, 47–56, and 531–35 (on nightclub design). See also Sylvester, *No Cover Charge*, 89. The phrase "gilded ghetto" appears in St. Clair Drake and Horace R. Cayton, *Black Metropolis: A Study of Negro Life in a Northern City*, rev. ed. (New York: Harcourt Brace, 1970), 2:xviii.

18. Jane Jacobs, *The Death and Life of Great American Cities* (1961; reprint, New York: Vintage, 1992), 33. See also James Sanders, Lisa Ades, and Ric Burns, *New York: An Illustrated History*, 2d ed. (New York: Knopf, 2003), 510–26; Stern, Mellins, and Fishman, *New York 1960*, 41–45; and Caro, *The Power Broker*, 984–1004. Oddly, Robert Caro's 1,200-page book does not mention Jacobs's crusade against the Cross-Manhattan Expressway in the 1960s.

19. Elizabeth Wilson, *The Sphinx in the City: Urban Life, the Control of Disorder, and Women* (Berkeley: University of California Press, 1991), 115–16. A gender-oriented new urbanist analysis is Dolores Hayden, *Redesigning the American Dream: Gender, Housing, and Family Life*, 2d ed. (New York: Norton, 2002), esp. chap 8.

20. On Studio 54, see Anthony Haden-Guest, *The Last Party: Studio 54, Disco, and the Culture of the Night* (New York: William Morrow, 1997). On Gatien's clubs,

see Frank Owen, *Clubland: The Fabulous Rise and Murderous Fall of Club Culture* (New York: St. Martin's, 2003); and Clifford Levy, "Impresario of the Night," *New York Times*, 31 July 1994, 13:4.

21. Paul Chevigny, *Gigs: Jazz and the Cabaret Laws in New York City* (New York: Routledge, 1991), introduction, 60–64.

22. Tricia Romano, "The Safety Dance: You Can't Dance If You Want To," *Village Voice*, 27 November–3 December 2002, 36–38; Ronald Smothers, "City to Recheck Night Clubs, Other Public Places," *New York Times*, 31 December 1975, 25; Robert D. McFadden, "The Knights of the Padlock Sweep Forth," *New York Times*, 31 March 1990, 27; Andrew Jacobs, "Dance Clubs Heeding Call to Tame Wild Life," *New York Times*, 31 August 1999; Jennifer Steinhauer, "After 77 Years, Cabaret Laws Face Rewrite," ibid., 24 June 2003, B1; Patrick Healy, "Ways to Flout Cabaret Law as Varied as Dance Steps," *New York Times*, 28 June 2003, B2; and *Newsday*, 25 June 2003.

23. On rave clubs, see Paul Chatterton and Robert Hollands, *Urban Nightscapes: Youth Cultures, Pleasure Spaces, and Corporate Power* (London: Routledge, 2003), chap. 9; and Phil Jackson, *Inside Clubbing: Sensual Experiments in the Art of Being Human* (Oxford, U.K.: Berg, 2004).

# Index

# Acknowledgments

This book is culled from more than a dozen years of research and writing. Other versions of the manuscript include details and subtopics that do not appear here. Readers who would like to inquire about this research are welcome to contact me.

Over the course of those years I received material support from generous employers and other institutions. Research in New York City began in 1994 with the assistance of a faculty research and development grant from The Colorado College. In subsequent years I benefited from a summer research grant from Middle Tennessee State University and from two Connecticut State University-AAUP research stipend and assistance grants. A great deal of the research was accomplished with the assistance of a six-month fellowship for college teachers from the National Endowment for the Humanities, an independent federal agency. I am particularly grateful for the extended inquiry that this assistance allowed me to undertake.

Essential help also has come from numerous archivists and librarians. The New York City Municipal Archives provided me with my earliest forays into the history of the city government. Director Kenneth Cobb and his staff also assisted me at crucial later junctures. The Billy Rose Theatre Collection at the Performing Arts Library at Lincoln Center, a branch of the New York Public Library, was invaluable for research on nightclubs. This collection and the NYPL's other pictorial archives provided me with most of the illustrations in this volume. The Manuscripts and Archives Division at the NYPL Humanities and Social Sciences Center houses the Committee of Fourteen papers and other sources. During my NEH fellowship the main reading room and Manuscript Division of the Library of Congress were essential resources. I am also grateful for the assistance I received from archivists at the La Guardia and Wagner Archive at La Guardia Community College, in New York City. The Internet barely existed when I began this project, but it came to revolutionize my research in countless ways; I owe gratitude to archivists, enthusiasts, and other web-page creators who have made catalogs, finding aids, and copious amounts of relevant material available online.

Many colleagues offered advice, assistance, and encouragement during the production of this book. Lawrence W. Levine probably provided this project with the earliest valuable direction in our many discussions in the late 1980s and early 1990s. For this reason and for many others, this book is dedicated to him. Patrick Miller and Kenneth Scherzer gave me vital early inspiration as I groped toward a definition of the topic. I benefited from the comments of audience members at presentations of an early version of Chapter 2 at a meeting of the New England chapter of the American Studies Association, a portion of Chapter 5 at the Mid-Atlantic Popular Culture Association, and a draft of Chapter 9 at a session of the Popular Culture Association. Colleagues and graduate students at the American studies program at the University of Regensburg, Germany, provided new perspectives during a presentation I gave during my time there as a Fulbright scholar. Lynn Dumenil, Lewis Erenberg, Timothy Gilfoyle, and anonymous press readers provided detailed and useful criticisms of early drafts of the entire manuscript. Robert Devens, an editor at another press, offered encouragement and valuable advice. Robert Lockhart at the University of Pennsylvania Press has been a collegial and effective critic and shepherd for this enterprise. I am very grateful to Christine Sweeney, the copyeditor, and Erica Ginsburg, who oversaw the book's production.

I hope that any of my colleagues in history and American studies who read this—colleagues past and present, near and far, with whom I have shared this project in any way (and even some with whom I have not shared it)—know how grateful I am for their encouragement, scholarly examples, and friendship over the years. I am most thankful to my family for their love and support. Its composition changed during the course of my work; my mother, my father-in-law, and others have passed away, but Jenny and I also celebrated the arrival of our daughter, Catherine. More than anything else, such sad and joyous events sharpen a historian's empathy for the lives and emotions of people past. Finally, as a historian of New York City who has never lived there, and who has partaken of the city's ordeal of the past five years from a distance, I am pleased to offer this work as a tribute to its residents.

www.ingramcontent.com/pod-product-compliance
Lightning Source LLC
Chambersburg PA
CBHW020338270326
41926CB00007B/231